D0078075

The Wagner Companion

The
WAGNER
Companion

Edited by
PETER BURBIDGE
and
RICHARD SUTTON

CAMBRIDGE UNIVERSITY PRESS
New York

First published in 1979
Published in the USA and Canada by
the Syndics of the Cambridge University Press
32 East 57th Street, New York, NY 10022 USA

Library of Congress Catalog Card Number: 79–50099

ISBN 0 521 22787 9 hard covers
ISBN 0 521 29657 9 paperback

© *This collection 1979*
by Peter Burbidge and Richard Sutton

Printed in Great Britain by
Latimer Trend & Company Ltd Plymouth

Contents

Contents
III. Prose Writings: Criticism: Bayreuth

Foreword

All great art work is unfathomable; but these essays convey a deep penetration into the philosophical, metaphysical and musical content of Wagner's mighty music dramas.

They are written not only for the expert, but for all those who wish to understand more truly and fully the phenomenon of the *Gesamtkunstwerk*.

Royal Opera House,
Covent Garden
November, 1978

REGINALD GOODALL

Preface

There are any number of biographies, guides to the operas, gossip and picture books, studies of one aspect or another of Wagner's work, but no single volume which provides discussion of the cultural, social and national factors which influenced his development as a creative artist, together with assessments of the various sides of his genius.

With *The Wagner Companion* we have, we believe, gone some way towards filling this gap. The *Companion* contains only original work. It is not aimed exclusively at one particular type of reader. It is intended to be as useful to the undergraduate sitting the music tripos as to the serious opera-goer, the student of German thought and culture, the commentators and programme-note writers, the reviewers and buyers of records, and the ordinary interested listener who has at some time felt the power and the magic.

There may be objections that the collaborative form deprives the volume of unity of thought, style, and even of personality. There is some truth in this; but we think nevertheless that the gain from having many contributors whose knowledge is close and profound in particular matters rather than a few who are concerned with generalities far outweighs the loss of the unifying factor.

Most readers will notice omissions. Some are intentional, some are for inclusion in a later volume. There is thus no detailed analysis of the plots of the operas. What Newman has adequately done we leave alone. That apart, there are important subject-areas which still need to be studied; for example, Wagner in a historical context rather than a musical or literary one; Wagner's use of his source material (myth, legend, chronicle); a study of the performance of the operas; an investigation into the reliability of *Mein Leben*; an updated iconography, discography, and bibliography; and so on.

Preface

The present bibliography has not been compiled with a view to amassing a comprehensive list of books with Wagner as their subject. This would have required a volume of its own; it would also have contained much material of doubtful quality. The intention has been to select works whose authors had something useful, interesting or illuminating to say, from Wagner's contemporaries to ours.

Among the great composers, Wagner stands out as a complex phenomenon. According to Tovey, Wagner was a natural genius: if he hadn't chosen to compose operas, he would have achieved comparable distinction in some other field. What he had to say was received sometimes with respect, frequently with adulation, often with hostility, but it was almost never ignored. Attitudes have undergone remarkable changes, from the worship of von Wolzogen to the hostility of Hanslick, from the reluctant idolatry of Thomas Mann to the slanted enthusiasm of some modern producers who think that the *Ring* is a Marxist tract.

A glance at the catalogue of any major library will show how much has been written on Wagner, with much dross among the gold. This volume, we hope, will add something to the gold—this gold more accessible and less corrupting to ordinary mortals than that at the bottom of the Rhine.

October, 1978   P. B.
                                                                                R. S.

I
Background Studies

ONE

Richard Wagner: Man and Artist

PETER BURBIDGE

'Suddenly he found the name "Wagner" on his lips.
As if unconscious he spoke it aloud: "Wagner . . .
Wagner". Where did the name come from? From what
shaft within himself? What was it driving at? Who was
Wagner? Wagner?'
HERMANN HESSE, *Klingsor's Last Summer*

WILHELM RICHARD WAGNER was born in Leipzig on 22 May 1813,
the ninth child certainly of Johanna Wagner, and probably of Karl
Friedrich Wagner, an official of the town court, though there are
grounds for doubt. A Jewish actor, Ludwig Geyer, lodged in the
household for some months before Richard's birth and, on the death
of Karl Friedrich when Richard was only six months old, assumed
responsibility for the family and married Johanna less than a year later.
Wagner himself suspected that he was Geyer's son: why otherwise
than to atone for a wrong would Geyer have been willing to devote
himself to the whole Wagner family? We can share Wagner's suspicions without resolving them. There is not enough evidence, nor is
there ever likely to be, to settle the question. It remains interesting,
however, on two counts. The first is that Geyer possessed a variety of
artistic gifts—he was a dramatist, actor, singer, painter—certainly not
possessed by Karl Friedrich and might conceivably have bequeathed
these in infinitely more generous measure to his son; and the second is
that there is a curious irony in the possibility that Wagner, dedicated
and persistent anti-semite, might himself have been a Jew.

His childhood was unremarkable. He was nervous and excitable, like other intelligent children; and, again like the intelligent, was impatient of authority. The theatre seems to have been his earliest passion. He approached it through the twin influences of Greek tragedy (studied in school) and the operas of Rossini and Weber (studied and sung by his sisters Clara and Rosalie). An uncle, Adolf Wagner, a cultivated but stodgy man of letters, introduced him to Shakespeare in his teens, which can only have done good, and to the crabbed and mannered style of German literary criticism, which clearly did harm. He played the piano in a desultory fashion; he studied scores, especially of opera, with enthusiasm and the closest attention; he made piano versions of Beethoven's Fifth and Ninth Symphonies. He saw the great singer-actress Schröder-Devrient as Leonore in *Fidelio* and was overwhelmed by the unforgettable musical and dramatic experience of the occasion.

He passed through the usual adolescent excesses of student days. He drank and gambled, but he also composed: a few concert overtures, a piano sonata and the C major Symphony date from this period. In appearance and manner he was already the striking and dominating character of later years, though the overwhelming force of his personality was yet to develop. In height he was diminutive, a trifle over five feet. He had an enormous head and expressive face: the eyes keen, piercing, the nose—'rudder of the face and index of the will'—bony and aquiline, the chin jutting sharply forward from the mouth. Some have seen his physiognomy as characteristically Jewish. He was always fastidious in dress, on occasion fussy and perverse; but he never bothered to match his manners to his appearance. Like Beethoven, he was more concerned with what he wanted to say or do than with the effect he was making. As a student he was desultory in attendance at class, assiduous in self-instruction. He began to read scores as others read prose. His innate musicality and enormous gifts resented and resisted humdrum day-to-day music instruction.

The facts of Wagner's adult life are too well known to need rehearsing here. The idea of Wagner as man and artist is an amalgam of what one derives from so many sources: the music and librettos, the prose writings, the letters, the portraits and photographs, the opinions of friends and enemies. His own view of friendship, and conversely of hostility, must be a major area of study for a full understanding of the man. The character of the mature Wagner began to harden and set during the period of exile in Zürich after the failure of the revolt in 1848. The traits of ruthlessness and egocentricity, which made ordinary friendship with him difficult to bear in any consistent way, were already apparent. He began to understand friendship only in terms of total surrender to his personality. He needed listeners, sympathizers, admirers, worshippers; and as with men who tower above others in personality and genius, dominating the surroundings like a redwood among scrub, he found the abandonment in the name of friendship of a need, a point of view, a plan, however trivial, utterly alien to his nature.

No ordinary friendship, then: his way was to inspire love or hatred, nothing between. Men either succumbed to the power and the fascination, or they shrank back, some in quiet but thoroughgoing detestation, others in violent repulsion. For his friends, the fine and noble spirit rose above everything else; for others, malice and treachery were predominant. Nor was it the weak and sycophantic who succumbed and the strong and independent who rejected. Such was the complexity of his nature and the extraordinary fascination of his physical presence that he inspired among all who were acquainted with him feelings as diverse and extreme as these acquaintances were themselves.

The key to his friendship was the friend's acceptance of domination. Many confessed to losing their identity in his presence. To Liszt he was 'a sort of Vesuvius in eruption'. To Hanslick he was 'egoism personified', he spoke 'continuously, and always of himself'. To Édouard Schuré, who knew him well in the days of writing *Tristan*, he was like 'a torrent bursting its dykes'.

> One stood dazzled before that exuberant and protean nature, ardent, personal; excessive in everything ... the frankness and extreme audacity with which he showed his nature, the qualities and defects of which were exhibited without concealment, acted on some people like a charm, while others were repelled by it ... his gaiety flowed over in a joyous foam of facetious fancies and extravagant pleasantries; but the least contradiction provoked him to incredible anger. Then he would leap like a stag, roar like a tiger. He paced the room like a caged lion, his voice became hoarse and the words came like screams; his speech slashed about at random. He seemed at these times like some elemental force unchained, like a volcano in eruption. Everything in him was gigantic, excessive.

The evidence is overwhelming: from all who knew him comes testimony of the need to dominate. Opposition depressed or angered him. 'He grows listless and loses his good humour when he is not allowed to dominate,' Cosima wrote to Judith Gauthier. This need, already evident in the early Dresden days, became so absolute in middle and later life that it percolated through to everything that he said and did from the greatest to the most trivial occasions. Cosima's was a mild judgement. To the ordinary observer, Wagner appeared to exhibit a vulgar egoism harnessed to the pursuit of uncontrollable personal desires. But it was not this at all: or rather, it was partly this and so much more. The self-criticism of ordinary people, the knowledge of self in any objective sense, were foreign to his cast of mind. He never seemed to confront the real nature of his personality in any mirror more demanding than the mirroring eyes of the most fervent of his admirers. Not for him the sharply revealing moment, the abrupt insight into himself as most others saw him. Every aspect of Wagner's character must be understood in relation to his own concept of the integrity of the artist as a great and noble ideal, not to be compromised in any detail whatever. Newman understood this as well as anyone, and puts it neatly: '. . . there were elements in him, as a man, that jar upon the taste of the purist in human character . . . but there is not a solitary instance in his whole career in which he yielded an inch of his artistic idealism for personal ease or profit'.

A curious and related feature of Wagner's character is the desire to 'communicate' his inner life to his friends. His passion for reading aloud is admitted in a wry and engaging passage in *Mein Leben*; and there is no doubt that he was extraordinarily accomplished in his performances. He was a man of ceaseless activity of mind, of great and continuous fertility in the production of books, essays, pamphlets, opera librettos—most of which he read aloud to a circle of friends, sometimes, as in the case of *Oper und Drama*, in extended sessions of no fewer than twelve consecutive evenings: not for egotism or vanity, not because it was the custom of the day (though people did read aloud more commonly in the nineteenth century than they do now), still less to test his ideas before a critical audience (for he needed only uncritical acceptance of what he read), but simply so that the indefatigable proselytizer in him, the inspired idealist, the man whose views, if properly communicated, would change the world, might find a means of expression. It is possible, too, that, so far as the librettos were concerned, Wagner saw his readings almost as preliminary performances. The completion of the *Ring* poem at the end of 1852 aroused the usual desire to read it to his friends in Zürich: and just to read it was important to him at a time when he was increasingly irked by isolation from the German musical and literary tradition. The desire grew stronger as he became older, and his dramatic skill seemed to develop with it. After the 1876 festival at Bayreuth, he read the poem of *Parsifal* to the delegates who had assembled to discuss the founding of a music school under Wagner's direction. One of them, Ludwig Schemann, confessed to being so moved by Wagner's marvellous reading that he failed to find the same feeling afterwards at a performance of the opera.

For such a man the years of exile represented deprivation and agony of spirit. In a moment of extreme intellectual loneliness, he described Zürich as 'a desert where I shall perish'; and almost in despair he wrote to Liszt: 'My whole intercourse with the world is through paper.' Liszt replied: 'your greatness is the cause of your misery'—a remark showing some insight into Wagner's capacity for self-pity as well as for suffering. When Liszt visited Zürich in the summer of 1853, Wagner went to meet him. 'We nearly choked each other with embraces,' wrote Liszt, '. . . he wept and laughed and stormed with joy for at least quarter of an hour at seeing me again.' Yet the Zürich years marked the beginning of the desire for withdrawal from the world, the real world in which he moved and spoke and worked, into the world of illusion, imagination, even of non-being. In a moving letter to Pusinelli he described himself as quite incapable of finding his bearings in the outer world, which puzzled and eluded him: it was the inner world which was real. In Zürich he began to read the literature of Buddhism, and felt keenly attracted to the doctrines of purification and non-attachment. He abandoned the *Ring* and turned to *Tristan*—for a host of reasons, prominent among them, of course, the relationship with Mathilde Wesendonk, but certainly among them as well the attraction of the mystical elements in the Tristan legend. His interest in Buddhism and his absorption in *Tristan* enabled him to live simultaneously at different levels, not just as an artist and as a man, but as a mystical lover (with Mathilde) and as a worldly lover (with his wife Minna). Nothing in his relations with one seemed inconsonant with his relations with the other; and for all his emotional involvement with both, he could, through his pursuit of non-attachment, see both objectively, in all their virtues and in all their failings, an observer and critic of them as well as of himself.

Hardly ever in his life was he especially aware of a logical hindrance to pursuing simultaneously two contradictory ends. The Minna/Mathilde relationships were sexually motivated, and were at least consistent at that level; but in some of his dealings with King Ludwig II of Bavaria the contradictions were quite baffling. At no time was he more intent on securing from Ludwig an annuity or pension, for example, than during the post-*Tristan* period, when he was insisting to the young king that he was weary of the world and more than ready to retire to a life of poverty and contemplation. It was as though reality were one sort of 'reality', fantasy another—though no less real; and, as in so many aspects of Wagner's life, the instinctive dramatist deployed on the fantasy the full resources of his art. One of these resources was verbal fluency, the ability to expound a case endlessly, enlarging, developing, decorating, until the eloquence itself carried a sort of conviction—to him above all others. And so the real world and the fantasy world twisted around each other, merged, and became indistinguishable.

Along with non-attachment as an intellectual aim went a curious sort of mental and emotional detachment, partly willed, partly involuntary, from stresses and excitements around him. At the first performance of *Rienzi*, Newman tells us, Wagner 'sat for most of the time in one of those semi-cataleptic states that were frequent with him in moments of crisis'. The tumultuous applause at the end of the opera, Wagner tells us in *Mein Leben*, affected him more as though it were a natural phenomenon—a torrential rainstorm or gale-force wind, for example—than as something directly connected with himself. His aloofness, puzzling to his friends and distressing to players and singers, could hardly have been studied, nor could he have failed to care very deeply that his opera should succeed; yet so distant did he seem during performances of his own work, from the earliest days to the festivals in Bayreuth, that he could only have resorted to what can now be seen as an instinctive self-preservation, a state of mind where pleasure, delight, exaltation, apprehension, anxiety merged into a condition of bemused preoccupation. The best-known example of this condition is the oration at Weber's reburial in Dresden in December 1844. In delivering the oration, Wagner, whose special gifts equipped him for this sort of rhetoric, slipped into a state of such detachment as to see himself from without as another person, stopped talking altogether, and waited for the other to continue. There can be no doubting his emotional turmoil, nor his defence against it. Weber's death, he wrote in *Mein Leben*, was a 'terrible blow', and the second interment 'stirred me to the very depths of my being'. Yet it is hard to resist the impression that the highly accomplished dramatist saw this and other

events in his life in theatrical terms, and could hardly have been un-
aware of the effect on others of his slipping into remoteness and un-
reality.

The revolutionary activities which led to his exile were only marginally
political. The despair of the artist and the anger of the man—the one
the culmination of a long series of failures and frustrations as Kapellmeister at Dresden, the other a ferocious reaction against the poverty
in which he lived—were the likely impulses which drove him to the
barricades. He revolted for art, for a society which would value art and
encourage its expression. Not that he was untouched by the plight of
the masses as a whole; but he responded more readily to suffering
humanity than to suffering people. Pity for those doomed to suffering
by the very nature of the lives they led and of the world in which they
were forced to live was, he told Mathilde, the profoundest source of
his art. Towards the end of his life, on a visit to Naples, he was appalled by the luxury of the few and the dire poverty of the many, by
the sheer loveliness of the countryside and the awful squalor which
represented man's use of it. As so often before, he felt alienated and
baffled by a world which he clearly failed to understand and for which
he felt no sympathy.

For all this, his own love of luxury, his extravagance, his perpetual
indebtedness to tradesmen of all kinds, his willingness to borrow from
any friend or acquaintance who would lend, are all key elements to the
understanding of Wagner himself. As a student and as a young man he
borrowed and spent with a reckless disregard for the consequences. 'I
must have money,' he wrote to Apel, 'or I shall go mad.' The flight
from Riga ('Better to be a cab-horse in Berlin than a Kapellmeister in
Riga') and the first years of extreme poverty in Paris saw the beginning
of the deterioration of his character so far as money was concerned.
The theatre in which he worked brought together, as was common in
the nineteenth century, people in poverty and in affluence; and the
contrast between the luxury of the rich mediocrities and his own poverty was the starting-point of his bitterness against society as a whole
and of his casualness about financial probity. In Paris he felt the first
real humiliation of the role of repeated borrower—a role which not
unnaturally revealed some of the most unattractive aspects of his
character. Throughout his life as a borrower—and, even in this context, what remained dominant was the single-mindedness of the artist

—he distinguished between lenders who were quite consciously devoting their money to the artist and his cause, perhaps making genuine sacrifices on his behalf, and who were therefore owed gratitude, and lenders who were simply helping an impecunious man, providing nothing more than a common charity, and were owed none. Peter Cornelius, who observed some of Wagner's financial dealings with King Ludwig, and whose admiration of the artist did not obscure his detached view of the man, remarked that Wagner seemed willing to allow 'his mental greatness to cover all his moral weaknesses'. For example, money provided by Ludwig to discharge Wagner's debts was only partly used for this purpose. Large sums were also spent on luxurious living in Munich, on the development of a style of living which could only result in further debts, and consequently in further calls on the king's purse.

Wagner's view of all this was characteristically lofty and detached. His larger creditors, the king, Pusinelli, Otto Wesendonk and others, were simply providing on account funds which would be easily repaid in the form of operas. In a sense this was not unreasonable, though all the circumstances were not in Wagner's favour. His early operas, in spite of their popularity throughout Europe, brought him very little money, since the concept of royalty payments had yet to be developed. Creative musicians were paid for a first performance—usually about a quarter of the fee paid to a principal singer—and nothing thereafter. Singers were paid for every performance, the composer for one only. Copyright law was rudimentary, but rights could be sold, and Wagner raised considerable sums of money in this way. In this, and in the sale of manuscripts, he was unbusinesslike to the point of chicanery. It repeatedly escaped his memory, for example, that while negotiating with Breitkopf and Härtel for the sale of rights in *Rienzi*, *Der fliegende Holländer* and *Tannhäuser*, these had already been conveyed to Pusinelli; that the rights in *Das Rheingold* and *Die Walküre*, which were sold to Schott, had already been sold to Otto Wesendonk years previously; and that the rights in the *Ring* as a whole, paid for many times over by King Ludwig, were eventually sold by Wagner to individual theatres for his own profit. For all this, he consistently maintained that he was indebted to no one, that the world itself was forever in arrears in paid acknowledgement of his art in material recompense for the gift of so much beauty.

Yet Wagner's debt to Ludwig was prodigious, and not only in material terms. Unlike the ministers and advisers of the Bavarian court, Ludwig was capable of seeing Wagner the artist separately from Wagner the man. The king's confidence in the probity of the man suffered damaging blows through his financial involvement with Wagner and through his gradual understanding of the liaison with Cosima; but none of this had the slightest effect on his devotion to and overwhelming admiration for the artist. The emotional intensity of the relationship with Ludwig is one of the odder features of Wagner's middle life. Their meetings were 'love scenes' conducted with 'the glow and ardour of a first love'. The language of *Mein Leben* and of the letters is rapturous, even ecstatic. The hint of homosexuality is there; so is the quite conscious withdrawal into an unreal, magical, fantasy world. With Wagner's music as the ruling passion of his life, it was not unnatural that the young neurotic king should have seen himself as Lohengrin and Parsifal; but what was unnatural, even sinister, was that Wagner, self-styled Gurnemanz, the wise counsellor and friend, should have seen his relationship with the king as a path to political power. The intense hostility of the professional courtiers prevented the development of this side of the friendship and eventually forced Wagner's retreat from Munich; but by then the sadness of reality was evident to Ludwig, and over the years he learned with pain that the greatest man of the age had something of Kundry in his nature, that he could destroy as well as create.

Wagner married twice. His first marriage, to Minna Planer, was twenty-eight years old when Wagner met Ludwig, and was destroyed in all but name. The two were divided by an incurable bitterness and hostility. In the beginning it had been different. As a young woman Minna was pretty, practical and affectionate. At seventeen she had an illegitimate daughter, Nathalie, whom she passed off as a sister. Already wounded and vulnerable, she had no lasting defences against Wagner's voluble, brilliant, impetuous wooing, became his mistress and, a few months later, on 24 November 1836, his wife. There is no doubting Wagner's love for her, nor his gratitude for her fidelity and patience during the years of extreme hardship in Riga and Paris. There is equally no doubting her love for him, nor, unfortunately, her almost total inability to comprehend either the nature of her husband's genius or his fanatical conception of artistic integrity. Her misfortune, her tragedy even, was to find herself, an actress of ordinary ability, limited intelligence and little imagination, bound in marriage to a man who represented one of the great artistic forces of the century. Even when not suffering actual privation, it seemed to her nothing less than perverse and wilful that a man of her husband's undoubted and recognizable gifts should refuse to compose in the manner of Rossini or Meyerbeer when to do so would have allowed them to pay their bills, eat enough of the right food and sleep warmly. His account of her in *Mein Leben* begins tenderly and lovingly, becomes steadily less sympathetic, and is finally heartless and bitter; and his portrayal of her in the operas takes a similar path. She is the warm, self-sacrificing Senta in *Holländer*, the cooler, doubting Elsa in *Lohengrin*, and the critical, self-righteous Fricka in *Rheingold* and *Walküre*. A disease of the heart caused Minna to age before her time; and as her beauty faded, so did the warmth and affection in her nature, until, in her later years, she became shrill and censorious, suspicious and jealous, something of a scold.

All this was not, to her, without cause. Throughout his life Wagner preferred the company and companionship of women to men. They were more immediately responsive to his personality and more superficially responsive to his art. It is some distance from this to the love that knew no bounds of expression or trust or sacrifice, which was a major theme in his work and a constant preoccupation in his life; but from the early passion for Minna to the final years with Cosima he felt always the need for feminine society and attachments, and seems never to have hesitated in entering into a relationship in which either the body was more than the spirit (as with Jessie Laussot and Judith Gauthier) or the reverse (as with Mathilde Wesendonk and Mathilde Maier). Yet it is clear that the passively feminine, readily yielding, type of woman to whom he was instinctively attracted left unsatisfied in him an important need: a need that was not finally satisfied until he discovered in Cosima von Bülow that a woman could combine animation and a natural sexuality with strength of personality, articulate intellectuality and day-to-day administrative efficiency.

It was the affair with Cosima rather than the devious wrangles over money that undid Ludwig's view of Wagner as an honourable man. This remarkable woman, daughter of Franz Liszt and Marie d'Agoult, wife of Hans von Bülow, and mistress first, then wife, of Wagner, was so exactly suited to the role of guide and protector of genius that a brief account of her is necessary in any account of Wagner himself. Her dominant characteristic was intellectual seriousness. She had the kind of intelligence that was at once penetrating and limiting: it probed without illuminating. Like Wagner in one of his less admirable aspects, she judged a question from the restricting viewpoint of a number of prejudices, most of which were formed early in her life. Her dedication to art and philosophy, especially his art and his philosophy, was beyond question; so was her quite conscious sense of self-sacrifice, both in her marriage to Bülow, whom she did not love, and in her liaison and later marriage to Wagner, whom she loved beyond any doubt, though he overwhelmed and consumed her, leaving on occasions no trace of an independent personality. She served him both before and after their marriage with unwearying devotion, and accepted without hesitation everything that he said and did. Her passions and prejudices led her into numerous follies of thought and expression. In detecting the influence of the Jews, for example, in all opposition to Wagner, she allied herself with the lunatic elements in German society, and showed to her discredit that she was more willing to follow a convenient prejudice than to work out an objective opinion. This apart, she was an earnest and not unaccomplished seeker of knowledge and instruction, an indefatigable reader—mostly in literature, history and art—a prolific correspondent and, above all, an ideal consort for Wagner. If at times her relationship to him appears as that of 'curator to a historical monument', as Gutman said, she nevertheless believed in him as man and artist with an unwavering, unshakeable intensity of conviction. She could have been, and perhaps did become, a prig; but she was saved, as a younger woman at any rate, by natural high spirits and an unrepressed sexuality. She shared Wagner's love of self-dramatization; and she had more than a touch of his self-pity. She was the only woman ever to be consulted about problems in the composition of the operas.

The affair with Wagner began secretly, as an intrigue. Both were married. But Minna Wagner died in January 1866, and, in April, Ludwig rented on Wagner's behalf the house Triebschen near Lucerne. In the early summer Cosima joined him with her three daughters; and Bülow visited them from time to time. Nevertheless, gossip spread, a scandal developed, and Ludwig was finally compelled to acknowledge that the two were lovers. A son, Siegfried, was born in 1869. In the following July, Bülow divorced Cosima, and on 25 August 1870 Cosima and Wagner were married. In the same year, a scheme was developed for a festival theatre at Bayreuth, and on Christmas Day,

Cosima's birthday, the *Siegfried Idyll* was first performed on the staircase at Triebschen. In 1872 Wagner moved to Bayreuth to supervise the building both of the theatre and a larger private house for the family; and in April 1874 he, Cosima, the children and a staff of servants took up residence in the splendid Villa Wahnfried.

A new aspect of Wagner begins to emerge: that of the cultivated artist of substantial means. Once settled at Wahnfried, the family developed a new and stable way of life, almost a routine. The house was large and comfortably furnished, it was well provided with servants both inside and out, and there were innumerable dogs. Under Cosima's direction, the manner of life became increasingly formal: children rose on entry of either parent, hands were kissed, and dinner taken in correct style—though the impish side of Wagner's nature led him occasionally to caper and jest, a total abandonment of the Olympian manner which Cosima considered a proper reflection of his greatness. On the whole, though, he was sympathetic to Cosima's objective of presiding over a formal household, and especially welcomed a routine which allowed him seclusion in the midst of family life.

It was a routine familiar in the lives of creative artists in their later years. He took breakfast with Cosima in their bedroom. Then, at about ten o'clock, he went to his study and worked until one. Lunch was taken with the children, then coffee with Cosima, in the garden when fine, otherwise in the drawing room. A glance at the *Bayreuther Tageblatt* was followed by a short rest. He was then joined by Cosima for work on the day's letters, she in the role of secretary or amanuensis. Later in the afternoon, there was a drive or a walk with the children. At seven there was supper, again with the children; and then, at eight, Wagner and Cosima settled to their evening: reading if alone, talk and music-making if joined casually by friends, more formal entertainment if there was a planned dinner party. It was an agreeable and relaxed way of life, especially in the first few years of occupation of Wahnfried; but it became increasingly marred by chronic anxieties over the finances of the theatre and by bickerings and tensions among the singers.

To these Wagner added a difficulty of his own making: a deep and irreversible anti-semitism. In 1850 he had published the notorious *Das Judentum in der Musik* under the pseudonym 'K. Freigedank' (though he made no attempt to disguise his highly personal style and quickly admitted to its authorship) in which he propounded the view that Jewish composers debased Western music by contaminating it with the musical traditions of the ghetto. Wagner's hostility to the Jews was determined partly by his accepting the conventional attitudes of the German bourgeoisie, partly by his desire for revenge for the humiliation and hardship of the Paris years when he considered his work to have been maliciously obstructed by Meyerbeer and Halévy (both Jews), and partly again by his sheer frustration and anger at the ignorant and biased criticism of his work in the press (mostly owned, or so he thought, by Jews). If it seemed ill-judged to publish the paper in the first place, it seemed positive lunacy to publish a second edition in 1869: even to his friends, even to Cosima, it seemed no less than a wilful attempt to kindle ugly passions, to arouse divisive hatreds. True, in the year before, at the first performance of *Die Meistersinger von Nürnberg*, Beckmesser's serenade had been hissed on the mistaken assumption that Wagner was parodying the chant of the synagogue; and it is easy to feel particular resentment over an occasion when, for once, no offence was intended. Through all this, it is difficult to determine the real extent or the exact nature of his anti-semitism. At best, his attitudes could be described as ambivalent: an erratic, irrational dislike of Jews in the mass (and of some whom he thought of as enemies anyway) went along with a deep personal attachment to individual Jews—men like Joseph Rubinstein, Angelo Neumann and Hermann Levi who were willing to work closely with him and to ignore, because of his genius, the antipathy of his anti-semitism in general and the wounding nonsense of *Das Judentum in der Musik* in particular.

Not that these attachments prevented Wagner from displaying grotesquely offensive behaviour to Levi during the preparations for *Parsifal*. King Ludwig was providing orchestra and chorus, and along with both went the king's Kapellmeister, Hermann Levi. Wagner tried first to get Ludwig to dismiss Levi, and when—to the king's credit and Wagner's annoyance—this was refused, he urged that Levi, the son of a rabbi, should be baptized before the first performance of the opera, though he had on earlier occasions claimed to feel some respect for Jews who resisted the temptation to Germanize their names. An objective consideration of Wagner's behaviour to people like Levi and Neumann is painful; but to reflect on the perverse pleasure which, during Levi's visits to Wahnfried, Wagner derived from taunting him with stories about progress in the preparations for his baptism is positively distressing. Periodic rancour against those

Jews on whom he depended for the proper performance of his work and a general hatred of the Jewish race were part of the improbable background against which *Parsifal* was prepared for the stage.

Less persistent but no less rancorous than his anti-semitism was his dislike of the French. Again, the hackwork and near-starvation of the years in Paris, the fiasco of the revised *Tannhäuser*, with hooligans from the Jockey Club systematically destroying the three performances, and finally the political tension in the 1860s between France and Germany, were contributory factors in converting a natural antipathy into a thoroughgoing hatred. A recurring theme in his prose writings of this period was the shallowness of French culture and the degeneracy of French life in all its aspects, in contrast to the profundity, freshness and vigour of all that was German. The notorious *Ein Kapitulation*, a patriotic farce for the stage written in 1870, is the culminating expression of this hatred. It ridicules the horrors of the siege of Paris and makes merry on the theme of the misery and starvation of the French. Newman (who consistently defends Wagner against unfair and uninformed criticism) describes it as 'tasteless, witless, loutish'. What is really indefensible is Wagner's decision to publish in 1873 after an interval of three years. It is just possible to account for the writing of it at the height of the passions engendered by the war; impossible to account for publication after the passions had cooled.

Ein Kapitulation was trivial and ephemeral. Not so the nationalistic appeal of *Die Meistersinger*, in which Wagner uses the full maturity of his genius to glorify 'imperishable' German art. Against the negative hostility to Jews and French must be set the overwhelmingly positive admiration for German art, the German people and Germany itself. 'I am a German,' he wrote to Liszt at the beginning of his exile, 'and I carry my Germany in my heart.' The art of the Masters, according to Sachs, is 'deutsch und wahr' ('German and true'); and if the German *Volk und Reich* should ever crumble under foreign domination and be subjected to foreign (French?) cultural influences— 'welschen Dunst mit welschen Tand' ('foreign mists with foreign vanities')—even then 'die heil'ge deutsche Kunst' ('holy German art') would remain, imperishable, indestructible. The passage has been variously interpreted to mean anything between straightforward admiration for the art of one's country and an incitement to racial war. The truth is midway. No longer a revolutionary, Wagner yearned, in common with the mass of his compatriots, for the rebirth of Germany as a nation; and art, once the regenerative impulse of a divided people, had become a refuge, a dream-image, something to lift and comfort, like religion, above sordid reality and worldly distress. Older passions misled him from time to time; but what part of him seems to be urging Sachs to say is that art is beyond personality, though not beyond nationality.

It is easy, with these considerations in mind, to pass over the fact that *Die Meistersinger*—that 'glorious, golden score'—is one of the great *comic* masterpieces of the lyric theatre, with only *Figaro* and *Falstaff* as anything like its equal, and that the man who wrote it had a huge and gusty sense of humour, sometimes playful and boisterous, sometimes delicate and touching, occasionally cruel and malicious. He romped with animals, climbed trees, stood on his head, hung by his feet from balconies. He improvised comic pieces on the piano, played with his children and took part in their pantomimes. His letters are full of puns, and there is even a good deal of verbal humour in the librettos. The ancient device of *Stabreim* was revived by him to give point and direction to purely musical impulses; but the temptation—if that is what it was—to exploit verbal virtuosity independently of any musical significance occasionally overcame him. Hence

> Freia, die Holde,
> Holde, die Freie . . .

in *Rheingold*; hence the rather feeble 'good runes' of Gutrune; hence the positively silly Tantris (as a disguise)—jokes which, whatever success they had in their time, do not now amount to very much. Nor is it easy to respond wholeheartedly to Beckmesser's humiliation in *Meistersinger*, for Wagner's onslaught, though it starts with genuinely comic theatrical material, depends in the end on cruelty and ridicule—excessive punishments, as we now see, for the offence of pedantry and the presumption of wooing Eva.

What dominates every consideration of Wagner is his consummate genius as a musician. It needs an effort of the imagination in our contemplation of Wagner nearly one hundred years after his death to understand that, for him, music was not everything in his creative and intellectual life. The great length and complexity of his prose writings, the huge number of letters, the dabbling in politics and philosophy, are all witness to the many-sidedness of the man's mind. There were some years after the completion of *Lohengrin* when music, or at least the composing of music, seemed a secondary activity. For him, the completion of one work did not automatically imply the start of another. It was not so much that creative energy, used up in the titanic and exhausting task of composition, needed renewal, as that the artist in Wagner required the musician to draw on deeper and different levels of imagination, so that no opera would repeat the artistic experience of another. One effect of this was that the operas required longer periods of gestation as the artist matured (though the subjects of all of them existed in notes or prose sketches from a comparatively early period in his life); another was that Wagner came to possess, in a degree probably unprecedented in the history of music, an absolute sense of the best functioning of his musical imagination.

For all this, there were times in his life when he seemed torn and oppressed by the enormous burden placed on him as a creative artist. How could the pleasures, comforts and satisfactions of ordinary men mean anything at all to the man who knew that he had to write the *Ring*? And because of the very nature of a project which began as a single opera of daunting complexity and developed into a cycle of four, the stupendous difficulties of conception and composition multiplied rather than diminished as the years passed. It is no exaggeration to say that he faced a task more exacting in its demands, more appalling even, than that of any musician before or since. Throughout the Zürich years, the music of the *Ring* was a constant preoccupation, and some motifs, as we now have them, crystallized at that time; but he worked fitfully at both libretto and music, tormented by the fear that the work would be impossible to perform, and harassed by the struggle to reduce the inchoate masses of dramatic and musical material to an articulate and organic whole. How to begin, how to find the creative moment from which all else would develop? The unassailable need to answer the question haunted him for years. What finally happened is well known. Wagner lay one afternoon, weak with fever, on a couch in a hotel at Spezia, intending to rest, concerned only to recover his health. He was overtaken instead by what he described as one of the most profound creative experiences of his life. In a trance-like state he seemed to sink deeply into fast-moving water, whose movement caused the tonality of the E flat major chord to sound in his ears, extended and unmodulated, with arpeggios rising unceasingly above it and then developing into melodic figures, the chord itself unchanging. The question was answered. What he had heard was the prelude to *Rheingold*. He sat down to compose the opera at the beginning of

November 1853, finished the composition sketch by the middle of January, and completed the orchestration by May 1854.

When the moment came and was recognized, Wagner worked quickly. Like Berlioz, he composed at a desk, not at the piano; and like Beethoven, he was driven, in his highest flights of creative activity, to a condition of 'raptus', an ecstatic, dream-like state described by Mathilde Wesendonk, and later by Weissheimer, who interrupted Wagner during the composition of *Meistersinger*:

> I knocked at his door, and when he did not answer I assumed that he had gone to the hotel to dinner. I was just on the point of seeking him out there when I heard a commotion inside. I knocked again. At last he appeared at the door: his features were completely changed, almost wild. 'I am in the thick of it', he said, and ran back shyly into his bedroom, where he remained until he had calmed down.

The piano, he told Cosima, he used only to recall things, not for invention; no new ideas ever came to him at the keyboard.

As he grew older, the 'raptus' came to depend more and more on external circumstances: light and warmth were essential, so were deep carpets and heavy curtains in his room, silk or velvet on his body. The harmony of colour stirred his imagination as readily as the tonality of sound. It is easy to dismiss these 'necessities' as no more than a morbid craving for luxury—an understandable reaction to the penury of his earlier life—and most superficial accounts of Wagner have so regarded them; but (while there is no specific evidence for this) it can be convincingly conjectured that a musician working in an idiom for which there was no precedent needed to sink into an atmosphere as unlike that of the ordinary world as could be contrived. That the luxury was not for its own sake, as it were, is clear from Wagner's changing the colours of satins and velvets to suit his mood and to suit what he wanted to compose. He was not organized as other people, he said on a number of occasions: and it was the only subject on which he ever appeared to be defensive. In the ordinary world, he told Pusinelli, he felt alien, disorganized, incapable of finding his bearings; what was real for him was the inner world, the world of the creative imagination. Luxury of a highly specialized and personal kind insulated him from what was alien and external, and made it possible for him to compose: a state of affairs puzzling to his friends and sympathizers, positively inimical to his enemies.

Nor did he respond, as most composers of operas have responded, to the exhilaration and excitement, the sense of power and authority, generally felt by a composer who rehearses and produces one of his own works. In Wagner, such an experience induced unhappiness in the theatre and profound depression outside it. He derived from it none of the normal satisfactions of self-expression and self-fulfilment. He cared little for fame and adulation. He did not even care for money in the sense that 'caring' had any influence on what he did. He cared only for artistic integrity. It was remarked on numerous occasions that, when his creative work was going well, his mood was one of extraordinary elation. Whether he was gay or depressed, exhilarated or unhappy, had no connection with his external circumstances, but only with the circumstances of his inner life. A good deal of *Die Meistersinger* was composed at the height of what Newman called Minna's 'malignant war' on him—absolute evidence of his ability to insulate his creative from his daily life.

He showed little interest in contemporary composers and their work: an attitude partly self-protective. It was another aspect of his artistic integrity. Most of what was put before him in score was mediocre stuff: to look through such music was disagreeable to him, to hear it positively painful. Wagner was not the man to spare the feelings of those who consulted him, and nothing could prevent him from saying what he thought. The sillier among them, in their pique, took Wagner's attitude to be jealousy; the more sensible, with their larger vision, accepted the unpalatable facts, and one at least took consolation from the envy of posterity at his contact with the great man.

Studied self-protection became the more necessary the more he strove to keep intact the workings of his musical imagination. Later chapters in this book, particularly those concerned with the concept of the 'whole art work' and with the method of composition, examine how this imagination worked and with what results. What is said there objectively and analytically was subjectively and lyrically expressed by Newman more than sixty years ago. His words are still relevant, still evocative:

> We can speak of the Wagnerian imagination as we can speak of the Shakespearean imagination; Wagner's is the only imagination in music which can be compared with Shakepeare's in dramatic fertility and comprehensiveness. It pours itself over the whole surface of a work, into every nook and cranny of it. It is a vast mind, infinite in its sympathies, protean in its creative power. For drastic incisiveness of theme he has not his equal in all music; each vision instinctively, without an effort, finds its own inevitable utterance. In the works of his great period every motive has a physiognomy as distinct from all others as

the face of any human being is distinct from all other faces. The motives are unforgettable once we have heard them. They depict their subject once for all: who today, enormously as the apparatus of musical expression has developed since Wagner's time, would dare to try to find better symbols than these he has invented for the tarnhelm, the fire, the Rhine, the sword, the dragon, the potion that brings oblivion to Siegfried; or for any of the men and women of the operas—for Wotan, for Siegfried, for Mime, for the '*reine Thor*,' for Herzeleide, for Hagen, for Gutrune, for Brünnhilde, and for a dozen others? . . . They are what they are because they combine in the fullest measure and in impeccable proportion the two great preservatives of all artistic work—a piercing personal vision and consummate style.

TWO

The German Intellectual Background

RONALD GRAY

WAGNER'S WORK is one culmination of the 'German Renaissance', the one that began in the middle of the eighteenth century, quickly rising in literature to the heights of Goethe and Schiller, in music to Mozart and Beethoven, and, in politics, from Frederick the Great's victories, through the War of Liberation against Napoleon to the unification of Germany under Prussian rule in 1871. *Der Ring des Nibelungen*, with its dedication of 1876, 'Composed in confidence in the German spirit', may be seen historically as a conscious apotheosis of over a hundred years of national aspirations. Yet any acknowledgement of Wagner's astonishing achievement must also take into account the deep aversion it called forth in a man who was at least his equal. Nietzsche's progression from enthusiastic praise to almost total denunciation must concern anyone who looks for some understanding of Germany and Europe in the last two hundred years or so.

As early as the 1760s, Lessing had called for a truly German theme in literature and proposed Faust as a typically German subject, a suggestion which Goethe soon took up. Herder had followed with a call for national self-realization for every nation. The early thirteenth-century manuscript of the *Nibelungenlied* (*Lay of the Nibelungs*) had been discovered not long before; other manuscripts of German medieval epics followed, and became the subjects of Romantic plays, poems and paintings. The brothers Grimm travelled about, collecting German folktales. The Rhine began to be celebrated as the great river of the Fatherland. Gothic cathedrals became a symbol of Germanic creativity, and the completion of the one at Cologne—then still unfinished after several hundred years—was regarded as a spiritual equivalent of the *Zollverein*, the Customs Union which heralded the political union of Germany's splinter-states. As a contemporary of Wagner's wrote in

34

1842, in words evidently meant to recall the Nibelungs: 'The Cathedral is the greatest of Germany's bulwarks which she will either guard or perish, and which will only fall when the blood of the last Teuton has mingled with the waves of Father Rhine.'[1] Sulpiz Boisserée actually saw the cathedral as a kind of national Valhalla.[2]

Friedrich Schlegel, in his 'Conversation on Poetry', had spoken of the need for a myth, comparable to the myths by which the poets of Greece had been inspired. Wagner in effect supplied or revived a large number, and contributed in no small way to the solidarity of the German Empire.

But German unity in and after 1871 was in a tenuous, ambiguous state. The Empire lasted only forty-seven years, and the signs of disaster appeared almost as soon as it had been founded. Was it significant that the *Ring* opened and closed in similar ambiguity? The thought is less fanciful than might appear.

One of the strangest features of the literary revival was the distrust with which some of its leaders regarded literature. Goethe's *Wilhelm Meister*, a novel which Friedrich Schlegel accounted equal in importance with the French Revolution, began as the story of a young man with a 'theatrical mission' to realize himself by becoming an actor; the novel ended with his complete rejection of the theatre in favour of a practical job as a surgeon. It was accepted by almost all the German Romantics that literature must always be presented ironically, in awareness of its partiality, its 'one-sidedness' in comparison with the 'many-sidedness' of the whole of reality. There was thus a particular quality to the taunt Nietzsche threw at Wagner after he had turned away from him, that Wagner was more of a mime, a man of the theatre, than a musician. Nietzsche had by that time developed a very low view of the theatre, which he did not appear to have had when *Die Geburt der Tragödie* (*The Birth of Tragedy*), a work full of praise for Wagner, was published in 1872. But the same swing to a contrary view had already been present in *Wilhelm Meister*, and there was something in the intellectual climate that invited it. Nietzsche was enlisting Goethe for the prosecution.

Almost all German thought from the late eighteenth century onwards was concerned with ambiguities. Kant's concern was still rational: with the greatest of logical pains, he demonstrated that Reason, the touchstone of eighteenth-century Enlightenment, must lead to contradictory conclusions about certain cosmological problems. In the one column of a chapter in the *Critique of Pure Reason* appears the demonstration that the world must have a beginning in space and time; in the adjoining, parallel column the demonstration that it cannot have a beginning; and so on through four sets of similar antinomies. For Kant, this was an intolerable paradox. Only by means of the 'categorical imperative', the intuitive knowledge of the moral law, was it possible to have any certainty about what lay beyond space and time: moral torments pursued a man indefinitely, no matter how old the offence. And here lay the escape from the antinomies, so far as there was one at all: in the very insistence of the conscience was a demonstration of eternal law.

For Hegel, however, the contradictions of the polarities presented no such problem; rather they were the way in which the Spirit of the universe had to manifest itself. In Hegel's philosophy, Spirit, which is very close to what Schopenhauer later designated Will, was that which turned itself into real beings in the world of phenomena. Unlike God, who created beings other than himself, the Spirit could only divide itself into contradictory opposites, and this division must always remain unsatisfactory. Yet, to restore unity, it was necessary for the Spirit in an individual to embrace the opposites in his own person, to embody them in his personal unity, however terrible that undertaking might be. To grasp the contradictions fearlessly—to march through the flames, one might almost say—and so embody them in oneself was to become at one with the Spirit, to be, in Hegelian terms, a 'world-historic man'.

Already general parallels with the *Ring* suggest themselves. For 'world-historic man' it is tempting to read 'Siegfried' (or Wagner). Kant's agonizing experience of Reason 'in itself confounded' could be paralleled in Wotan's horror in *Die Walküre* at finding Brünnhilde, the very instrument of his own Will, acting against him. Yet there is no need to suppose that Wagner had either Kant or Hegel in mind. The history of German philosophy throughout the whole first half of the nineteenth century is a continual turning about of the opposites. Hegel had seen Man as 'alienated' from the Spirit—alienated, that is, in the sense that it was Man's tragedy to be separated from the Spirit, to be an individual over against the cosmos, capable of redemption only through becoming one with the Spirit again, or, at all events, through seeing some great man represent that one-ness for him. Feuerbach, on the other hand, who influenced Wagner in his early days, reversed the argument: it was the Spirit who was alienated from Man, and Man, to become himself, must realize himself in the totality of all his potentialities. Marx in his youth actually seemed to believe that each individual was potentially all individuals, and that only alienation prevented him from making the potentiality real. The 'Young Hegelians' generally put their emphasis on actual full realization here and now of the Spirit which Man had within him: they were revolutionary where Hegel, accepting the status quo as inevitable and great, was politically quietist. They expected to make reality become ideal rather than recognize reality as being already as ideal as could be.

Marx declared in *Das Kapital* that he had found the truth in Hegel standing on its head, and that his own aim was to turn it right side up again. In effect, as we shall see, Nietzsche was in a similar relation to Schopenhauer. Everywhere the polar opposites of Kant take on a new shape: in Schiller it is the 'naïve' (*naiv*) and the 'reflective' (*sentimentalisch*) poet, in Goethe it is the poet Tasso and the man of affairs Antonio, in Hegel and Marx the thesis and antithesis, in Heine the 'Hellene' and the 'Nazarene', in Nietzsche the 'Apolline' and the 'Dionysian'.

Parallels with forms of Oriental thought, especially the Yin and the Yang of Taoism, are self-evident, not surprisingly since German scholars had been translating the Orient to the West for some generations before Wagner's birth. Schopenhauer was explicit: on the last page of the main section of *Die Welt als Wille und Vorstellung* (*The World as Will and Idea*) he drew attention to the similarity between his own doctrine of the total abnegation of the Will and the Buddhist Nirvana. He also maintained that his work could not be understood except in relation to Kant. Thus the ideas among which Wagner grew up were not only prevalent in almost every sphere of German thought, but were echoed in the great 'new' religion from the East, the possible alternative to Christianity.

Add to this that, since Hölderlin had had his vision of the renewal of classical antiquity on German soil, many others had begun to believe in Germany as a new Greece, and you will appreciate how Wagner was inspired to see himself as a modern Aeschylus. As he wrote in a letter of 1860 to Berlioz, 'I took my stand on the position which art once occupied towards the public life of the Greeks.' Bayreuth was to be the new Theatre of Dionysus.

Wherever one turned, every trend seemed to converge towards a supreme manifestation of German power, spiritual and political. The gods whom Hölderlin had thought alive only 'above our heads, aloft in another world', would await only the moment

Bis dass Helden genug in der ehernen Wiege gewachsen,
  Herzen an Kraft, wie sonst, ähnlich den Himmlischen sind.
Donnernd kommen sie drauf.

(Brod und Wein)

(Until heroes enough have grown in the iron cradle,
  And hearts, as before, resemble the Heavenly in strength.
Thundering then they come.)

(Bread and Wine)

Hölderlin, though he did not know it, had dreamed of Siegfried.

Wagner enjoyed not only a German inheritance. Without Shakespeare and his influence on German drama, Wagner could not have conceived of music-drama as he did. One of his earliest compositions was a much adapted version of *Measure for Measure*, and Shakespeare was, for many Germans, the symbol of national self-realization. Nor was English influence only literary and dramatic. Without Berkeley there would have perhaps been no Kant, and so no Schopenhauer. Yet it was in a mainly German atmosphere and tradition that, in 1854, the once revolutionary poet Herwegh introduced Wagner to Schopenhauer's work. *The World as Will and Idea* had by then been published thirty-five years (the enlarged edition only ten years), but had remained almost unknown until 1853. As Ernest Newman says, however, Wagner's enthusiasm did not mean that he took his philosophy from Schopenhauer: the philosopher 'merely reinforced his emotions and intuitions with reasons and arguments'.[3] The refinement on Newman that has to be made is that these emotions and intuitions were apparently derived from tradition and atmosphere rather than from pure self-examination.

Wagner had, before 1854, been very much concerned with practical revolution. The state of the world was unendurable, but it was to be changed politically, on lines suggested by thinkers like Proudhon and Bakunin. (The aftermath of such ideas was what inspired Shaw to write *The Perfect Wagnerite* (1898), interpreting the *Ring* as propaganda for Socialism; he was mistaken, though Hans Mayer still defends the general idea.) After 1854, political revolution ceased to be Wagner's concern. The unendurable state of the world was recognized by Schopenhauer too. The difference was that Schopenhauer proposed no political scheme of improvement, no heaven on earth such as Marx in his youth was able to envisage. Schopenhauer, like the Buddha, had nothing else to offer but 'The Naught', and this was the new goal that Wagner now set himself.

Within the tradition of dialectical thought, this was not such a very remarkable change. It was, in a sense, as though Wagner had abandoned the Matter of Marx for the Spirit of Hegel, or as though Wotan were to welcome the destruction of the gods which Siegfried must ultimately bring on, rather than create the power of the sword which should effect the overthrow—both essentially his own decisions. The dialectic continued throughout, only the position of the actors had changed. In Marxist thought, the ultimate was the annihilation of all individuality, the breaking down of all walls, whether of the family or of property. But this was a physical equivalent to the annihilation of the individual in Nirvana. Wagner had believed with Proudhon in the annihilation of property; he now believed with Schopenhauer in total annihilation. Either way, division would cease, the barrier between individual and the whole would disappear.

It was also not alien to the dialectical tradition that, despite his belief in self-denial, Wagner remained in his personal life, as Ernest Newman says, a man who 'knew no law of life except the full realization of himself at the moment'.[4] Egotism was at least as strong a force in Germany as any other system of thought, and Wagner's sometimes incredible disregard of other people's interests was not ordinary selfishness, but was buttressed by arguments which almost all the intellectuals so far mentioned had subscribed to or put forward to some degree (as George Santayana sets out in his book on *Egotism in German Philosophy*). A dialectician like Hegel found no difficulty in reconciling supreme egotism with complete self-renunciation.

There is no doubt, all the same, that it was to Schopenhauer that Wagner chiefly looked, philosophically, for the remainder of his life, though Schopenhauer did not reciprocate his admiration, and even said on one occasion that Wagner did not know what music was. The philosopher was an old man by now, rather given to egotism himself. His sarcastic comments in the margin of the poem of the *Ring*, of which Wagner sent him a copy, show little sympathy, though it is true that he may not have troubled to note passages which he liked.[5] Schopenhauer probably never knew that Wagner had tried to obtain a chair of philosophy for him at Zürich, or how similar to his own thought Wagner's was. Wagner, on the other hand, even though the operas were not translations of the philosophy into music, saw the relationship as vital. He wrote at length on Schopenhauer in the essay on Beethoven and in his autobiography, and was particularly indebted on account of what the philosopher had written about the role of music in life. An outline of the main features of Schopenhauer's system will help to make clear the nature of Wagner's debt.

The title of Schopenhauer's main work is difficult to translate, though *The World as Will and Idea* is the title by which it has usually been known in the English-speaking world. The implication that 'the World' is both at once, both Will *and* Idea, is clear enough. But Will does not mean here what it usually means in English; it has nothing to do with personal determination or resolve. It is rather akin to what Kant called 'the thing-in-itself' (though more dynamically active): in other words, reality as it is, independently of any personal view of it, before and after we see it; it is akin to Hegel's Spirit or Marx's 'forces of history'. In Wagner's terms, it is very similar in some ways to 'Rhinegold', though it is also closely related to the Will of Wotan, as he describes it in the dialogue with Brünnhilde at the end of *Die Walküre*. Schopenhauer's Will is inchoate, ruthless, brutal, 'the essence of things', and yet unknowable to any individual consciousness, just as Freud's 'Unconscious' or Jung's 'Collective Unconscious' are. (Both Freud and Jung claim to be able to tell us a good deal about these unknowables, but questioning their authority to speak is outside our range here.) The only way in which the Will becomes known to individual human beings is through what Schopenhauer calls *Vorstellung*.

For this, 'imagination' will not do; it has too many unwanted overtones, though it is one of several meanings which *Vorstellung* has. Taken to pieces, *Vorstellung* is composed of *Vor*, 'before', and *Stellung*, 'placing' or 'position'. When a German says, 'Ich stelle mir vor,' he means, 'I imagine,' but he says, literally, 'I place before myself.' To understand Schopenhauer's meaning, therefore, it has to be seen that the Will makes its appearance in the world by placing itself (or a mirrored image of itself) before itself. The Will feels hunger, which is nothing but hunger until it takes shape as teeth. The Will feels sexual desire, which is nothing until it becomes genital organs. Yet the teeth and the genitals, although *Vorstellung*, are not opposed to the Will; on the contrary, they are intimately connected with it, as an artist's drawing is connected with his deepest creative impulse. Until the drawing takes shape, the nature of the impulse remains hidden. But, like an artist, the Will is continually impelled to show forth what it has in itself, and what it shows is the world we see.

At the same time, the world we see is not identical with the Will. Here Schopenhauer takes up the problem with which Kant and other idealist philosophers were faced: how is it possible for an individual human being to claim knowledge of ultimate reality beyond his own subjective imaginings? At this point, the sense of 'imagination' in *Vorstellung* has a more appropriate part to play. We imagine the world, 'wir stellen uns die Welt vor', but we are frequently aware that this *Vorstellung* is inadequate and needs correction. If we accept Kant's argument (thought not all philosophers would) we conclude that we can never get beyond *Vorstellung*, never know the 'thing-in-itself', except in so far as we have knowledge of the moral law through the categorical imperative. If we go with Hegel, we believe that certain great individuals are capable of knowing the essential spirit of the world, and that these great individuals gain a following precisely because lesser individuals recognize in them the spirit which they are unable to realize effectively in themselves. In Schopenhauer, however, the process is different.

In Schopenhauer, we have to recognize that the world is not necessarily the dual arrangement of subject and object which it seems to us to be. It is only when the Will creates its own *Vorstellung*, when it 'places itself before itself', that it splits up into object and subject: before that moment there is (mythically speaking) perfect unity. And yet, to our imagining, the division is plainly there. We are individuals beyond any doubt, and what one individual sees, thinks, hears, feels is different from what another sees. This is so rooted in our experience that we are unable to see the concealed identity. In reality, Schopenhauer argues, there is no such division. The dilemma of Kant about the unknowableness of the 'thing-in-itself' was a delusion. We are not separate individuals, because the Will 'realizes itself', in other words, makes itself real, in each of us. The Will is 'that which is known to everyone without intermediary', and since the Will is a unity, its manifestations, its *Vorstellungen*, are a unity. Thus Schopenhauer can say 'the world is Will, through and through', and at the same time 'the world is *Vorstellung* through and through'. There is no insoluble paradox about this, he says, since the *Vorstellung* is the mirror of the Will. The paradox is rather in the inability of human beings to recognize their essential unity. In the Sanskrit saying which Schopenhauer quotes, that unity is clear enough: 'Tat tvam asi': 'That art thou': each of us is the Will in all its aspects, consoling as well as terrifying, inspiring as well as nauseating. To recognize that I am the bomb or the tiger which destroys me is the root of wisdom.

There are objections to this line of argument which could not be even sketched in the space available here. The important fact, so far as Wagner is concerned, is that Schopenhauer sees the world as a mirror of the Will. The idea is of some antiquity. In Jakob Böhme, for instance, the Silesian mystic of the early seventeenth century who inspired William Blake as well as many of the German Romantics, the creation of the world is seen as a violent desire in the Naught, which preceded the creation, to produce a mirror-image of itself; when it does so, the mirror-image becomes a kind of female counterpart and lover of the primal Naught. No such sexual symbolism appears in Schopenhauer, even though the Will is erotic. Yet there is little doubt that Wagner echoed Schopenhauer, whether consciously or not, in several passages of the *Ring*. The end of *Rheingold* is a case in point. If the parallel between the gold and the Will is accepted at all (it does not tally perfectly), the song of the Rhinemaidens becomes a kind of lament that the Will has passed into the world of *Vorstellung*. The gods pass over in triumph into the new Valhalla, pursued by the mocking irony of Loge, the god who knows that the division between the depths of the Rhine and the heights of the rainbow-bridge is an illusion. But though the deceiver Loge promises the Rhinemaidens that the mirror-image, as it were, will suffice, since the gold will still be there in the world of 'appearances':

> Glänzt nicht mehr
> euch Mädchen das Gold,
> in der Götter neuem Glanze
> sonnt euch selig fortan!

> (Though no longer
> The gold gleams on you maidens
> Yet in the gods' new radiance
> Sun yourselves blissfully henceforth,)

the Rhinemaidens know otherwise:

> Rheingold! Rheingold!
> Reines Gold!
> O leuchtete noch
> in der Tiefe dein lautrer Tand!
> Traulich und treu
> ists nur in der Tiefe:
> falsch und feig
> ist, was dort oben sich freut!

> (Rhinegold, Rhinegold,
> Pure gold!
> If only still shone

In the depths your sheer glitter!
  Tender and true
  It can be only in the depths.
  False and cowardly
Is all that rejoices up there.)[6]

The gold which the gods have appropriated to their own use is still the same Rhinegold, just as the Will which becomes *Vorstellung* in the world is still the Will. But both gold and Will are perfect only in their undisturbed state, in the depths of the Rhine or before the division into subjectivity and objectivity. At the same time, the words with which the maidens sing of the gold have curious overtones. 'Dein lautrer Tand' is reasonably translated as 'your sheer (or pure or mere) glitter'. But *Tand* is a pejorative word, not really the kind of word you would expect the maidens to use if they were simply praising the gold. *Tand* is akin to 'tinsel', 'tawdry'; Wagner uses it in *Die Meistersinger von Nürnberg* to decry French music. It is as though the maidens were half-recognizing the essential nothingness of the gold they have been guarding.

The Will is, after all, really nothing. It is the Naught which mirrors itself in the world, and to recognize its nonentity is the only way in which one can escape from the nonentity of existence into the Naught of Nirvana. Perhaps there is no real difference between the two, only our imaginings: we imagine distinctions which in the deepest sense do not exist, so the sequence of thought runs. Yet the implication, that the deepest things themselves are only *Tand*, is disturbing. As Yeats wrote: 'Empty eyeballs knew/Mirror on mirror mirror'd is all the show.' The Naught, mirrored, could only be Naught. No quality, whether trivial or superb, could ever be attached to it. Was Loge's irony directed not only at the gods' fleeting possession of the ring, but, *via* the maidens, at the ring itself?

The image of the mirror recurs in *Die Walküre* in the relationship between Siegmund and Sieglinde, each of whom sees in the other his or her own self. As Sieglinde sings to Siegmund:[7]

        Im Bach erblickt' ich
          mein eigen Bild
      und jetzt gewahr ich es wieder.

        (In the stream I saw
         My own image
        And now I see it again.)

But not only Siegmund and Sieglinde reflect one another. Sieglinde sees in Siegmund a resemblance, or more than that, to Wotan:

> Deines Auges Glut
> erglänzte mir schon:
> So blickte der Greis
> grüssend auf mich,
> als der Traurigen Trost er gab.

> (The blaze in your eyes
> Has shone on me before.
> So the old man gazed
> At me in greeting
> When he brought comfort to me in my sadness.)

Both brother and sister are something like mirror-images of Wotan himself, and 'Tat tvam asi' applies very well to them.

The progression of events in Schopenhauer does not end with this 'objectivation' of the Will in the world of real phenomena. As this objectivation goes on, it produces a self-awareness in the Will: it is a process of self-realization, the very word that was used earlier for Germany's political development in the nineteenth century. The Will—which, it must be remembered, is not the superficial will of any one individual, but a deep driving force in him of which he is unconscious—recognizes itself more and more clearly in the mirror presented to it by the world of phenomena, and as it does so, it is increasingly filled with revulsion. What had before been blind impulse now becomes self-aware, and at the point of complete self-awareness, as Schopenhauer describes it, one of two things happens. The Will either affirms itself ('bejaht sich'—'says yes to itself') or denies itself. If it affirms itself, the situation is like this:

> having been presented in its objectivated state, that is, in the shape of the world and life as a whole, with its own essential being, completely and clearly, in the form of *Vorstellung*, this awareness does not inhibit its willing in any way, but this very same life is willed by the Will just as it is; although whereas before this was without awareness, as a blind impulse, it is now with awareness, consciously and soberly.[8]

Here the Will is not put off by the sight of its mirrored self, but goes on as before, knowing just what it is doing. This is, in effect, the course which Nietzsche took, refusing to allow any insight into human nature to destroy his 'will-to-live'—though there is nothing 'sober' in Nietzsche's decision; on the contrary, he insists on gaiety.

The other possibility shows when the will-to-live (roughly a synonym for the Will) denies itself. This occurs

> when, upon that awareness [i.e. the total mirroring of the Will] all willing ends, and then it is no longer the individual phenomena, of which the Will has become aware, which function as motives ['Motive'] of the Will, but rather the whole awareness of the essence of the world, which has come to maturity through the conceiving of the [Platonic] Ideas, now becomes a quietus ['Quietiv'] for the Will, and the Will thus freely annuls itself.[9]

As Schopenhauer himself says, some of this is hardly intelligible, but the general intention seems to be that there is not so much a renunciation of the Will (or by the Will), as a cessation of activity when the full mirroring of the Will has occurred. One further point also needs to be made. When Schopenhauer speaks of the Will annulling itself, he uses a word of ambiguous meaning. 'Und so der Wille frei sich selbst aufhebt'[10] ('and the Will thus freely annuls itself') is also capable of meaning 'and thus the Will freely lifts itself up to a higher state in which it preserves itself', for *aufheben* means both to 'lift up' and to 'preserve', as well as to 'annul' or 'cancel'. Hegel freely uses the word in all three senses, and often ambiguously.

It would be hard to assert that Schopenhauer uses *aufheben* deliberately in an ambiguous sense in this passage. Yet, in the final paragraph of the main section, he does seem to allow of a certain ambiguity. Confronting the possible charge that if all he has to offer in place of this world is a mere nothing, a gloomy recognition that behind all virtue and all sanctity there is merely a void, he answers that what remains after the total annulment of the Will is certainly, for all those who are still full of Will, Nothing. 'But conversely for those in whom the Will has turned about and denied itself, this so very real world of ours with all its suns and Milky Ways—is Nothing.'

In these final words Schopenhauer uses 'Nothing' in a sense different from the one in which he uses it in the sentence before. He suggests that there is or may after all be some supreme realization, greater even than the starry heavens (compared with which they are as nothing), for those in whom the Will is annulled. But he may also be read as declaring that the suns and the Milky Ways are themselves, being Nothing, the blissful state to which the world aspires. In other words, to lose one's life is to save it, or, in Goethe's words:

Und so lang du dies nicht hast,
Dieses: Stirb, und werde!
Bist du nur ein trüber Gast
Auf der dunklen Erde.

(And so long as you have it not,
This 'Die, and grow and live!'
You will be but a sorry guest
On this gloomy earth.)

Wagner is in accord with this, though even more with Goethe's indication in the same poem ('Selige Sehnsucht', 'Blissful Longing') that the way to this death and life is through a desire for a *höhere Begattung* ('higher sexual union'). Wagner is, in fact, more explicit than Schopenhauer, and less ambiguous. When he first wrote the poem of the *Ring* he included lines for Brünnhilde, just before her self-immolation, which pointed in so many words to the continued existence at least of love after all else had vanished. Neither gold nor glory nor marriage nor morality should be retained:

Nicht trüber Verträge
Trügender Bund,
Nicht heuchelnder Sitte
Hartes Gesetz:

(Neither the deceptive bonds
Of gloomy contracts
Nor the harsh law
Of hypocritical morals)

—but in contrast, the total acceptance which only love could bring:

Selig in Lust und Leid
Lässt—die Liebe nur sein.

(Blissful in joy and sorrow alike
Love alone—lets be.)[11]

This, dating from the time when Wagner was still a positive affirmer of Life, a 'Yea-sayer', as Nietzsche would have put it, no longer seemed appropriate when he took up *Götterdämmerung* again in 1869. True, at the moment she would have sung this, Brünnhilde is about to give up her life, but the words suggest that the world of phenomena is, to the eyes of love, still and always acceptable. Love lets be, whether the experience is of joy or sorrow. Influenced by Schopenhauer (it may be), Wagner deleted the words and tried to substitute others which would

46

accord more closely with the philosopher's ideas. In the end, however, he abandoned these as well, believing that the music expressed with greater precision all that he wanted to say.

What remains in the music is not pure Schopenhauer after all. After the destruction of Valhalla, the audience is left confronting not an awful emptiness, no gaping, terrible Naught, but the love motive. But Love implies beings, relationships which Schopenhauer's 'Naught' cannot tolerate. The similarity with Wagner is rather in Goethe's *Faust*—in the final scene which Mahler used for the Eighth Symphony —in the lines:

> Blitze, durchwettert mich!
> Dass ja das Nichtige
> Alles verflüchtige,
> Glänze der Dauerstern,
> Ewiger Liebe Kern.

> (Lightnings, so shatter me,
> That all of mortality's
> Vain unrealities
> Die, and the Star above
> Beam but Eternal Love!)[12]

—an image quite close to that of the gold returned to the Rhine. Wagner presents the synthesis nakedly: the burning gods before our eyes, and the love motive in our ears, very much as Ibsen does in the conclusion of *Brand* (written in 1865), when the avalanche descends while a voice speaks out of the roaring destruction: 'He is *deus caritatis*.' (Thomas Mann draws attention to other parallels with Ibsen in his *Sufferings and Greatness of Richard Wagner*, near the beginning.)

Wagner does not necessarily follow Schopenhauer very closely. In several of his operas, the conclusion is not Nirvana but continuance of love beyond the grave, which sometimes has more affinity with Novalis's *Hymns to the Night*. But Schopenhauer provided Wagner with more than the stimulus of ideas. Equally welcome were the comments on music in paragraph 52 of his major work, and in the supplementary essay, 'On the Metaphysics of Music'. For Schopenhauer, all art stood in some relation to the Will, to the 'thing-in-itself', but arts such as architecture and literature were at one remove from it. What was to be had from these inferior arts was a recognition of Platonic ideas, these ideas being objectivations of the Will. Music, however, was the highest of all the arts, being itself a direct objectivation of the Will, the Will itself speaking of the essence, without any intermediary.

Even here Schopenhauer was not the sole inspiration. Similar views had been expressed not long before, by Wackenroder, Schumann (and later by George Sand), while Friedrich Schlegel claimed that music constituted, as it were, the only universal language in existence. E. T. A. Hoffman saw in music not only a healing power but a means to conjure up 'those mighty spirits who stir up fear, horror and hopeless yearning in man's soul'. All this was part of Wagner's inheritance and he was all the less likely to question it.

Nor do Schopenhauer's much more questionable views on tragedy seem to have aroused Wagner's opposition. Hegel, after all, had placed tragedy rather than music highest of all the arts, whereas Schopenhauer accords it a lower position: one is entitled to think any such hierarchy meaningless. Yet it is easy to see how Schopenhauer's view of tragedy must have appealed to Wagner: he sees it as essentially showing the protagonist freely yielding up his life, the will-to-live having perished. This was very close to what Wagner had seen as tragic in *Der fliegende Holländer*, and was to repeat in the *Ring* and *Tristan*, though, of course, it will only fit the facts of a very small number of tragedies in the whole history of the genre. Far more rewarding to Wagner was the assertion that music was directly concerned with the essence of things, and, more than that, presented a vision of all possible events in life and in the world:

> For music [Schopenhauer writes in *The World as Will and Idea*] is, as we have said, different from all other arts in that it is not an image of the appearance, or rather of the adequate objectivation of the Will, but a direct image of the Will itself, and thus presents the metaphysic to all physicality in the world, the Thing-in-Itself of every phenomenon. Accordingly, one could just as well say of the world that it is music incarnate, as that it is Will incarnate; from this it becomes explicable why music makes every picture, every scene of real life and of the world stand out with a higher meaning—the more so, it is true, the more analogous its melody is to the inner spirit of the phenomenon concerned.[13]

When Wagner was so intent on expressing the whole cosmos in his music, these must have been very gratifying words indeed.

Yet, in his gratitude, Wagner could easily have overlooked the lack in Schopenhauer of any critical standpoint about music. Clearly, not all music of whatever kind can possess that essential quality which Schopenhauer claims for it. He was probably thinking of Beethoven, but the issue still remains: *which* music, even of Beethoven's, is a direct image of the Will? Schopenhauer admits as much, in saying that the higher meaning is more evident, 'the more analogous the melody is to the inner spirit . . .'. It is not merely by the fact of being music that music has such value, and it seems highly doubtful whether, philosophically speaking, any such claim can be made for it at all.

Music was, for Schopenhauer, what the categorical imperative was for Kant, and Christ was for Luther: direct access to the heart of the mystery. But Schopenhauer goes beyond Kant's claim, in that he sees music not merely as one way of glimpsing the eternal, but as a microcosmic version of the macrocosm, that is, as the whole world in miniature. It is difficult to go all the way with Schopenhauer here, even for those who believe that music is life. He suggests, for instance, that there is confirmation of his view in the fact that the groundbass corresponds to the lowest stage of objectivation, a kind of stirring of the Will, while the higher voices not only arise in accordance with it, but correspond to the mineral (tenor), vegetable (contralto) and animal (soprano) kingdoms. This is a rough symbolism of the kind fashionable among Romantic writers and others in Schopenhauer's youth—like Goethe, he wrote a theory of colours which corresponded more closely to his philosophical ideas than to empirical facts. The symbolism may yet be relevant to the fact that *Rheingold* opens with a long passage of almost unchanging bass notes.

More relevant is Schopenhauer's theory that music expresses essences, so that it does not merely convey a joy or a grief, but Joy and Grief (*die* Freude, *den* Schmerz). Again, one may question on philosophical grounds whether any such reference to absolutes is helpful: the joy of Beethoven's Ninth Symphony is quite unlike Zerlina's when she is reconciled to Masetto in *Don Giovanni*. But the function of Wagnerian leading-motives, when they bear or are given names like 'Impotence', 'Menace', 'Renunciation', 'Love', 'Atonement', seems meant to convey a sense of the absolute qualities in each case, and even if the philosophical claim is questionable, the implicit suggestion within Wagner's cosmological framework is part of the effect he wants.

Music is not the supreme good in Schopenhauer's whole system. It is the supreme art, but it releases the artist only temporarily from the conditions of living, which are in all truth infernal. Our life, he says, 'is in its origins and essence hopelessly evil' (but he does not conclude what would perhaps follow, that music is so). Even though the tragedian may point towards this realization, or a painter such as Raphael or Correggio may portray a glimmer of 'that peace beyond all understanding . . . that deep quietude, that unshakeable confidence and serenity' which precedes a final evanescence of the body, there is ultimately nothing but the Naught, and the only path towards serenity is to experience the suffering of the whole world to such a degree that one becomes identified with it. Sympathy, in its original sense—more immediately conveyed by the German *Mitleid*, 'co-suffering'—is the one thing necessary. To suffer with all men, to realize that all men are oneself, 'Tat tvam asi,' is to break down the walls erected by the *principium individuationis*, the alienation from the whole which occurs through the very fact of being an individual. When *Mitleid* is complete, at the same time that the recognition by the Will of its own relentless brutality is complete, all selfhood is renounced. One ceases to will or to want anything, death becomes welcome, a complete quietism emerges such as was practised by Bodhisattvas, pietists, quietists and the 'beautiful soul' whose spiritual life Goethe portrayed in the sixth book of *Wilhelm Meister*. Schopenhauer quotes with approval the quietist Madame de Guyon, 'All is indifferent to me; I *can* will nothing more: I often do not even know whether I am here or not.' And this, as he sees it, is the consonance of his philosophy with Christianity. 'All love (*agapé, caritas*) is sympathy. All love that is not sympathy is self-seeking. Self-seeking is Eros. Sympathy is Agapé.'

It was just such a feeling as Madame de Guyon's that Wagner expressed in his letter of December 1854 to Liszt, a yearning for 'complete unconsciousness, total non-existence, the vanishing of all dreams'. And although Wagner denied having had more from Schopenhauer than the addition of another note to his spiritual discords, it seems significant that *Tristan* was conceived just at the time, in the autumn of 1854, when he had been so impressed by the philosopher's book. *Parsifal*, of course, is rooted in Schopenhauerian sympathy.

Yet, when we look more closely even at *Tristan*, the essentially Wagnerian interpretation becomes apparent. Tristan is not seeking Nirvana when he tears off his bandages, and such a suicidal act would, in any case, never have had Schopenhauer's approval: suicide for Schopenhauer was merely one more act of self-assertion, in this case against the necessity to go on living. The death of Tristan is a means towards going on loving Isolde (however paradoxical that may be, if neither of them exists separately beyond the grave):

> Mit blutender Wunde
> Erjage ich mir heut Isolden

(With bloody wound
I gain today Isolde.)[14]

The paradox of love beyond self-annihilation is something Schopenhauer never contemplated, though it is the theme of opera after opera of Wagner's before and after his encounter with the philosopher, and is perhaps present even as early as *Rienzi*.

Wagner also diverges from Schopenhauer when he comes to the conclusion of *Parsifal*. Whereas when Tristan tore the bandages from his wounds there was no earthly help for him, when Amfortas exposes his own wound he is cured not by himself renouncing the world, but by the touch of the same spear that wounded him, and this spear has both Christian and phallic overtones: it bleeds in sympathy with Amfortas's wound, but is held erect; it is not a cross, but a rod that saves. Also foreign to Schopenhauer is the notion of a redeemer. Nothing in Schopenhauer suggests that there is anything but the Naught in view, nothing corresponds to the restoration of the Grail to the community of knights, or to the idea of one man restoring life to many.

In any case, it may be questioned whether Wagner's music can ever be held to state the verbal proposition which the text affirms. Music, it must surely be said, has no philosophical or religious meaning at all such as can be put in words.

It was therefore strange in a way that Nietzsche should have chosen to make his break from Wagner on account of the so-called Christian qualities of *Parsifal*. Wagner did, it is true, astonish Nietzsche by speaking of his deep repentance, and of his leaning towards Christian dogmas, so much so that Nietzsche could only believe that it was all inspired by sycophancy towards the allegedly Christian rulers of Germany. The opera itself was nothing like so Christian, and perhaps it is even impossible to say what significance the touch of the spear actually has—at all events the symbolism is complex. Yet Nietzsche's eventual opposition to Wagner calls for our close attention.

Nietzsche had grown up with Wagner's music, and was wildly enthusiastic at an early age.[15] When he played the piano score of *Tristan* in 1860, he was only sixteen, thirty-one years younger than Wagner. Eight years later he seized with alacrity the chance to meet Wagner. In 1869 he was appointed to a chair of classics in Basle, not so far from Triebschen, where Wagner was living by that time, and, from then on, for a while did everything in his power to defend and promote Wagner's reputation, not only as a composer, but as a German composer. *The Birth of Tragedy from the Spirit of Music*, written during the Franco-

Prussian War of 1870–71 which led to the foundation of the Reich, had a preface addressed to Wagner, and included as a part of its argument the statement that the last words of Wagner's Isolde expressed the very combination of the Apolline and the Dionysian that Nietzsche saw as the essence of Greek tragedy. The work was written at a time when Nietzsche was enthusiastic in the German cause, and the claims on Wagner's behalf seemed to chime with this.

Only a few years later, however, Nietzsche was disillusioned. The new Germany of Bismarck was not what he had hoped for, and in his *Thoughts out of Season* he went over to the attack. The chief error his contemporaries were making, he now declared, was that German victory in battle meant a victory for German culture. He feared 'the extirpation of the German spirit in favour of the "German Reich" '. Wagner could no longer be praised as the great German composer; he was rather, Nietzsche believed, one of the great Germans who were more than Germans (*überdeutsch*), one who chimed not with the present condition of Germany, in the 1870s, but with the future. The lesson Germany must learn from Wagner was to be like Wotan, to give up power in the knowledge that power is evil; like Brünnhilde, to give up knowledge out of love; like Siegfried, to be free and fearless, 'to grow and blossom in innocent selfhood'.

Nietzsche's turning away from Wagner can, then, be understood as the outcome of his further disappointment: within only a few years both Germany and Wagner successively proved to have feet of clay. Wagner had given up the daring opposition to the values of German society which Nietzsche had supposed him to represent. Wagner's optimism and his belief in Greek gaiety and serenity (*Heiterkeit*) had been undermined by Schopenhauer, from whom Nietzsche had also turned away. Wagner had been diverted from his social and political revolutionary aims into a quietistic, subjective quest for individual fulfilment, and his attempt at establishing through Bayreuth a community of renouncers of the world was now no more than a cynical supplying of what an exhausted society needed: 'brutality, artificiality and innocence'.

All this was in *Der Fall Wagner* (*The Case of Wagner*), published in 1888, though already in *Human, All-too Human* Nietzsche had made allusive attacks on both Wagner and Cosima. (The reference in para. 164 to geniuses who take themselves to be gods was meant to apply to Wagner, while para. 430 implicitly condemns Wagner for allowing Cosima to bear the brunt of attacks on him. There are many scattered references, too, in *The Will to Power*,[16] and a section in *Ecce Homo*.) He went on then to make that accusation already mentioned, that Wagner was more a mime, a man of the theatre, than a musician. Wagner was not a musician by instinct, but became one because he was an actor; he made music an adjunct of drama. More than that, he had turned music into 'Idea', or, in other words, had provided equivalents in music for what were supposed to be absolutes—a notion Nietzsche could not tolerate. And worst of all, Wagner was a representative of mass-culture and of the advent of Bismarck's 'Reich'.

Nietzsche's criticism, despite the fact that he was nearing insanity when he wrote it, is worth attention. It is, basically, that Wagner has, in *Parsifal* at all events, pretended that a performance in the theatre, in which one does not participate as one does in a religious service, can in some way be an equivalent for the religious service: that what is only contemplated aesthetically, can matter as much as what one loves with all one's heart and soul and strength. (Tolstoy's case against Wagner, in *What is Art?*, was similar.) Nietzsche is opposed, in short, to what in modern parlance would be called 'camp'—the detached enjoyment of something to which one is not devoted. He is also opposed to the alternation between the ideal of *Tristan* and that of *Parsifal*:

> Modern man presents, biologically, a contradiction in values, he sits between two stools, he says 'Yes' and 'No' in one and the same breath. What wonder then, that it was in our own times that falsity became flesh, and even became a genius? that Wagner 'dwelled among us'?[17]

Wagner was, in Nietzsche's eyes, a man who essentially followed Hegel in his affirmation of contraries, whereas for Nietzsche there were only two alternatives, Zarathustra or Parsifal. Or so he felt, though his own ambiguities are at least as pervasive. The works of his last years are shot through with his preoccupation with Wagner—*Götzendämmerung* (*Twilight of the Idols*) is a derisive allusion, and *Nietzsche contra Wagner* continues the attack.

But there was not only opposition, there was also desperation in Nietzsche's awareness that, after the first Bayreuth festival of 1876, he was deprived of the one bold spirit he had looked to:

> [I was] weary too, not least from the grief of a merciless suspicion that from now on I was condemned to distrust more deeply, despise more deeply, to be alone more deeply than ever before. For I had *nobody* but Richard Wagner . . . I have always been *condemned* to Germans . . .[18]

The bitterness of that famous cry suggests how much Nietzsche cared for and looked to Wagner. It also strikes the keynote for the main trend of later discussion, so far as Germany's leading intellectuals were concerned. Was Wagner a representative of the best in Germany or the worst, or of both simultaneously, in the 'modern' spirit as Nietzsche defined it?

It is a sad thing that Nietzsche's criticisms of Wagner are so unspecific. No one was more devoted to Wagner than he had been, and the sudden reversal (akin to so many other contradictory attitudes in Nietzsche's life) makes one impatient for detail. He excuses himself on the ground that he once loved Wagner, and with that we must be content. Yet, if we probe past the often merely sarcastic remarks, some more precise picture of what was in Nietzsche's mind can at any rate be suggested.

The wildest of the criticisms is that Wagner continues the line of 'life-denial' with which Luther had crippled the Renaissance, a criticism which could not be made of, say, *Die Meistersinger*, and which seems to contradict the accusation that Wagner is ambiguous. One probably does best to regard each opera as the exploration of a possibility rather than a philosophical statement, though Wagner certainly invites, theoretically, a philosophical criticism. Certainly, Nietzsche was aiming a shrewd blow at Wagner the man, and the author of *Parsifal*, when he spoke of the current trend to combine Christian charity with anti-semitism. His disgust is comprehensible, though it should not extend to the paradoxes of the operas. But it often seems as though Wagner were not aiming at a consistent philosophy at all. The sheer individual fulfilment of *Tristan* gives way to the communal fulfilment of *Parsifal*: Wagner might have said he had always wanted both.

Another thrust of Nietzsche's is the charge that all Wagner's heroines, stripped of their mythological covering, become 'almost indistinguishable from Madame Bovary', in other words from the model of sentimentalized Romantic love-ecstasy. The operagoer who wants to test Wagner's power need only compare his heroines with Flaubert's. Whatever conclusion he reaches, there is no denying Nietzsche's charge that Wagner is devoid of ironical detachment. Whether he deserves the barb that he is the German Victor Hugo is another matter. At the root of Nietzsche's criticism is the accusation that the lack of detachment is so great as to produce a stifling adherence to the emotion of the moment —'The way Wagner's emotion holds its breath, refuses to let go an extreme feeling, achieves a terrifying *duration* of states when even a moment threatens to strangle us'—this is one more form of the criticism that, far from being self-renouncing, Wagner's music was grossly self-indulgent.

But more probing than any other criticism of Nietzsche's was the charge that Wagner blithely disregarded realities which he could not properly dismiss. At times, this sounds like mere rationalistic criticism, as when Nietzsche absurdly suggests that we strip Parsifal of his medieval armour and consider him, in modern terms, as a candidate in theology. A fairer proposal occurs when Nietzsche could seem to be at his most flippant:

> Siegfried 'emancipates woman'—but without any hope of progeny.— One fact, finally, which leaves us dumbfounded: Parsifal is the father of Lohengrin. How did he do it?—Must one remember at this point that 'chastity works miracles'?—*Wagnerus dixit princeps in castitate auctoritas*. (Says Wagner, foremost authority on chastity.)[19]

A scrupulous critic will object to this coupling of one opera with another, and of both with Wagner's own life. The Parsifal who refuses Kundry need have nothing to do with Lohengrin, in another work. Yet what Nietzsche is driving at is shown when he accuses Parsifal of rejecting 'the very conditions of life'. Without sexual love there is no life, and by seeming to ignore this, Wagner was avoiding one of the deepest truths. 'Have you ever noticed,' Nietzsche asks, 'that Wagner's heroines never have children?' It was a profound enough question; and if we choose to consider what Isolde's love would mean in terms of real life, we have only to compare her with Anna Karenina. The operas, however much one may admire them, take place in a world which has no contact with the social reality of Wagner's or our own world. The symbolism has no backing from the world of bodily experience; it is never truly incarnate. This is what Nietzsche meant when he classed Wagner along with the *Hinterweltler*, the 'backworldsmen' or 'metaphysicians', who looked for fulfilment in non-human conditions.

Nietzsche's criticism of Wagner's music was similar. Principally, it was that it had lost contact with the body, that one could not dance to it as one could to Mozart (again, this is not true of passages from *Die Meistersinger*), that it had become chaotic, that it threatened to swamp the human in the name of the metaphysical, as Nietzsche believed the German nation to have done. Wagner was dictatorial, and showed it nowhere more than in his plots, which were arbitrary. (Why, in fact, should Tristan bring about his own death at the moment when the dearest woman on earth is about to be restored to him? Does not philosophy override a natural human response here?)

If there is any guiding thought in Nietzsche's attack, it is, then, an insistence on the human condition, *das Diesseitige*, and on a healthy, deeply grounded love, here and now. He rejected Wagner after *Parsifal* because, as he saw it, the composer could not provide an art which, while remaining profound, would answer to reality, take on the flesh, in the fullest sense. Whether the love between Walther and Eva in *Die Meistersinger* met his expectations he never said; Wagner might have replied that he had taken the measure of that, too. And indeed, Wagner had made the same point about music that could be danced to, the same point about the need for body and spirit to be one.

Yet the full complexity of Nietzsche's position is not realized until one remembers that his own philosophy was always at least as much interrelated with Christianity as was Wagner's music, not only in *Parsifal* but also in *Tannhaüser*. To castigate Wagner for turning to Christianity was illogical in a man who never lost sight of the idea that every human being has his own crucifixion to undergo. Nietzsche's Superman is not simply a 'blond beast': he is one who has gone to the uttermost limits of self-awareness, who knows what a Christian might call the sinfulness in himself, through and through. 'There has only ever been one real Christian, and he died on the cross': that saying of Nietzsche's, double-edged as it is, expresses his own ambiguous relationship to Christ. When the philosopher finally broke down, Jakob Burckhardt was able to detect the madness that had now enveloped him through the signature on Nietzsche's message to him: 'The crucified Dionysus'. That was one last sign of the dichotomy which marks all Nietzsche's writings, and not least his criticism of Wagner.

Thomas Mann was inclined to see in Nietzsche's criticisms not an attack but a panegyric: 'it was love-hate, self-castigation', and 'rather a stimulus to enthusiasm than a crippling of it'. That is going very far indeed, and yet stays within the spirit of these dialectical confrontations. Nietzsche was very close to Wagner, even in rejecting him, just as he was to Socrates, Christ and the German nation of his own day, however much he might oppose them. Even Nietzsche's opposition to Wagner's anti-semitism was ambiguous; it is easy to find passages in Nietzsche's own writings which despise the Jews as a race, and so it is with everything he wrote: the simultaneous 'Yes' and 'No' which Nietzsche detested in Wagner is equally apparent in his own work.

Mann, the chief figure in the later intellectual tradition to make both Nietzsche and Wagner into foci of his thought, remains in the same ambiguity. His first novel, *Buddenbrooks*, represents Wagner's music as a turning-point in German history. Yet the deep doubts that Mann maintained, even in his early twenties, are shown by the fact that Hanno Buddenbrook's Wagnerian improvisation on the piano in the final pages takes the form of a sexual orgy for one. Mann had taken in the force of Nietzsche's criticism, yet could not resist what he felt as Wagner's allurement. His stories 'Tristan' and 'Blood of the Volsungs' deal directly with the perverse and even lethal effects of Wagner's music, as Mann saw it. *Doctor Faustus*, in representing the fate of Germany in the twentieth century through the life of a composer (Schoenberg thought, very reasonably, that he himself was intended) is closely connected: the music of Leverkühn, the modern Faust, is an eerie combination of the angelic and the diabolical, even, *per impossibile*, an identification of the two. Throughout his life, Mann could never escape from the ambiguity. In 1911 he could write that 'as a mind, as a character, [Wagner] seemed to me suspect, as an artist irresistible, even if deeply ambiguous in relation to the nobility, the purity, and the healthiness of his effects'. Yet, at that time, Mann was inclined to think that Wagner's star was waning. Wagner was 'essentially of the nineteenth century', and the masterpiece of the twentieth century would be —echoing Nietzsche's criticism?—logical, formal, clear and healthy.

Even then, however, Mann could not resist the call of Wagner's 'shrewd and sensuous, romantic and wily magic'. The strange contrasts are in evidence again. And some twenty years later he could still not evade them.

By 1933, the dubiousness of Wagner seemed to some critics to be confirmed by the fact that he was enthusiastically adopted by the Nazis (Hitler, it may be recalled, was swept off his feet by *Lohengrin* at the age of twelve.) Nietzsche became a prop to the new régime in much the same way, along with Hölderlin, Kleist, Meister Eckhart and, indeed, most of the German pantheon, if Alfred Rosenberg was to be believed. (For Rosenberg, in *The Myth of the Twentieth Century*, though he made some shrewd criticisms of the operas, Wagner revealed 'the essential quality of all Occidental art'; he found the Nordic ideal of beauty in Lohengrin and Siegfried, the highest values of what he styled 'Nordic-Occidental man' in Wotan, King Mark and Hans Sachs.)

Mann had no need to make any great effort to shrug off the exploitation of Wagner's work by Nazi apologists. Wagner, as he observed, had not abandoned the 'bourgeois age' in which he was born to exchange it for 'a totalitarianism that murders the spirit'. Yet—and here the intricacy of the background becomes most apparent, when one considers how firmly opposed Mann was to everything that Nazism stood for—

there is a curious echo of Rosenberg in that Mann also accepts Wagner as showing the essential German nature.

There *was* a difference, all the same: for Mann, Wagner represented German qualities, while at the same time, like Mann himself, he stood at a distance from them. Thus, even in the middle of his own panegyric, Mann could write:

> ... *apart from the fact* that this *oeuvre* is an eruptive revelation of the essence of German-ness, it is also an actor's representation of it, a representation so intellectual, so garish and like a poster (*plakathafte Wirksamkeit*) in its effects that it amounts to a grotesque parody and seems intended to inspire a world-wide public, inquisitively and shudderingly attentive, to cry out 'Ah ça c'est bien allemand par exemple!' ... Wagner's art is the most sensational self-portrayal and self-criticism of German nature that one could well imagine....[20]

The truth of this characterization is not so important at the moment as the indication it gives of the prolonged ambiguity in the relationship of outstanding Germans to Wagner's music, an ambiguity that continued until at least the middle of the twentieth century. To understand that ambiguity, one has to remember that the combination of an extreme positive with an extreme negative has been essential to the dialectical tradition ever since Hegel. Mann does not see the German-ness Wagner portrays as wholly beneficent—the 'shudderingly attentive' population of the rest of the world must have had some cause to shudder, and Siegfried's 'Funeral March' is barbarously splendid enough, in all conscience. Yet there are times when, for Mann, the full assertion of German-ness in all its contradictory qualities is equivalent to a full statement of all that matters in humanity. In such a frame of mind, none of the contradictions in Wagner matter, any more than it matters if Nietzsche's attack was really a defence. The opposites resolve themselves into a single identity which has cosmic portentousness.

Against the background of German thought between Hegel and Mann there is, in fact, no place for criticism, only for a continual inter-pretation and circulation of opposite poles. Within that tradition, Wagner becomes one more of those who spin the dialectical wheel, and it does not matter very much whether one or other of the opposites emerges uppermost, whether Wagner is closer to Nietzsche or to Schopenhauer, since the interlinkings between them all are so complex and subtle.

From outside the tradition the whole question changes. When one is mainly concerned with the success or partial success of particular works in various aspects—music, drama, language—the need to reconcile opposites disappears. We do not expect Shakespeare, after all, to reconcile *Lear* with *As You Like It*, and it is only because Wagner's work seems to be meant more as a unified whole, and to have a unitive philosophy, that these difficulties about his work arise. Once the issue becomes a purely musical or literary one, the grandiose schemes disappear, and the operas are better appreciated, in many respects, without them. Wagner's genius was neither literary nor philosophical, it was musical, and it is to musical considerations that we should look for the true measure of his achievement. The great dramatic qualities of his music at its best have little need of philosophy: they make their effect on the pulses; words will never convey more precisely what they signify.

THREE

The Literary Background

POETRY, POETIC DRAMA
AND MUSIC DRAMA

MICHAEL BLACK

WAGNER KNEW that he was not merely a German composer, or a writer of operas, or a 'Romantic' artist. He was giving the whole of European musical and dramatic art a new direction by turning the stream of fully developed orchestral music into the 'dried bed' of opera. His metaphor is appropriate: opera had drained away into the sand and pebbles because it had lost direction and depth, and it needed to be brought back to its expressive purpose and its relationship with the community in order to become national and popular at the deepest level. To make it once again express that kind of personal and social consciousness, Wagner had to re-create it. Like many reformers, he did so by going back *ad fontes*, to the spiritual and social spring-head. So all dramatic endeavour since the Greeks was to be summed up anew in his work, completed, and given a new direction.

This chapter is a prelude to an account of that music-drama; the themes traced here are the intrinsic and historical relationships between poetry and music, poetic drama and musical drama, written by one interested primarily in poetry and drama.[1] From that point of view, Wagner's own account in his prose works necessarily seems incomplete or biased in detail, in the way that a great practitioner's preconceptions must be, if they are to under-pin his own art. But the historian and critic can still be guided by that powerful beam, using his small torch on the shadows it creates. It is remarkable how much of Wagner's account can be taken over unchanged.

It is a commonplace that song and gesture are more immediately and richly expressive—more primitive—than everyday speech, which is usually cliché. Speech, to become more adequate, rises by one step to

60

poetry, and now by a further step to song. But we only have to go back to the European Middle Ages to find that, in popular art, poetry *was* song; there were until recently oral poets in Europe who could not produce a poetic verbal form until they sang it. We resort to gesture when lost for words: hence mime and dance. Art is, in one aspect, expressive power, part of the urge backwards from the shared conceptual commonplace to the directly felt. Individual arts have often claimed that adequacy, immediacy, richness and complexity of expression have been at their command only; have been jealous of their own powers, and always fearful that a neighbour art is a trespasser. The relationship between poetry, poetic drama, music and opera since the Renaissance has these striking aspects: that the two great periods of expressiveness in literature coincide with those of music, and that in both periods the two arts have converged and tended to struggle for primacy. In the first (what we call the baroque), dramatic poetry was the dominant partner, at first tolerant, possibly even contemptuous of the beginnings of opera, yet finding itself encroached on at the end of the seventeenth century. In the second (what we call the Romantic period), music was overwhelmingly more powerful, socially more powerful—more used, more 'consumed'. Poetic drama was a mere revival, fearful for its own continuance in the face of music, and above all of Wagner. In the eighteenth century, the barren literary period between the baroque and Romantic eras, the causes which atrophied poetry and poetic drama also affected opera; yet it was opera which in that period flourished best as a social art form. The twin links between the two vital periods—the continuing literary traditions which kept alive the hope of a revival of poetic drama and, by extension, of a popular music-drama—were the tradition of Shakespearian performance, translation and criticism; and the related growth, first in Germany and then in France and England, of a critical tradition and a fruitful aesthetic which replaced the canons of neoclassicism. This produced a revival of poetic drama and a great flourishing of lyric poetry. Yet it can be argued that the main beneficiary was finally opera, and above all Wagner's music-drama. That is the basic outline of this chapter.

But we must first look back to Greece, as all subsequent art has looked back, especially when reform had to be grounded in classical precedent. Greek tragedy in its first recovery at the Renaissance seemed to offer artists prestigious forms and motifs; it was primarily apprehended at the formal level. To Wagner it offered the more profound precedent of a socially rooted art. To the members of the Camerata in Florence at the end of the sixteenth century, thinking that music might be raised to its antique Orphic power by returning to the Greek combination of music and dramatic poetry, it offered the example of a union of song, dance, mime and declamation. For Wagner, it also offered the idea of an entire community on social-religious festival occasions, participating in a performance which was also a rite; re-enacting the myths which gave the place its numinous identity and the people their common stock of religious feelings. The social-religious link was myth, and in regularly re-enacting the myth the actors and their audience participated in something which, in a sense, they understood, yet which for ever transcended their understanding. We think now that myth is functional: that ritual performs necessary social or religious operations. It is reductive to think that is all. A proper analogy with myth is the work of musical or dramatic art itself. Its performance links people in an understanding which is partly shared, partly personal: where new understandings from the individual mind may win the assent of others; where the 'meaning' is inexhaustible, cannot be adequately paraphrased, can only be performed in a 'total' way that involves gesture, song, the inspiration performers give each other, the way audience and performers affect each other. Such a complete performance of a work of art is the nearest analogy we have to the epiphany, the divine showing-forth, which is one subject of myth.

The 'art' poetry of the Renaissance, where it was not dramatic, was lyrical in a limited sense. The poet had in mind the classical prototype: the sacred frenzy of the bard, striking his lyre and singing his inspired improvisatory verse. The poets of the Italian Renaissance, and then those of France—especially the poets of the Pléiade—and of England, did expect their poetry to be set to music. But, partly because music had already become a professional skill, the arts had separated. Increasingly from the fourteenth century—except for rare cases like Machaut or Campion, who were both poets and musicians—a composer was needed to supply a subsequent setting. Hence the long history of the 'art song'. This sequence—poetry is written, then set—made poets give themselves the primacy. Ronsard said, unhistorically, that music was 'the younger of two sisters'. The convention lingered: Milton later talked of the 'sphere-born harmonious sisters, voice and verse'. But that was to ignore that in England a generation before, in the writing of Donne and his imitators, poetry had split into two streams. One was a prolongation of the lyrical tradition; the other was new, and can only be called 'dramatic': marked by its adherence to the rhythms, intonations, vocabulary and intentions of passionate speech, the speaker being in a specific emotional state—a dramatic situation. This was inevitable, for England had between the 1580s and 1630s seen the rapid rise of its own national drama, culminating in the work of Shakespeare. The poetry of the drama had commanded a national audience and produced its own form and language, in iambic blank verse. This was taken over into Donne's satires and similar poems. The accepted dominance of the dramatic form turned the true lyric into something elegant and minor, tending to the trivial. And, in the poetic desert of the eighteenth century, the iambic couplet of Pope and Crabbe, still a 'spoken' form, preserved a vigour derived from its use in the playhouse.

The absolute pre-eminence of drama in the baroque period was a European phenomenon. The three great nation-states of Europe— Spain, France, England—contested for political hegemony, which also meant cultural hegemony. The literary sequence was this: Spain and England both produced a popular poetic drama in which, though there was no close cultural contact, there were extraordinary parallels. Somewhat later, the French drama, also initially popular, evolved into a classical form. The perfection of French drama coincided with French political hegemony under Louis XIV. For a whole century thereafter, the dominance of neoclassicism meant the dominance of French artforms, supported by the canons of neoclassic criticism. One could say that *opera seria* was its main achievement in the eighteenth century. When, towards the end of the century, Romantic art was being established, it had to escape French dominance: to become national again, to become popular. The true appreciation of Spanish drama, especially Calderón's, and English drama, especially Shakespeare's, was one essential plank in the Romantic platform. In this revaluation, German critics and scholars contributed as much as, or more than, the English and Spanish. The Germans had a national literature to create, and were looking for models of freedom. Wagner is the final beneficiary of that tradition of critical thought and dramatic endeavour.

Independently, towards the end of the sixteenth century, both Spain and England produced their popular national drama. Even the theatre buildings were alike: open to the sky like the Greek theatre, with the audience in a circle round a platform-stage: the audience itself being drawn from all the social classes, who were united in their appreciation of an art which was primarily verbal. The actor, among this community, had by his voice and gestures and movements alone to project a drama which the poet conveyed in words alone.

In the broadest sense, the subject of drama is always the national consciousness. In England and Spain it was a nation still in touch with its religious and political origins: the two things being indistinguishable. It was also moving towards a modern consciousness—specifically the conflict between the individual and the group, the stuff of tragedy. Politically, the history plays of Shakespeare and others appealed to the Englishness of the English and their cohesive sense of the past; certain other plays catered for the 'ballad' interest in the contemporary or historical event, local or foreign, or drew upon the imaginative world of the romance. But much more important, the English evolved a theatre where tragedy was possible. At this deeper level, it appealed to what Wagner would have called the 'common need' of spectators: not just their political or sectarian consciousness, but their 'pure humanity'; and in Shakespeare's tragedies and romances one sees how history, romance, ballad and folktale are given the depth and complexity of myth. Think for a moment of the plot of *Lear*, of *Macbeth*, of the final plays: their imaginative freedom is not grounded in mere actuality.

It was also a poetic drama in the sense that poetry was the primary constitutive element, not an accessory. Lessing over a century later made a penetrating remark in the *Hamburgische Dramaturgie*: looking back to Shakespeare, he saw in the 'primitive' London theatre, with its open stage and its absence of scenery, not a poverty but a richness, a total freedom; he quoted Cibber's remark that 'there was nothing to help the spectator's understanding or to assist the actor's performance, but "bare imagination" '. Nothing, that is, but the verse and the acting for which it was the score. The poet had to do it all in words, and it is a natural analogy to say that Shakespeare's verse—and Racine's later—does with spoken words only what Wagner does with sung words and orchestral accompaniment.

At the simplest level of dramatic convention, this is a matter first of evoking a place, the setting of the action, then of creating the characters who inhabit it and interact with each other. A past has also to be conveyed to the audience. Then an action must take place. None of these elements is an end in itself: the place must be part of the tonality of the dramatic experience; it is created by the poetry for the sake of that part in the total effect. And like the narrative element—the plot, 'what happens'—it is not significant unless it takes us deeper into the consciousness of the main characters; and that too can only be conveyed by what they say. Everything tends to be internalized in the sense of being taken into the characters' consciousness and expressed through it:

64

narrative does not just recount the past; it tells us the *meaning* of the past, or about the narrator, and we see the hearers react significantly to it. We are drawn within these constellated centres of consciousness and adjudicate among them, as we must do if we are to understand their fatality. What is evolving is not a 'plot', but a relationship between a group of inner worlds which we need to understand both as individuals and as part of a patterned whole.

The 'style', the 'poetry', is that succession of felt verbal effects by which we, the spectators, re-create the whole structure in our minds as it is performed before us. None of this is merely information we have to have clumsily conveyed to us if we are to understand what is going on. When the drama is mature, these elements are themselves part of the structure, vehicles of meaning. Hence much misconception in discussions (by Newman for example) of the difference between drama and music-drama. A lot is thought, patronizingly, 'acceptable in the bustle of the drama', the mere setting-up of a situation. It is thought undesirable in the more spiritualized music-drama. But in neither is it mere scaffolding. It is part of the total effect, and this is a musical effect—the analogy is forced on us. Verse has its own natural music, and in Spanish drama this was very varied, and the spectators knew the forms and their expressive functions. The varying line and tempo of an interchange between characters are determined by the charge of meaning which their words are evolving. The long speech at crucial moments, or the soliloquy, was structured musically like a strophic or through-composed aria. Indeed, we should not *have* arias in operas if in poetic drama the tirade and the soliloquy had not provided the pattern. They are in both arts our most direct and profound way into the consciousness of the characters; and you can make quite specific parallels between the structure of a tirade by Racine and a recitative and aria by Purcell.

A brief and familiar example must suffice to establish these points. Take the tonal effect, first noted by Herder, when, in *Macbeth*, Duncan approaches Macbeth's castle. We are all conscious of the lightening, the note of grace, as he and his party see the nests of the house martins in the walls within which he is to be murdered. Anticipating dutiful hospitality—one symbol of an ordered social life—they infer a fatally misconstrued omen. The passage runs:

DUNCAN: This castle hath a pleasant seat; the air
           Nimbly and sweetly recommends itself
           Unto our gentle senses.

BANQUO: This guest of summer,
            The temple-haunting martlet, does approve,
            By his loved mansionry that the heaven's breath
            Smells wooingly here: no jutty, frieze,
            Buttress, nor coign of vantage, but this bird
            Hath made his pendent bed and procreant cradle:
            Where they most breed and haunt, I have observed
            The air is delicate.

The irony is obvious. Less obvious are the filaments of significance which tie this piece of 'poetry' into the whole structure. The bird itself contrasts with other birds which convey tonality. 'The raven himself is hoarse,' Lady Macbeth says grimly, 'that croaks the fatal entrance of Duncan under my battlements.' As Duncan is murdered, the owl, 'the fatal bellman', gives 'the stern'st good-night'. As Macbeth ponders Banquo's murder, looking out over the darkening land, he sees the birds 'make wing to the rooky wood'. These are 'night's black agents': he invests them with his own evil. By contrast, the martins stand for natural good: the note of 'pendent bed and procreant cradle'—natural sexuality leading to fulfilment in parenthood—is hideously inverted in Lady Macbeth's invocation of evil: she calls on the dark powers to unsex her, to denature her as mother; at one moment she claims the willpower to murder her own child in the furtherance of evil; at another, when she knows herself better, she fears the 'compunctious visitings of nature' (the martins are also nature's visitors). Even the words 'temple-haunting', linking with 'heaven's breath', make their tiny contribution; while the major theme of building (in 'mansionry') brings in all those things people try to establish in life—building a trust in someone, basing a hope on something, having ambitions, believing intuitions or predictions.

So the poetry is radically thematic, and the themes are capable of development and transformation, of creating and linking tonalities. These tonal effects are related to deep insights into the consciousness of the characters. The themes run through the play, fuse with each other, are capable also of inversion and harmonic treatment.

Shakespeare's poetry, in his great plays, or Tirso's poetry, or Calderón's, is a web of thematic material, forcing on us the musical analogy. Or it does *now*, since we live after Wagner; but in the great age of European theatre, from 1580 to 1680, the analogy was the other way. The dramatic analogy was forced on poetry as a whole, and on music. To musicians, the height of expressiveness at that time would have been dramatic; they would want to capture, and to heighten, first in the polyphony of the madrigal and then in monody, the accent of the passionate voice putting the hearer in possession of an external situation and an internal reaction to it. Monteverdi came, in the time and place where vocal music was attempting dramatic declamation; and, within a generation, poets might have felt a kind of threat. Sidney had earlier conceded that music was 'the most divine striker of the senses', and behind much Renaissance thought about music lay the possibilities touched on in the Orpheus legend. This was never so aptly demonstrated as in Purcell's *Ode for St Cecilia's Day* of 1692, where the feeble words of Nicholas Brady veer away from the Christian saint to the pagan demigod; and the music triumphantly does what the words only gesture towards. Of music itself Brady allows

> Tis Nature's voice, through all the moving wood
> And creatures understood:
> The universal tongue, to none of all her num'rous race unknown.
> From her it learnt, the mighty art
> To court the ear or strike the heart,
> At once the passions to express and move;
> We hear, and straight we grieve or hate, rejoice or love . . .

This was sung at the first performance 'with incredible graces' by Purcell himself. It was a climactic moment, or might have been, in English art, for music was making a claim to be the dominant partner. Dramatic poetry was dying in England; might opera take its place?

In England and Spain one can see a certain convergence of music and drama. English visitors were going both to Venice and to Paris, and were in both places impressed by the spectacle of opera. For Spain, the whole Mediterranean area was its cultural sphere. There were musical adaptations of Shakespeare in England, but these were essentially refurbishings to suit a new taste. In Spain, Calderón collaborated with composers, but there was no musician of continental stature. In England theatrical tradition as a popular poetic form never fully recovered from the Puritan interregnum and the closure of the theatres; then Purcell died tragically young and the possibility of a national opera was blighted: opera became an exotic taste for the rich, sung in a foreign language, and performed mainly by foreign virtuosi.

Purcell's eyes and ears had turned naturally to France. It was there that opera was for the moment at its strongest, and the relationship between the greatest composer, Lully, and the greatest dramatist, Racine, included actual collaboration. Cavalli had come to Paris in 1660 and created a taste for opera: Lully and Quinault had laid the basis of a native French operatic tradition in the 1670s. Racine had collaborated with Boileau and Lully in *La Chute de Phäeton* and later wrote the words of *L'Idylle de la paix* in 1685. It was in France that the crucial convergence of the two arts took place.

Music historians tell us that the characteristic of the early French operatic tradition is the strength and weight of its recitative, which tended to be syllabic. It was directly modelled on the declamation of the best actors; Lully is said to have studied the delivery of Mlle Champ-meslé, Racine's mistress and leading lady, whom he lovingly coached to deliver the verse as he conceived it—that is, musically. (Pepys showed the same kind of interest by getting one of his music teachers to record in musical notation Betterton's delivery of 'To be or not to be . . .' at much the same time.)

Wagner thought, and we still tend to think, of French classical drama as 'cold' and 'correct': the copybook exemplar of classical decorum as opposed to Shakespearian freedom. This stereotype was created first as pro-French propaganda in the Voltairean Enlightenment, and then as anti-classical propaganda in the Romantic period. It is important to point out that both Corneille and Racine were passionate and wilful writers who, during their lifetime, found a theoretic straitjacket of Aristotelian decorum being imposed on them by critics, and who in their theoretical writings often covered themselves by pretending to have conformed to the rules they had broken. Corneille's natural mode was a heroic lyricism: at the crisis of *Le Cid*, his hero, torn by the conflict between love and the necessary renunciation of love, bursts into an aria, the famous *stances*, which happen to be declaimed, but might equally well be sung. Both Corneille and Racine were archaic by the critical standards being evolved in their time: this lyricism, expressed in *stances* or massively sustained soliloquies, was an inherently poetic medium, at odds with the naturalism (the key term was *vraisemblance*) which classical theorists were trying to impose. This was a new criterion which moved towards total illusionism or realism, and finally killed poetic drama truly conceived: for people do not naturally speak to each other in verse; we do not naturally overhear people delivering long and superb-ly constructed soliloquies; nor, or course, do people inform each other at such length of situations of which both are well aware. The neo-classical canons were the first step towards nineteenth-century natural-ism, if not towards the end of all drama. In the seventeenth century there was meanwhile an inconsistency between what theorists said and what Corneille and Racine wrote. In the eighteenth century, it was comfortably assumed that they *had* written in accordance with the canons. In the nineteenth century, they were cited, according to party, as the patron saints of right thinking or the sources of all dry academism.

Yet Racine is the greatest poetic dramatist after Shakespeare, and the structure of *Phèdre* is as musically organized as *Macbeth*. One could also make a direct analogy with *Tristan*. Most characteristically, in *Phèdre*, only two characters address each other at length, and with the kind of intensity inconsistent with speed; very little 'happens', except that there are occasional large swings in the plot brought about by an announcement, an arrival, a painful outburst of truth, a death. The same past is more than once retailed by one character to another; not because information has to be conveyed, but because a meaning has to be extracted. With each rehearsal of the past, a deeper meaning is elicited, and the characters are carried further into an understanding of their fate. The themes are of love and death; a leading image is darkness and light; at the end, the heroine is free to die since the fatality of her life is finally clear to her. She is released into the night.

That is to obscure the disparities—but they are spiritual, not formal. Phèdre's self-laceration and final self-punishment are the polar opposite of Isolde's ecstatic acceptance of release: the entire morality of Racine's play is inverted by Wagner's opera. But the kind of structure could hardly be closer, and the final acceptance that what happens is an expression of an inner compulsion, a personal fatality—that we brew our own potions—is common ground.

Racine's drama is musical in the same two senses as Shakespeare's or Calderón's. The verse is most exactly structured and paced. The French heroic couplet is a more formal structure than the fluid English iambic; and both are less variable than the patterns of Spanish verse. The Alexandrine in France was basically two lines of twelve syllables each, divided into half-lines or hemistichs, with a caesura in the middle of the line and a rhyme at the end—four measures, linked by a harmony. (Berlioz tended to write his libretti in a loose Alexandrine, and you can hear the verse-structure in the music.) The form is immensely variable: the speech-unit can go down to a half-line or even to a single syllable; the caesura can be slid back and forth along the line. So characters can, in very swift recitative, exchange a mere exclamation, or rapid half-lines like sword-thrusts; or epigrammatic couplets; or larger structures. These build up into strophes of 4, 8 or 12 lines; and the huge tirades (arias) are built up of several large strophes which convey a magically controlled development of sense which is also a control of line and

tempo—and, of course, of theme. The thematic structure of *Phèdre*
is as dense as anything in Wagner, and in a sense less arbitrary, for the
themes are derived directly from the myth. Phaedra (etymologically
and with awful irony 'the light-bringer') is descended from the sun-god,
and married to the slayer of the Minotaur. The theme of light carries a
natural inversion (darkness, guilt, death). Its development in the play is
by disclosure—through false guilt to the revelation of true guilt. The
blackened innocence of Hippolyte is revealed as true innocence; but the
light shed on Phèdre reveals pollution. The second theme associates the
monstrosity of the Minotaur (natural human evil) with the labyrinth
(the recesses of the personality, the self). The characteristic movement of
the play is a recurrent bursting out, in which people cannot restrain
themselves from a guilty utterance or act, but are carried away. The
monstrous element in them breaks out. It is summed up and completed
in the actual monster which kills the innocent Hippolyte. He is a virgin
and a hunter; he is associated with Diana and Neptune, and with sub-
themes of free wild young animals being broken in or hunted, or
sacrificed. The linking theme is blood: the racial inheritance of a
polluted stock; that which is poured out in appeasement; that which is
innocently shed; that which is demanded by the monster as tribute. In
the end the monsters turn out to be the people you love or are loved by,
and you kill them or they kill you at the end of the labyrinth. The line of
Phèdre which everyone knows—

C'est Vénus toute entière à sa proie attachée

—means in this world that the goddess of love is a predatory wild beast
which scents the shed blood of the stricken deer (Petrarch's old cliché
given a new lease of death), leaps on to its back and drags it down.

As a structure, *Phèdre* is inexhaustibly rich in its links and reverberations, and manages to be both calculated and spontaneous-seeming to an
inconceivable degree. Like Shakespeare's plays, it is a totality, a
'system', to use the modern term. It is not paraphrasable, though one
has to try to talk of its 'meaning'. The only satisfying interpretation is
an adequate performance. It shows a profound grasp of the potential of
myth as something to be imagined, entered, explored, received, but
not allegorized or otherwise explained away.

Indeed, looking at what Quinault and Lully were doing with opera,
and especially their *Alceste*, Racine made remarks indicating that he
thought they were trivializing myth. That tendency too was inherent
in the new neoclassical principles. Myths, being classical, are therefore

respectworthy; but if you care about *vraisemblance*, many myths are embarrassingly improbable, and must be somehow circumvented. Hence the comfort derived from Boileau's doctrine that myth provided a well-known 'fable' which might in most cases be given an allegorical significance, and was at best, or perhaps at worst, the 'ornament' which might lengthen out agreeably some otherwise abstract enlightened message.

Racine uncharacteristically followed Lully and Quinault in giving his *Iphigénie* an 'operatic' conclusion: one of those dénouements where tragedy was avoided. A god descends to offer a solution, perhaps to take the intended victim up to heaven. From Monteverdi's *Orfeo* to Strauss's *Ariadne auf Naxos* opera has used these conventions. They are sanctioned ultimately by Euripides, but derived immediately from a delight in those courtly ballets and masques where an aristocratic audience is flattered by a happy ending and impressed by the use of elaborate scenic machinery descending from the flies to deliver the god and take up another passenger. On the whole, myth and popular drama prefer a death; so that when Mozart's *Don Giovanni* goes down to hell to appropriate orchestral harmonies, opera was being put back in touch with the people.

Meanwhile, Racine's *Iphigénie* spawned many operas. Generally, he welcomed the most demanding myths—even the Christian ones. His *Esther* and *Athalie* are significant in this account, in that after years of writing verbal music he finally took actual music into his drama. *Athalie* in particular, the savage story of Jehovah's preservation of the line of David, from which the redeemer has to spring, has God himself speaking through the mouth of the Archpriest Joad, and it presents a powerfully unified and uninterrupted form in that, being set in the Temple of Jerusalem, there can be a choir (the Greek chorus restored), and between the acts this communal voice actually sings psalm-like choral comment on the action. The verse is fine; the music, by Moreau, is relatively feeble; and it may have confirmed Racine in the feeling that, while the experiment was interesting and abundantly worthwhile, he had managed better on his own. Like Calderón, he had 'done it all in words' before, and the achievement was not less, but greater.

In the seventeenth century, then, in England, Spain and France, but especially in Paris in the 1670s, the dramatic power of music and the musical power of drama first approached each other. The drama was overwhelmingly the stronger partner. But the convergence took place at the close of a whole artistic era. Poetry, and with it poetic drama, had no inherent sense in the eighteenth century: it was thought merely an ornamental way of saying things and not, as it had been, the *only* way of saying certain things. The doctrine of universal paraphrasability, style as 'choice' and art as ornament, are the death of deep meaning, of the correspondence of form and function and therefore of organic form. These things had to be rediscovered in Romantic poetry and criticism.

Partly for these reasons, the successful continuators of the classical dramatic tradition in the eighteenth century were not the Italian, French, English, Spanish and German authors who wrote a lifelessly correct tragedy, but the librettists and composers of *opera seria*. These are more vital works precisely because the form allows the music to supply the lack of true dramatic poetry. The essence of these dramas is an internal struggle of the kind Corneille and Racine had depicted. A noble personage displays his magnanimity by resisting some impulsion, usually a forbidden love, and rising to a height of self-abnegation which is also the affirmation of a higher self. His struggles, in eighteenth-century language, are flat: in eighteenth-century music they can be sublime. An aristocratic audience could genuinely feel that its values had been displayed, tested and given depth, and that this form of drama was therefore serious.

Neoclassic tragedy, and the criticism of Voltaire and the French classic theorists from D'Aubignac to La Harpe, are, so to speak, the law and the prophets of the old dispensation. Voltaire felt himself to be the continuator of the French classical tradition, which was to be the European ideal. The beautiful, it was pointed out, was in all places and at all times the same, just as reason was self-consistent. If the beautiful had been evolved and codified in classical France, it was for the later French, and those who wanted to be their equals, to write in the same way. Voltaire's plays have some interest still, but though they are in verse they are not poetry; they strike us as literary rather than human, or the humanity they appeal to is merely social. *Zaïre* has moments of warmth, because it borrows from *Othello*, as *Eriphyle* does from *Hamlet* and *Mahomet* from *Macbeth*. Voltaire had during his English stay in 1726 admired English science and empiricism, and taken a large-minded interest in the intuitive skills of the fertile barbarian Shakespeare, still performed by the parochially minded English as the best thing they had in that line. This was reported in 1733 to the consciously superior French.

The first real dent in this cultural armour was made by Lessing, a more genuinely urbane critic. Lessing started from the position that

72

Germany had no national drama, and needed one. If Germans looked beyond their frontiers, their eyes fell on France: culturally self-confident, not to say colonialist. In their modesty, Germans like the pliable and mediocre writer Gottsched might accept that the French model *was* the European model, but they would be wrong—'those who boast of having had a theatre for a hundred years, aye, who boast of having the best theatre in all Europe, even the French have as yet no theatre, certainly no tragic one. The impressions produced by French tragedy are so shallow, so cold.'[2] In combating French neoclassicism, Lessing took Voltaire's plays and the theories of the neoclassic doctrinaires as truly representative of the greatest achievements, as the real thing: a comprehensible error at the time, but one which prejudiced the terms of the discussion for ever after.

Lessing put forward as alternative model the poet Shakespeare: 'Shakespeare and Shakespeare only and alone.'

> But is it always Shakespeare, always and eternally Shakespeare who understood everything better than the French, I hear my readers ask? That exasperates us, since we cannot read him. I seize this opportunity to remind the public of what it seems of purpose to have forgotten. We have a translation of Shakespeare.[3]

This was Wieland's prose translation of 1762–6, the inauguration of the great tradition of German translation culminating in the Schlegel–Tieck version of 1796–1810. Shakespeare became naturalized in Germany: he was performed (notably by Friedrich Ludewig Schröder in Hamburg in 1776); he was understood from Herder's time to be a popular poet—in contradistinction to the *style noble* of classical France —and therefore to offer a model for a German national and popular poetry; he was translated; he was understood and felt; he called for and received the first modern criticism.

Even in France something of the same kind occurred: indeed, the tradition of translation began earlier, though it was not imprudently literal for a long time. The eternal Voltaire, feeling that in his well-meant patronage he had been a Frankenstein, took offence, and in 1776 poured scorn on the taste for the Shakespearian dunghill and its scattered jewels, to use his own phrase.

The after-life of Spanish drama was similar. Calderón's *En esta vida toda es verdad y todo mentira* has a plot and characters like Corneille's *Héraclius*. Which was the earlier play? In probable fact, neither influenced the other; but Voltaire found himself arguing that Calderón, the barbarian, must have been first, so that Corneille could refine his crudity. It is natural, he said, that Corneille should have found a little gold in this other, Spanish, dunghill. In his *Dictionnaire philosophique*, under the heading 'Art dramatique', Voltaire mocked at Calderón's *autos* (one ultimate source of *Parsifal*). He could see no symbolical sense in them; in any case, it was just wrong, in the eighteenth century, to express religious feelings—especially popular feelings—as drama. Literature was a secular art for a literate, courtly and leisured community which might, as a matter of principle, have a set of beliefs, but would not have the superstitions of the mob.

But the effect of Voltaire's unexpressed anxiety, beneath the confident generalizations, was great. When Voltaire lost his temper, Europe attended. The result of this first-class literary row was to draw attention to English and Spanish popular drama, and to Shakespeare above all.

The argument in France was inevitably conducted in the old terms: decorum *versus* licence, inspired ignorance *versus* the classical rules. In Germany, a whole new set of terms was evolved at the same time as a national drama was being founded. German drama—pre-eminently that of Schiller and Goethe—was influential internationally: for neither England nor France had a new drama of comparable importance at that date. England never did again, and French Romantic drama came later. Yet neither drama nor lyric poetry are the main achievements of German Romantic literature; the tradition of German literary and philosophical criticism is one of the glories of European culture: profoundly influential in Germany itself, and, sometimes in concealed form, influential in England and France, since it is the foundation of modern aesthetics, criticism and scholarship.

The master-ideas of the German critics can be summarized. They derive from the opposition of the sympathetic historical understanding to the prescriptive universalism of the neoclassic rules. Art springs from and is *of* its time. National art is, first of all, popular, and it was a prime need to recover the native spontaneity, imaginative strength and figurative expressiveness of a popular art. A developed art attentive to its own needs, and not to rules, is characterized by an organic form. Things are not composed by being put together to a conventional plan from prefabricated components: the full expression of a complex idea produces, as Lessing was the first to say,

> another world, a world whose chance events may be connected in a different order, but must still be connected logically . . . a world of genius which transposes, reduces, heightens the particles of the present world in order to form a whole therefrom . . . [This 'whole' is] rounded

74

in itself and complete, fully explained in itself, where no difficulty arises to which a solution is not found in [the author's] plan. We ought not to be forced to seek a reason outside, in the general plan of things.[4]

Related to the rediscovery of the national is the rediscovery of the need for myth (the basic or primitive form of figurative expression); the relationship between primitive religion and its poetry and mythology; the sense of poetry as natural primal utterance. Poetry, said Herder, is a natural kind of prophesying. Hence it became clear that the Bible was poetry; that poetic myth is the stuff of natural religion; that a science of hermeneutics or interpretation would be as needful in religious as in literary studies; that in both it would take its departure from the consideration of *form*. Shakespeare and the Greek dramatists, the Spanish dramatists, came into a new focus: not as primitives for whom a classically minded person could find extenuations, but as the summits of previous artistic traditions that a new drama (and perhaps, Schiller thought, and Schelling thought, a future opera too) might emulate.

These critics—Lessing, Herder, Goethe and Schiller, Kant and Hegel, Schelling, the two Schlegels—performed crucial functions. They inaugurated a national literature which was truly German. Since their wide-ranging tastes and knowledge made them free of the whole of world literature, the new writing could avoid Franco-centrism and became a new thing rooted in its own soil. In particular, they saw the theatre as an organ of communal life, the most truly social art. By presenting Shakespeare as a European parallel to the Greek achievement, they offered the model of a freely constructed but organic dramatic form. They watched over the birth of German drama. They implicitly provided Wagner with most of the planks in his ideological platform, and they fostered the second convergence of opera and drama.

Friedrich and August Wilhelm Schlegel deserve particular mention. Friedrich first (1797) pointed out the degree to which Shakespeare was a deliberate, a conscious, artist—not the neoclassical stereotype of the wild intuitive genius at all. August Wilhelm is more important for this history in that he was a consummate translator *of* Shakespeare and Calderón; his writings, especially the lectures on the history of drama, had an international circulation and influence: and he gave Madame de Staël a good deal of the education which she, in turn, gave to the English and French in her *De l'Allemagne* (*On Germany*). It was he who talked of Shakespeare as 'systematic', described his 'musical symmetry' and his 'gigantic repetitions and refrains'. Shakespeare for him is an 'abyss of deliberateness, self-consciousness, and reflection'. His remarks on form strike us as consistently modern:

> . . . in the fine arts all genuine forms are organic, i.e. determined by the content of the work of art. In a word, form is nothing but a significant exterior, the speaking physiognomy of everything . . .[5]

The Schlegels are the link between Germany, France and England; indeed, August Wilhelm's influential comparison of the *Hippolytus* of Euripides and Racine's *Phèdre*, the *Comparaison des deux Phèdres*, was written in French and published in Paris in 1807. It was a wilful disparagement of Racine, and it may have been here that Wagner found his stereotype of French drama. Madame de Staël's *De l'Allemagne*, first published in England, is an encyclopedia as well as a travel-book: German literature was now presented as the pre-eminent European literature of its time, the leading shoot of a Romanticism defined by German critics; and French cultural chauvinism was tactfully and pertinaciously corrected. Among the natural consequences were Constant's version of Schiller's *Wallenstein*, and, later, Nerval's of Goethe's *Faust*. In general terms, Madame de Staël helped to turn French attention outward, to Germany, and England.

The Schlegels and Schelling stand also behind Coleridge, whose eclectic criticism is partly practical and intuitive, partly theoretical and based on other men's theories as well as his own. His importance is twofold: much English critical theory is founded on the *Biographia Literaria* and the Shakespeare lectures; and he influenced Poe and therefore Baudelaire and Mallarmé. The German with whom Coleridge had most direct contact was Schelling, with whom he shared a theological interest in hermeneutics—leading to a view of the spiritual unity of the Bible through the idea of evolving communal experience; and to the distinction between myth and allegory. Schelling had said that a people is a *Gemeinschaft des Bewusstseins*—a 'community of consciousness'; that poetry is the expressive product of myth, not an allegorical form which uses myth to explain and trivialize it; that religion is itself an evolving area of racial consciousness in which the 'primitive' or mythological stage is not to be discarded *as* primitive; that myth tends to emphasize its own form, whereas in allegory form is only a veil, where the 'meaning' is real substance; that 'symbol' itself is an unsatisfactory term suggesting a dissociation of image and sense. Indeed, Schelling adopted Coleridge's term 'tautegory': the myth contains within itself a significance which cannot be otherwise expressed. Ritual, re-enactment, takes precedence over doctrine, which is an attempt to express in words what is best expressed in performance. The relevance of all this to the *Ring* is worth pondering.

Romantic criticism formulates insights and aspirations not realized in Romantic drama—but in Wagner. After Goethe and Schiller, every major Romantic poet attempted the drama, and knew that it must be, somehow, a poetic drama. But even *Faust*—universally acknowledged as the great dramatic work of its time—is a doubtful achievement. Friedrich Schlegel said flatly that 'Goethe's works have no unity, no totality: only here and there is a faint beginning'.[6] One might in a concessive mood agree that Part I of *Faust* has a form implied by its own freedom; but Part II is an outright assemblage of disparate elements which do not begin even to be dramatic. Romantic drama produced fine plays of a less ambitious kind: Schiller's *Wallenstein* and *Maria Stuart*, Byron's *Marino Faliero*, Vigny's *Chatterton*, Musset's *Lorenzaccio*, Hugo's *Ruy Blas* among others. There were also the 'closet' plays: Wordsworth's *The Borderers*, Byron's preposterous *Manfred* (an attempt at an English *Faust*), Shelley's *Prometheus*, Hölderlin's *Empedocles*. The successes and failures can be ascribed to common debts: the domination of Shakespeare was exercised through a narrow range of his plays; and this gave the Romantic poet-dramatists a conventional and surprisingly shallow notion of what a poetic drama was—what constituted freedom from the constricting mould of French neoclassicism.

Friedrich Schlegel gives a clue to this process. He was interested in a national drama as expressive of the national consciousness; it was natural to turn to Shakespeare's histories as models. *Henry V*, he asserted, represents the summit of Shakespeare's power. Schiller's 'passionate rhetoric', Schlegel knew, was not poetry, but it was effective drama of its kind, and Schiller's political energy, in *Don Carlos* for instance, was inevitably found sympathetic by nascent liberalism. The same note, characteristically shortcircuited by Goethe's ultimate insouciance, is heard in *Egmont*. One sees with what ease Goethe ends the play with what Schiller called a '*Salto mortale* into the operatic'. The national hero, about to be politically martyred, is comforted by seeing his own apotheosis, and the drama loses all its edge. The political concern which makes Schiller an activist could, in other dramatists, be turned into something merely theatrical—spectacular, histrionic, 'epic' in the Hollywood sense. It was Shakespeare's histories which gave the Austrian dramatist Grillparzer some of his characters (his Ottokar is a mixture of Macbeth and Richard III; his Rudolf is Henry V), and gave him also his form, his iambic, and even literal verbal echoes. But knowledge of *Macbeth* taught Grillparzer nothing about tragedy. It took Victor Hugo's genuinely epic imagination to turn that kind of heroic pageant into something original and stirring—in *Hernani*, for instance, where, in his colossal soliloquy before the tomb of Charlemagne, Don Carlos turns before our eyes into the 'world-historical man' Charles V, having begun the play as a standard Romantic anti-hero. *Hernani* shows another Shakespearian influence: that of *Romeo and Juliet*, which had had since Lessing's advocacy a peculiar power—leading in due course to *Tristan*.

The histories and *Romeo and Juliet*: they make two kinds of fatality accessible, neither of them necessarily or intrinsically tragic. The first is the fatality of historical process—the working-out of vast political and dynastic processes on a European stage. The two really great achievements in this line are Schiller's *Wallenstein* and Hugo's epic moments (in *Hernani*, in *Cromwell*, for instance). This was a real feeling, an excitement; and in the era of Napoleon, that active self-realizing energy was a natural interest. But it is the self inflicting itself on the world in action. The corresponding tragic irony—the insignificance of mere action or the blind reversal of fortune—is equally simple and external. The second fatality is that of young love frustrated by those same impersonal social forces—politics, religion, dynastic interest. This is more tender, more lyrical; but only a self-aware passion has tragic possibilities. Romantic drama has an enormous sense of the theatrical: the *coups de théâtre* in Schiller and Hugo are still electric, the 'strong curtains' still impress. What was lacking was inwardness, inevitably associated with the absence of poetry—all this verse was at best rhetoric or epic inflation. All the ends are external.

So romantic drama has force but lacks depth. Its lowest aspirations were expressed by Stendhal. He had no feeling for Racine's passion or Corneille's moral energy: he saw them as presented by their neoclassical whitewashers. Corneille was only a poet, he thought, and it was amazing that he thought a tragedy was a poem. What Stendhal wanted, and what he thought he saw in Shakespeare, was a prose pageant-drama on French national history, where actual places and people and events could be taken into heroic drama, where people could be killed on stage; where you could ask what time it was and be answered 'midnight' (and not 'the stealthy hand of time e'en now approaches the dread hour of . . .', etc.), and where you could talk about pistols and not 'dread engines breathing fiery death'. He was given what he wanted in due course; in *Hernani* Don Carlos says simply '*Quelle heure est-il?*' and

gets the simple answer, '*Minuit bientôt.*' At this, presumably, neoclassical blood froze in the veins of the staid part of the audience on the night
of the celebrated 'battle of Hernani'—one of those climactic nights in
the Parisian theatre when first Shakespeare (in 1822 and 1827) then
Hugo (in 1830) and finally Wagner (in 1861) had to be booed before
they could be afterwards applauded.

Much grand opera of the early nineteenth century is evidently
parasitic on (not to say a parody of) Romantic drama. Hence all that
picturesque European history, with its costume-detail and local colour,
dwelling most lovingly on Schiller's Counter-Reformation period.
Hence all those processions, convent scenes, coronation scenes, *autos-
da-fé*, with their opportunities for scenic display. Hence all those romantic cloaked and masked figures; all those robber bands with noble chief-
tains, all those princes in disguise, all those romantic assignations
between thwarted or doomed lovers, all those cells, inquisitions, threatened tortures, all those last-minute rescues and sudden revelations of
identity, all those exclamations, dark utterances, solemn threats, curses:
they ring fundamentally false and ridiculous in our ears. But for the
music, we shouldn't tolerate them for a moment. Above all, it is shallow
and external: an external fate twitching at stock characters. The English
know it also: that theatricality, surviving in the novel, in the worst parts
of Dickens—those flashing eyes and heaving bosoms: 'My curse, my
bitter deadly curse, upon you, boy.'

For the novel, too, until it became entirely self-sufficient in form,
was partly parasitic on the drama and also inherited its falseness and
staginess. Walter Scott and Edward Bulwer Lytton (author of *Rienzi*)
ally the folkloric to the bad theatrical. Strange that what is immemorial
in those dramas is the tendency to discover that an improbable number
of young people with long-lost parents are in fact the children/siblings
of those by whom they are just about to be murdered/married. Now
that is the stuff of myth, provoking deep questions about identity and
relationship, going back through Lessing's *Nathan*, even Voltaire's
Zaïre, through Shakespeare to the Greeks. But, in Romantic drama, all
else is local colour, mere action and thrilling suspense, and almost
nothing is significant. Where myth does get treated, as in Kleist's play
Penthesilea, one finds with a chill that it is seen as representative of
sexual psychopathology. So we are prepared for all that heated treatment of the Salome–Herodias theme at the end of the century (including
the inevitable operas), and ultimately for Freud's reductive labelling:
this myth 'means' *that* complex. Alternatively, in Grillparzer's dramatic

trilogy, *Das goldene Vlies*, the tale of Jason and Medea is stripped of its mythic horror, abridged and turned into the account of a 'modern' blocked emotional relationship like Grillparzer's own—fundamentally a realist reduction.

Successful Romantic drama had the virtue of its defects: if it was often shallowly theatrical, it was at best very playable, and strongly effective in its way. The malady at the heart of the revival of poetic drama is shown by those poets and critics who held that a true poetic drama could only take place within the reader's mind. The theatre was a place of vulgar showmanship: the poet was either too sensitive, or his language too subtle, or his conceptions too vast (as in *Faust*); they could only be travestied by greasepaint, painted canvas, sweat and flaring lights. The Romantic poet like Keats or Wordsworth made his obligatory theatrical essay and returned to his proper sphere. It became the 'sensitive' thing to say, as Lamb did, that even Shakespeare—or Shakespeare above all—could not be adequately played.

Romantic drama in its more virile mood could lead naturally to grand opera, to early Verdi, or to Wagner's *Rienzi*. The native German romantic tradition of Hoffmann and Weber, sturdily linked to the naïve strengths of German folktale and ballad and Viennese pantomime, could lead to *Tannhäuser*, *Lohengrin* or *Der fliegender Holländer*. But nothing in romantic drama could either match Shakespeare or Racine, or even show them to be understood as exemplars in terms of form; nor could it fulfil the aspirations of Romantic criticism. It took *Tristan* to do the first, and the *Ring* to do the second.

Romantic poetry at its greatest is not dramatic, still less popular: it is the personal, individual utterance; the single point of view, the aristocracy of sensibility. The reader does not follow the poet's dramatic self-projection outward into a clash of characters, he replicates the poet's projection of the world inward on to the screen of his unique consciousness. At its nearest approach to the dramatic, it is soliloquy; at its most impersonal, it approaches song. The brief stanzaic utterance, resonant and charged, of Wordsworth, Blake, Hölderlin and Goethe, bears that clear musical analogy—and Goethe had the good fortune to be set by Schubert. But that was fortuitous; for the most part the great Romantics, and especially the later French Symbolists, were elaborating a music of words: a tight organic form based on associative structure, logical ellipsis and image-transformation. Some outward trigger—a sight, a sound—sets off the poetic process, and the poet embeds this accident in a pearl of layers of meaning, a symbolic structure.

It was in Paris, in the 1860s and after, that the most consciously reflective and ambitious writers of their time, Baudelaire and then Mallarmé, pondered the phenomenon of Wagner's music-drama, and in Mallarmé's case wondered if literature had become the minor art. Baudelaire's attitude was frank admiration, as between equals. His essay *Richard Wagner et Tannhäuser à Paris*[7] makes a generous case for Wagner, who had just had his opera hissed by the Parisian philistines. Essentially, Baudelaire saw Wagner as a master of the same kind of art that he aimed at himself; to penetrate the hearer, to operate on him the kinds of internal transformation made possible by *'une totalité d'effet'*. Baudelaire's calm pleasure in the work of a fellow artist sprang directly from a sense of the equivalence: a successful poem would operate like a piece of music; therefore, a successful piece of music would be the analogue of a great poem. In both one observes the perfect reader, the perfect hearer, responding exactly to the complex structure of effect meditated by the artist. What is omitted is precisely the drama: nonetheless, something deep in Wagner spoke to something akin in Baudelaire; in his letter to Wagner printed as a preface to the essay, Baudelaire speaks of the effect of Wagner's music on him. In particular he felt— apart from the ordinary synesthesia—something which is best expressed verbally in his own poems; the correspondences between sensations of expansion and liberation, the intensity of yearning for, the joy of the rediscovery of, primal satisfactions, felt as bodily sensation, further back than words, though words too can evoke them. He never heard it, but one can imagine Baudelaire listening to the 'Liebestod' with peculiar sympathy. As Isolde fancies she sees a movement of the dead Tristan's breast, a breathing, a return to life, the music begins analogically to stir. It sets up a gentle rise and fall, which turns into stronger waves, which are naturally associated with swimming movements and with love-making. As the sense expands, becomes universalized, the thundering rise and fall becomes the *wogender Schwall* of the whole universe—*'in des Welt-Atems wehendem All'*—into which Isolde is liberated; and whether she is there breathing or dying or swimming or flying or drowning or in the throes of sexual ecstasy is all one. Baudelaire would remember that that was what he was implying in poems like 'Elévation'. His language seems tightly controlled, but that makes the implications exact.

Au-dessus des étangs, au-dessus des vallées,
Des montagnes, des bois, des nuages, des mers,
Par delà le soleil, par delà les éthers,
Par delà les confins des sphères étoilées,

Mon esprit tu te meus avec agilité,
Et comme un bon nageur qui se pâme dans l'onde,
Tu sillonnes gaiement l'immensité profonde
Avec une indicible et mâle volupté.

Baudelaire had no great dramatic ambitions: Mallarmé once had. He faced a world in which Romantic poetic drama was dying, partly because it was no longer 'box-office'. The melodramatic *drame* or the *pièce bien faite* brought to the height of perfection (if that is the word) by Eugène Scribe offered a narrow range from coarse theatricality of a popular kind to a skilful manipulation of dramatic convention which caused the drama to become the art which destroys art by too effectively concealing it. Mallarmé's original ambition for his *Hérodiade* was that it should be performed; but he was advised that his first sample was too 'poetic'. Never finished, its three fragments figure in his work as among '*Autres poèmes*'. The striking thing about it is its musical ambition: it opens with an 'overture', delivered by Hérodiade's nurse as an 'incantation'; and it is an outpouring of densely interlocked thematic material floated on a stream of rich verbal tone. The 'scene' which follows is 'undramatic' partly because it is so operatic: the nurse feeds Hérodiade's tremendous bursts of arioso. The final fragment is St John's strophic song at the moment of his beheading. *Hérodiade* turned into a poem instead of becoming a drama by a process natural to Mallarmé. He may have been disheartened, even disgusted, at the thought of the theatricality of the theatrical world, its incomprehension, the impossibility of acquiring a popular audience for what he was doing. More important, his natural bias, from the time when as a youth he acted a play in which he took all the parts himself, was towards his own kind of internalization of the drama. This was a systematic extension of the early Romantic view that the great poetic dramas can only be played in the reader's head; combined with an equally systematic extension of the typical romantic poem—the reverie—in which the reader re-enacts an internal transformation in the poet, usually solitary, usually in a landscape, and using the universe as a theatre in which he discovers grounds or hints for an inward or spiritual evolution in some way related to the scene (the so-called pathetic fallacy).

Mallarmé is the crown of that whole movement: his usually brief, dense poems, usually in a domestic décor, are a set of algorithms, discovery procedures, in which the heroic reader by dint of finally decoding the text thereby liberates the effect, and breaks through into a world of significances, on a cosmic scale, revealing the ideal world behind the real. These structures of effect are a verbal music in which the poet, like Orpheus, 'sings the world' (to use Rilke's term, borrowed from Mallarmé); or like an alchemist transmutes the ordinary into a recovered golden world, which mirrors the ideal. This is a religion of art, and its rituals would take place either in a theatre which had recovered its true hieratic purpose, or in any formal circumstances (even a public lecture) in which a performer, before an audience, produced in that audience the effect he intended. In the last resort, it occurs when any reader opens a book and, by the operation of linked printed words on the page, is transformed as the poet meant.

With ideas of that kind already forming in his mind, Mallarmé was introduced by Baudelaire's essay, by Villiers, Catulle Mendès and Judith Gautier, to Wagner's work; and he must instantly have felt—perhaps feared—that here was a giant who had done what he, Mallarmé, theorized about, and had done it not by retreating into an internal world, but by taking the old despised theatre by the throat and *making* it serve him, writing for it a revitalized poetic drama: national, mythopoeic, articulating the ideal. He had already, and would have increasingly, huge live audiences. He converted other arts to his uses, and made them ancillary to the music. Was this truly the art-form of the future?

Mallarmé's response was to reiterate the equivalent claim for poetry, and he does it most significantly in the sonnet 'Hommage' which he wrote for the *Revue Wagnérienne* of January 1886. A tribute to the dead Wagner, it simultaneously makes Wagner's claims and Mallarmé's, and does the second by showing how it is possible to do the first, in words only. It operates a set of dualist transformations: a temple-tomb decked with black is transformed into a theatre blazing with light and sound; silence, mourning and the dread of oblivion into rejoicing, fame and apotheosis; the dead artist is shown epiphanizing: reborn as a god every time his works are performed; black is transformed into gold (a synesthesia of tonality based on the alchemical reference); orchestrated chaos into the dominance of a master-theme on the gleaming trumpets; the black on white of a notated score into the synesthetic polychrome of the performed music (seen also as the taking off into the azure of a host of hieroglyphic birds), and therefore into the performance of a rite in which art, which is civilization, is invoked and is operant. All that, in fourteen very cryptic lines. The poetry does indeed rise into a blaze at the end, the sestet is a steady soaring upward from a dull hubbub; the trumpets are made finally to sound, announcing the awaited name, the new god, Richard Wagner. Mallarmé just manages to write from a position of assumed equality: basically he is implying 'we can do that too, all in words. We reclaim for poetry *son bien*, appropriated by music.' Whether you feel that Mallarmé's poetry *can* do as much, as richly and immediately, as Wagner's music is quite another question.

Here in Paris, in the period 1860 to 1880, poetic drama and music-drama converged again, as they had in Paris in 1660–80. This time poetic drama was incomparably the weaker of the two—more or less moribund. Poetry had retreated from the stage, and has never effectively returned. It has become the dense verbal structure long elaborated by the poet, printed, silently read and exfoliating in the mind. There it effects complex mental evolutions, and if you concede that all process is dramatic, then it is the silent drama of the solitary consciousness: no longer a popular art, no longer public, rising at best to song. There have been poetic impulses in dramatists, and dramatic essays by poets, in the twentieth century, but these do not amount to a live, still less to a popular poetic drama. If it were to revive, we should not perhaps recognize it, because we should expect it to have familiar forms, and the fulfilment of that expectation caused the debility of Romantic drama. Meanwhile we have still to assimilate Wagner as, arguably, the greatest European dramatist since the seventeenth century. It is his music drama which has most fully realized A. W. Schlegel's ideal formulation:

> The theatre, where many arts are combined to produce a magical effect, where the most lofty and profound poetry has for its interpreter the most finished action, which is at once eloquence and an animated picture, while architecture contributes her splendid decorations, and painting her perspective illusions, and the aid of music is called in to attune the mind, or to heighten by its strains the emotions which already agitate it; the theatre, in short, where the whole of the social and artistic enlightenment which a nation possesses, the fruit of many centuries of continued exertion, are brought into play within the representation of a few short hours, has an extraordinary power over every age, sex and rank . . . .

FOUR

The Musical Background

JOHN WARRACK

No figure, however lofty, stands wholly separate from
his human surroundings; every German is related to his
great masters in something, and this something is by the
very nature of the German capable of a great development, and therefore needs a slow development.
RICHARD WAGNER

ON PALM SUNDAY 1827, Wagner was confirmed in the Dresden
Kreuzkirche. He would have heard the beautiful Dresden Amen,
already long part of his childhood church-going, in the old melody's
harmonization by an earlier *Kapellmeister*, J. G. Naumann. The Amen
was never to lose its place in his imagination as associated with the gift
of grace descending: he makes early use of a version of it as part of the
orchestral prelude to the nuns' 'Salve Regina' in Act I, scene 2, of *Das
Liebesverbot*, in a tender wind scoring; it suffuses the chorus announcing that grace has been visited upon Tannhäuser at the very end of the
opera; and, of course, it plays an integral part in the invention of
Parsifal, the soaring scale finally merging with the theme of Parsifal
himself as the redeemer is redeemed, to close the entire score, and with
it Wagner's own creative career.

It is not hard to see how a musical idea associated with a powerful
emotional experience would reverberate in the mind of so receptive a
young man as Wagner; and throughout his formative years, he was
acutely alert to what would be of most help in the development of the
musical language he needed for his dramatic ideas. First and foremost,
he had been a dramatist; and discovering himself to be a musician as
well, he heard music with a dramatist's ear. No major composer of the
nineteenth century has escaped the examination of his idiom by critical

85

douaniers to see what is being smuggled through from other sources, and the discovery of evidently contraband material has led to the laying of charges that should never stand up before anyone who has given serious thought to the nature of the creative mind. For Wagner, with his rapacious intelligence, the need was to find whatever he could that might, when put through his own imaginative processes, serve his ideas most fully. The early nineteenth century was an age of much novel music, with a wealth of original ideas often buried in works whose composers could light upon something of charm or excitement or dramatic pungency but less often summon the creative resources, in a time when the classical certainties had receded, to give all their ideas successful large-scale form. It is part of the essence of Wagner's gifts that he should have had from his earliest years the instinct to sense the full creative implications of what was in its original form often merely a harmonic gesture, a turn of melody, an effective piece of scoring, or an exciting or touching dramatic effect, and to allow it to work in his mind until it could emerge in its most complete expressive form, and as part of a music-drama on the largest scale.

To deny a composer the right to make the most of what history has offered him is to ignore the fact that a creative mind must first root itself before it can hope to grow. It is what the artist makes of his heritage that should concern the critic, and the interest in tracing its course in his work lies only in appreciating how the creative faculties have been applied so as to make new imaginative use of it. Moreover, the musicological sport which the Germans call *Reminiszenzjagd* generally leads to the hunt barking up the wrong tree; for not only is it difficult to show conclusively that one musical gesture has been the source of another, but almost impossible to be certain of where some of the most basic musical gestures have their ultimate origin. Mere coincidence of notes does not prove an influence, or we should be committed to a *post hoc ergo propter hoc* argument, to believe that one of Clementi's piano sonatas influenced Mozart's *Die Zauberflöte* overture and the opening of Beethoven's *Pastoral Symphony* the opening of *Wozzeck*. What alone can constitute an influence worth examining is when something in the works familiar to a composer has so impressed him as to lead him to give it new musical and dramatic life by his own gift. It is merely plagiarism, the appropriating of the great by the lesser, that should concern the *douaniers*.

The earliest, and most reliable, pages of *Mein Leben* give ample evidence of the kind of resonance that could be set up in the young Wagner's mind by a musical impression such as that of the Dresden

Amen. The sound of an orchestra tuning up, peculiarly evocative for any musician, is for him something more:

> The mere tuning up of the instruments put me in a state of mystic excitement; even the striking of fifths on the violin seemed to me like a greeting from the spirit world—which, I may mention incidentally, had a very real meaning for me. When I was almost a baby, the sound of those fifths, which has always excited me, was closely associated in my mind with ghosts and spirits.[1]

The thrill of the discovery of Beethoven's Ninth Symphony, which led to him making his own piano score of the work, strengthened his feeling for the sound of bare fifths; and the opening of the *Allegro con brio* of his early C major Symphony, a work across which the shadow of Beethoven falls strongly, lies almost exactly between the opening of the Ninth and the opening of *Der fliegende Holländer*, where the bare fifths have come into their own in Wagner's imagination in their association with the spirit world. Beethoven, Wagner was always ready to admit, formed the most inspiring influence of his youth. In the early years of the nineteenth century Leipzig was notable for its popularization of Beethoven in the Gewandhaus concerts, and Wagner was well aware that his D minor Overture showed the influence of *Coriolan*, while in failing to recognize his C major Overture at a surprise performance later in life, he observed that it was a mixture of Beethoven and Bellini but obviously by neither. But the crucial experiences of Beethoven, which served to summon him to his real vocation as a composer of music-drama, were the repeated rehearsals of the Ninth Symphony he attended in Paris, and still more—'If I look back on my life as a whole, I can find no event that produced so profound an impression on me'[2]—the performance of Wilhelmine Schröder-Devrient as Fidelio.

No contemporary voice dissents from this admiration. Both Moscheles and Chorley preferred her Fidelio to Malibran's; Schumann, who wrote 'Ich grolle nicht' for her, called her Fidelio 'nobly projected' and declared her to be the only artist who could survive with Liszt acting as accompanist; she was responsible for making Goethe revise his unfavourable view of Schubert's 'Erlkönig'. She was, however, by no means a complete singer. Weber, who considered her the best of all Agathes and to have outstripped all he thought he had put into the part, was already observing in 1822 (a year when she sang Fidelio under Beethoven) deficiencies that were to increase to the point when in 1842 they seriously disturbed Berlioz: admitting her qualities, he disliked the exaggeration that had overcome her acting, her tendency to steal scenes and introduce irrelevant 'business', especially her habit of introducing so much parlando that whole stretches were virtually spoken and the great cry of 'Töt' erst sein Weib!' in the dungeon scene of *Fidelio* became merely a shout. What clearly impressed Wagner, in his reaction against Italian singers and their methods, was her concept of opera as primarily a dramatic art. She had herself begun her career as an actress in Vienna, though she must have acquired a versatile technique from her Italian training to be able to include in her large repertory, as well as Fidelio and Weber's Agathe, Euryanthe and Reiza, roles as different as Cherubini's Faniska, Spontini's Olympie, Spohr's Jessonda, Gluck's Iphigénie and Alceste, Mozart's Donna Anna, Rossini's Desdemona, Bellini's Romeo and Donizetti's Anna Bolena. Her greatest triumphs in these roles, however, came before the sad vocal and personal decay of her later years. In her prime, 'young, beautiful, ardent', as Wagner found her, she swept him off his feet; and, as he wrote to her in his famous letter after her Fidelio, 'that evening made me what I then swore it was my destiny to become'.

The effect of Wilhelmine Schröder-Devrient upon him serves also to indicate the unsatisfactory state of the theatre which he attended. The author of the fearful *Leubald* has clearly acquired the less happy tricks of *Schauerromantik* without also responding to such inspiration as was to be found in the contemporary Romantic drama. He seems to have remembered less from serious drama than from the popular Viennese theatre he enjoyed. It was a characteristic of the Viennese *Posse* to indulge in fantastic plots thronged with fairies and genii, often tasting the humour of transferring a plain Viennese citizen to these fairyland surroundings while also touching on moral issues. The best-known contemporary dramatist was Ferdinand Raimund (1790–1836), praised by Wagner in *Über Schauspieler und Sänger*, whose pieces, such as *Der Diamant des Geisterkönigs* (1824—a *One Thousand and One Nights* plot) and *Das Mädchen aus der Feenwelt* (1826), deal, as their titles suggest, with contact between the spirit and the human world; in *Der Alpenkönig und der Menschenfeind* (1828), the King of the Alps impersonates the misanthropic hero in order to cure him. It is not hard to see how such conventions influenced *Die Feen*, and, in greatly subtilized form, colour *Der fliegende Holländer*, *Tannhäuser* and *Lohengrin*; indeed, throughout his career Wagner remained responsive to the influence of the magic theatre in certain corners of his plots. This is the less readily observed since the contact of the human and the supernatural, on the level at which we encounter it in Wagner, relates much more importantly to the Romantic preoccupation with the division between instinct and reason which was felt to have occurred in the Enlightenment, and which is symbolized in the many legends that treat the question of trying to re-establish contact, or even bring about an actual marriage, between the human and the spirit worlds. Even the sudden interruption of such a marriage ceremony, which plays a part in versions of the Undine legend, was to impress Wagner with the dramatic effect he had seen in other operas when he came to write *Lohengrin*.

It was, however, outside German-speaking lands that Wagner was to find much of what he wanted. Italy tended to provide him only with powerful general impressions, and what he called the 'musikalisch zu nennende Gefühl', the urge to put things into music. The musical vision of the *Rheingold* prelude came to him while resting in La Spezia; a voice singing in the night impressed him while he was working on Act II of *Tristan* in Venice; and from the Palazzo Rufolo in Ravello he was able to write home, 'Klingsor's magic garden is found.' However, *Das Liebesverbot* is a practical expression of the German Romantic *Sehnsucht nach Italien*; and for all his need to take up, like Weber, an artistic position against Italian opera, he recognized where its virtues for a German lay:

> The long-drawn melodic form of the Italian opera composers, such as Cherubini and Spontini, could not issue from the German *Singspiel*; it needs must have its rise in Italy . . . From it Auber, Boieldieu and myself have learnt much. My closing chorus in the first act of *Lohengrin*, for instance, derives rather from Spontini than from Weber. From Bellini, too, one may learn what melody is. The moderns are distinguished by a poverty-stricken melody, because they hold by certain prominent weaknesses in Italian opera, but neglect the composers' merits.[3]

'Gesang, Gesang und abermals Gesang, ihr Deutschen!', he cried in an unsigned article in the local paper before conducting *Norma* in Riga,[4] and he claimed that he had learnt the art of melody here as 'Herr Brahms und Cie.' had not. Yet even in his praise of Italy, in the letter quoted, he acknowledges implicitly that some of the most effective Italian influence has come by way of France. And that meant the Opéra.

Between 1839 and 1867, Wagner was in Paris eight times, on three occasions making extended stays. The Opéra, as he encountered it, was at the height of its influence as the home of the *style Empire*, which in the splendour of its spectacle had evolved from the old baroque opera as a Grand Opera to satisfy the taste of a prosperous and self-assured but culturally inexperienced middle class, who wanted plenty of evidence, in the opera house as elsewhere, that they were getting their money's worth. The operatic landmarks of the years leading up to Wagner's first visit were the premières of Spontini's *La Vestale* (1807), *Fernand Cortez* (1808) and *Olympie* (1819), Auber's *La Muette de Portici* (1828), Rossini's *Guillaume Tell* (1829), Meyerbeer's *Robert le Diable* (1831) and *Les Huguenots* (1836), and Halévy's *La Juive* (1835). Each reflected the interest in a style of presentation harnessing new mechanical inventions to the desire for grandiose spectacle; and the chief architect of this movement was Pierre-Luc-Charles Cicéri (1782–1868), a gifted stage artist who specialized in splendid panoramic effects. Closely associated with him was Louis-Jacques-Mandé Daguerre (1787–1851), famous as a pioneer of photography but in his earlier days the director, from 1822, of the Diorama, a theatre which dealt in the exhibition of magnificent pictorial effects: surviving pictures include what was obviously a thoroughly vivid representation of an eruption of Vesuvius. In the same year, 1822, Daguerre joined Cicéri at the Opéra. While Cicéri excelled in scenes of snow, of misty valleys dominated by castles, of huge palace halls, Daguerre made their representation possible in more convincing form by his banishment of the old Italian system of wings, forming corridors and denying perspective, in favour of three-dimensional scenery and such effects as clouds moving across the new panorama he installed, trees that cast actual shadows, exact historical detail in sets and costumes and photographic accuracy in landscape. But it was the move of the Opéra to the rue Lepeletier in 1821 that gave Cicéri his real chance. The installation of gaslight enabled Cicéri and Daguerre to open, suitably, with a piece by Isouard, *Aladin, ou la lampe merveilleuse*, that made splendid capital of the new device. In 1829 they used, for a *ballet-pantomime* by Scribe, Aumer and Hérold, *La Belle au Bois Dormant*, a *panorama mobile*. This was a painted cloth which unrolled on drums to provide moving décor behind a rocking boat as the Prince journeys to the castle; and the device was much used in later productions still in performance during Wagner's visits. The most famous of all their spectacles was the eruption of Vesuvius in Auber's *La Muette de Portici* in 1828, when the stage was manned by a team of machinists that even contained a director of pyrotechnics, Ruggieri, whom Cicéri had brought back from Italy. Cicéri's designs for *Robert le Diable* included a splendid cloister, of which three sides were fully built, probably in imitation of the cloister of Montfort l'Amaury. Many of his designs survive, showing his sense of the dramatic effect of vast landscapes, often viewed through the columns of a great hall and with woods and houses in the middle distance, crowned by a great mountain peak. Between 1833 and 1848, a famous quartet of Cicéri's pupils, Despléchins, Diéterle, Séchan and Feuchères, took this example up, and to the magnificent outdoor scenes added the excitement of elaborate transformations and especially of even more thrilling natural cataclysms and the conflagration and collapse of mighty castles beneath them. In making décor organic but also dominant, Cicéri and his followers were with reason reproached for replacing one orthodoxy with another; but the long-enduring popularity of some of the productions (*La Muette* lasted until 1882, *Les Huguenots* until 1914, *Guillaume Tell* into the 1920s) shows how powerful was their effect. Not only did *Rienzi* take much of its nature from Wagner's appreciation of this impressive set of theatrical conventions; here also are to be found the imaginative origins of much of the magic paraphernalia of the *Ring*, while as late as *Parsifal* there are still working in Wagner's imagination the dramatic possibilities of the *panorama mobile*, of Cicéri's lofty halls and his collapsing castles.

Wagner was the more responsive to French influence through the nature of the operatic repertory which had surrounded him since his earliest years. Weber had quickly recognized that the only hope for founding a German Romantic opera lay, not with native *Singspiel*, but in French opera as it had so impressively developed with the Revolution and Empire; and his Prague and Dresden repertories were dominated by French works. Weber's own music was, of course, for Wagner a profound early excitement, as was the actual presence in Dresden of the sick, limping composer himself: *Der Freischütz* was still a national sensation, and Wagner saw *Preziosa* under Weber with his own sister Rosalie in the title role, and *Silvana* with his sister Louise. In Leipzig he also saw *Idomeneo* (which he failed to appreciate), Marschner's *Der Templer und die Jüdin*, Spontini's *La Vestale*, Auber's *Muette* and *Le Maçon*, Boieldieu's *La Dame blanche* and Rossini's *Guillaume Tell*. In Prague he again saw *La Muette*, as well as for the first time encountering Hérold's *Zampa*, a work which in 1832 had become a typically Viennese mania; and it was in Vienna at this time that he also saw some of Raimund's *Zauberdramen*. The pattern of his youthful experience of opera is filled out the more clearly by a study of the works which formed the repertory of the theatres at which he was employed.

Wagner arrived at Würzburg in the second half of January 1833; here he found already installed his brother Albert (who had made his début as George Brown in *La Dame blanche* in 1830). As solo and chorus *répétiteur* he was responsible for, in February, *Zampa*, Paer's *Camilla*, Cherubini's *Les Deux journées*, *Der Freischütz* and *Fidelio*. In March were added *La Muette*, Rossini's *Tancredi*, Auber's *Fra Diavolo* and Weber's *Oberon*; after Easter there was the excitement of the first local performance of Meyerbeer's *Robert le Diable* with Albert in the title role (the Paris première had only been in November 1831). The season closed on 30 April; during the summer Wagner worked on *Die Feen*, and the theatre reopened on 29 September with Marschner's *Der Vampyr*, to which was added his *Hans Heiling* in the following month. Returning to Leipzig at the beginning of 1834, Wagner probably saw Auber's *Le Bal masqué*, and certainly saw Schröder-Devrient in Bellini's *I Capuleti ed i Montecchi*.

At the end of July 1834, Wagner took up his position as conductor at Magdeburg;[5] the company was actually out on summer visits until October, and on the 12th the season opened with *Don Giovanni*. The repertory, an outstanding one for so small a town, continued with *I Capuleti ed i Montecchi* (14 October: much repeated, including with Schröder-Devrient the following April), *Zampa* (22 October), Bellini's *La Straniera* (24 October), Rossini's *Il Barbiere di Siviglia* (30 October) and *Tancredi* (4 November), *Le Maçon* (?10 November), *Fra Diavolo* (14 November), *Le Secret* (21 November: this was a one-act comedy by Jean-Pierre Solié that was then popular on all German stages), *Der Templer und die Jüdin* (2 December: the first German opera so far), *Les Deux journées* (12 December), Weigl's *Die Schweizerfamilie* (23 December) and, as the last new production of the year, *La Dame blanche* (30 December). The year 1835 opened with Schröder-Devrient in Rossini's *Otello* (15 January), and continued with Weber's *Preziosa* (25 January) and *Oberon* (30 January); during February were added Gläser's *Des Adlers Horst*, *La Muette*, Paisiello's *Die Schöne Müllerin*, and *Der Freischütz*. In April, Schröder-Devrient, who had sung in *Der Freischütz*, returned for *Fidelio*; and new works later in the year included Schenk's popular *Der Dorfbarbier* (15 October) and, a novelty for smaller German theatres, Spohr's *Jessonda* (11 December). The first new production of 1836 was Auber's *Lestocq* (3 February: less than two years after the Paris première); and on 29 March came Wagner's own *Das Liebesverbot*. The company then dispersed; Wagner returned to Leipzig, making a visit to Berlin, where he saw *Fernand Cortez* in May before travelling on to Königsberg at the end of July.[6] Here the difficulties that prevented him from working fully in the theatre confined him to only a few performances, but he did hear the first local performance of Bellini's *Norma, La Muette* (as his wedding Benefit), *Euryanthe, La Juive* and Bellini's *I Puritani*, before the company went bankrupt. Returning early in the summer of 1837 via Berlin to Dresden, he again saw *La Juive*, as well as watching the Warriors' Dance in *Jessonda* performed by the garrison soldiers, which he cited as the model for the military dances in *Rienzi*. In August, he arrived to take up his post in Riga.[7]

Here he found in Karl von Holtei an impresario who was not greatly interested in extending the repertory; he was therefore confined to more performances of fewer works, conducting in his first year eighty-five performances of sixteen operas, as follows: *I Capuleti ed i Montecchi* (10), *Der Freischütz* (9), *Norma* and Adam's *Le Postillon de Longjumeau* (8), *La Dame blanche, Zampa* and *Fra Diavolo* (6), *Die Zauberflöte* and *Il Barbiere di Siviglia* (5), *Don Giovanni, Le Nozze di Figaro, Die Schweizerfamilie* and *La Muette* (4) and Méhul's *Joseph, Le Maçon* and *Les Deux journées* (2). The second year saw him conducting eighty-two performances of twenty-two operas: *Robert le Diable* (9), Winter's *Das unterbrochene Opferfest* (7), *Der Freischütz* and *Le Postillon de Longjumeau* (6), *Norma, Fra Diavolo* and Adam's *Le Fidèle berger* (5), *I Capuleti* and *Otello* (4), *Joseph, Fidelio, Jessonda, Zauberflöte, Barbiere* and *Preziosa* (3), *Don Giovanni, Figaro, La Dame blanche, Oberon, Die Schweizerfamilie* and *Zampa* (2), and *La Muette* (1); he also conducted an act of *Die Entführung aus dem Serail* and rehearsed *Der Schöffe von Paris* by Heinrich Dorn—Wagner's Riga successor, later to be a bitter enemy and, ironically, the composer of an opera *Die Nibelungen* in 1854.

These three repertories at Würzburg, Magdeburg and Riga represent a fair sample of the normal German operatic diet of the day outside the capital cities; and it was in some of these works, and others of similar kind, that Wagner was to find sometimes a hint, sometimes a strong example, sometimes an actual device or incident that would prove of service to him in the formation of his own mature style. In this he was consciously the follower of Weber, whose music had surrounded him from childhood (and in one of whose pieces he had actually appeared, as an angel with wings strapped onto his back). From Weber he learnt where to look for guidance; and in Weber's own music he was to find much of value. He was, in general, much influenced by Weber's handling of the orchestra. Though his liking was for a softer blend of tone than is typical of Weber, whose beautiful handling of individual instruments within the orchestra was to be a stronger influence on Berlioz and

still more on Mahler, he was much impressed by the example of operatic music in which the interest is often contained primarily in the
orchestra, with the vocal line growing out of it. The clearest examples
are to be found in *Der fliegende Holländer* (which, together with *Die
Feen*, is Wagner's most Weberian work), not only in the handling of set
numbers within the composition but also in the characterization of the
Dutchman himself on his first appearance: the 6/8 section of 'Die Frist
ist um' is a natural growth from Oberon's 'Fatal vow', which had already
inspired Arindal's 'Wo bist du, ach' in *Die Feen. Lohengrin* and
Tannhäuser owe much of their nature to the vocal style of *Euryanthe*,
together with its flexible movement between recitative, arioso and aria;
and in *Lohengrin* the whole concept of the opposition of a dark pair of
lovers and a virtuous pair derives from *Euryanthe*, with the grim oath
which Lysiart and Eglantine swear being reflected, in almost literal
detail of invention, in the oath sworn by Ortrud and Telramund. The
overture may have given Wagner the example for the exuberant Prelude
to Act III of *Lohengrin*, and *Euryanthe* also showed him the effect of
distant horns used in a distinctive manner which he was to recall in
Act II of *Tristan*. From *Oberon*, too, came not only much in *Die Feen*,
but perhaps the peculiar lilt of Roshana's Flower Maidens; though there
is a caution for those who tend to regard influence as a matter of conscious imitation in the known fact that the theme for the *Parsifal* Flower

Ex. 1

Maidens actually occurred to Wagner when he was writing, of all things, his American Centennial March. Certainly 'Ocean! thou mighty monster' provided not only the thrilling sound of the trumpet striking up through the texture for the sword motive, but the immediate example of the heroine greeting the sun (see page 94). The direct ancestor of this music is Weber's Reiza, as she hails the sun after the storm:

Ex. 2

However, Wagner had another example to mind, in one of the most obscure of the works he conducted at Magdeburg, Gläser's *Des Adlers Horst* (1832). It is quite an impressive work, in which Wagner may well have observed the effect of the ironic juxtaposition of happiness and despair, and seen how even so modest a talent as Gläser's could build up dramatic tension by means of insistently repeated figures; but he must also have remarked the manner in which Rosa follows Reiza in greeting the sun three times over in the opera's first aria:

Ex. 3

ROSA

Die Son - - - ne

The instances of this particular dramatic effect do not end there, and can indeed serve as something of a warning to reminiscence hunters; for the apostrophe to sun and light was a regular event in operas written in the aftermath of the Enlightenment, whose German name, *Aufklärung*, was, indeed, taken from the frontispiece to one of the key works of the movement by Germany's representative rationalist, Christian von Wolff, showing the sun bursting through clouds. It is, as in other instances, less a case of one composer copying another, with Wagner at the end of the line, than of certain ideas and symbols being in general currency, recurring naturally from work to work and reaching particularly potent expression in the music of Wagner as the climactic artist of Romanticism.

Wagner was always ready to admit at any rate part of his indebtedness to other composers, though he made a sharp distinction between what he was willing to concede privately and what he chose to publish. It was not mere politeness that led him to acknowledge his debt to Rossini on his famous visit to the composer himself, while publicly finding it necessary to take a stand against much of what Rossini represented; and Richard Pohl incurred the Master's severest displeasure for a breach of Wahnfried security:

> There is much that we freely admit among ourselves, for instance that since my acquaintance with Liszt's works I've become quite another fellow as a harmonist to what I used to be; but if friend Pohl babbles this secret to the whole world as a summary review of the *Tristan* Prelude, that's at the very least simply indiscreet, and I can't concede that he was authorized to such an indiscretion.[8]

Wagner's irritation is justifiable, in the atmosphere of hostility he felt he had to overcome, and on other occasions he was more wary. Sometimes he was silent, sometimes dismissive about works that had influenced him; and he was capable of drawing the scent off to minor features of a work whose effect on him had been more subtle and more profound than he liked to admit. For French opera he had the respect of someone recognizing where part of his ancestry lies; and for Auber, 'the most purely French of all composers' as he called him in the charming and eloquent *Erinnerungen an Auber*, he had a personal musical affection. It did not extend to everything the prolific Auber wrote, and in his disappointment with *Le Domino noir* (1837) and *Les Diamants de la Couronne* (1841) he was able to compare Auber unfavourably to a barber who lathers from force of habit but seldom applies his razor. Yet he was tolerant of *Le Maçon*, a work which had a long career on the German stage as *Maurer und Schlosser* but in which it is hard to see anything Wagnerian, and well-disposed towards *Lestocq* (1834), describing it as 'une de ses productions les plus spirituelles et les plus solides'.[9] Apart from the powerful choral writing which is a distinguishing characteristic of *Lestocq*, there seems little to have held Wagner's imagination; but it was quite another matter with *La Muette de Portici* (1828).

What Wagner claimed for *La Muette*, setting it far above *Guillaume Tell*, was chiefly the dramatic fervour of the subject and the technical flexibility with which it was handled:

> There had never been an opera subject of this vitality; the first real five-act drama with all the attributes of a tragedy and, moreover, provided with a tragic denouement . . . The novelty in this music for *La Muette* was the exceptional concision and the drastic concentration of form: the recitatives shot to and fro like lightning; one moved from the recitatives to the choral ensembles as if in a storm; and in the midst of this chaos of fury, suddenly came energetic exhortations to calm or renewed summonses of a new furious intoxication . . .[10]

Admitting the effect the work had upon him, Wagner cannot bring himself to reveal the full extent of its influence. As H. F. Redlich has pointed out, in a close examination of the influence of *La Muette* on Wagner,[11] it is one of the models for *Lohengrin*; but the parallels go further than general similarity. There is a resemblance between the two bridal processions, with a solemn march accompanied by chorus and the suggestion of a distant organ, and the handling continues in strikingly similar manner, with Fenella's sudden interruption of the pageant reflected in the interruptions by Ortrud and Telramund. Wagner might also have noted with admiration the handling of the Wedding March as a reminiscence motive, reappearing affectingly when Fenella, the *muette* of the title, explains by gestures that it was Alfonso's promises of marriage that caused her to yield to him, and dropping dramatically from C into B flat minor as she indicates that he is already married: there is a parallel here with his handling of Elsa's motive and, in the

D

superb stroke whereby the poisoned Masaniello repeats his stirring C major call to arms in D flat but breaks off and tails away hopelessly, a brilliant example of how thematic material may be dramatically distorted. The fact of Fenella's dumbness also served to give Wagner an example, one which he would already have marked in Weber's *Silvana*, of how in a scene with a silent heroine the burden of expression must pass with striking effect to the orchestra: there was much here for him not only in the general formation of his style, but as a specific example when Elsa in Act I answers the King only by signs; and in Act III when, her oath broken, she cannot meet his eye. The demands this placed upon the eloquence of Auber's harmony drove him to an exceptional degree of chromaticism (as when Fenella describes her incarceration) which must have been suggestive. But above all, it was the example of opera on a large scale in which the dramatic interest was not subordinate to strictly musical demands which impressed Wagner, as he wrote in *Oper und Drama*, where he also finds a fanciful analogy between Fenella and the Muse of Drama struck dumb and wandering broken-hearted through the world until finally she makes away with herself in the artificial fury of a stage volcano.

But though he rarely expressed himself with such warmth about an opera, Wagner was moved to public enthusiasm not only by Auber. He freely acknowledged his own debt to the work with which Weber had shrewdly chosen to open his Dresden Intendantship (and in which Wagner's stepfather Geyer had taken a part):

> I found the thorough study of Méhul's opera *Joseph in Egypt* [1807] very stimulating. Its noble and simple style, added to the touching effect of the music, which quite carries one away, did much towards effecting a favourable change in my taste, till then warped by my connexion with the theatre.[12]

As is evident, this was written of a time when Wagner had grown weary of the theatrical tawdry he found all about him; he can hardly fail, also, to have observed Méhul's motivic technique, which is capable of going beyond *Reminiszenzmotiv*, the comparatively simple recall of a theme as identification of a person or to recall a past event, and can anticipate the characteristic features of leading-motive. In Méhul's *Euphrosine* (1790) a motive symbolizes not only jealousy but its action, its object, and the intention to implant it, and in *Mélidore et Phrosine* (1794) a motto-theme is identified with the words, 'Love, be our guide', as the main-spring of the opera. Wagner must also have remarked the originality of instrumentation which could lead Méhul to score his *Uthal* (1806) without violins, thereby producing a peculiar swarthiness of texture well suited to the depiction of the dark, mist-wrapped forest on which the curtain rises. Possibly, too, he took note of the elegant scoring of Adam's *Le Postillon de Longjumeau* (1836), which, particularly in its imaginative use of woodwind and horns, at times suggests an almost Berliozian orchestral quality. In Hérold's *Zampa* (1831), which, as we have seen, he knew intimately, there was the example not only of a certain squareness in passages, such as the opening chorus, which have a similar ring to much early Wagner chorus writing, but of the motivic use of the chords for the statue, darkly scored on closely packed horns, bassoons, trombones, ophicleide and drums. But it was the conjunction of *Zampa* with the Viennese popular theatre that must have come to his rescue when he found himself in a quandary with the plot of *Götterdämmerung*. There is no reason why, after Siegfried's death, Hagen should not take the Ring and achieve his purpose: he is, with a feebleness that can go unnoticed in the powerful intensity of the atmosphere, prevented by Siegfried's dead hand rising in warning. There can be little doubt that Wagner was succumbing to Viennese memories of *Zauberpossen* and of the scene when the pirate Zampa places his ring on the finger of the statue of his rejected bride, at which the statue closes its fingers and crosses its arms; Ernest Newman points out another legend in the *Deutsche Mythologie* of the brothers Grimm concerning a statue that raises its hand away from supplicants to whom it does not wish to yield its rings.

Adam, Hérold and even Méhul, however, meant less to Wagner than did Boieldieu. He liked *Jean de Paris* (1812), and was known to give vent to his high spirits when on a family outing by singing the page Olivier's aria. Whether or not he knew *Les Deux nuits* (1829), which had a certain success in Germany, he must have encountered one of its tunes as a number popular in Paris vaudevilles; this did not escape the eye of Berlioz, who duly reproved him for deriving his *Lohengrin* Bridal Chorus from what Berlioz declared was already 'un pauvre morceau', 'La belle nuit, la belle fête':[13]

Ex. 4

Certainly in *La Dame blanche* (1825) Wagner recognized a work of unusual quality, one with a touch of what he called 'symbolic Romanticism'. There is much in the work to show that the example of *Der Freischütz* had fallen on fruitful ground in France: Weber himself was so enthusiastic when he heard it on his way through Paris in 1826 that he immediately sent word home to Dresden recommending it, and the impression it made on Wagner is strikingly evident in his own music. A few turns of phrase in *La Dame blanche* that seem to recur in late Wagner are in reality no more than melodic commonplaces put to different expressive purposes: it is more in the construction of the drama that he found points to admire. The Auction Scene he considered a model of French art, and it is indeed admirably constructed; and Marguérite's *fileuse*, which he was known to have sung at the piano with approval one evening, was certainly a model for the Spinning Chorus in *Der fliegende Holländer*. Jenny's ballad, moreover, has a dramatic effect similar to that of Senta's Ballad, and even in her contribution (not that of the chorus) some musical kinship; these are further instances of a familiar operatic device being used with particular effect by a gifted composer and thus awakening a powerful response in Wagner.

However, his greater enthusiasm was reserved for Halévy, possibly as providing fewer direct resemblances but certainly for the example in the dramatic handling of large forces. Glasenapp recalled Wagner in the summer of 1878 extolling the virtues of Halévy's music and taking down a score of *La Juive* (1835) to play extracts in illustration; he admired the work's power of establishing the feeling of a certain epoch without recourse to a confusing wealth of detail. This, and the renunciation of a stereotyped style of modern French opera for the sake of larger dramatic gains, he praised in an article covering four numbers of the *Revue et Gazette musicale*, 'Halévy et *La Reine de Chypre*' (in which numbers, incidentally, Berlioz was also writing).[14] He makes his article the occasion for a declaration of his own dramatic beliefs, opening with an unequivocal statement:

> To make a good opera there is necessary not only a good poet and a good composer, but also for there to be sympathetic agreement between the talent of each. If both were equally enthusiastic about the same idea, so much the better; but for a perfect work, this idea would have to occur at the same time to both musician and writer . . .

And he goes on to declare that such a union is ideal rather than practical, deploring the situation whereby routinely 'effective' librettos consistently fail to inspire composers to proper heights. This is his text for praising, in *La Juive* and *La Reine de Chypre* (1841), 'two monuments in the history of music'; and even his revered Auber is held up as an example of mere *opéra-comique* routine and of rhythmic dullness beside Halévy's freedom from convention and his breadth of conception. Only in the later instalments does Wagner come round to discussing *La Reine de Chypre* itself, and he remains reticent about details which might be thought to have had an influence on him, such as the chromatic harmony in the overture, the use of sinister melodic figures under tremolos, the development of rhythmic figures over repeated notes to generate tension, the freedom of movement between chorus, recitative and arioso, perhaps even a specific resemblance between the harmony at a point he does describe—the orchestral delineation of the devious policy of the Council of Ten—and his own Tarnhelm motive. But it is, in both works, the larger issues that have aroused his respect, especially Halévy's capacity to be the master of the grand opera style and not its victim; and it was this which led him to press Halévy upon German composers as a model.

Halévy was not the only composer to have mastered the demands of musical drama as conceived by the management of the Paris Opéra. *Guillaume Tell*, with its passages of eloquent nature painting and of national aspiration, could not really reconcile Wagner to Rossini. But praising Cherubini and Spontini, alongside Méhul, he declared that in their works 'there is fulfilled all that Gluck desired or could desire'.[15] Cherubini in particular he saw as Gluck's successor, the inheritor of classical tragedy in opera, and he admired the symphonic nature of Cherubini's operas—perhaps also the quality of his overtures as lying between those of Gluck and of Romantic opera. The overture to *Les Deux journées* (1800), an opera deeply admired by the Romantics and one whose score is said to have lain on Beethoven's desk, even contains a prominent and repeated figure which it would be absurd to say Wagner actually copied for his Spear motive, but whose downward striding scale, first with dotted notes and then in plain crotchets, can hardly have failed to impress him with its dramatic effectiveness:

Ex. 5

But in Spontini there was the example of a man of great strength of will and authority in the theatre, able to impose effective performance of enormous and elaborate works upon the theatres of three countries. Wagner was dazzled:

> The most important artistic experience I had came to me through the performance of *Fernand Cortez*, conducted by Spontini himself, the spirit of which astonished me more than anything I had heard before . . . I gained a fresh insight into the peculiar dignity of big theatrical representations, which in their several parts could, by well-accentuated rhythm, be made to attain the highest pinnacle of art. This extraordinarily distinct impression took a drastic hold of me, and above all served to guide me in my conception of *Rienzi*.[16]

In Spontini's three greatest works, *Fernand Cortez* (1809), *La Vestale* (1807) and *Olympie* (1819), there was an example of theatrical effect on the grandest scale which was not lost on the enthusiastic Wagner. As Berlioz was the first to remark, the triumphal march in *Olympie* is a direct ancestor of that in *Rienzi*; but it was really the opportunity for such triumphal marches and religious processions provided by the conventions of the Opéra and answered by the pomp of Spontini's public style that showed Wagner the way. The use of historical subjects impressed him, even though their pageantry can ring hollow in Spontini; for the *style Empire* undoubtedly encouraged, in a composer whose gifts lay naturally with grandeur rather than character or subtlety of idea, a pomposity whose four-square manner of expression it was to take Wagner some time to outgrow. However, there was also the example of some unusually rich and inventive orchestration, and of a real attempt to break free from the confines of number opera, whose implications were not lost upon the German Romantics and in particular on Wagner. Some of the more obvious accoutrements of Spontini's operas were to be no more than a starting-point for Wagner, but in the first of the three major operas, *La Vestale*, Wagner had involved himself personally with his careful preparation for the Dresden performance in 1844 (for which he even composed the bass tuba part), and this is the work which entered his consciousness most profoundly. There is the example of the effect of a busy accompaniment figure kept constantly on the boil; and in the Prelude to Act III, the use of dark horns with timpani, answered by woodwind and then an ostinato string figure, has an atmosphere and colour that we now feel to be Wagnerian. Further, of various ideas which have been put forward as the origin of the Death motive in *Die Walküre*, one of the candidates is the figure associated with death in Act I of *La Vestale*, and returning in Act III, to the announcement, 'Julia va mourir'.

However, the grand opera style of Auber and Halévy to texts by

Scribe that had so impressed Wagner found its most complete expression in the music of the composer who was the cleverest at exploiting what had by then become an elaborate theatrical artifice. Meyerbeer's defection first to Italy and then, when he calculated more effectively, to Paris, had roused the patriotic fury of his ex-fellow pupil Weber; but Wagner was willing to look for the virtues in Meyerbeer's success in Paris. One of these, of course, was success itself. As a fellow German trying to make his way in what was then the most important opera house in Europe, Wagner could not ignore Meyerbeer's achievement, but his letter approaching Meyerbeer with the score of *Das Liebesverbot* includes in the necessary flattery a just remark about Meyerbeer's talent when he suggests that it is in the nature of the German to take the best features of foreign art so as to render his own genius universal—an observation about German art which he was neither the first nor the last to make. For all that has been written about the relationship between the two composers, what Meyerbeer exercised upon Wagner was really an effect rather than an influence. It is possible to isolate certain ideas as having previously occurred in Meyerbeer, as, for instance, the curse in *Le Prophète*; but as Robert Gutman points out, there is throughout Wagner's work a fascination with 'the dramatic motive of a curse frequently followed by madness and a journey, often expiatory, that in turn led to redemption through a lover's act of benevolence'.[17] The curse is a hoary theatrical device, occurring long before Meyerbeer; equally, to cite Meyerbeer's stage prayers, such as those by four of the principals in *Les Huguenots* or by the chorus of monks in *Robert le Diable*, as the example for Rienzi's 'Allmächt'ger Vater' or Wolfram's 'O du mein holder Abendstern' is to forget that these were days when a tenor's evening was hardly complete without his *Preghiera*. In the brilliance with which he handled grand opera, raising to its maximum pitch of effectiveness a genre almost exclusively devoted to effect, Meyerbeer set before Wagner an irresistible example; and the skill with which Wagner responded in *Rienzi* was in turn to affect the construction of *Le Prophète*. But when one studies the actual music of the two men side by side, it becomes clear that the real ancestor of *Rienzi* is *La Muette de Portici*, and that in general Wagner took Meyerbeer's Paris operas as an encouragement to succeed in the same manner, but that for his specifically musical models he turned to less synthetic composers.

For all his interest in French opera, these composers certainly included a number of his German seniors and contemporaries. Of the minor figures whose music featured in his own repertories, it is difficult to imagine Weigl and his fresh, tuneful little *Die Schweizerfamilie* (1809) contributing much to Wagner's imagination, and he himself declared that though this work and Winter's *Das unterbrochene Opferfest* (1796) showed an appreciation of what Mozart had done, the Mozartian manner had here become merely pretty. Schenk's *Der Dorfbarbier* (1796), a work of incredible popularity in the first two decades of the nineteenth century and one which Wagner in *On German Music* called 'excellent', is remarkable chiefly for its mixture of aria forms; of its fifteen numbers, only nine are arias and lieder, and those very varied in scope. There is greater interest, however, in the work of Peter Lindpaintner, whose music has been suggested as a source of Wagner's style.[18] Lindpaintner's own model in *Der Vampyr* (1828) is obviously Weber and the atmosphere of Romantic horror put into currency by *Der Freischütz*: there is a very Weberian opening chorus interrupted by a chain of sinister diminished sevenths as Balbine arrives to announce, 'Ach! Isolde ist entfloh'n'; there is even a Bridesmaids' Chorus, later presented (as in *Der Freischütz*) in subtly perverted form, a melodrama, and a cavatine for Lorette that makes her kin to Aennchen. Much else, such as the fondness for polonaise rhythm, is of the common stock of Romantic opera; but Wagner may have remembered the powerful effect of a steady running figure under a tremolo, a characteristic of Lindpaintner's style, when he wrote the opening storm in *Die Walküre*, perhaps also the sinister tremolo chords in *Der Bergkönig* (1825) at the appeal to 'dunkle Mächte', an obvious *Euryanthe* reminder of which Wagner would have had no need. Certainly, there is in the striking overture to Lindpaintner's music for Goethe's *Faust* a remarkably Wagnerian use of stormy tremolos, dramatically reiterated figures, violent contrasts and chromatic harmony. It was a time of harmonic experiment, yielding results which, as with so much else, are now entirely associated with the greatest figures in the Romantic movement, but which often owe their origins to minor, even incidental effects in long-forgotten works. Whether or not Wagner knew and remembered the work, there is certainly a remarkable similarity between Isolde's swoon in *Der Vampyr* (1828) and the Magic Sleep motive of *Die Walküre* in the dramatic idea of a harmonized descending chromatic scale covering four bars.

Over and over again, in the minor works of the basic German operatic repertory of these early decades of the nineteenth century, we shall find effects of harmony and of figuration that were to be given their most vivid definition in the context of a great work of art by Wagner. He himself was well aware that he had constructed his musical language from the materials available; and the tendency of every contemporary operatic composer to search for new sensation in harmony so as to match the demands of particular effects of Romantic horror or erotic intensity was one of the factors that contributed to the enlarging of the tonal system with a new vocabulary of harmonic effects. E. T. A. Hoffmann, responsible for so much that gave Romanticism its peculiar colour, affected Wagner only as a writer, though by Wagner's own admission it was many years before he completely absorbed his infatuation with Hoffmann. His actual music, much less adventurous than his prose, did little for Wagner, though it may not be only coincidence that the end of his opera *Undine* (1816) (a work made famous in Romantic lore by Weber's review) includes a *Liebestod*. Yet though Heilmann, a spirit, announces 'O stille, des Himmels milder Wille hat ihn zum reinen Liebestod erkoren', there is no Wagnerian colour here or in the ensuing chorus.

Ex. 6

There was more for Wagner in the *Undine* opera by Lortzing, an underrated figure whose operas contain, alongside numbers of routine cheerfulness or pathos, some remarkable and prophetic passages. His *Undine* (1845) concludes with one of Romantic opera's many crashing palaces, here in conjunction with the rising of the river to burst its banks and flood the scene, suitably illustrated. Harmonically, Lortzing was often ahead of his time, as in the very Wagnerian bars accompanying Hugo's death:

Ex. 7

As so often, what strikes us as novel, and entirely associated with a certain composer, not only has precedents but even then may consist of a long-familiar harmonic device, even a single chord, given new effect by its handling. In *Rolands Knappen* (1849), for instance, the opera of Lortzing's in which his feeling for chromatic harmony is at its most intense, there are some prefigurations of much that was to become wholly associated with *Tristan* (begun in 1857). There is a horn fanfare which can share with the *Euryanthe* horns the distinction of preceding the effect Wagner drew upon for Act II, and Amarin's Romanze, in Lortzing's Act I, includes the following:

Ex. 8

What is striking here, more than the actual chords, is the particular pungency with which Lortzing puts to work, in close juxtaposition, that Romantic maid-of-all-work, the diminished seventh, followed, after its resolution onto the tonic, by a dominant minor ninth and immediately preceded by what is none other than the so-called '*Tristan*

chord', on the same notes as those on which Wagner first sounds it. Wagner certainly knew Lortzing's music, and his offhand dismissal of *Hans Sachs* (1840) arouses suspicions of a more than passing interest. The common source of *Hans Sachs* and a significant part of *Die Meistersinger* lies in Johann Deinhardstein's play (1827), but both here and in *Der Waffenschmied* (1846), which includes a Sachs-like figure in Stadinger and a lively group of apprentices, Wagner found some stimulating ideas. Many of the figures and events which Lortzing used in his setting of Deinhardstein recur, much developed, in *Die Meistersinger*, from the very Beckmesser-like figure of Eoban Hesse and his public humiliation, to Sachs's fascination with dreams as the stuff of poetry. Probably Wagner would have seen, in Lortzing's agreeable but modest little opera, more opportunities missed than taken. But there is the coincidence of the sequence of dances before the denouement, and of the chief apprentice Görg being reproached, like Senta, for dreaming while the others toil away; when he does rouse himself to sing a Weber-ish song to words by Sachs, the introductory bars end with a figure in the bass that anticipates his descendant, David:

Ex. 9

Over Spohr, Wagner was still more equivocal, especially in the different opinions he expressed at various times over *Jessonda* (1823). Of Spohr's operas, *Der Berggeist* (1825) includes some elaborate chromatic harmony and quite a fluent sense of *Durchkomponierung*; but it is hardly possible to open the score of *Jessonda* at any page without lighting upon some Wagnerism. There is an example for the opening of *Lohengrin* and Henry the Fowler's pronouncements about the Brabantians and the Hungarian foe in the similar address by Tristan d'Acunha to the Portuguese about the Indians; but it is in the harmonic language that Wagner would have discovered the most interesting novelties. Spohr's chromaticism and his enharmonic modulations, something of a mannerism in much of his work, are here applied to proper dramatic ends; and Wagner's characteristic liking for suspended chords of the seventh or ninth, surprising enough when found prefigured in Lortzing, is seen to have considerably earlier ancestry in Spohr, as Jessonda tells Amazili to dry her tears:

Ex. 10

Close as this already seems to the world of *Tristan*, there is a much stronger resemblance at the moment when Nadori, transfixed by Amazili's beauty, fails to complete his announcement that she must die according to Indian law, and the orchestra takes over—a supremely Wagnerian example of the 'Blick' and its portrayal by the orchestra when words fail:

Ex. 11

In this remarkable work, we even meet a direct anticipation of another sort. Wagner himself, complaining of the dullness of the first recitative, incautiously added after a scornful music example, 'one was all impatience for a re-entry of the full orchestra with a definite tempo and a set melody';[19] and the effect of the latter upon him will be readily observed by all who remember the beginning of Pogner's address:

Ex. 12

DANDAU

Aus die - ses Tem-pels heil' - gen Mau - ern

With Marschner, there was a much stronger community of ideas, not least in Marschner's capacity to make the supernatural not merely a salting of fairy tale or magic designed to add a delicious shudder, but the emotional centre of the drama. Wagner knew his work well, and even added an Allegro to Aubry's 'Wie ein schöner Frühlingsmorgen' in *Der Vampyr* (1828). Many of the work's gestures are taken from *Der Freischütz* and from the *Schauerromantik* apparatus of contemporary drama; but we are half-way between *Der Freischütz* and *Der fliegende Holländer* in the conception of Emmy as a pure maiden under the threat of Lord Ruthven's need to find three female victims for the Devil if he is not to be claimed by Hell, and in the conception of Ruthven as not merely a black villain, like Kaspar, but a character knowing and loathing the destructive evil in himself, a reluctant, tragic sinner whose legend and personality captivate Emmy. Her ballad has something of the effect of Senta's; and there is, at the least, coincidence in her singing, 'Sieh', Mutter, dort den bleichen Mann', immediately before Ruthven's actual appearance. *Der Templer und die Jüdin* (1829) is, by contrast, a grand opera taking its example from *Euryanthe* and foreshadowing *Lohengrin* and parts of *Tannhäuser*. Wagner would have observed here, as well as from Weber and others, the effect of Marschner's characteristically dramatic use of orchestration, his tendency to give the orchestra rather than the voices the burden of the argument, and his increased fluency of movement between numbers. He praised the scene in Act II, when Bois-Guilbert reveals that he is not all bad, as 'a creation of the greatest originality of feeling'; and there is much of Elsa in the scene of Rebecca waiting hopefully for her champion.

But it was, above all, in the work about which Wagner maintained a careful silence, admitting only its influence upon *Die Feen*, that sources for some of his ideas are to be found: *Hans Heiling* (1833). Here we meet not only an altogether larger treatment of the theme of the split between the spirit and human worlds than in the various *Undine* operas, in a manner well on the way to all Wagner was to discover in the idea for *Holländer*, *Tannhäuser* and *Lohengrin*, but some important points of technical effect. These include the use of sequences as well as reiterated figures to generate tension, the effect of plunging an audience straight into the centre of a drama, and a heightened dramatic use of orchestration. A good deal of *Heiling* is still rooted firmly in Weber, such as the *Bauernhochzeitsmarsch* and the on-stage band in the Finale to Act I, with its gradual dying away, to say nothing of the general aspect of the vocal line and a distinct whiff of the Wolf's Glen in No. 9 of Act II. But it is in this latter scene that we find the most unmistakable signs of the effect Marschner could have on Wagner, in the *Durchkomponierung* of the events of Anna lost in the wood and the chorus of gnomes, with tremolo octaves low on violins and violas, and octaves on trombones below the stage, joined by a succession of low thirds on cellos and bassoons under the chorus; above all a direct anticipation of the *Todesverkündigung* as the Mountain Queen herself appears:

Ex. 13

Finally, Wagner remained indebted throughout his entire life, not only to the host of composers both major and minor whose works formed the musical surroundings of his early years, but also to his contemporaries and friends, Liszt and Berlioz. Wagner's admission that since coming to know Liszt's music he had become 'ein ganz anderer Kerl als Harmoniker' has been quoted earlier; he also admitted to Liszt the likeness between the opening of *Parsifal* and Liszt's *Excelsior!*, a resemblance of which Liszt made beautiful and poignant use when he wrote his elegy *Am Grabe Richard Wagners*:[20]

Ex. 14

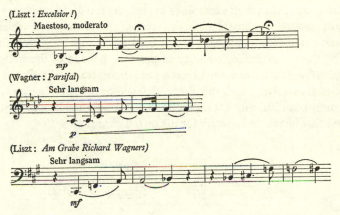

(Liszt : *Excelsior !*)

(Wagner : *Parsifal*)

(Liszt : *Am Grabe Richard Wagners*)

Wagner is also said to have admitted in private the resemblance between the four arpeggiated common chords of Sieglinde's awakening and the similar set of augmented chords opening Liszt's *Faust Symphony*, to which Liszt good-naturedly replied that at least they would now be heard—a story which, whether true or not, is characteristic of both men. There is even the most vivid of all *Tristan* anticipations, as Humphrey Searle has pointed out,[21] in Liszt's love-song 'Ich möchte hingehen' (*c.* 1845); and there are other passages not hard to find in Liszt's music which show that his own development of chromatic harmony, along lines independent from those of Wagner, often came to similar or even further-reaching conclusions. And in the manoeuvrability which this gave Liszt in his handling of thematic transformation, Wagner was enabled at last to make of the old and familiar device of motive (the *Reminiszenzmotiv* of the late eighteenth and early nineteenth century which had become something more in the hands of Weber and his successors) an expressive device whose implications were inexhaustible.

For all the occasional edginess of their relationship, Wagner was hardly less in Berlioz's debt, not only for suggestions of an illustrative manner in music that he also observed in Liszt, but for several crucial hints on the handling of dramatic music. By far the most important of Berlioz's scores, for Wagner, was *Roméo et Juliette*. Impressed by the work, he proposed to write for Berlioz a libretto on *Wieland der Schmied*, and planned the dramatic symphony on *Faust* of which only the first movement survives as his *Faust Ouvertüre*. His present of a score of *Tristan* with an admiring dedication was an act of confessed gratitude: in *Roméo* he could see an example of symphony fertilized by poetry and turning towards an abstract music-drama, not of the kind which he himself could follow, but one which held many ideas for him. Prime among these was Berlioz's ability to pass the burden of dramatic expression from verbal enactment on to pure orchestral meditation, at key emotional moments, with the *Scène d'Amour* and what Wagner called 'the most beautiful musical theme of the century', holding at least one phrase that he was to intensify for his own *Tristan*:

Ex. 15

(Berlioz) (Wagner)

There was much for *Tristan*, too, in the opening of Part Two of *Roméo*, with its chromatic straining of unaccompanied violins, and the oboe love-theme that had, in *Tristan* fashion, originally been associated with death in Berlioz's cantata *La Mort de Sardanapale*. Bowled over by Berlioz's music, by *Roméo et Juliette* in particular on hearing it in Paris in the winter of 1839–40, Wagner acknowledged the revelation of a new world of music; and though he had sharp reservations about the total success of *Roméo*, in his later years he would not hear a word against it.

But by then he was more fully aware of the difficulties of conferring new order and meaning upon a tradition that was in the process of fragmentation. The diversity of the music upon which he drew is witness to the extent of that fragmentation; but it is stronger witness to his own powers in forming of so many disparate elements a cohesive language, in which the ideas of Romanticism reach their fullest expression, and are made the matter of great art. From the enthusiastic absorption of the immediate examples around him in the early works, to their eventual outcome in the subtle, elaborate conceptual language of *Tristan*, the *Ring* and *Parsifal*, there is no great artist who has travelled so far.

II
The Dramatist
and the Musician

FIVE

Wagner the Dramatist

RICHARD DAVID

THEORY

WAGNER PERSUADED HIMSELF that his music-dramas were unique, 'the works of art of the future', precisely because they combined all the arts into an indissoluble whole in which each element reacted upon the others to produce a multi-dimensional effect beyond the range of any single art. From this standpoint it may seem a barren exercise to dissect out one of these elements, drama, for particular examination. Yet Wagner's chief critical work, *Oper und Drama* (*Opera and Drama*), studies the separated elements in great detail as a preliminary to prescribing the means for their recombination. To ask, then, how Wagner in practice knitted the one with the other, and what his work gained from the extra dimension, should not be meaningless questions.

Some definition of terms is necessary, for Wagner in his critical works[1] uses the word 'drama' to mean the composite work in which speech (*Dichtkunst*), music (*Tonkunst*) and mime (*Tanzkunst*) are the three mutually supporting arts. In what follows I shall particularly study the contribution made to Wagner's music-dramas by the third of these, which, because it includes the overall spectacle as well as the individual miming, might better be called the art of the theatre. Such a study would, however, be largely pointless without reference to the end-product, the 'drama' as Wagner understood it.

For Wagner, the unanimous co-operation of the arts, in drama, perished with the decline of the theatre of classical Greece. His avowed object was not so much to revive Greek drama, for it was his belief that drama must grow organically from the actual conditions of the life of the people; and the conditions under which Greek drama flourished had long since disappeared and could not and should not be reconstituted. He proposed rather to re-create drama out of modern conditions, taking over from the Greeks the essential prerequisites of drama as he saw them exemplified in the tragedies of Aeschylus and Sophocles. These prerequisites were, first, that its subject must be immediately recognized by the generality of people as 'real', in the sense that it is a part of the common experience (in this, the relationship between the chorus, as the mouthpiece of generalized experience, and the protagonist, who particularized it, was all-important); secondly, the experience must be concentrated by the poet and all side-issues pared away; thirdly, it must be directly communicated to the feeling of the audience with nothing left over that needs to be ferreted out by the intellect.

Wagner has analysed at length the peculiar characteristics and effects of drama as a form of communication, and the part that music should play in it. Though his exposition is often turgid and his style of writing sometimes unfashionably flowery, his conclusions have a boldness and breadth that are immediately taking. They may be summarized as follows. Drama externalizes and gives objective shape to what would otherwise appear the personal, subjective propositions of the poet, and so transforms into shared experience what might otherwise seem no more than intellectual theorizing. Music assists the process through its unique capability for directly transmitting feeling. In this it can be likened to gesture, which can corroborate or, on occasion, even take the place of speech. Through this capability of music, stirrings of emotion that cannot yet be crystallized into speech may be immediately communicated; future developments in the action can be foreshadowed before the characters of the drama are aware of them; the inner meaning of past events can be brought out; and the drama is thereby both emotionally enriched and enormously strengthened in its organic connections. In absolute music, these potentialities of the medium are wasted, or become barren, because they can there create at best only fantasies, at worst mere mechanical constructions. Music needs to be attached to reality in the form of presented action (that is, drama). The essential bases of this action can, in turn, only be defined by words.

A significant statement is the letter of 15 February 1852 to Theodor Uhlig,[2] in which Wagner explains how Beethoven, for him the greatest of musicians, failed to achieve ultimate communication:

> The thing about the great compositions of Beethoven is that they are really poems, in which the aim is to represent an actual subject. The reason why they are hard to comprehend lies in the difficulty of identi-

fying with certainty the subject represented. Beethoven was completely possessed by a subject: his most significant musical constructions are wholly imbued with the individuality of the subject that engrossed him. He was so aware of it that he thought it unnecessary to identify his subject otherwise than in the sound-picture itself. Just as our literary artists really address themselves only to other literary artists, so Beethoven here of necessity addressed himself only to the musical artists. Even the pure musician, by which I mean the man who makes patterns with abstract music, could not understand Beethoven, because this pure musician is obsessed with the 'how' and not with the 'what'. The layman, on the other hand, was bound to be utterly confused by these pictures in sound. At best he could derive pleasure only from that which to the composer was merely the material means of expression.

And in a particularly inflated passage in *Das Kunstwerk der Zukunft* (*The Art Form of the Future*, 1849)[3] Wagner described the solution to which Beethoven ultimately resorted, in his last symphony: after his voyage through the turbulent seas of absolute music he cast anchor on the terra firma of universal art, and his anchor was the World.

In his later writings,[4] after he had adopted Schopenhauer's doctrine of music's absolute supremacy among the arts, Wagner allowed music an independence and leading role that quite contradict these earlier theories. The operas from *Tristan* onwards reflect this change of emphasis, which is well charted in Jack M. Stein's *Richard Wagner and the Synthesis of the Arts*. I shall later argue that it was in fact always Wagner's music, as the primal partner, that shaped his dramatic writing to its peculiar needs rather than, as he himself sometimes suggested, the opposite. In the meantime I state as an axiom that, without the music, none of the dramas could ever have come into being, and that they are wholly conducted in the medium of music, which conditions their structure and the quality of their actions, and provides the means by which their dramatic effects are achieved.

PECULIARITIES OF MUSIC-DRAMA

In adopting music as the medium for his communications in dramatic form, Wagner of necessity accepted certain conditions that are inherent in music as a language: music takes longer than words alone to put over a complicated message, though it can communicate a simple message instantaneously; and it possesses a unique ability to present several messages simultaneously. The first characteristic means that rapid or subtle dialogue (or, for that matter, soliloquy) is lost in music, which can move fast but cannot then convey a great burden of meaning. To take an extreme example outside the Wagnerian range, patter songs are effective as gymnastic displays, but can have little expository function. Rapid music can suggest a mood—of hilarity, anxiety or anger—but no more. Wagner's fastest interchange, the confrontation in *Siegfried* of Alberich and Mime outside the dead Fafner's cave, brilliantly pictures their mutual hate and provides a strong musical contrast to the meditative flow that is to follow; but it consists of little more than the traditional school-boy insults of 'Yah!', 'Beast!' and 'Same to you!' Probably few spectators of this scene catch the one dramatic point: the irony in Mime's threatening to set on Alberich that 'Siegfried and his sword' that within minutes are to be his own destruction.

Wagner, unlike many other librettists, including even such sensitive ones as Hofmannsthal and Auden, knew well that in music genuine dialogue, intended to reveal the interaction of one character with another or otherwise to develop the 'argument', must be allowed a pace at least as deliberate as the *stichomythia* of the Greeks, which, while appearing hasty, is in fact extremely formal. An example from *Die Meistersinger von Nürnberg* is the wary interchange between Beckmesser, who has pocketed the prize song, and Sachs who has just realized that he has done so: a passage sandwiched between Beckmesser's two outbursts, of anger and of joy, which are purely emotional and emotive. A more extended instance in *Siegfried*, equally well pointed and spaced, is the argument between the Wanderer and Siegfried on the way up to Brünnhilde's rock. Here the musical conditioning of the scene is even more apparent. It is in the nature of music, at least of music before Webern, that climaxes, if they are not to lose their power, must not follow too closely upon each other. A breathing-space is needed between the Wanderer's great cry of renunciation and the actual disappearance of his empire with the shattering of his spear. Young Siegfried's questioning of Mime about his own history, or Gurnemanz's interrogations of Kundry and Parsifal, are other dialogues in which, although the tone is peremptory, the pace is stately. Indeed, Wagner is open to the accusation of being more deliberate than he needed to be. Extreme examples of this tendency are his famous pauses or silences: the first meeting of the Dutchman and Senta, Sieglinde's longing look at Siegmund as she is packed off by Hunding to bed, or Tristan and Isolde after the drinking of the love-potion. Music can support such moments of extravagantly attenuated action which must in spoken dialogue collapse, but Wagner has stretched them to the very limit.

If the effects in music-drama have to be simpler and broader than in spoken drama, they may also be more intense. A *coup de théâtre*, supported by the full orchestra or by one of the great variety of striking sonorities included within it, has a resonance quite beyond anything that can be produced on an ordinary stage. When, in the first scene of the last act of *Die Meistersinger*, Walther, in festival garb, at last appears to Sachs and the anxious Eva, what makes this one of the most overwhelming moments in the whole of drama is the orchestra, which blazons his coming with an ecstatic version of the theme already associated with summer nights and young love. Similarly, music has the same power as poetry (but raised to a higher degree) to establish a mood, set a scene, create an emotional context which may define, or even extend, the implications of the action. Constant references by the characters bring the moon on to the stage of Shakespeare's *A Midsummer Night's Dream*. The moon enters even more forcefully into the first act of *Die Walküre* when, to *fortissimo* held notes in the woodwind, pulsating chords in heavy brass, and a flurry of harps, the door of Hunding's hut flies open to the spring night.

The other characteristic of music in drama, its rich allusiveness, is succinctly exemplified by the passage in *Götterdämmerung* where Siegfried and Gunther, in the toils of Hagen's plot, swear blood-brotherhood. The shaky foundations of the pact are revealed by the orchestra, which counterpoints the oath with, in Ernest Newman's words, 'tuba and trombone ejaculating "Hagen!" '.[5] Indeed, there is hardly a bar in *Götterdämmerung* that does not refer forward or back or sideways or all three, as well as to the situation in hand.

Occasionally, Wagner uses the device too naïvely. Siegmund relates how he returned from an expedition to find his father gone. Gone where? Siegmund does not know; but the trombones nudge the audience with a whispered, 'Gone to Valhalla!' This letting the spectator into a secret that is not known to any character on the stage (Hagen's plot is, after all, Hagen's) has a somewhat coy effect. The richest use of the technique is in the revelation of motives or feelings that do not appear on the surface. Act III of *Die Meistersinger* opens with a theme representative of Sachs's awareness of the vanity of human wishes, a theme that later introduces his *Wahn* monologue. It has, however, appeared earlier as a counterpoint to the last verse of the cobbling song with which Sachs has crowded out Beckmesser's serenade, and on that occasion Eva, listening in the shadows, has confided to Walther beside her the inner meaning of the song and the disappointment that lies behind the outward boisterousness. In the last scene of all, the crowd greets Sachs's entrance with a full-throated rendering of his own hymn. It is, in a sense, his proudest moment; but though Sachs is touched by the people's recognition, the same theme, harmonized in the strings, shows that resigned melancholy is still his dominant emotion.

From such purely musical resources derives a whole palette of dramatic ironies. Furthermore, the web of dramatic implications can be so thick that action, in the sense of physical movement, business, is not so urgently needed to keep the drama under way. Wagnerian drama, despite the forging of the sword and the killing of Fafner, has on the whole very little action of this kind. But to say this in no way implies that there is little 'going on'.

One other quality of music must be mentioned: its power to sustain correspondences and to make cross-references over an enormous time-span, with the second term in the comparison so varied that between first and last a great development seems to have taken place. The forms of classical music are mostly based on repetition and variation. Wagner used this property of music to provide not only the structural members that articulate and bind together his vast dramatic edifices, but also to generate a great enrichment of their emotional content.

WAGNER'S QUALIFICATIONS AS MUSIC-DRAMATIST

Wagner the musician was endowed with certain capabilities that ideally fitted him to be a music-dramatist. Chief of these qualities was a genius for inventing musical phrases that perfectly express a point of character or action. It may be said, using his own idiom,[6] that his musical 'gestures' were wholly appropriate and so 'corroborated' or reinforced the dramatic point being made. To take a very simple example: the motives of the sword and of the Rhinegold are, both of them, little more than arpeggi on the notes of the common chord; yet by their shape (the dotted notes of the sword), extension and instrumentation (trumpet initially against horns), the one becomes as exact a symbol of the hard glitter of the sword and of its promise of action as is the other of the basking laziness, the primeval passivity, of the gold. When the thing to be expressed is less solid and objective than these, the expression can still be recognized as exactly correlated. The dissolving of Isolde's scruples in desire is as plain in the swirls of the woodwind (a descending run followed by upward zigzags) as is the cutting edge of the sword in its octave drop and succeeding climb to the tenth above. And, indeed, the sword itself is something very much more extensive than the physical object which, when the theme is first heard, does not even exist—is no more, as the saying goes, than a gleam in its creator's eye.

Between the extremes of visible stage property and nuance of feeling, for every element in the drama Wagner has a musical equivalent that is both a marvel of conciseness and instantly convincing. The buoyant cello theme that accompanies Tristan's ship from Ireland to Cornwall perfectly suggests an easy swell and a following wind. The brute menace of Hunding in *Die Walküre* is made immediate by the Wagner tubas with their staccato chords that warily shift tonality. Sunrise and gathering dusk, flickering fire and the swaying of water, the mystery of the Tarnhelm and the wryer mystery of the potion that robs Siegfried of his memory, Beckmesser's spite in *Die Meister-singer* or Kundry's self-disgust in *Parsifal*: whatever it is, Wagner has music for it.

Not that the musical expressions are exact images, still less onomato-poeic representations, of what they express. It is rather that the listener, when given his cue by the Word, immediately and enthusiasti-cally recognizes the theme as an apt symbol for the object or idea, and thereafter instantly reacts to it with the same associations, even when, under new emotion, it is transformed: the slow swell of the sea under Tristan's ship becomes dancing excitement as port is sighted, and the solemn, backward-looking theme of the Volsungs generates energy and resolve as Siegmund in *Die Walküre* swings the sword that may re-establish the fortunes of the clan. The practice, roundly condemned by Deryck Cooke,[7] of labelling such musical themes with portentous names is convenient for reference but risks reducing Wagner's ripp-lingly organic musical language to a cabinetful of ossified specimens.

Here it may be as well to make another attempt to undo the mis-understanding created by Debussy's joke about Wagner's characters having each his *carte de visite* which is formally presented on his every appearance. In fact, few of Wagner's 'leading-motives' or themes stand for persons at all. There is no Wotan motive, though there are at least a dozen themes that are associated with Wotan in one aspect or another. The Siegfried motive is first and foremost the actual sound of his horn, boyishly blown; its transformation at the beginning of *Götterdämmerung* does not so much announce a new or transformed personage as indicate to us that the boyishness has been shed, has given place to a new maturity as the result of Siegfried's union with Brünnhilde. It signals a quality not a person. Similarly, the Brünnhilde motive that wells up from a turn in the bass clarinet to permeate the whole string texture is not so much the new Brünnhilde herself as the womanliness and humanity that the warrior-goddess has won from the same union.

The nearest that Wagner ever gets to the *carte de visite* is probably the knightly theme connected with the young hero of *Die Meistersinger*. Certainly it heralds his arrival at the song trial in Act I and again for the prize song in the Act III finale. But Walther is himself a symbol, of the fresh and free ideas invading the Masters' settled world of fixed forms and bourgeois conventionality. The so-called Walther theme represents one aspect of the new ideas embodied in von Stolzing: their youthful, aristocratic *élan*. Other qualities have other gestures: human warmth appears in the four-note phrase that begins the prize 'after-song', questing imagination in the sequence from the trial song that haunts Sachs under the elder tree. Parsifal, too, might be said to carry a label, and the device of answering Gurnemanz's prayer for a deliverer with the 'Parsifal theme' *fortissimo* as the swan that he has shot falls on to the stage, may seem naïve, though it has also been hailed as a theatrical masterstroke. Here, again, it is a mistake to equate the theme with the person, to whom, indeed, at this stage in the story, such a positive and confident signature does not at all correspond. Parsifal's theme, like Walther's, is not so much a person as a way of life. A genuine *carte de visite* can be seen in Verdi's not very successful experiment with Aida, who follows her motive on to the stage as constantly and inevitably as Mary's little lamb followed Mary.

Another myth, also concerning the nature of Wagner's melodic invention and its use for dramatic purposes, requires to be similarly exploded. This myth was fostered not by another musician but by Wagner himself, though the truth is one of many demonstrations that his practice was often very different from his theory. In *Oper und Drama*[8] Wagner insists that the writer of music-drama should exactly reflect in the melodic and harmonic shifts of the music the shifts of meaning in the words that he is setting. He takes as an example the sentence 'die Liebe bringt Lust und Leid', and prescribes fairly exactly the modulations that must take place between *Lust* and *Leid*, with the word *Lust* instinctively (*unwillkürlich*) sung to the leading note that determines the shift to the new key. Nothing quite like this is actually found in the operas. Though J. M. Stein[9] argues attractively that it is, at least in *Lohengrin* and the first two dramas of the *Ring*, I think that he exaggerates Wagner's skill in this direction. Certain practices that are self-evidently advisable are followed: a keyword will be placed on a strong beat or isolated from the rest of the sentence by a marked difference in pitch. Yet, with the real masters of musical declamation, with Monteverdi or Bach, who shape every interval and chord to reflect the feeling in the words, Wagner does not even offer to compete, and still less with the efforts of a Janáček to make music reproduce the inflections of a speaking voice. There are many passages where the orchestra makes the essential statement, the voice merely moving among the inner parts by whatever are reasonably convenient intervals. When the voice part is exposed, its line is almost wholly dictated by musical considerations: it creates or repeats themes that are musically satisfying in themselves, or that are suitable to musical development and musical extension. In this sense, again, Wagner is achieving dramatic ends through the medium of pure music, not adapting music to a verbal role.

CHOICE OF PLOT: THE PROGRESS TO MATURITY

Whether it was that Wagner's music needed a message of a kind upon which it could precipitate itself, or that his message sought expression in a medium—music—which demanded certain conditions, the dramatic actions that Wagner chose to set were, at least after he had found himself, peculiarly apt to music in general and to Wagner's music in particular. They were bold and simple structures upon which his music, like the varying light upon Monet's depictions of Rouen Cathedral, could develop a wealth of differing resonances. He found such actions in legend, often not far removed from archetypal myth. His claim that such myths, being spontaneous creations of *das Volk* ('the Folk'), were purer, truer, more universal than the sophisticated fabrications of intellectuals must be taken as a rationalization, and even then as applicable only in part, for he seldom accepted them as given, but reworked them assiduously, combining and blending the folklore motives from more than one source. It was still a right instinct for himself that chose to rework pebbles rounded by the waters of time rather than sophisticated modern artefacts. As he came to know himself better, he insisted more and more on plots pared of all inessentials; unities of time and place, as well as of action, were more closely observed; and in place of the extended poeticisms of the conventional librettist he adopted and adapted the old alliterative stressed verse (*Stabreim*) which, at least in intention, allowed no room for slack in the meaning and offered close and punchy accents for the music to fasten on.

It is the absence of these later stringencies that accounts for the comparative weakness of Wagner's first three operas. The critic must also remember that even when the third of these, *Rienzi*, was being written, the author was no more than twenty-seven years old. It is still puzzling that so very little of Wagner's mature *dramatic* power comes out in these early works.

Die Feen has a legendary subject, but one that had already been sophisticated by Goldoni's reworking. As one might expect with a novice opera, many of the effects are borrowed from other operas in which their effectiveness had already been demonstrated (Ada, the sorceress-heroine, evidently recruits her ladies-in-waiting from the same agency as does Mozart's Queen of Night). The plot is diffuse, and attention is distracted from the central issue (the testing of the hero Arindal's character) by several subordinate themes, such as the invasion of Arindal's sister's kingdom, which are promisingly raised but come to nothing. Such real dramatic conflict as there is occurs, significantly enough, in the internal doubts and divisions of the hero himself, Arindal, whose frantic self-communing casts a shadow at least as far ahead as Tannhäuser. What is fascinating about the opera is that so many of what in later works are to be key ideas are already present here in embryo: forbidden inquiry, fairy garden, magic weapons, final transfiguration.

The music of *Das Liebesverbot* is notoriously derivative and slight, but this refashioning of Shakespeare's *Measure for Measure* has been characterized as Wagner's 'unique success in the realm of the well-made play',[10] and one might therefore expect to find in it some foretaste of his later dramatic mastery. In fact, the handling is extraordinarily vapid and amateurish. The opportunities for theatrical effect, for example, the first entry of Friedrich (Shakespeare's Angelo) to chill a fooling crowd, are muffed, and the unmaskings of the final dénouement, which even in Shakespeare have attracted some ribald comment, are here quite ridiculously perfunctory. The nearest to real drama is the interview between the condemned Claudio and his sister Isabella. Though Claudio's lines are a travesty of Shakespeare's 'Ah, but to die . . .', their expression (with sombre ejaculations for trombone) is not without force, and the agonies of brother and sister do at least interlock. The greatest failure in the opera is, after the partial success with Arindal in *Die Feen*, a curious one: Wagner's character-divided-against-himself, Friedrich/Angelo, is a wholly cardboard figure. Again, a main theme of the opera is one that will later assume overwhelming proportions: the opposing forces of natural instinct and arbitrary decision.

Rienzi is much more single-mindedly dramatic than its two predecessors. Indeed, it is, as Wagner himself admitted, more traditionally theatrical than any other of his works.[11] This is because, in taking over Bulwer Lytton's plot without much alteration, Wagner came nearer than at any other point in his career to accepting a librettist other than himself. The opening scene of the thwarted abduction of the heroine and the resulting confrontation between patricians and plebeians might well form a part of an opera by Verdi and is composed with something of Verdi's urgency and verve—qualities that do not in this precise form reappear in Wagner's works. Yet one feels throughout that the drama is factitious not organic, that the situations are contrived to spark off a particular and momentary dramatic effect and do not constitute an inevitable progress. For instance, Rienzi's absolute refusal to pardon the treacherous nobles in Act II, followed by his sudden relenting in answer to the prayers of his sister and of her lover, are too obviously theatrical taps for turning on, first, an Anxiety Trio and, then, a Grand Reconciliation Finale. The lover Adriano's vacillations in Acts IV and V are not much better motivated. Such opportunistic dramaturgy would be scorned by Verdi's predecessors, let alone Verdi. One has to go back to Handelian opera to find an action so frankly manipulated to provide the pretexts for a series of contrasted musical numbers.

Der fliegende Holländer is the first opera of Wagner's maturity, and this is signalled by the choice, for the first time, of a true myth or folktale as subject. On this occasion the myth is almost too simple. As Carl Dahlhaus points out in an admirable analysis of the nature and quality of Wagner's dramatic actions,[12] the opera is little more than the ballad dramatized; Senta and the Dutchman are the only characters of any importance; Erik is necessary merely to provide a precipitation of the catastrophe, and his patently mechanical employment robs the part of any feeling or interest. Then, too, because of the narrowness of the subject and the expansiveness of the verse, the work is wordy. Compare the Dutchman's first soliloquy with, say, Wotan's narration in Act II of *Die Walküre*. Wotan has been called prolix, but he has much to say and says it succinctly. The Dutchman is verbose. In *Tannhäuser* two myths are combined and set up a series of reverberations the one with the other; but the fusion is not exact and again too much is said about too little. The plotting, moreover, has something of the artificiality and staginess of *Rienzi*, and to this we will return. Altogether, the opera is something of a throwback after *Holländer*, which appears a more characteristically Wagnerian work. In *Lohengrin*, all the lines do lead to the centre, and the verse shows a greater tautness, though *Stabreim** only makes its appearance with the *Ring*. Though dramatically there is little in *Lohengrin* that is not better done again later, it is the first of Wagner's operas to combine the seriousness and intensity of *Holländer* with a complex action moving determinedly and coherently to a logical conclusion. After *Lohengrin*, Wagner's ultimate objectives were never really in doubt, though he often found cutting the path to them a long and laborious process.

OVERALL STRUCTURE

Der Ring des Nibelungen is at once the most elaborate and the most characteristic of Wagner's dramatic constructions. Too much has been made of the occasional loose ends and inconsistencies, the unconformities resulting from the size of the structure and from the changes of plan that occurred in the long period of its creation. To ask 'What happens to Alberich?' is as irrelevant to this drama as investigations into Desdemona's actual opportunities for infidelity are irrelevant to *Othello*. What matters is to notice how unerringly Wagner has seized on the key moments in at least fifty years of mythic history: key moments in two senses, for they are the crucial turning-points in the action as a whole as well as those incidents in it that are the most susceptible of presentation as objective drama. The subject of the *Ring* is, simply, choice. To say 'choice between good and evil' is to put it too baldly, for the problem that faces the personages of the drama is often of the kind that Eliot's Becket has identified as 'the right deed for the wrong reason', and the choice itself may take the

* The poetical form pointed by stress rather than by strict metre and with alliteration and assonance in place of rhyme.

disguised form of reason *versus* instinct, power *versus* love, self-interest *versus* the general benefit. The eighteen scenes of the action hinge on the moments of significant choice: Alberich's rejection of love and acquisition of the gold; Wotan's surrender of the ring to ransom Freia; Siegmund's defiance of order and convention in acknowledging his true affinity to Sieglinde, and Wotan's reversal of this choice at Fricka's urging; Siegmund's sacrifice of his chance of Valhalla to his loyalty to Sieglinde; Wotan's anguished recollection of the false choice forced upon him and his consequent mitigation of Brünnhilde's sentence; Brünnhilde's refusal to give up the ring, to her the token of her lover, in any power-political bargaining. Most of these nodal moments are marked by the nobly serious motif that has been much too narrowly catalogued as 'the renunciation of love'. True, it sounds for the first time when the Rhinemaidens tell Alberich that the price of the gold is renunciation, but it is not renunciation when Siegmund or Brünnhilde expressly choose love. It is the theme of serious or heroic choice.

Wagner's revisions of the original plan have, it must be admitted, impaired some of the particular connections of the action. The yoking of different dramatic and musical genres in *Walküre* and in the last act of *Siegfried* will be studied in other connections. Here, where we are concerned with structure, I will only examine the first act of *Götterdämmerung*, which seems to me awkwardly constructed. It is not merely that the succession of four scenes makes for an unwieldy length. The real trouble is that these scenes are too disparate, and one has to wait until Act II for the focused intensity that characterizes Wagner's best work. Three of the scenes are prologues, but prologues on levels as different as those of the prologues to Goethe's *Faust*. None is dispensable. The Norns are necessary to give the action its cosmic dimension. The scene between Siegfried and Brünnhilde is required not merely as a recapitulation of the end of *Siegfried*, which is the starting-point of the new opera, but to establish that the relationship of the two is:

> Whole as the marble, founded as the rock,
> As broad and general as the casing air.[13]

Only if this is emphasized at the outset can the magnitude of the deception attempted by Hagen and the devastating effect of its success upon Brünnhilde be measured. The third scene, in the Gibichung hall, is the plot-prologue or exposition. The act would be less ungainly if the break came after this scene. One might argue that, dramatically considered, Siegfried's second conquest of Brünnhilde belongs to development rather than to exposition, and that the second act, devoted to Siegfried's enterprise on his blood-brother's behalf, should run from Brünnhilde's meditation alone on her rock, before the assault begins, to Gunther's discovery that the enterprise was not, as he thinks, carried out in good faith, and his turning from trust to revenge.

There are, I suspect, two reasons why Wagner did not adopt this solution. The first is his instinctive adherence to the unity of time: the scene on the rock belongs to the same day as the first scene in the hall, and the second night in Brünnhilde's cave rounds off the act as the first night rounded off the preceding opera. The second reason is the importance of the placing of Brünnhilde's scene with Waltraute, before Siegfried arrives to overpower her. That scene is to have vibrant echoes in the very end of the *Ring*, and this structural correspondence is clearer if the scene concludes the first large movement of the opera than if it opens the second.

Elsewhere, the shape of Wagner's actions can seldom be faulted. That is to say, the separate acts in each opera are well balanced with each other and the relation between them is firm. Critics have objected that Act III of *Die Meistersinger* is inordinately long. The first part of it is a rather traditional construction consisting of a string of arias and duets (though at this stage in his career Wagner's duettists sing consecutively and not in ensemble), and it is followed by a very extended finale, including Sachs's excursus on German art which Wagner was inclined to cut but which his Cosima insisted on his retaining. I do not find any of this out of scale, and the excursus, in emphasizing the Masters' view that music is a social (and therefore a national) activity, deepens the significance of their contribution to the final marriage of instinct and experience. I am less happy about what seems to me Wagner's failure in *Parsifal*, despite the searching prelude to Act III, to convey the great gap of time and feeling that divides this final act from what has gone before. Other doubts about Wagner's general dramaturgy concern, even more than this one, not so much the structure as the quality of his dramatic actions, and to this we now turn.

THE QUALITY OF THE ACTION

Tristan und Isolde is frequently taken as the quintessence of Wagnerian theory and practice,[14] but this is misleading. It is perhaps true that *Tristan* is the most purely musical of Wagner's music-dramas in that the drama is carried on more nearly in terms of music alone than it is in any other of his works. It is arguable that, of all Wagner's works for the stage, *Tristan* is least spoilt by a performance without stage action and would still make a not inconsiderable part of its proper effect if the words, too, were dispensed with.

A model analysis of the third act, considered both as music and as drama, has been given by Joseph Kerman.[15] He shows that the force of the act is contained in two great musical surges or *crescendi* (the two 'fits' of Tristan's delirium), of which the second is a reflection but at the same time an enhancement and enrichment of the first. It may be observed that the other two acts, which Kerman seems to pass over rather disparagingly in favour of the last, are built on the same principle of the double surge, a series of waves that reflect each other. In the first act, a chain of musical links (the sailor at the masthead, Isolde's rage, the ship at sea) is matched by a second chain in which the individual links are varied and reordered, with new links added (Kurwenal's insolence, Isolde's death-wish, the crew's shanty). A third chain follows the second, the divisions being marked by the opening or closing of the curtains round Isolde's 'cabin'. In the love scene of the second act a whole series of movements (Brangaene's warning, the lovers' 'little death' and their rallying to the affirmation of 'So stürben wir, um ungetrennt') is repeated in a varied form, shortened but at the same time heightened, breaking off with the irruption of the hunting party to a hideous distortion of the horn call with which, at the beginning of the act, the hunt had faded with the day.

It is, however, a mistake to deduce from these parallelisms and from the lush musical texture of *Tristan* that Wagner's drama is always subjective or that in his works (to quote an epigrammatic statement) 'action is passion'.* This is not true even in *Tristan*, admittedly the extreme in this regard. The dramatic context in which the lovers are placed is not a creation of their own imaginations: they inhabit a real and orderly world. The values of that world, though they conflict with the instinctively established values of the lovers and are eventually rejected by them, are widely accepted values. The audience can appreciate that to steal the wife of a benefactor to whom one has sworn absolute loyalty, or to give oneself to an enemy who has killed one's betrothed, might by some be considered treachery. The predicament

* Francis Fergusson, *The Idea of a Theater*, Princeton, 1949, p. 81: '*Tristan* . . . the most perfect instance of drama as "the expression of emotion": the doctrine which identifies action with passion.'

of Tristan and Isolde would be less complex and therefore less interesting if they did not recognize themselves as traitors. The Night and the Day may be symbols, but unless they symbolize positive values, the second act of the opera, which is largely devoted to a discussion of their opposition, would be sheer delirium. Unless Marke has just cause to feel injured, his two great laments are excrescences.

At the other extreme from *Tristan* are scenes of Wagnerian drama in which the action is pure dialectic. Obvious examples are the last three scenes of *Rheingold*. It may be objected that this is because *Rheingold* is no more than the exposition section of the complete *Ring*, and therefore unrepresentative of a tetralogy which as a whole is as much a fantasy as *Tristan*. Yet this exposition section has itself a beginning, a middle and an end, and is self-contained.

The first scene of *Rheingold* presents, in broad primary colours, the elements of the situation: the state of natural innocence (the Rhinemaidens are animal, mischievous, but not evil), and human intelligence which, thwarted, prefers power to humanity as symbolized in 'Liebe und Weibes Werth'. Alberich's rejection by the Rhinemaidens is, through the musical (and ritual) device of repetition, nicely varied, but otherwise the presentation is simplicity itself. The second scene begins to show the implications and the effect upon others of the letting loose of the gold upon the world. Wotan's security, in his dreamed-up fortress of Valhalla (tubas and trombones in sonorous D flat) is broken by Fricka's anxious reminder (B flat minor recitative) of the price that remains to be paid for it. The extended dialogue, mostly in expressive recitative but time and again broadening naturally into arioso and aria, brings out more of the essentials of these key figures: Wotan's complacency and his wilfulness, Fricka's possessiveness and her jealousy of the male world. Fricka's plight is as sympathetically presented, in the F major–D minor aria 'Um des Gatten Treue besorgt', as is Wotan's pride of achievement and his all-too-patronizing yet real affection for his goddess. Though in the action Donner and Froh are to be little more than walking gentlemen (and Freia a mere sex-symbol), we learn that all 'the men' were in the plot together, all ready to sacrifice Freia to their desire for position and material comfort. The cross-currents, already quite subtle ones, set up in this dialogue are further complicated by the entry of the giants, and later of Loge. The two giants are themselves stongly but simply contrasted: Fasolt open, straight, trusting; Fafner secret, devious, suspicious. Loge's cynicism, his delight in deceit for its own sake, as a recreation, counterpoints the basic issues but does not obscure them. The giants are already divided in their motives for acquiring Freia. Fasolt wants her as a human companion, Fafner because her removal from the gods will drain them of their power as well. In other words the dichotomy *Liebe/Macht* (Love/Power), which informs the whole drama, also in germinal form conditions the psychology of the giants as it has been seen to condition that of Wotan and of Fricka. Throughout the scene, echoes of Alberich's choice confirm that this is both the genesis of the dramatic action and its continuing inspiration. This action, although its quality is very different from that of *Tristan und Isolde*, is still (as in *Tristan*) wholly conducted and shaped in terms of music. Recitative swells into arioso as ratiocination expands into feeling; harmonic shifts and changes in orchestral timbre reflect the changing relations of the characters to each other and to their situation. Though Wagner's theories about matching the music to the sense were never implemented, in the way that he suggested, in relation to individual words, the musical expression does, in general, exactly reflect and present the drift of the action.

The third scene, in Nibelheim, can be analysed in the same way and will be seen to possess the same musical dialectic, as subtle as that of the preceding scene but more closely co-ordinated; for, at least after Alberich has come upon his unwanted guests, the dialogue is concentrated, recitative and aria are more closely integrated and are bound together by the repetition and variation of three vigorous musical themes: the anvil motive, a scale bustling energetically up from the bass and seeming to express Alberich's sense of command, and the theme which is rather pompously known as 'Arrogance of Power' (*Machtdünkel*), but which can rather be felt as a self-hugging exultation. The exercise of the ring's power on the Nibelung slaves, once in Nibelheim and again when Alberich has been dragged into the upper air, produces two colossal musical climaxes.

The last scene, after Alberich has 'tripped away home', continues and consolidates the argument, but is in my view the least successful of the four. This is chiefly because of the over-simplicity and rigidity of the giants' themes, qualities which derive in part from the very nature of the giants as Wagner wishes to portray them, but in part also from inadequacies in Wagner's technique at this stage in his career. In consequence, a second altercation with the giants was bound to pall. Other awkwardnesses are the intervention of Erda and the sudden appearance of the sword theme as a signpost (at this point in the action an illegible one) to the next stage in Wotan's progress. Both are ill-fitted and incongruous patches on the drama, and at a later date Wagner would surely have managed these transitions more effectively.

Tristan on the one hand and *Rheingold* on the other represent the extremes of Wagner's dramatic texture. The other dramas fall between the two or combine their qualities. To continue for a moment with the *Ring*, the first act of *Die Walküre*, though it presents the essential data of the action crisply enough, is nearer to the *Tristan* idiom than to that of *Rheingold*. The second act, too often under-estimated, juxtaposes—this time without damage to continuity or coherence—the lyrical and the dialectical. The scene between Wotan and Fricka closely follows the technique of their similar arguments in *Rheingold*. Their first wary fencing is recitative; Fricka's 'O was klag' ich um Ehe und Eid' is pure aria, and a splendid one. Yet the dialectic, the gradual inching out of Wotan from one defensive position after another until no logical refuge is left to him, is undeviating and cogent. There follows Wotan's great soliloquy (Brünnhilde, his audience, is expressly addressed as a part of himself and, even without this, can be said to fill the same role as Miranda in her first scene in Shakespeare's *Tempest*—to draw out and to diversify her father's confession). Beginning in pure recitative, it grows organically in both passion and complexity to conclude in a shattering climax. Brünnhilde's deep dismay, a postlude, gives way to the first sounds of the manhunt as the fugitives enter. The scene that follows is a more convincingly realistic presentation in music of agitation and despair than any that had gone before it. As Sieglinde falls into the sleep of exhaustion, the music broadens into the *Todesverkündigung*, a ritual (note the repeated questions and answers) of great solemnity and impressiveness. With right instinct, Wagner conducts the business necessary to round off the act with the utmost economy and rapidity, the combatants meeting and their protectors appearing above them as in lightning flashes or the shifts of a kaleidoscope.

In this act the apparently disparate actions are in fact one action. The predicament of Siegmund and Sieglinde is a part of Wotan's predicament, and Brünnhilde's predicament, developed in the final act, is to stem from that also. Wotan's predicament is itself strongly conditioned by his whole relationship with Fricka. Although, in this act, almost every musical style available to Wagner and every dramatic device has been employed, they have been fused into a whole that is dramatically seamless.

VISUAL EFFECTS AND THE SENSE OF THEATRE

Wagner's obsession with the need for realistic presentation and his personal involvement in the actual staging of his music-dramas are on record.[16] The kind of would-be objective, solid *mise en scène* for which his works were conceived is now outmoded, yet the very elaboration of settings and properties that Wagner demanded show that he strongly visualized his dramas as he composed them. It is therefore surprising to discover how limited and rare in his work is the sort of visual drama—the physical confrontations, the counterpointing of one movement with another, the ironic juxtaposition of one character with another—that is such a feature of, say, Shakespeare's or Chekhov's plays. The big spectacular effects are there in plenty, and splendid they are. Valhalla burns and Klingsor's magic garden collapses. The haunted ship looms out of tempest, the dragon rears up from his cave, and the burghers of Nürnberg engage in a full-scale riot on stage. There are performing animals galore and a flying ballet of mermaids. The childish gusto of most of these happenings belongs rather to pantomime than to serious drama. Even in the *coups de théâtre* described earlier, powerful as they are, there is a touch of staginess. What one looks for in vain is the kind of overtone generated when the Macbeths, joint authors of Duncan's death, make their separate excuses to a suspicious court; when the doors of the Wild Duck's attic (into which Hedvig has just disappeared with a pistol) stare at the audience through the farcical scene of Ekdal's packing; or when, on the night of the fire, the presence of the Three Sisters' old nurse at first escapes and then outrages the managing sister-in-law.

Wagner's nearest approach to such visual irony is Isolde's frenzied drawing of the curtains to reveal Tristan in distant isolation—an effect that producers often go out of their way to mar; and the presence of Hagen is, on a comparatively simple level, almost always ironic, whether he is holding the drinking horn for the blood-brothers Gunther and Siegfried, his puppets, or the spear on which Brünnhilde and Siegfried successively swear their incompatible truths. Even when all the ingredients are there, Wagner sometimes fails to make the most of them. There could be no more powerful visual contrast than the Dutchman's ship, weather-beaten, dark and silent, and Daland's ship, dressed for harbour and all lit up in more senses than one. Yet the effect remains undeveloped: the Norwegians sing a jolly song and the

Dutchmen a grisly one and that is that. The simplicities of Wagner's visual imagination are shown up all the more in comparison with his aural inventions, which, as might be expected, are brilliantly suggestive. The sailor at Tristan's mast-head, the scratching of the chalk behind the Master Marker's curtain, the echoing of Hunding's cowhorn in the corrie below the pass where Siegmund makes his last stand—all these effects succeed in precisely the way in which Shakespeare, Ibsen, Chekhov succeed with their visual effects.

The comparative naïvety of Wagner's visual presentation is carried over into his handling of the action on the stage. In Act II of *Die Meistersinger*, Sachs is extraordinarily (but conveniently) wayward in deciding whether, at particular moments, he will work indoors or out. In the first part of the last act of the same opera, the characters time their entrances and exits with equal artificiality so as to avoid each other. The repeated interventions of Ortrud and Telramund in Lohengrin's wedding procession are clumsily managed; and if this may be excused on the ground that the opera is an early work, what can one say in defence of Brangaene's feat of climbing into the castle of Kareol, which, however dilapidated, is defended, while Marke and Isolde remain shut out? This is a manipulation that, unlike the neglect of Alberich's fate, may draw attention to itself while the action is still in progress and so create an unfortunate distraction. Yet even this crudity is relatively easy to swallow. Shakespeare, too, never jibbed at a time-saving short cut, and could withdraw two momentarily superfluous characters from the action with no more than, 'Hark! one word in your ear'. The music, or the poetry, covers all.

Yet if, as stage designer or director, Wagner appears a little naïve, as actor he clearly possessed outstanding natural gifts. His perceptiveness as to how a part could be put over and his skill in communicating the perception to others shine through his own account[17] of rehearsals with Schnorr von Carolsfeld, the first Tristan, and are particularly exemplified in the creation of all his smaller parts. With very few exceptions (Erik and Freia have been mentioned, and Klingsor will be touched on later) these have all the crisp solidity of Shakespeare's minor characters. Even the eight non-principal Mastersingers and the eight subsidiary Valkyries, though their names may be confused, have their own distinct personalities. What is more, every one of the smaller parts is, in theatrical parlance, eminently 'practical'. The actor of Mime, of Gutrune or of Kurwenal is shown what to do, for the wheedling guile of the one, the pliant ingenuousness of the second, the doggy loyalty of the third are given more concrete articulation in the music than they could ever receive from the fullest stage directions.

DRAMATIC PRESSURE

There is another quality which is essential to drama, but which is hard to define except by negatives or analogies. I use the dynamic or electrical analogy in order to distinguish pressure from current. There are plenty of operas—for example, the comedies of Rossini—in which the current runs strongly and briskly but the pressure is low. In Wagner's work, too, there are moments when the music generates an irresistible surge: 'Siegmund heiss' ich, und Siegmund bin ich!' cries the hero to hammering sextuplets in the woodwind, and the spectator says to himself 'We're off!' as he settles himself contentedly in his seat. But on these occasions it is musical impetus that provides the excitement, not dramatic pressure which may be strongest at those moments when the music pauses. Nor is pressure the same as suspense, which is a product of certain arrangements of the plot. The second act of *Götterdämmerung* has always seemed to me to be, once Hagen's colloquy with Alberich is over, on a lower level than the rest, precisely because, thrilling though it is, the thrills derive more from suspense and less from the dramatic pressure that loads every other scene in the opera. The melodrama of the final trio and the staginess of the call for 'Siegfrieds Tod!' are an index of this.

The case of Gluck is instructive. His operas, at least the later ones, exhibit the quality of dramatic pressure in a large degree. Because, dramatically considered, they so obviously possess this high potential, critics have been much exercised to find the explanation in the quality of Gluck's music: because the effect of, say, *Iphigénie en Tauride* is so powerful, the music must be 'great' in its own right. This is not so; it is, in the best sense, *Gebrauchsmusik*, suited and shaped to the one end, drama. Wagner himself noted this when he characterized Gluck's music as 'musical prose'. On the other side stands Berlioz. Compared to Gluck's 'prose', Berlioz's highly idiosyncratic and expressive music is pure poetry. Furthermore, his imagination is strongly 'dramatic', as the word is commonly used: when Mephistopheles suddenly materializes or Aeneas starts from his bed to meet Hector's ghost, the effect is electric. But Gluck's continuous dramatic pressure is a quality that Berlioz simply does not command. His would-be dramatic works, between the sudden nodes of excitement, fall into static periods, lyric, elegiac, maybe even epic, but certainly not dramatic. Wagner's works are strongly marked by this quality of dramatic pressure, but the full potential was not developed early, and *Tannhäuser* provides the clearest demonstration of the initial weaknesses. The one instance of true dramatic pressure in *Tannhäuser* is in the overture, when into the clear atmosphere of the pilgrims' chant steals the first whiff of the exotic world of the Venusberg. What pipes and timbrels! What wild ecstasy! The alien and the erratic impinges sharply on sober certitude. Yet when this conflict is played out in full in the Venusberg scene, even as revised for Paris in 1861, all dramatic pressure is lost. Some of the ache of unformulated and unsatisfied desire may still be there (the sirens' song), but Frau Venus herself is a cold abstraction and the device of raising the pitch of Tannhäuser's declaration by a semitone on each of its two repetitions may look well on paper but in the theatre is mere ineffective academicism. In the second scene, the recognition of Tannhäuser by his old comrades brings a moment of interest, but the attempt to consolidate and expand this in the vast ensemble that follows merely creates a monument and not a drama. The second act is little better. The climax, when the outraged knights encircle Tannhäuser with drawn swords and Elisabeth throws herself between them, has all the makings of a theatrical sensation, and her plea, 'Ich fleh' für ihn', is a superbly effective tune. Yet neither comes to much because the ensemble that follows is, again, wholly static, the jagged phrases divided between the lower voices, and designed to liven the otherwise cumbrous mass, only serving to spotlight its cumbrousness. It is only in the last act, with Tannhäuser's despairing narration of his pilgrimage to Rome and his repulse by the Pope, that the true dramatist appears.

I have already suggested that *Tannhäuser* was, after *Der fliegende Holländer*, something of a throwback. Its successor, *Lohengrin*, is from the point of view of the dramatic critic a very marked step forward. Wagner achieves the same *frisson* when Elsa first speaks of *her* supernatural visitor, the knight of her dream, as when Venus' bacchanal first insinuates itself into the overture to *Tannhäuser*; but this time the tingle is even greater when the hint expands into full realization and the knight's swan-drawn skiff actually appears. The chorus is used with a new authority and definition; its comments, short and pregnant, whip on the action rather than retarding it in the way of the pachydermal ruminations of its counterpart in *Tannhäuser*. The feeling of *Lohengrin* is hieratic and its mode is the mode of ritual, but in contradistinction to its predecessor it is genuinely dramatic.

The full measure of Wagner's development as a dramatist can be gauged from a comparison of these early works with the first and third acts of *Parsifal*. The middle act is curiously unsatisfactory. To begin with, Klingsor is, like Friedrich in *Das Liebesverbot*, no more than a stage villain. Though the magic sleep of *Walküre* has added its contribution to his spells, this demon king is not half so convincing a sorcerer as the authentically pagan Ortrud in *Lohengrin*. Their supernatural powers are expressed by very similar figures, falling and rising for Ortrud, rising and falling for Klingsor; is it mere prejudice that finds Ortrud's theme genuinely disturbing and Klingsor's mere mumbo-jumbo? The Flower Maidens are, perhaps intentionally, pure kitsch, and though Kundry's first calling of Parsifal's name is dramatically striking, the long temptation scene between them is apt to pall. It has some kinship with the last scene of *Siegfried*, in which Brünnhilde makes the transition from godhead to womanhood. This has been acclaimed as a psychological study of the greatest subtlety, but I do not find it so, largely because it is such a jumble of musical patches and, for me, the dramatic connection snaps as one is switched from 'period *Götterdämmerung*' to the discarded string-quartet fragment and thence to the clog-dancing fourths of the theme so solemnly named 'Love's Resolution'. The Kundry–Parsifal scene, though musically rather more homogeneous, suffers from something of the same weakness. It is both monotonous and bitty, and the dramatic pressure is in consequence low.

The first and the third acts are a very different matter. Action, in the sense of physical events, is even more restricted than in the middle act, yet the pressure, the feeling of a destiny ineluctably unrolling, is never relaxed. This is particularly true of the first part of the last act. There are only three personages, and of these Kundry speaks only two words, the broken 'Dienen! dienen!', and Parsifal is silent for the first half of the scene. As in Act I, it is Gurnemanz who 'tells the story', but it is not so much by him or through him as round him or behind him that the action is developed. Here, for once, Wagner's visual imagination makes a crucial contribution. The air of dilapidation, of fading hopes and of patient resignation, which pervades both people and properties, is counterpoised by the signs of newly emerging spring, and against this freshness is set in turn the sombre, silent and discordant figure of the knight in black armour which, like Richard III's, is 'marvellous ill-favoured'.[18] The pace is never hurried or urgent, and though the music may dawdle here and drift into a brown study there, its continuity is never broken and eventually swells into the most characteristic of all Wagner's musical surges, the 'Good Friday Music', which naturally and cogently crowns the action. 'Natural' and 'cogent': these seem the right words for the scene as a whole. The world it creates is not the live world, but a symbolic or allegorical one. Yet, to the spectator in the theatre (the visual element is vital), it has an immediacy that is more vivid than life.

MUSIC AND DRAMA

Oper und Drama begins by diagnosing the sickness of nineteenth-century opera. Its cause, said Wagner, was that 'a means of expression (music) has been made the end, while the end of expression (the drama) has been made the means'.[19] Again, in *Eine Mitteilung an meine Freunde* (*A Communication to My Friends*), he wrote: 'I will speak primarily of [my] poems, not only because in them the connection between my art and my life is most clearly displayed, but also because I must through them establish that the organization of my music, my method of operatic composition, was conditioned by the essential nature of these poems.'[20] Here, and in many similar passages, Wagner asserts that music was no more than the means, the material, with which he sought to create his ultimate object, drama. On the other side Deryck Cooke can say, as a musician, that Wagner's dramas would in themselves have soon been forgotten and that what lives is his music.[21]

Cooke's statement, I think, goes too far. I concede that what Wagner called the 'stuff' of his dramas was not as elemental, as original, or as universally significant as he imagined. *Das Volk* ('The Folk'), whose identification with the dramas was ultimately to vindicate them, has so far appeared in no more convincing shape than the aesthetic clique which (after Ludwig of Bavaria) first took up Wagner's works, and the Nazi party which later made something of a mascot of them. It seems an injustice to Wagner to suppose that he would have accepted either of these as good witnesses or as worthy of his cause. Though the 'stuff' with which he chose to work had undeniably a high potential, there is in Wagner's transmission of it something missed or muddled so that the full power is never developed. To put a finger on the fault is hard. One may indicate its existence in this way. The question, 'What am I to feel, or think?' is as pertinent at the end of *Tristan* or

Götterdämmerung as at the end of *King Lear*. Whether or not it is answerable is irrelevant; what is significant is that the question itself seems less important in Wagner's case than in Shakespeare's.

Acknowledge, then, that Wagner had not the capability to make as much of the Nibelung or Grail legend as Aeschylus made of the story of the house of Atreus. His contribution to drama (and not only to music-drama) was still immense, taking the form of an enormous enlargement and enrichment of the means of representation. His boast that with the orchestra he restored the function of universalizing the drama which had formerly belonged to the Greek chorus was not a vain one. Justified, too, was the claim that his technique of motival variation added a new dimension to communication, enabling the hitherto inexpressible to be expressed. His intricate musical forms, not externally applied but each newly invented for a specific purpose, gave unity, cohesion and carrying power to dramatic actions even when extended over a very long span.

These means, the material of this contribution, were wholly music, and music employed with such skill that one is tempted to conclude that the musician generated the dramatist and not vice versa. The letter to Uhlig about Beethoven is also significant in this aspect.[22] It suggests that Wagner could not trust himself to 'pure' music, but felt that the music that he had it in him to write could not be self-sufficient and needed a host-plant, 'the Word', to nourish it. That at least is true: Wagner's music would go for little were it not attached by the Word to an actual physical context and expressly given a human relevance. Yet Cooke is right in saying that it is the music (music, granted, that has been fertilized by the Word) that obsesses the memory, and not the drama. Ultimately Wagner is of Beethoven's rather than Shakespeare's party.

SIX

The Total Work of Art

MICHAEL TANNER

I. PROLEGOMENON: WAGNER AND CRITICAL ARGUMENT

'RICHARD WAGNER is the most violently controversial artist known to history.' Wilhelm Furtwängler, Wagner's greatest interpreter, began with these words his magnificent essay *Der Fall Wagner, frei nach Nietzsche*'[1] in 1941. Fifteen years later, Curt von Westernhagen began his book *Richard Wagner: Sein Werk, sein Wesen, seine Welt* by quoting the same words. And I have no doubt that they will come in handy for many future commentators on Wagner as they attempt to get under way in stating what they see as the truth about 'the case of Wagner'. His art, it would seem, is inherently controversial in a way that is not true of any other artist of comparable significance. There is this difference between now and one hundred years ago or less, that it is absurd any longer to pretend that he is *not* significant: and Nietzsche, his most virulent critic, never made the mistake of dismissing Wagner as in- consequential, even though his tactics of exalting *Carmen* at Wagner's expense may be seen as an attempt to do that. But Nietzsche had too sure a sense of priorities to waste his energies on an unworthy figure, and he devoted more of them to attacking Wagner than to any other single figure, even Socrates or Christ.

Simply because Wagner remains so controversial, it is tempting to think that the greatest achievement a critic of his work could possibly dream of would be an account of Wagner such that every intelligent, sensitive and disinterested reader would be persuaded that, after almost a century and a half of fierce critical battles, 'the common pursuit of true judgement' (T. S. Eliot's definition of criticism) had at last reached its goal. Or that it had come as close to that as one can hope to in the case of any major artist. I have certainly been tempted by such an ideal, and during the twenty-five years of my own fanatical attachment to Wagner I have, whenever opportunity offered, attempted to 'make converts' and to rebut the nearly incessant stream of absurdities that still flows strongly in books, magazines, and so on by critics who, as it has always seemed to me, felt incited by listening to, or simply thinking about, Wagner to perpetrate them.

My love of Wagner is no less strong or deep than it ever was; and I am still appalled by the nonsense that otherwise sensible men tend to talk about him, and I feel as incensed as ever when a critic tells us that Mime, or Beckmesser, or Klingsor is clearly intended to be a Jew. But while there should be no relaxation of vigilance in resisting the mistakes and mendacities which anti-Wagnerians seem to need to produce, I have come to feel that it is a distinctive feature of Wagner's art that he does provoke powerfully opposed responses, and that that is not a limiting judgement on his greatness. It is a large critical error to think that more than a certain degree of agreement about art is necessary or desirable, an error fostered by the notion that if there is not such a thing as *the* true judgement to be made about any given work, then we have only the alternative of total subjectivism. This error is neatly encapsulated in the passage from Eliot from which I lifted a phrase in the last paragraph. He says, in his essay 'The Function of Criticism', 'The critic, one would suppose, if he is to justify his existence, should endeavour to discipline his personal prejudices and cranks—tares to which we are all subject—and compose his differences with as many of his fellows as possible in the common pursuit of true judgement.'[2] As a partial statement of the aims of criticism, this couldn't be improved on. But it has, if treated as an account of the whole task of the critic, a disabling defect; for there is the implication that whatever individuates people in a critically significant way can be dismissed, or at least characterized, as 'personal prejudices and cranks—tares to which we are all subject'. But I take it that Eliot would not have denied that it's a good thing that we do have individual personalities, which are inevitably reflected in our preferences, artistic and otherwise. One of the tasks of the critic which is least often performed is that of sorting out those elements in works about which agreement in attitude and feeling is to be sought and is to be expected, and those elements about which it would be absurd to demand agreement—absurd in the same way that it would be to expect or think that everyone should fall in love with the same person, or even like or dislike, as opposed to ad-miring, say, or disapproving, of that person.

I'm not writing an article on aesthetics, nor even summarizing one, but certain commonplaces of criticism, or of critical theory, seem to need restating rather firmly in some contexts, and especially when a frightened, or worse, an arrogant retreat into subjectivism is likely. And because of the chronic disagreements about Wagner's works everyone, apart from the fanatics on either side, may be reaching the stage where they don't want to spend any more time in fruitless disagreement, and so agree to differ, though it's not clear that *such* an agreement is going to be found; rather it's an admission of necessary sterility. My aim is a more delicate one than is usually required of the critic: for in Wagner we have an artist about whom it has come to seem foolish to expect agreement among critics at all, except perhaps in respect of certain technical aspects of his art, where a limited amount of progress has been made.

Does this have, *a priori*, any consequence for his standing? One might think so, for the following reason: the area where one *does* expect, and try for, critical agreement is one which concerns our common humanity. The reason why some works assume a central position, or are touchstones, and accepted as such, is that they are concerned with the needs and impulses without which we wouldn't be men at all. That is why 'centrality' is not a cant critical term, but an indispensable one. Now one might claim either that the works which are touchstones of aesthetic worth are so in respect of the area they concern, or in respect of the specific views they take towards it. Thus, in a society where the family is of key importance, a work might be claimed to be of worth on the grounds (though not, of course, only on the grounds) that it dealt with issues involving the family, or that it dealt with issues involving the family *and* proposed or suggested specific solutions or ways of regarding them. Both positions—which have not usually been sorted out adequately, which is my excuse for separating them rather brusquely here—are, and have been, widely held. There is a pronounced critical tradition in which the major values invoked *are* precisely 'seriousness', 'maturity', 'moral intensity', and where it is admitted, if not explicitly, then in the light of the most highly esteemed works, that there are more ways than one of being serious, morally intense, or even mature. But alongside or within this tradition there has been another one, which is concerned that art should not only give every evidence of seeking the truth, but that it should have found it.

The fact that there *are* these two importantly different traditions should alert us to a further fact: that, as a consequence, the value of many works will be both felt and expressed in the same terms, though some of the critics using those terms will actually differ from some others. For instance, one critic might praise D. H. Lawrence for his seriousness and moral intensity while not at all agreeing with his view on the subjects to which his intensity was directed, and another critic might both approve of the intensity and also share Lawrence's actual views. Yet it is often curiously hard to find out which of these two lines some critics, even very important ones, are taking, possibly because they are not perfectly clear on the question themselves.

One might, indeed, suggest that it is a characteristic of critics who take art seriously, and has been since the beginning of the nineteenth century, to vacillate between these two positions. I mean by 'critics who take art seriously' those critics who don't think that art is the only thing worth taking seriously, nor think that art, if it *is* serious, has to be assimilated to something else. Wagner's art has been treated in both those ways: some people have been 'Wagnerians' in that they felt that Wagner's art was self-sufficient, and that one could spend a life well simply responding to it: one might take Ludwig II, mildly inaccurately but with symbolic rightness, as representative of that group. Other people have been Wagnerians in that they felt that Wagner's art was essentially doctrine, prophecy, and a means of redemption: Cosima and Houston Stewart Chamberlain (whose books on Wagner are nevertheless worth reading) were the founder-members of *that* approach. The correct approach—whatever its conclusion—has been less often tried.

The vacillation that has characterized criticism since the Schlegels is a consequence of the fact that most of the works of the past that we value have been composed either with a background of Christian belief, or a background of Greek or Roman beliefs, multifarious as those were. Since most of the great critics of the nineteenth and twentieth centuries, and also most of their great artists, have not been Christians or Graeco-Roman pagans, the consequence has been that the great art of the past is appreciated without its presuppositions, or often, its upshots, being endorsed. One reason why Shakespeare is so appealing to everyone is that he does not make the requirement of that colossal suspension of disbelief in Christianity which can be so exhausting when it is demanded for the length of the *Divine Comedy*, for instance. We shall see in detail later how Wagner's complex relations with Christianity make some of his works appear, to many earnest souls, too hot to handle.

But the main point here is that—even granted, as in the cases of

143

Shakespeare or Beethoven, a great deal of conflict about which of their works are greatest, and why—there is nonetheless a consensus that within the *oeuvre* of each of them centrally human issues are dealt with, and in a way that commands respect or awe, if not always love or mild affection. But there is no such consensus about Wagner's *oeuvre*, even though it incontestably deals with questions of life and death, the basis of morality and politics, and the nature of the personality—among other things. For many people, the manner in which he broaches these subjects is so crude and bludgeoning that he doesn't so much carry out explorations (and the 'creative' is closely linked to the 'exploratory' in much of the most valuable criticism) as assaults or rapes. Are we to admire this admittedly demonic force, who can hardly be denied Nietzsche's title 'the most impolite of geniuses' (unless we reserve it for Nietzsche himself)?

Well, it would be idiotic to claim that dealing with central human questions was a sufficient condition of artistic greatness: it would allow in both the hopelessly cheap and the viciously perverted. So critics who denied Wagner's greatness could freely agree that he deals with the momentous issues that it is characteristic of the greatest art to concern itself with. What, they may claim, is unacceptable is his mode of doing so: to put it at its gentlest, his art's 'robust exploitation of subtleties, its vigorous handling of fragile profundities, and its wicked appeals for goodness',[3] in Erich Heller's characteristic words; and it can be, and often is, put much less gently, in a tradition inaugurated by Nietzsche—not that he was the first person to abuse Wagner, of course, but that he set the pattern for referring to him as 'that old Klingsor', 'a helpless decadent', and a major cultural disaster. But there's a difficulty: could Wagner have been, or still be, a major cultural disaster without being a great artist? Put like that, it sounds as if we have only to make up our minds about whether art, to be great, must be 'true' or 'right', or at any rate not catastrophic. But it's a decision that proves, the moment we brace ourselves for it, appallingly difficult to take. Suppose that one feels (as I do) that Christianity is, or was, a moral and metaphysical (in other words, a religious) disaster: does one stop listening to the *St Matthew Passion*, the *Missa Solemnis*, not to mention the huge bulk of church music from the thirteenth century onwards that a musically sensitive person may easily be overcome by? And what of the majority of Western visual art and architecture from the Dark Ages to the eighteenth century? If one is going to be aesthetically ascetic, the rigours will indeed be hard to bear. And it is a misfortune for criticism that the few who have inflicted on themselves such rigours have felt that they might as well go the whole hog while they were about it: hence Tolstoy's notorious rejection of very nearly all art. What we have much more typically is criticism in favour of 'improving' works, where the improvement comes from having one's ideology (Marxist or Christian, say) backed up by a 'moral tale'. Clearly Wagner is not going to prosper under those conditions. Just in case anyone might think that Wagner was an 'improving' artist for believers in one particular ideology, namely that of National Socialism, which was what the Nazis themselves thought, all one needs to ask is: How? Since the works that the Nazis concentrated on were the *Ring* and *Meistersinger*, it's perhaps worth pointing out, very rapidly, that there is no conceivable interpretation of the *Ring* which gives anything like a comprehensive account of it and which tallies with the Nazi *Weltanschauung*; and that the whole weight of the Nazi admiration for *Meistersinger* falls on the last five minutes, which, in the work, clearly concerns art and not politics. But, the person who sees Wagner as all too readily playing into the Nazis' hands will reply, it's not the specific content of the dramas, it's the general 'feel' that suited them so well, the mist-shrouded atmosphere of Nordic gods, blood-brotherhood, permanent hysteria, incipient or actual, the *Schwung*, of an unusual kind, which led Francis Fergusson to his memorable comparison of *Tristan* with Riefenstahl's film, '*Der Triumph des Willens*' (The Triumph of the Will).[4] That is a more intelligent point, with which I shall be dealing later. It is again, I may add, a Nietzschean criticism *au fond*, in that, so far as Nietzsche makes any points more specific or thought-provoking than his wilful paradoxes, they are concerned with the spiritual climate of Wagner's works—a climate which he has been widely felt to share. But *that* aspect of Wagner needs exceptionally careful handling—not in order to smuggle him out of the Nazi camp, but to ascertain exactly what the climate is, and why his alleged Nazism is as libellous an allegation as Nietzsche's, or as D. H. Lawrence's 'proto-Fascism'.

I have set off several diverse but connected lines of thought: the one to which I wish briefly to return before I close this section is the challenge that Wagner presents to criticism. It is easy to carry on to no good purpose about his endless and seemingly inherent capacity for engendering controversy. Yet it remains a unique phenomenon: any intelligent Wagnerian will have to concede that there are musically and dramatically sensitive people who are revolted or bored by Wagner, in a way that simply doesn't happen with any of the other towering figures in the arts, or not to the same extent. There are anti-Proustians, anti-Miltonists; there were anti-Beethovenians—Stravinsky, for example; but then the reaction against a particular figure at a particular time is something quite different. There are *still* anti-Wagnerians, even though it is at last possible to compose music or listen to it without having Wagner looming over one, as it hardly was seventy years ago. It may turn out to be the case that the fundamental for-or-against feeling for Wagner is prior to the content of his works, and defeats analysis or the possibility of argumentation. But if that conclusion is the right one, it should be postponed, like all conclusions of its kind, for as long as possible. And even if it is accepted, it should still be possible to delineate the uniqueness of the phenomenon by drawing a line around it, so that it needn't be merely *named*. In fact, I believe that a great deal of the unease, as well as the awe, that Wagner evokes can be dissolved or rendered harmless. Meanwhile, anyone who hates him has a duty to justify so vehement a response, as one always does have with hatred, unlike love. And those of us for whom Wagner is a figure who evokes intensities of positive reaction that are incommensurable with those vouchsafed by any other artist (and I don't mean to suggest that any of my fellow-contributors is in this category, though I imagine some may be) also have a duty to ourselves to clarify the extraordinary significance that he plays in our lives.

2. GESAMTKUNSTWERK AND TOTAL WORK OF ART (I)

Wagner's theory of the *Gesamtkunstwerk* is a bore, and in this section, after briefly dealing with it, I shall explain why I am using an English term sufficiently portentous to sound as if it's a translation of Wagner's term. The notion of the *Gesamtkunstwerk*, as expounded by Wagner himself and his epigones, is what Thomas Mann calls 'bad nineteenth century'. It indicates a grandioseness of ambition which is quite unlike what Wagner actually created, and in any case his reading of Schopenhauer led him, as everyone knows, to give music a pre-eminent place in his work.[5] Certain aspects of the theory, such as that of the 'redemption' of sculpture by moving actors, and, only mildly less foolish, the incorporation of the art of painting into the designing of backdrops, amuse or embarrass according to one's mood; sometimes both. Otherwise his theory comes simply to the fairly old view that *dramma per musica* is a possibility, and in the context of Meyerbeer and Donizetti a necessity; and to the novel view that music-drama transcends any other art form. My own view is more circumscribed: music-drama practised by Wagner transcended any other art form, and as practised by some other great artists—Monteverdi, Gluck, Mozart, Beethoven, Bellini, Verdi, Mussorgsky, Pfitzner, Janáček and Schoenberg at their best—equals any other art form. In other words, it is not the art form, it is the artist working in the form which determines how great it is. Not a very striking view; but I'm prepared to agree with Wagner, and to argue on his behalf, that music-drama practised supremely *is* supreme. The sheer idea of arguing for a ranking of the arts is universally considered absurd at the present time, and I shan't be able here to argue with the thoroughness which is required both by the subject and by the historical position in which I am arguing it. I hope, incidentally, to be able to use the latter factor to my advantage.

I take my cue from an unexpected source (in this context): D. H. Lawrence. It is well known that he made claims for the novel as the supreme art form. Characteristic formulations are, for example:

> The novel is a great discovery: far greater than Galileo's telescope or somebody else's wireless. The novel is the highest form of human expression so far attained. Why? Because it is so incapable of the absolute. In a novel, everything is relative to everything else, if that novel is art at all.[6]

And a little later in the same article, he gives his reasons:

> You can fool nearly every other medium. You can make a poem pietistic, and still it will be a poem. You can write *Hamlet* in drama: if you wrote him in a novel, he'd be half comic, or a trifle suspicious: a suspicious character, like Dostoevsky's Idiot. Somehow, you sweep the ground a bit too clear in the poem or the drama, and you let the human Word fly a bit too freely. Now in a novel there's always a tom-cat, a black tom-cat that pounces on the white dove of the Word, if the dove doesn't watch it: and there is a banana-skin to trip on: and you know there's a water-closet on the premises. All these things help to keep the balance.[7]

Again, in another article he argues for a similar conclusion from different premises:

> Now I absolutely flatly deny that I am a soul, or a body, or a mind, or an intelligence, or a brain, or a nervous system, or a bunch of glands, or any of the rest of these bits of me. The whole is greater than the part. And therefore I, who am man alive, am greater than my soul, or spirit, or body, or mind, or consciousness, or anything else that is merely a part of me. I am a man, and alive. I am man alive . . . For this reason I am a novelist. And being a novelist, I consider myself superior to the saint, the scientist, the philosopher, and the poet, who are all great masters of different bits of man alive, but never get the whole hog.[8]

147

It's worth noticing that in this article ('Why the Novel Matters') he also says, 'The Bible—but *all* the Bible [Lawrence, like Nietzsche, preferred the Old Testament to the New]—and Homer, and Shakespeare: these are the supreme old novels.' So he could easily be attacked for using the well-tried method of saying something alarming and bold, only to be discovered meaning something much less drastic a bit later on. But that would be to miss the point, which is, I take it, that we can only see Homer or the Bible or Shakespeare (elsewhere he adds Plato) as novels now that we have paradigmatic ones in terms of which to read Homer, etc. I don't deny that there is an inconsistency between what he says about *Hamlet* in the first article, and his inclusion of Shakespeare as a novelist in the second. But it doesn't much matter. The central points are that the novel is the only medium that deals with the whole man; and, related to, but distinct from that, the novel is the only medium in which an artist can't get away with didacticism; if he tries, by 'putting his thumb in the scale', to persuade us of his own views, he will be betrayed by the substance of the novel, or else (presumably) the novel will be too blatantly biased and bad for us to take it seriously in the first place.

The general reaction to these views of Lawrence's is, I suspect, that they are 'stimulating', i.e. can be ignored except for use when composing examination papers. And anyway, he *was* a novelist, so can be expected, and allowed, to be extravagant in defence of his art, which is often taken far too lightly. The same could be said for Wagner's theoretical writings—indeed, it often has been: opera is always in danger of collapsing into frivolity, thanks to the vanity of singers who can perform prodigies of breath-control and produce spectacular trills, top C's, and so forth; or, in Wagner's day, opera was in danger of capitulating completely to the taste of a public that wanted to be reminded of imperial splendours, so that the twin distraction of 'machines' and twittering divas led to the impostures of Meyerbeer and the suppression of the true function of opera, a function which could be performed by nothing else.

Wagner's theoretical writings, though it's always clear that they are the product of an extraordinarily rich mind, are notoriously turgid, full of special pleading, and, except when he is being practical, or hits the odd inspired phrase, lacking in the astonishing energy and resource of both the man and his art. By contrast, Lawrence's writings about art are almost always unqualifiedly wonderful, while his art often, after the supreme achievements of *The Rainbow* and *Women in Love*, dismays

by its shrillness, diffuseness, and Lawrence's misplaced faith in everything he wrote possessing its own organic form. From his critical
writings we can learn to state with the closest precision what is right,
and what is wrong, with his art: and the same is true for what he says
about the novel and all literary or dramatic art. If he's right, applying
his principles of judgement, the novel will survive more often than any
other art form. And it will do that because of the criterion, which is
obviously of central concern, of the internal balances of the novel, the
inability of the novelist to get away with anything. My claim is that, just
as, using this criterion, Lawrence is rapidly led to call Homer, the Bible
and Shakespeare novels, so he should supremely have claimed that
music-dramas are novels—or, if the playing fast and loose with nomen-
clature is becoming too absurd, as I think it is, that he should have conceded that music-drama can do at least as well as some other forms of
artistic expression the things that matter most. Of course he didn't,
because he wasn't particularly sensitive to music, and never said anything that suggests he realized its importance as a mode of expression.

A general argument about the nature and value of music is something
that I need to produce, but which, to be convincing, would have to
take up a disproportionate part of this essay—the whole of it, in fact. I
agree with Schopenhauer and with Wagner after he had read Schopenhauer, that music occupies a unique position among the arts, or indeed
among all modes of human communication, on account of its capacity
for catching and rendering directly the movements of the will. I do not
use a capital for 'Will' because I do not want, at least here, to invest in
the whole Schopenhauerian metaphysic. What I *do* mean by 'will' is
best given by yet another quotation from Lawrence, this time when he
is writing to Edward Garnett about the difference between *The Rainbow*,
on which he was working, and *Sons and Lovers*:

> You mustn't look in my novel for the old stable *ego*—of the character.
> There is another *ego*, according to whose action the individual is un-
> recognizable, and passes through, as it were, allotropic states which it
> needs a deeper sense than any we've been used to exercise, to discover
> are states of the same single radically unchanged element. (Like as
> diamond and coal are the same pure single element of carbon. The
> ordinary novel would trace the history of the diamond—but I say,
> 'Diamond, what! This is carbon.' And my diamond might be coal or
> soot, and my theme is carbon.)[9]

Without grasping that point, one can't begin to understand *The
Rainbow* and *Women in Love*, and even when one does grasp it, there
are passages in both novels that remain inpenetrable; and it is significant

that in his subsequent fiction, both successful and unsuccessful, Lawrence deals much more with the old stable ego than in those novels. My claim for music is that it can, though it does not necessarily, concern itself with an immediate expression of the carbon which is the ego according to whose action the individual is unrecognizable: that the movements and states of this ego are such that it is doubtful whether language used discursively, as it is even by Lawrence, can convey them: and that Wagner pre-eminently among operatic composers does. To put the case at its crudest: his characters speak in the way that we expect of 'the old stable ego—of the character', but the music to which, or to the accompaniment of which, they sing is that of the other ego. That is not the only purpose that Wagnerian music serves; but it often *does* serve that purpose, and increasingly so as his life's work progresses. It is not surprising that Wagner had almost a sense of *déjà lu* when he read Schopenhauer; for his own works, whose central characters are suffused with a need for 'redemption', are concerned to divine the workings of the carbon-ego; the diamond, which we might call the social ego, is one that Wagner was increasingly coming to see was not itself the subject, or object, of 'redemption'. But so long as the old operatic forms were adhered to, it was impossible to concern himself with the carbon-ego in the way that he needed to; hence he was led first of all to his mistaken, and never practised (by him) theory of the *Gesamtkunstwerk*, as we find it in *Opera and Drama, A Communication to My Friends*, and other writings of that period, in which he confused several issues and only incidentally threw light on particular works, while at the same time, in his celebrated formulation concerning the relationship between means and ends in opera and music-drama, he succinctly stated a truth about the recurrent degenerative tendencies of opera without seeing that they were not necessarily connected with the kind of opera which he wanted to replace. The red herring of the *Gesamtkunstwerk* could have wasted still more of his time if it had not been for Schopenhauer telling him what he had often glimpsed, but not previously formulated: that the musical element in music-drama not only was of peculiar significance because of the intrinsic nature of music, but that therefore its contribution to music-drama could not be regarded in a purely aggregative way, which is the unfortunate impression that the *Gesamtkunstwerk* theory gives: the more arts you have working away at the same time, the more impressive will be the effect. Of course Wagner would never have subscribed to the proposition stated thus baldly, but I can't see that his theory really avoids it. Not only did his grateful, and one must feel, relieved acceptance of Schopenhauer's theory of music enable him to exploit his musical powers more fully than, under the influence of theory, he might otherwise have done—though it's not likely; it also enabled him to realize his true aims, which he had never succeeded in making clear to himself or, *a fortiori*, to anyone else. One reason for the extraordinary copiousness of Wagner's writings during the five years when he produced no music was that he could not quite focus on his 'true need'. Actually, he was an instinctive artist, as he sometimes knew; but he had to believe that there was a theory he was working in accordance with, again like Lawrence, though Lawrence had a juster view of the relations between his novels and his theoretical writings ('polyanalytics') than Wagner.

The nature of music and the nature of the self: it was Schopenhauer's distinction to link them in a crucial way, and it is this linking which alone puts him in the first rank of philosophers. It is notorious that his philosophy has had extremely little influence on philosophers: not even Nietzsche was deeply influenced by it; but he has had a more powerful influence on artists over a shorter period of time than any other philosopher, even on figures as disparate as Tolstoy, who called Schopenhauer 'the greatest man who ever lived', and Thomas Mann, two violently antithetical figures, though that doesn't mean that a discussion of the contrasts between them would be valuable. Artists have found Schopenhauer appealing for various reasons, among which is his superb style. But they have found their activities as artists justified in his metaphysical system more impressively than in anyone else's, and not only justified but elevated to a position where no other activity is superior: that was naturally welcome in the age of Hegel, who placed art below philosophy and religion. Furthermore, for some of them his specific metaphysical views seemed more sympathetic than those of the dominant optimism which is so wearying a feature of the history of Western philosophy. But besides his congenial and slightly glamorous gloom, there was his emphasis on a dimension of human nature which was found still more attractive by artists addicted to brooding on the non-rational and possibly non-conscious elements in the personality: in other words, by characteristically Romantic artists, for whom other metaphysical systems either by-passed the deepest problems concerning the nature of the self, or else gave coarsely reductive accounts, *à la* Hobbes. As, disappointed by external reality and lacking conviction about a transcendental realm, Romantics looked within, they hoped, and in some cases demanded, to find there what had previously been posited outside or beyond. So far as analysis of the self went, Plato remained, as always, a possibility; but there may have been Romantics who felt what Nietzsche was finally to assert stridently: that Socrates inaugurated the era of Greek decline, and that Plato therefore had only the glory of being the greatest of decadents the first time round. Not only that, but his suspicion of all art except in the service of his own social ideals rendered him less useful as a guide in this respect: it was not until Schopenhauer that a philosopher, as opposed to a theorizing playwright such as Schiller, had the courage to take his stand on music for its own sake as the most direct expression of fundamental reality, because it dispensed with concepts. The latter claim, which I think is certainly true, is both the glory and the agony of music: self-evidently the glory, and only slightly less obviously the agony, because almost everyone is sometimes in their lives, when they are most moved by music, simultaneously most frustrated that they cannot say why, in the sense of saying what the music 'means' which so moves them. Schopenhauer provides an account both of the depth of their emotion and of its ineffability. Before he encountered Schopenhauer's works (three years after *Opera and Drama*, published in 1851), Wagner claimed that it was more of an agony than a glory that 'absolute' music was ineffable, and, taking Beethoven's Ninth Symphony, argued that it reached a point of such intensity that the only thing for it to do was to become vocal, and thereby verbal. Since he never explicitly revoked the doctrine of *Opera and Drama*, he did not explain how the Ninth Symphony stood in the light of Schopenhauer's teachings. He did, however, state explicitly in *Music of the Future* (1861) that poetry and music are of separate value and equal importance, and to be broadly matched rather than pedantically joined. That poetry is actually to be subordinated to music comes out by *Beethoven* (1870) and *On the Destiny of Opera* (1871); and also that the firm lines drawn by the drama allow the music to be more free and bold in form and impetus. And clearly enough what the music *is* doing, among other things—and one should never overlook the versatility of music—is giving us the deepest feelings of the characters who are singing, so that their words are given resonances of meaning which enhance enormously their significance and hence their effect, while simultaneously out of all the music's possibilities of expression that one is actualized by the text which is relevant for our understanding; music is harnessed and thus its freedom of movement, to put it loosely, is restricted: on the other hand it both fertilizes and is itself enriched by having its place in a precise dramatic context. That is the first part of what I mean by 'total work of art'. It is not, even approximately, what Wagner meant by *Gesamtkunstwerk*. But it is somewhat closer to what he meant after he had read Schopenhauer than before.

3. GESAMTKUNSTWERK AND TOTAL WORK OF ART (2) THE RING

I want now to return to the claims that Lawrence makes for the novel, because they amount, in a straightforward way, to the claim that the novel is the most complete form of human expression, at the same time as he stresses that one great thing about the novel is that it has no 'absolutes'. The claims are closely related: for absolutes entail a kind of discrimination and exclusion which Lawrence wants to avoid at every level. At the same time that we are meditating on this aspect of Lawrence's claim, we should remember his demand, in the wonderful opening passage of his essay on Galsworthy, that 'a good critic should give his reader a few standards to go by. He can change the standards for every new critical attempt, so long as he keeps good faith.'[10] The point is that while, on the one hand, we can't cope with experience without having criteria to judge it by, on the other we must always be prepared to revise our criteria. To explain how these processes work would take one into the logic, psychology and even sociology of art, and for that matter of science: but we all know that they do, or can, work. Now part of the refusal to have absolutes is the down-to-earthness of the novel, which Lawrence contrasts with *Hamlet*. And one might feel that if, as is clearly the case, false absolutes are the consequence of exclusiveness and grandeur, then Wagner is more prone to them than almost anyone else. And that is a claim that lies behind a lot of anti-Wagnerian criticism. Lawrence does not want us to forget that even the grandest people need 'a water-closet on the premises', and that *is* a significant point. But it is one thing to agree to *that* point, another to insist that an artist should produce work in which at no stage would the mention of a water-closet be out of place. Not that Lawrence does make that demand here: but it is useful when one wants to be reductive. It's made crudely by Aldous Huxley in his characteristic piece 'Tragedy and the Whole Truth',[11] where he argues that tragedy necessarily excludes what we can find in the nourishingly full-bodied pages of Fielding. As always, when a general argument is presented about art, one wants to say, 'But stick to examples, and remember that a paramount critical virtue is *tact*.' And that's only what one wants to *start* by saying: it would be absurd to argue that *any* grand style is out of place. I shall discuss later the view that some works of art are self-sufficient, in that though they may only be part of the truth (of course), they adequately present *that* part; and others are not, in the sense that they focus our attention on part of the truth by magnification, distortion and simplification. Meanwhile, the important Lawrentian point is not that tendencies to grandiosity can be checked in novels by occasional trips to the lavatory by the characters, but that there should be no absolutes in the sense I have specified. In *that* sense the novel can be a total work of art, in that the whole range of human experience can be accommodated within it, and if our frames of reference are shattered, so much the worse for them. That is a large part of the importance of the creative. Now the question is whether or not Wagner proceeds with absolutes, even if they vary from work to work; and if they *do* vary from work to work, whether the change in ultimate values takes place, as it were, between works or can be incorporated in them. For when an artist develops in a very spectacular way, as Wagner unquestionably did, and not simply by developing a mature and personal idiom from relatively callow beginnings, but also by treating of the same themes over and over again, and advancing in his grasp of them, we want to see, within his works, why he has changed, and how profoundly felt the change is. For an artist who is concerned as Wagner is with the fundamental springs of human behaviour, we need to be given insight at least as much into *movements* of the soul as into its states. And the more Wagner goes on in his prose writings about the 'purely human', the more we want to grasp *what* it is: we are back again at the carbon-ego, and its relation to the social self, the diamond ego. And the sense of values that we derive from Wagner comes from understanding the 'deepest need' (a favourite phrase, in various near-synonymous forms, of Wagner's characters) that his characters, in all their mythic-psychological depth, possess.

But what sense of values *do* we derive from Wagner, and are we convinced by his characters' 'höchste Not'? I'm afraid it would be foolish to expect anything less than an extremely complex answer to these questions, which is what the rest of this essay will be concerned to provide, in several stages. The first is to look at the manner in which Wagner brings us to feel what the values of his works are, and thus to discover whether there is a sense in which there are built-in checks in his works. He is normally taken to be the artist *par excellence* (if that is the *mot juste* in this context) who is determined to get us to believe whatever it is that he wants us to by, in Nietzsche's formulation, saying 'something so often—till one despairs—till one believes it';[12] and he is unlike Bizet, Nietzsche tells us, whose tragic accents are achieved 'without grimaces! Without counterfeiting! Without the *lie* of the grand style!'[13]—all of which we find in Wagner, Nietzsche famously claims. I am not concerned here with a general defence of Wagner against Nietzsche's often crude, but sometimes very shrewd, attacks;[14] but this is something that is too widely felt about Wagner, and too germane to the issues at hand, to be ignored. The question of repetition aside—*what* does Wagner say so often?—there is still the matter of what is normally taken to be his overwhelming rhetoric, by which some listeners are *hingerissen*, and others *abgekühlt*. Now the eloquence (as I hear it) of Wagner's music is not directed towards a simple propagation of one point of view per work: it is one of his most obvious characteristics that he gets inside most of his *dramatorum personae* to an extent which equals, easily, Mozart's or Monteverdi's (I think primarily of *L'Incoronazione di Poppea* here). In many situations it is perfectly clear where his sympathies lie; but then whose sympathies would lie elsewhere? He never betrays animus towards his creations—not even towards Mime, and certainly not towards Beckmesser or Klingsor—in the way that Beethoven does towards Pizarro, who is a straightforward villain of melodrama: if one sees *him* 'from the inside', there's very little inside to see. Wagner's music is eloquent on behalf of all his characters, though the eloquence may be temporarily withdrawn: we see Tristan in Act I almost entirely through Isolde's eyes until some way into the scene between them: we get inside Tristan at 'War Morold dir so wert'. Until then we have been able to have the luxury of sharing Isolde's entirely righteous rage (it's no luxury for her: 'Ungeminnt! Den hehrsten Mann steht's mir nah zu sehen! Wie könnt ich dies' Qual bestehen?' 'Unloved! The finest man stands nearby for me to see! How can I support this anguish?' Surely no line in opera or elsewhere in art is more desolate.) But time after time, when listening after being given a plot-summary, one expects to find that one's sympathies are unproblematically distributed, and that turns out not to be the case at all. Nothing could be more abysmally obtuse than Robert Craft's claim that '*Parsifal* is one of the most misogynistic works of art ever written'.[15] He primarily has Kundry in mind, incredible as it must seem to everybody *else* who has listened—or perhaps simply to *everybody* who has listened to *Parsifal*. Not only is she seen in the gentlest light, after her furious entry in Act I, but in the opening scene of Act II Wagner presents a more hideous portrayal of spiritual and psychological bondage than any artist has ever done. It is some of the most unenjoyable art I know, and has a horribly chilling effect; and yet, extraordinarily, not only do we feel with Kundry in her loathsome condition, but with Klingsor too. For Wagner is again unique in the intensity with which he makes us realize always how desperately miserable evil people are. There is no need for Alberich to tell his son 'Hagen, mein Sohn! Hasse die Frohen!' ('Hagen, my son! Hate the happy!'), memorable as the injunction is. It is clear from the beginning of the scene known as Hagen's Watch how miserable he is, and there is a terrible, painful longing as he apostrophizes Siegfried and Gunther on their journey: 'Ihr freien Söhne, frohen Gesellen' ('You free sons, happy companions') to a motive that occurs again only in the orchestral interlude that follows his meditation, and at the end of the unspeakably malevolent Prelude to Act II: a motive, so far as I know, never labelled by commentators, but which, if I were a believer in motive-labelling (as, on a small scale, one can hardly not be) I would call the motive of the Pathos of Evil: a name which not only has the authentic Hans von Wolzogen/Lavignac ring about it, but which does accurately sum up what is being expressed, above all the sense of frustration at being evil, and the envy of freedom. It gives us, coming when it does, the sense of the essential connections that there are between evil, bondage and misery. It is clear, too, in the similar pathos of Klingsor's line, 'Ha! Er ist schön, der Knabe!' ('Ha! The lad is beautiful!'), in which Craft manages to see only lip-smacking pederasty. It would be mistaken to say that Wagner takes a creator's joy in portraying every kind of character that comes to mind; he is too morally serious for that. Evil, as presented in Hagen or Klingsor, is no laughing matter, as it virtually always is for Mozart (Don Basilio, Don Giovanni in the repulsive trio in Act II—'Taci, ingiusto core!'). But it's one thing to present a character as evil; another to withdraw from him. One of Wagner's achievements is precisely to make us frighteningly enter into characters such as Hagen or his more complicatedly wicked father Alberich: no one would want to be either of them; there is no question that their existence is undesirable, and yet blame would seem childish in respect of them.

And here we come to a topic which, though it's rarely put explicitly in these terms, is one of the elements in Wagner's *Weltanschauung* which is as responsible as anything for dividing opinion: his view of people as saved or damned, sheep or goats. He seems to me to be in this respect like Shakespeare and Dickens, and unlike George Eliot, who is always nudging us not to be vengeful about, say, Hetty Prynne or

Rosamond Vincy, because they have been spoilt by other people whose bad tendencies in turn are explicable by the way they were brought up, etc.; the sole exception in her *oeuvre*—and a very powerful one—is Grandcourt, one of the most convincing figures of evil that realistic literature has to show, and one for whom no explanation is offered, and no extenuation. Wagner is also unlike Lawrence and Nietzsche, both of whom, far from taking up a *tout comprendre, c'est tout pardonner* attitude, acknowledge and indeed miss no opportunity of diagnosing evil, invoking a principle connected with 'life' as a basis for doing so; though in Nietzsche's case, at least, the vehemence of his denunciations is strikingly at odds both with his proclaimed *amor fati*, and the fatalism from which that proceeds.

It is odd how little success operatic composers have had with evil—odd, that is, granted that music makes available to them such rich resources for its expression. Not all that many of them have tried, though arguably they have shirked an urgent task: in *Die Zauberflöte*, for instance, the Queen of the Night is intended as an evil figure (at least from the beginning of the finale to Act I). But astonishing as her music is, if evil is what Mozart was attempting to depict, as opposed to impotent hysteria and rage, then his failure was grotesque. Though Nero in Monteverdi's *Poppea* is certainly evil, one of Monteverdi's most remarkable feats is to depict him as being compounded of childish tantrums and the passionate sexuality of maturity. I have already said how pasteboard a figure Beethoven's Pizarro is; Beethoven is marvellous, in such passages as the opening of Act II of *Fidelio*, and in some of the finale of Act I, at catching an atmosphere in which evil hangs heavily, but he doesn't, or can't, embody it. The same seems true of Verdi: one of the least satisfactory parts of *Otello* is Iago's creed, not because it isn't in itself a reasonably convincing, if superficial, portrayal of nihilism, but because it isn't clear how Iago moves from it to his strenuous and successful plottings. And oddly enough I can think of no depiction of evil in twentieth-century opera which can compare with Wagner's. In the bizarre world of Berg it is madness and violent frustration that we find most often, and Lulu is a figure from black comedy rather than from tragedy; and evil needs tragedy, or its transcendence, to be accommodated dramatically. As for Richard Strauss, and his attempts in *Salome* and *Elektra*—I feel forced to lapse into the language of old-fashioned school reports: tries hard but can't do any better. And what he does isn't nearly good enough; it may be, as Wilfrid Mellers has said, that those operas are all the nastier for being only skin-deep, but nastiness is one thing, and evil another. Strauss couldn't appreciate this, or most other important moral and emotional differences. Hence his incorrigible mediocrity.

Any portrayal of the human condition which can lay claim to comprehensiveness must include evil, though it should refrain from getting excited about it in the way that tragic theorists are especially prone to: nor need it talk about the 'fundamental mysteriousness' of evil, or for that matter of goodness. Given 'the facts' of our evolution, and our place in the world, I find nothing mysterious about there being good and evil in men and their actions. I'm more inclined to find it mysterious that some people find *that* mysterious, unless they are bent on this kind of thing:

> When tragedy has accomplished its work of rendering the unintelligible intelligible and the unendurable endurable, there remain still what the older moralists would call 'the mystery of iniquity' and 'the mystery of godliness'. The first is the baffling, tormenting mystery of the nature and origin of evil in the human soul [. . . and so on].[16]

Self-indulgence about tormenting miseries may be found not only in tragic commentators, of course: they are often incited to it by tragic artists. One of the reasons that Wagner causes resentment is that some things—the existence of evil being one of them—are simply presented by him as brute facts. Hagen's fearful plottings and Klingsor's attempts to undermine the society of the Grail are not things which Wagner surrounds, as he could so easily do with the apparatus at his disposal, with clouds of mystagogic vapour: he kept that kind of thing for his prose writings. Wagner is one artist whose good characters are more difficult to understand than his bad ones; there is a kind of transparency in his portrayal of villains, possibly a suggestion that evil is less deep than goodness. One consequence of this is that we rarely get in Wagner the sense of resolution which the great tragedies of our civilization allegedly give us. Or, to become intrusively personal, I do not get that sense; but then the sense I do get from the tragedies that I feel to be the greatest is much more one of bafflement mixed with impotent frustration than those people who write on tragedy in terms of affirmation, purgation and the rest say they do.

In what I've said so far about Wagner's treatment of evil, I may appear to have assumed that the criteria for distinguishing the evil from the good are self-evident in his work, and possibly also that they are the usual criteria of Western Christianity, broadly speaking. Wagner's relationship to Christianity is a dauntingly complex one, which I shall therefore discuss when I've sorted out less obscure issues. But in terms of the moralities of the last hundred years—the period since, to all intents and purposes, the remaining vitality was drained from Christianity—Wagner is a member of that fairly heterogeneous group who might, with some risk, be called vitalists: the opposition is to utilitarians, and relates to a set of opinions about the make-up of human beings which provides a rich complexity for a situation which is all too often dismissed as one of aridity, sterility and other, similarly depressing elements. One of the reasons why the name of D. H. Lawrence occurs so often in these pages is that my passionate attachment to both these artists, as to Nietzsche, is an attachment to a view of life which is in opposition to the utilitarian view. I am not at all inclined to sneer at utilitarianism in the current Anglo-Saxon way. But with its quantitative stress, its advocacy of a more or less hazy egalitarianism, its uneasy relations with justice, and its odd tendency to oscillate between democracy and paternalism—is what is best for people what they *think* is best for them or what better-informed people know (or think they do) is best for them?—utilitarianism has proved unattractive to a distinguished collection of aristocrats of the spirit, including some near-traitors within the walls. Wagner himself, so far as I can discover, never discussed utilitarianism, but it is clear that, at least until 1849 and the collapse of his revolutionary aspirations in Dresden, Wagner held political opinions which entailed some version of utilitarianism, and that he never explicitly rejected that kind of morality, even though he rejected the optimism, in a metaphysical sense, which is necessary for the efforts a utilitarian must make if he is to act out his moral beliefs. Actually Wagner was from the beginning, like nearly all great artists, an anti-egalitarian and an aristocrat, whatever may have been his touching and disingenuous hopes for free performances of the *Ring* for 'the people'. (I'm not implying, of course, that the audiences of the Bayreuth Festival over the whole period of its existence haven't been disastrously at odds with *any* hopes that Wagner ever had for the reception of his works.) Again like all great artists, he was above all concerned with what human life might be like, lived with the utmost intensity and purity. He may have hoped, in common with many of his contemporaries, that somehow humanity *as a whole* might ascend to a higher view and to nobler lives; but if he did, that drastic unrealism does not enter into and infect his music-dramas. If he is not openly contemptuous of the mass of humanity, as Nietzsche always and Lawrence nearly always is, that is because they are, mostly, irrelevant to his works. His only deeply political work is *Das Rheingold*, and 'the people', though they figure in *Meistersinger* as the ultimate arbiters of authentic worth, only do so through a complicated relationship, controlled by Hans Sachs, between themselves and *Wahn* ('illusion'). So Wagner belonged, whether or not he was aware of it, in the tradition of moral vitalism, by which I mean a tradition of thought that uses as the criterion of moral worth 'life'. This tradition is certainly as confused and, up to now, unsatisfactory as utilitarianism, and in so far as it has had connections with practice, they are disreputable, since it was in the name of 'life' that untold millions have been killed. But because unsavoury lines of influence, such as that from Gobineau and Wagner through Houston Stewart Chamberlain to Rosenberg, can be traced, that doesn't mean that we should feed back into our views of Wagner the unspeakable evils perpetrated by Rosenberg and his superiors. The tradition of moral vitalism (my own coinage, I believe) has been propounded less by philosophers than by artists, and that in itself is a significant fact.

Protests made in the name of 'life' against either a whole scheme of morality, or against specific actions undertaken in accordance with a moral code, are usually the result of feelings of unnatural constraints in those who make them; and it is not surprising that with the promise of heaven withdrawn, those ardent moralists who did not become 'awe-inspiring moral fanatics' (Nietzsche's phrase for George Eliot in *Twilight of the Idols*), asserting Christian morality all the more strenuously to compensate for their loss of faith in the Christian religion, should instead have felt Christian morality as meaninglessly oppressive of the qualities which define man when he is *not* defined as being made in God's image. And it is natural to think and speak of such oppressiveness as 'living death'; hence the criterion of 'life' comes in—as it had, indeed, with Christ, who said that he came to give us more abundant life. What is novel in the moral vitalists is their tendency to operate with 'life' as a self-explanatory criterion, rather than relating it to loving one's neighbour, for instance. As such, it tends to become as wayward and repugnantly subjective as any other brand of intuitionism. The three vitalists whom I am concerned with have all realized this, and all provide indications, often less clear than we might wish, as to what makes for life and what is inimical to it. And all of them envisage the possibility of a hero who is able to live more fully, having broken away from the shackles of Christian or other constricting moralities, and needs to be brutal to those who have failed to make the break, or who have made it in the wrong way. They are all consequently alleged to be proto-

Fascists, and their work tends to be aestheticized—i.e. neutered—in order to be made bearable. So Siegfried is nearly always thought of as a stupid and ungrateful lout: whereas it could not be more plain that Wagner's idea is that Siegfried's sense of life, and of its enemies, is so strong that he instinctively recognizes them, whether they become openly aggressive, as Fafner does, or whether they attempt to conceal their loathing for him, as Mime does. Siegfried *is* ruthless: it is amazing that there should be any argument either about *that* fact, or about the necessity for it. Zarathustra is ruthless in the same way; and though Lawrence does not have such unequivocal heroes as Siegfried or Zarathustra (the superman), his positive characters see what is 'death-eating', and know what they have to do: exterminate it. Hence the alarming quality of a great masterpiece such as Lawrence's story 'The Fox'; and even those of us who go in for armchair endorsements of acts of necessary violence, such as the culmination of that tale, would shrink from practising it, partly because acting in accordance with the dictates of 'life' is sometimes illegal, partly because most of us have not the degree of confidence that we are right about those dictates which is required to act accordingly. Of my three figures, Wagner had an extraordinary confidence, both in living and in his art, about what he had to do: he is consequently thought of as a monstrous egotist or even a 'characterless ogre' (as Robert Gutman describes him in later life[17]); Nietzsche, who preached the doctrine of hardness but was himself a very gentle person, tends to be a figure of fun for that among other reasons; and many people feel about D. H. Lawrence something of the same kind, if not to the same degree, that they feel towards Wagner: words such as 'impossible', 'detestable', 'insensate' are still commonly applied to them both.

A danger that Wagner's work suffers from in a way that Lawrence's doesn't is that it is so absorbing, seemingly so inclusive, so various and yet all so richly characteristic of its creator that it has proved possible for many people to live by it alone: Wagner as a way of life, and that means merely attending performances, or, in some ways still more drugging, merely listening to recordings of his work. It is an astonishing quality of the art that it can by itself provide enough emotional and spiritual nourishment to make even demanding people feel that they don't need anything else; but it is notoriously pernicious, and the 'Wagnerian' is a specimen loathed by everyone who really cares for Wagner's genius, and has been a justified object of attack at least since Nietzsche weighed into the species in *Der Fall Wagner*. In the end, our assessment of Wagner's art must depend on the extent to which it leads us out into life, and whether we are in a condition where we are better able to make sense of our experiences, and whether they themselves are enriched by what more we have to bring to them: in other words, the standard which we must apply to all art which matters.

So if Wagner is genuinely life-giving, he must propel us into life, not offer himself as a substitute for it. But the question remains: what is the criterion of life? It is all very well for Blake to say, 'Everything that lives is holy, life delights in life'—or rather, it's *not* all very well; both statements are evidently false, and therefore it is bad poetry. Many living things are not at all holy, and even Blake should have known that a great deal of life—one might remind him of vultures—delights in death. Given the conditions of living, there is much life that has to get rid of what stands in its way, as Siegfried needs to kill Fafner: Craft is wrong again in describing that act as 'wantonly disrupting the ecological balance'.[18] And it is simply no good muttering 'storm trooper' when Siegfried is mentioned.

We might, after this quantity of generality, test the nature of Wagner's sense of life by a consideration of Siegfried, while remembering that he is only part of a development which runs on to Parsifal. In the longest of his letters to Röckel (dated 25 January 1854) Wagner writes:

> Of course I do not mean my hero to make the impression of a wholly unconscious creature: on the contrary, I have sought in Siegfried to represent my ideal of the perfect human being, whose highest consciousness manifests itself in the acknowledgement that all consciousness must find expression in present life and action.

But with this, as with all of Wagner's glosses on his art, we must remember that Wagner also wrote to Röckel (23 August 1856):

> How can an artist expect that what he has felt instinctively should be perfectly realized by others, seeing that he himself feels in the presence of his work, if it is true Art, that he is confronted by a riddle, about which he too might have illusions, just as another might?

How indeed, especially when the work in question ended by taking a radically different course from that originally intended? It had been revised before Wagner wrote the letters which contain either quotation, and the revision makes one agree more readily with the second self-questioning statement than the first. For whatever Wagner's hopes may have been in portraying Siegfried, the collapse of them is surely evident from the first sketches of *Siegfrieds Tod* onwards. For this 'perfect human being' proves in the final work of what became a tetralogy to be helpless in dealing with the world of imperfect and evil beings, and indeed to be himself either corruptible or very gullible, depending on how one interprets what occurs in connection with the potion and the disguise in Act I of *Götterdämmerung*. But Siegfried's decline is less likely to worry people than his limitations at every stage: can Wagner really have wanted us to regard either the ignorant and vigorous boy of the first two and a half acts of *Siegfried*, or even the rapid developer of the last half-act and the duet in the prologue to *Götterdämmerung*, as an ideal? One feels momentary sympathy with those hostile commentators who regard Siegfried as the invention of an effete, hypochondriac intellectual, finding his ideal in everything that he himself is not. But earlier on, in his huge letter to Röckel of 25 January 1854, Wagner himself has said: 'Experience is everything. Moreover, Siegfried alone (man by himself) is not the complete human being: he is only the half', and proceeds to talk in his characteristic way about Brünnhilde as the other half. The point of the earlier quotation about Siegfried is then that his perfection consists in his highest consciousness manifesting itself 'in the acknowledgement that all consciousness must find expression in present life and action', as opposed to either remaining purely in thought, or alternatively in the hero's failing to achieve adequate consciousness. That is, there is no reason to think that Wagner thought the ideal man should spend his time frolicking in bearskins, fighting dragons and so on; Wagner was not a fool. Nor was he attracted by the notion of fools, as we shall see in dealing with Parsifal. Certainly he felt that the 'man of today', whom, he tells Röckel, Wotan represents, is in need of purification, and he wasn't entirely out of sympathy with the Romantic glorification of noble savages; but he wasn't entirely in sympathy with it either. There is no question that Siegfried, as we first encounter him, has everything to learn, and his development in the course of the eponymous work is, among other things, a development in consciousness: his profoundly moving meditations immediately before the so-called 'Forest Murmurs' are a clear indication that he wants to find out who *he* is through finding out about the fundamental conditions of all life; like many of Wagner's other characters, and like Lear, he wants an answer to the question, 'Who is it that can tell me who I am?' Unlike many of the other Wagnerian heroes, however, he does not want to discover his identity in order to transcend it (as do the Dutchman, Tannhäuser, Tristan, Parsifal), but in order to establish it more firmly. Wagner's implication, both in *Siegfried* and in the letter to Röckel, is that that central tendency, on which Hegel had presciently dwelt at length in his meditations on the nature of Romantic art, to retreat into the self and find value, or at least solace, there, is something to be questioned. In the context of the ever-increasing inwardness of nineteenth-century art, to which Wagner himself made some notable contributions, 'the acknowledgement that all consciousness must find expression in present life and action' is profoundly revolutionary, probably more so than its originator realized: if he had, he would have made more fuss about it in his writings, as well as composing a complete music-drama about it.

In the context of this remark, Siegfried's ignorance of fear and his desire to learn it is more striking than the incorporation of a quaint detail from a separate legend might suggest. For fear of the outside world (the attitude that regarded it as fundamentally menacing, and which Wagner shows Mime to be an especially acute victim of, just after the Wanderer has taken his leave, and again when he is trying to teach Siegfried the concept) was ever more typical of the artistic mentality as the century progressed, and in many respects ever more justified. Inwardness was no new feature of art—that should go without saying; but the kinds of inwardness which nineteenth-century art portrays and incorporates, and which music and the novel are pre-eminently suited to express, so that we should not be surprised that they are *the* great art-forms of Romanticism: those were something new. We shall need to examine these attitudes in some detail to see to what extent Wagner espoused them, and to what extent his work constituted a critique of them. Certainly Siegfried is himself not an 'inward' character, while the Wanderer is, and is vanquished by the champion of the new outwardness. But this hero is on his way to learning—to learning to love, and other things, which remain unspecified, though in the prologue to *Götterdämmerung* Brünnhilde tells him that she has given him 'what the gods taught [her]', indeed all her knowledge. Siegfried is doubtful whether he has absorbed it, so it is unclear, in what follows, whether the disaster which overtakes him as soon as he enters the hall of the Gibichungs is a result of his fairly marked tendency not to take much notice of what Brünnhilde is saying to him, or whether her knowledge proves of no avail to him as, in the second act, she laments its uselessness to her. The motif of the educated Siegfried, which is a transformed version of his horn motif in *Siegfried*, shows a sturdiness and pride, but hardly an advance in consciousness. What has happened is that the force of love has turned out to be much weaker than anyone expected, including Wagner. The renunciation of love in the interests of power is perhaps, according to the *Ring*, the beginning of all evil, if not of all mischief, as the Rhinemaidens have demonstrated in their unkind treatment of Alberich. But the force of love itself is at every stage less than one expects. One expects love to be *the* answer, simply because Wagner has shown, with great power and also a subtlety so rarely attributed to him that almost no one has understood what the *Ring* is about, that a world devoid of love is hateful: that is what makes *Das Rheingold* so chillingly impressive an experience, and increasingly so. Because it contains on the one hand so much glorious scene-painting, and on the other so much fascinating argumentation, it is easy to overlook what it does not contain, but what, as soon as one has felt it, one comes to see is the central point of the work; it is also why Act I of *Die Walküre* is an urgent necessity after *Rheingold*, for as soon as the curtain rises after the storm, one immediately has thrust upon one what was so conspicuously absent in *Rheingold*. Listening to the 'preliminary evening' of the trilogy in this light, it becomes an extraordinarily powerful dramatic experience. And, as I suggested, it is sufficiently alarming to make one feel, as Wagner intended and may well often have felt himself, that love would make the world go round. But after Act I of *Walküre*, when hopes on both sides of the footlights have been raised extremely high, love is defeated; first Wotan's love for his children: then his children's love for one another, and Brünnhilde's love for them: then her love for her father, and his for her. *Die Walküre* is primarily about the painful illusoriness of the feeling of strength that love gives, whether it is sexual, parental, protective or whatever. At the same time it is one of the most moving demonstrations of tenderness, again felt in a variety of relationships, that art can offer. And though, taken by itself, as up to a point it should be, since Siegmund and Sieglinde's pitifully brief love is entirely contained in it, it is a tragedy of defeat, it is one of those rare cases of a tragedy which enhances one's belief and trust in what is defeated. What so many tragic theorists take as paradigmatic, which is an affirmation carried through in the face of apparent disaster, and what so many of the greatest tragedies do not conform to, is exemplified to perfection in *Die Walküre*. That is why it is impossible to be overenthusiastic about the scene of the Annunciation of Death: it is simply sublime, though it isn't simple. Siegmund's contemptuous rejection of Valhalla's 'paltry splendours' ('spröden Wonnen'), which at first causes Brünnhilde such bewilderment, and then effects the change in her which precipitates the peripeteia of the whole drama, makes us know and feel, just as surely as it does Brünnhilde, that his love for his sister,

even if it is doomed to almost immediate catastrophe, is more valuable
than anything that Wotan can offer. And Valhalla, which is clearly
Wagner's image of any desirable life after death, is given a more
devastating blow by this lofty lack of interest on Siegmund's part than
by all Nietzsche's diatribes, brilliant, penetrating and witty as they
often are, against 'other worlds'. Furthermore, the Valhalla which
Siegmund is rejecting is, as it is described for him by Brünnhilde, a
hedonist's paradise; it is not simply because he would not be happy
without Sieglinde, though of course he would not, that Siegmund
refuses to follow Brünnhilde there. The fierce immediacy of his response to Brünnhilde's extraordinarily noble, stern and beautiful summons comes from a level which is simultaneously prior to, and transcends, considerations of happiness. The force with which the scene
works on us is such that we cannot but acknowledge, with Brünnhilde,
the greater depth of Siegmund's humanity over her goddess's wisdom.
Of all the love-deaths of Wagner's characters, it is Siegmund's which is
most affecting *as* a death, because neither he nor we are deluded into
thinking that it is a prelude to anything further; yet it is also likely to be
his death that strikes us as the most moving—or would, if it were given
the kind of overpowering grandeur that the Funeral Music imparts to
Siegfried's death. Wagner took a huge risk in making Siegmund and
Sieglinde so warmly sympathetic; for they are not the central figures of
the *Ring*, and it is the life and death of their son with which Wagner is
more concerned. We, as 'men of today', like Wotan, are more likely to
respond to a moderate-scale hero with a desperately miserable past,
than to a fearless boy whose heroism consists in forging a sword, killing
a dragon and a dwarf, breaking a spear, and passing through a wall of
fire, none of them acts which intimidate him in the least, since Mime's
attempts to teach him fear are futile.

It is inevitable, then, that we are going to feel that Siegfried's hour of
glory is also the hour of his death. In the wonderful narration to the
vassals, which never ceases to have one hanging on Siegfried's every
word, even though he is only telling us what we already know, in the
gathering excitement of the music as he remembers that he awoke
Brünnhilde, in the moment of utter horror we feel as Hagen runs him
through, in the final invocation to Brünnhilde (like Verdi in *Otello*,
Wagner was not afraid to use old operatic devices when it suited him),
and then the funeral music itself, and finally in the second part of
Brünnhilde's huge peroration ('Wie Sonne lauter strahlt mir sein
Licht'): all these put Siegfried in a different light from anything that

had preceded them. Is it because this is music-drama that we are so beguiled? For at this point we recall Lawrence's remark, quoted earlier, that in the novel, as opposed to other art forms, 'everything is relative to everything else'. It may easily come to seem that in Wagner the music is, ironically (in the context of his views), absolute. And the case of Siegfried may seem as good evidence as any for this view: to simplify a little, could it not be argued that there is one Siegfried presented by the poem of the *Ring*, and another, quite different, presented by the music? Of course, for much of the time—the whole of *Siegfried*, at least—they are perfectly welded: all Siegfried's major characteristics as given in the poem are reflected and intensified by the music—impatience, enormous energy, bewilderment, tenderness and so on. But *Götterdämmerung* has always seemed to some critics to be problematic: musically, they have felt (and rightly) it is by far the greatest of the four works, but dramatically, for too-often-recited reasons, it is atavistic, clumsy and slipshod, and crudely melodramatic; and its ideological tendencies make nonsense of the rest of the work, or vice versa. I do not think that any of those charges is true, with the possible exception of that of clumsiness: Siegfried's disguise, bewilderment when Brünnhilde claims that he stole the ring from her, and Gunther's confusion are either unthought-out by Wagner, or else complex in a non-contributory way.[19] But no doubt Wagner would say, as again to Röckel: 'It seems to me that you have attached more importance to the connecting links and parts of the great chain than they, as such, deserve.' One can sympathize with that, while regretting that Wagner himself wasn't guilty of the same fault, which would have prevented countless commentators from wasting their and their readers' time. And over certain matters, such as the question of what power the ring itself has—since it certainly does not give any of its owners the power that the Rhinemaidens tell one another it has—Wagner is culpably vague. However, in the specific instance of *Götterdämmerung*, we have still to settle the question of the relationship of words and music, in so far as they concern a possible glamourizing of Siegfried. Does he deserve the funeral music? Or is Wagner finally showing us in those shattering minutes what music-drama itself could not show us? It would be heavily ironic if he were, since it would mean that the funeral music then occupied a place closely analogous to that which Wagner had claimed that the *Leonora No. 3* overture occupied in relation to *Fidelio*: that it made the opera superfluous.

On balance—and it *is* a matter of balance, however difficult that may be to maintain in Wagner's presence—I feel that Wagner does finally show us, posthumously, the greatness that is implicit in Siegfried but which he never has a chance to reveal until his last hour—or perhaps it is only through the relived experience of his life that he becomes what he *does* unquestionably become, and so merits the funeral music. Until then he has taken all too seriously his creator's description of him: he has lived in the present without incorporating into himself his past. Most of Wagner's characters, from the Dutchman to Kundry, are haunted by their past, and spend their lives, which threaten to be eternal, trying to atone for what it contained. Clearly a point came when Wagner felt that the idea of redeeming time past was idiotic, or impossible: hence he conceived of his man of the future. His art is always an art of exploration, growth, and instinct, as he knew it had to be. To keep out the non-instinctual it was necessary to unburden himself at those annoying lengths in prose, sometimes brilliant, usually obscure. So as he groped his way forward in the *Ring*, he produced his magnificent specimen of manhood, who, so long as he lived entirely in the present obstinately refused to become a hero: *Siegfried* is both the greatest testament and the severest critique of the Noble Savage. Yet again Wagner's great letter to Röckel is our most helpful guide. He quotes Erda's words to Wotan in *Rheingold*, and says:

> We must learn to *die*, and to die in the fullest sense of the word [i.e. not survive and enter another existence]. The fear of the end is the source of all lovelessness, and this fear is only generated when love itself begins to wane. How did it happen then, that this feeling which imparts the highest blessedness to all living things was so far lost sight of by the human race that it finally came to this: all that mankind did, ordered and established was conceived only in fear of the end? My poem sets this forth.

These are wonderful words, in a way more wonderful than the poem which they are allegedly a gloss on. For what has happened there is that in creating a being who does not fear the end, indeed does not fear anything, Wagner has produced a *Naturkind* who is not similar enough to us to suggest how we might regenerate ourselves, as we most certainly need to do. But he has created someone who 'learns to die': for whatever criticisms may be made of the young Siegfried, and all of the usual ones are silly and ignorant, there can be no question of his heroism—his spiritual heroism—as he dies. There is no question of 'transcendence'; to make *that* clear we see Valhalla going up in flames half an hour later: his last words, a greeting to Brünnhilde, are mirrored

168

in her last words: 'Siegfried! Siegfried! Selig grüss' dich dein Weib!'
But the blessedness and ecstasy are in the realization of the value of a
relationship which had been betrayed, but which is understood for *all*
its worth only at the end: we should not be surprised about that, since
the last orgiastic shouts of *Siegfried* are, strangely (it may seem):
'Leuchtende Liebe, lachender Tod!' ('Radiant love, laughing death!').
The manic mood of those apostrophes is very different from Siegfried's
last whisperings, or from the noble exaltation of Brünnhilde from the
point where she ignites Siegfried's funeral pyre. In between they have
learnt too much to recapture the careless rapture of *Siegfried*, but what
is central is their welcoming death, since it must come, or as Wagner
puts it:

> . . . the necessity of recognizing and yielding to the change, the many-
> sidedness, the multiplicity, the eternal renewal of reality and of life.
> Wotan rises to the tragic height of *willing* his own destruction. This is the
> lesson that we must learn from the history of mankind: *to will what
> necessity imposes*, and ourselves bring it about. The creative product of
> this supreme, self-destroying will, its victorious achievement, is a fear-
> less human being, one who never ceases to love: Siegfried.

What makes the huge letter to Röckel, from which all these excerpts
come, so fascinating, is the give-and-take between the works as finally
realized by Wagner, and what he tells Röckel about them. Until the
final clause of the last quotation, we have a superb commentary on the
central theme of the *Ring*. But Siegfried as 'one who never ceases to
love'? One is more inclined to feel that he never begins. The excitement
he shows in the duet in *Siegfried* is not so much the excitement of love,
as of prospective fulfilment of more primitive needs; and in the Prologue to *Götterdämmerung* Brünnhilde's intensities place Siegfried's
as being those of a maturing extrovert. But he does learn that he loves,
and what that meant, only when he uses all the resources of his *memory*
(i.e. when Hagen has given him another drink half-way through his
narration).

The fundamental difficulty facing both Wotan and Wagner is this:
how to get the act of returning the ring to the Rhinemaidens accomplished by someone who is ignorant of all that the ring can do, all that
it stands for, yet who is a true hero. That leads to the question of how
ignorant a hero can be. Wagner clearly wants 'the man of the future' to
be, if not ignorant, then innocent of, among other things, apprehension,
arrière-pensée, greed and meanness. But the cost of freeing him from
having these qualities is that he lacks also many others which are in-

volved in having these; Siegfried is at least as remote from us as Homer's heroes are. Wagner tries to bring him closer by giving him 'consciousness', in the sense that they lack it. But however much Wagner hoped that he could lead us forward by his vision and presentation of Siegfried, in fact he leads us back: the required combination of 'psychology' and 'myth', to use Thomas Mann's famous pair of near-antithetical terms, fails in this instance, as it does not anywhere else in the *Ring*, or indeed in any of Wagner's works. Siegfried is not the prehistoric stormtrooper that he is often dismissed as; but it is hard to see what inner resources he could have relied on to avoid being converted by a propagandist of Hitler's gifts; just as he fails to sense the evil in Hagen. Wagner's failure is the kind that is not uncommon in art, and that has been shown to exist by Dr Leavis in *Middlemarch*: Will Ladislaw is clearly the only failure in that novel, and that is because George Eliot wasn't able to imagine him: all she could do was to endow him with the qualities that Dr Casaubon notably lacked, and not to give him the qualities which Dr Casaubon regrettably possessed. So he is a mere inanimate list of qualities, or virtues, positive and negative. Fortunately Siegfried is not an artistic catastrophe on that scale, partly because Wagner has imagined him vividly, up to a point, partly because of 'the power of sound'. His final consciousness—which is a consciousness of the past seen in relation to the present—and the surpassingly moving threnody and celebration of him cast huge shadows back to his earlier life, and indeed to his conception. Wagner is not cheating here, because he has shown us something deep and true, even if it is not the truth he set out to show us. He has shown us, in a definitive way, that the kind of simplification of existence glorified in the Noble Savage will not work: he has put something to a test, a genuine artistic test—that is, at every point we are free to react to Siegfried, to see whether he is a true artistic creation (I don't deny the difficulty of applying the requisite criteria, and indeed of knowing what they are), and to see whether we are being nudged or bludgeoned into taking a favourable attitude to him. It seems to me that we are not. His downfall is the downfall of innocence and spontaneous vitality and joy in living, and it is tragic, but it is not for us so overpowering and involving as Brünnhilde's end, because in her we have complexity, psychological sophistication, moving weaknesses and failures of sympathy—she is, in other words, her father's daughter, though the Wotan of *Die Walküre* rather than *Das Rheingold*.

Wagner held a rather different view, for he felt that, in his scene with the Rhinemaidens, Siegfried demonstrates that he 'has grasped the highest truth and knows that death is better than a life of fear—he keeps [the ring] only as a proof that he at least has never learnt what fear means'. Actually Siegfried says that he would give them the ring for love, but not on the basis of threats, and that 'Leben und Leib, seht:— so—werf' ich sie weit von mir!' ('For life and limb, see—thus I fling them far from me!'), which is not the same as showing that he 'knows that death is better than a life of fear'. It *is* carefree, grandly heroic, but the all-important comparative *judgement* that Wagner attributes to Siegfried at this point is surely smuggled in. If there is a place where Siegfried shows an awareness of the endless renewal of Nature, and himself as part of Nature, it is in his wonderful cry to Gunther: 'Nun floss gemischt es über; der Mutter Erde lass das ein Labsal sein!' ('Now mixed, it overflows; let it be a refreshment for Mother Earth!'). It is a magnificent moment, and stands out all the more because of the un-typical sentiment coming from Siegfried.

If we return to the quotation from which my discussion started, that 'all consciousness must find expression in present life and action', we find that the 'hero' of the *Ring* is not one character, not even Brünnhilde, though she comes nearest to exemplifying the requisite 'acknowledge-ment', but Wagner himself; or if that is too dangerous a formulation, since it suggests a kind of intrusion of personality that is not to be found in the work, we may alternatively say that the work shows us the truth of something which is exemplified by the whole drift of events in it, and which is what leaves us, unquestionably, exhausted but ex-hilarated by it. Exhausted, of course, because of the huge dimensions of *Götterdämmerung*, and its astounding economy and concentration, which do not allow any respite, except a little at the beginning of Act III; but exhilarated and exalted because an unimaginable complexity of experiences has been summed up triumphantly, without simplifica-tion or exclusion. Though the final scene is Brünnhilde's, and could not be anyone else's by that stage, it does not belong to her in the same way that Siegfried's narration necessarily belongs to him. We believe in her enlightenment—'Alles weiss ich, alles ward mir nun frei' ('I know all, everything is clear to me now')—because it is our enlighten-ment too. She has not done anything to gain enlightenment. When she comes majestically forward after the dead Siegfried has raised his arm and Hagen has recoiled in terror, she is clearly in command; yet the last time we saw her she was beside herself with vengeful rage, and we do not have any information about what has been happening within her or to her between times. Her new state of knowledge and her capacity to bring events to their ordained climax are readily believable, but it would be a mistake to think that it is *she* whom we should primarily be concerned with during the last half-hour of the work. The understanding that she has, and that we share, is vouchsafed us by the music: the system of leading-motives, though not the rigorous or ridiculous thing that it has often been thought to be, *is* a loose-knit system which does enable Wagner to draw the whole of the work together, in the Funeral Music, and then from 'Starke Scheite' onwards. In that amazing last sequence, when nearly every crucial motive in the work appears, seemingly with complete spontaneity and inevitability, we have the clearest proof that music-drama is *the* supreme form; what metaphorical resources can do in poetic drama, as Michael Black demonstrates in his essay in this volume, is moving, ironical, anyway charged and potent; but it pales before the end of *Götterdämmerung*, because the resonances set up by music are simply not conceivable in language, even when Shakespeare is using it. In the end, the *Ring* is exhilarating because of an identity of form and content of a unique degree: it bears testimony to limitless creativity, and is itself limitlessly creative, inexhaustible in its fecund suggestiveness, in a way that makes *Finnegans Wake*, which attempts the same kind of thing, seem what it is—something for expert crossword-solvers and Ph.D. students. The suggestiveness of the *Ring*, though it has no doubt earned many an academic advancement, is of a kind that ministers in the most immediate and powerful way to life. After Brünnhilde has leapt into the flames and the music of destruction has receded, we are left first with the song of the Rhinemaidens—the song of innocent, pre-moral Nature; then Valhalla, building to its greatest climax, a climax of true grandeur as opposed to the deliberate grandiosity of the end of *Das Rheingold*, so that the theme achieves supreme fulfilment as that which it represents goes up in flames— Wagner's point being that Valhalla, the symbol of human creativity and the urge for immortality, both for oneself and for the products of one's labours, will ultimately perish, while none the less being a very glorious spectacle; and then the theme on the violins which has suffered the title of 'Redemption through Love' from its earliest days. All that one need ask is: What is redeemed? for that label to be exposed as absurd: it has nothing to do with redemption, in any sense of that term, including the Wagnerian one (on which, see below), when it first appears in Act III of *Die Walküre*, or when it recurs in Brünnhilde's last moments of ecstasy, or at the end. If Ernest Newman is right in saying that it 'spreads consoling wings over the whole stupendous drama',[20] that is not because it looks like wings on the page, though it does; nor because it is 'sublimely irrelevant', a typical critic's escape-hatch; but because it is the theme which expresses the possibility and exuberance of new conscious life; Sieglinde had sung it when, knowing that Siegmund was dead and she herself was soon going to die as well, she yet knew that new and valuable life was stirring within her: Brünnhilde had sung it when, preparing for her self-immolation, she concluded the whole sequence of events that has been the tortuous story of the *Ring*; and Wagner ends by having his violins sing it—those instruments that are nearest to the human voice—while simultaneously unconscious Nature rolls peacefully forward, and human creativity, wonderful but containing the seeds of dissolution (how Lawrentian Wagner was!) is celebrated without irony even as it is incinerated, and the mis-named Redemption theme promises that there will be new conscious life. The excuse for the misnomer must be that when Western man's thoughts turn to the best that can happen, he inevitably thinks in Christian terms, and then of being redeemed, even though the idea is evidently nonsensical in the context.

So, in the *Ring*, Wagner has sung of 'what is past and passing, and to come', and he came very close to answering to Yeats's more detailed specifications:

> ... The young
> In one another's arms, birds in the trees
> —Those dying generations—at their song,
> The salmon-falls, the mackerel-crowded seas,
> Fish, flesh, or fowl, commend all summer long
> Whatever is begotten, born, and dies.
> Caught in that sensual music all neglect
> Monuments of unageing intellect.

Well, not quite all; but Wotan, like the Yeats of 'Sailing to Byzantium', though concerned to erect a monument to unageing gods not necessarily intellectual, finds himself, in his great scene with Erda in Act III of *Siegfried*, willing that he should be replaced by Siegfried, whom he calls, carried away by his own eloquence, the 'ever-young'. No one, and nothing, is ever-young; but the banal painfulness of ageing and dying may be lessened or annihilated when we are reminded, in adequately splendid terms, that even if we don't know what will replace us, something will: that is the promise held out by the final theme in the *Ring*: never was anything more appropriately named a 'cycle' than the great work. For it ends where it begins, except that the first chord was E flat major and the last is D flat major; a little progress has been made, the tone of the world has been slightly raised by the cataclysmic events that constitute that cycle, even if the tonality has been lowered. And before that world of gods, men and dwarfs perished, but only just before, in the dusk, the owl of Minerva spread its wings, as Hegel said it did in his single memorable remark. For a brief moment Brünnhilde and we understood, thanks to the unique power of music to bring together disparate elements, if not into harmony, at least into counterpoint. In talking or writing about the *Ring*, I find, and I suspect that other people do too, that there are moments when one seems on the verge of being able to express its significance; and then one thinks, or someone else says, something that unfocuses it again. It would be foolhardy to think that one had said the last word on the work, because it remains for us, as for its creator, a 'riddle'. My point has not been even to try to say the last word, but rather to suggest that while the necessary detailed discussion and analysis of motifs, motives, and all the other musical and dramatic ingredients of the *Ring* continue, and may well remain endlessly disputable, what we can hold steady, and what encourages any amount of labour, is that the creativity that it manifests to such an incredible degree is also what it is, at least in large measure, about.

It is easy to play fast and loose with 'creativity' and cognate terms, so that orgies of destruction are glamourized as being *au fond* the conditions of new creation, and so forth. But I am not concerned here to sort out the murky purposes to which this notion can be put; only to insist that Wagner in the *Ring*, and above all in *Götterdämmerung*, is concerned with the conditions for new life: that when he tells Röckel that Wotan rises to the supreme tragic height of willing his own destruction, it is in order, he immediately goes on to say, that he may be replaced by Siegfried. It might not be necessary to stress these elementary points if it weren't for the absolutely relentless use of *Götterdämmerung* whenever Hitler's last days in the Bunker are described or referred to: even the most distinguished writers on Hitler quite naturally slip into it, so conditioned are they by their more propagandizing predecessors. It is perfectly clear that in his conduct of the last stages of the war, Hitler was determined that, as he was to perish, so was everything else that he still retained any power over; indeed, the 'motive of annihilation' is the only consistent and coherent one running through his life, as J. P. Stern has recently shown in his excellent book *Hitler: the Führer and the People* (while making the inevitable Wagnerian reference). Wotan's willing 'Das Ende!' springs not from hatred of the possible future, but from the knowledge, venomously brought home to him by Fricka, that he is morally bankrupt, yet still the guardian of right: having excluded or ignored love for power politics, and then tried to right political wrongs by moving out of the public realm back into the private, so that the supremely intimate and tender love of the Volsung twins is to be used by him, he hopes, to redeem his public wrongdoings, he finds only that he is bound by his own fetters: so he bitterly wills in Act II of *Die Walküre* what he welcomes in Act III of *Siegfried*, and what reaches its end at the conclusion of the whole cycle. How *can* people go on drawing analogies between Wotan in Valhalla and Hitler in his Bunker? The fact that the comparison would have delighted the Führer himself doesn't seem adequate reason for continuing with it. The Third Reich was, in a straightforward way, destructive and self-destructive: the *Ring* is, in a straightforward way, creative and a celebration of creativity.

None the less, there is still, even if this account is accepted, a leading question: one can't simply be creative—something has to be created. And to talk of creating new life simply won't do, because there remains the question of what *it* can do, apart from continuing the task of creation. This is another form of the doubt that I began this section by expressing, as to the nature of moral vitalism. 'Nothing matters but life,' says Lawrence; and no doubt he is right. But not all life matters, as I have already argued. Some criterion still has to be found to distinguish valuable life from superfluous or malignant life. In the *Ring*, Wagner combines heroic vitalism with an ethic of love. It is love which is supposed to be creative; but it turns out to be inadequate as a defence against the forces that are concerned to triumph over it, including the power of simple lust. When the ring, which has ceased to be a symbol of the possibility of world-domination, and has become the symbol of Brünnhilde's and Siegfried's love, is used by Brünnhilde to repel the advances of Gunther/Siegfried, it proves powerless. And love can also be seen as making Siegfried more, rather than less, naïve and stupid; for in *Siegfried* he feels the strongest revulsion against Mime, and is not taken in by his cajolings in Act II (we need not go into the significance of tasting Fafner's blood). At every stage in *Siegfried* he does the right thing, even though he is untaught. But once Brünnhilde has given him her lessons, and he is ready to go forward to new deeds, he is unable to detect evil intentions any longer, and the potion, which is best understood as a device for telescoping a long process of corruption by the non-heroic and anti-heroic, turns him into a randy youth distinguished only by his toughness.

Once again, I would feel embarrassed by the obviousness of the points that I'm making if they were not completely missed by nearly all commentators. The two most notable critics to have made these points before me, Morse Peckham in *Beyond the Tragic Vision* and Robert Raphael in his monograph *Richard Wagner*, have not made their case out as strongly as they might have done, because, in the case of Peckham, he treats the words and the music altogether separately, while Raphael treats all the operas as if they were plays by Ibsen. They thus make Wagner seem simpler than he is, though more complex and valuable than do most commentators. There is simply no denying, if one takes the music into account, the heroic nature of Siegfried's and Brünnhilde's love; and in the first of their two duets, the process by which Brünnhilde comes to a finally joyful realization of her womanhood, as opposed to her goddesshood, while at the same time Siegfried matures from a boy who alternates between regarding Brünnhilde simply as a mother-figure and simply as a sexual object into seeing her as an equal in love—processes the consummation of which necessitates the final dionysiac fugato—those developments are as valuable as anything in the *Ring*, even if the altitude at which they take place makes them less moving than the development of Siegmund's and Sieglinde's love in Act I of *Die Walküre*. The duet at the dawn of *Götterdämmerung* is hugely exhilarating and thrilling, but the very simplicity of the response that it evokes should warn us that this love is vulnerable in a way that Brünnhilde and Siegfried can't believe, and that we can only believe when we see, or rather hear, to our dismay, Siegfried's memories of Brünnhilde sliding away, and when we incredulously hear Brünnhilde call Waltraute 'du fühllose Maid' just after she has described in one of the most moving of all scenes in world drama, Wotan's plight, after he had kissed Brünnhilde to sleep. Childishly over-confident of the nature and power of their love, both of them have been reckless and callous to all needs other than one another's, with the result that it is precisely one another's needs which they finally, and fatally, betray.

Brünnhilde and Siegfried are like their creator at least in this respect: they make enormous demands on life, while absolutely refusing to 'transcend'. The attack on transcendence begins, in the *Ring*, with the questionable moral status of Valhalla; it looks wonderful, but isn't the price too high? It turns out that it is, and anyway, as we've seen, Siegmund delivers a more shatteringly immediate critique of Valhalla to Brünnhilde. But is Valhalla an adequate symbol of transcendence, it will be asked. Isn't it earthly, all-too-earthly? It is as adequate a symbol for transcendence as anything can be that remains intelligible. Wagner's intuitions about the boundaries of meaningfulness turn out to be surprisingly robust. With that forthrightness which Erich Heller characterizes as 'his vigorous handling of fragile profundities', Wagner always explores any 'beyond' that his works posit. And his estimate of Valhalla is roughly that it's the place where old warriors go not to die, but to fade away. At the same time Wagner realizes that you can't achieve anything worthwhile on earth simply by being happily in love: Brünnhilde's opening words to Siegfried in *Götterdämmerung* are 'How would I love you, if I did not let you go forth to new deeds, dear hero?' But while propelling Siegfried 'zu neuen Taten', she is strangely content to stay on her rock, waiting for him to return. And Siegfried may seem to be too intent on 'being a hero', in the Sartrean sense of abdicating responsibility for his actions by feeling that he's got a role to play. His opening words to Gunther: 'Nun ficht mit mir oder sei mein Freund!' ('Now fight with me or be my friend!') are a touchingly comic expression of his newly acquired self-consciousness: he's saying the kind of thing that heroes have to say. So neither of them is clear about how they are to be fulfilled, now that Brünnhilde has been won and imparted her wisdom, such as it is, to Siegfried. It isn't as if Wagner himself was at a loss for profitable activities for his characters to involve themselves in—or rather, he persistently explored, with the pertinacity of the supreme artist, the possibilities of living for people who were not supreme artists. Given the absolute fulfilment that he found in his own art, and finally in his life too, it is astonishing that he never rested on his inordinately hard-earned laurels. Finding a destiny for 'the man of the future' *was* his artistic mission, pursued with ruthless single-mindedness. The attractions of enormous vitality were very powerful, and that is why Siegfried is so marvellous a creation. But vitality wasn't enough: less so for Wagner than for Nietzsche, who replaced the nonsensical idea of the Christian hereafter with a not less nonsensical idea of the eternal recurrence, and the supreme achievement of man, or superman, as willing that what was going to happen an infinite number of times whether he willed it or not *should* happen. And less so for Wagner, too, than for Lawrence, whose most positive suggestion was of 'a new phallic tenderness', by no means to be sneered at, but scarcely possessing the breadth or depth that was needed and is needed for providing adequate spiritual nourishment in the first stages of the decisively post-Christian era.

The *Ring*, then, though it leaves us braced, refreshed, invigorated by suggesting the vital flow that comes from unconscious Nature (the Rhine and the Rhinemaidens) and moves towards a creativity which is self-destructive as soon as it attempts to erect monuments that are unageing, leaves open the crucial question as to how the essential human capacity for generation, metaphorical as well as literal, is to be deployed. Wagner had hoped, both before he launched on the enormous *Ring* project, and during it, that he could find an answer in *some* kind of love, but none of the attempts had led where they were meant to: and his absolute integrity means that the painful truth emerges through whatever rhetoric Wagner may employ to disguise the repeated rebuffs that 'the facts' administered: the truth emerges both within each work, and in the fact that, definitive as, say, *Tristan* may sound, no sooner was it finished than something that was at least superficially very unlike it had to be created.

4. TRISTAN UND ISOLDE: THE MOST BEAUTIFUL OF DREAMS

Wagner's letter to Liszt is famous:

> Since I have never enjoyed in life the true happiness of love, I shall erect a monument to this most beautiful of all dreams, in which from beginning to end this love shall for once be completely fulfilled: I have sketched in my mind a *Tristan and Isolde*, the most simple but full-blooded musical conception. (Letter no. 168 in the Wagner-Liszt correspondence.)

Most commentators on *Tristan*, taking that as the keynote, slip easily into taking the great work itself as what Wagner would have liked to have in life: and no doubt Wagner partly thought that that was what he wanted. He gives, in the letter, an account of the genesis of *Tristan* which makes it sound straightforwardly as if it is a wish-fulfilment or compensation, or one of the not very large range of things that popularizing psychoanalysts tell us that it is, the only distinguishing feature being that in Wagner's case the nature of what he is producing is abnormally evident to its author. And this not very complex account of the nature of *Tristan* fits in well with a pendulum-type view of his works, as he moves from extremes of eroticism to extremes of revulsion from the flesh, ending in *Parsifal* with a decidedly gamey glorification of chastity.

On the other hand, if we look more than casually at the text of the poem of *Tristan*, we find the lovers expressing themselves in terms which either take the notion of romantic love to its limit and glorify it, as de Rougement argues in *L'Amour et l'Occident,* or else yearn for something which is very far from what most lovers, even or especially most romantic lovers, have wanted: death, surcease, nothingness, unconsciousness—all these terms, or rather their German equivalents, are used. Indeed, the last three words of the work are Isolde's 'Unbewusst, höchste Lust!' ('Unconscious, highest bliss!'). With this in mind, it is not difficult to convince oneself that, far from being a glorification of romantic love, *Tristan* constitutes an exposé of it—not difficult, that is, if one ignores the music. Doing exactly that, Morse Peckham and his disciple Raphael argue for that view of the work, and very persuasively, though one's faith in a commentator who calls Morold 'Isolde's uncle'[21] is less than total; but then most Wagnerian commentators are highly accident-prone in respect of the actual events in the works.[22] This is Raphael's summary of his central thesis:

> In [*Tristan*] the metaphysical dream of all lovers, their transcendent vision of love as a realm of everlasting and supreme value, is subjected to the most thoroughgoing scrutiny, and with the expected result. The transcendental vision of the lovers becomes unmasked for what it really is: emotional quicksand, a deceiving and destructive 'wave', whose illusion eventually submerges their identities and engulfs their lives, exactly as we see happen in the instance of Siegfried and Brünnhilde.[23]

Morse Peckham is still more drastic:

> The love scene in the garden is entirely an analysis of how two lovers exploit each other's emotions. Their whole effort is to merge their two identities and together vanish away into night and nothingness, to become one with the universe. Unfortunately reality intrudes, as it always does. Death is the only gateway that leads to this goal, but when you are dead you can scarcely enjoy the loss of identity. Transcendental erotic love, then, is an unrealizable ideal, because it pursues a symbol and not a reality. It is an insanity. Far from being an apotheosis of love, *Tristan* strips the mask away from one of mankind's most cherished orientative gratifications and reveals it as an illusion.[24]

One's immediate reaction to Raphael and Peckham—and I've tried these passages on a fairly large number of intelligent Wagnerians—is: But that's not how one feels while listening, or for some time after. In this case we are presented especially acutely with a problem that recurs in the appreciation of a great deal of art, if not all of it, when it makes an immediately strong impression: the problem, namely, of the gap between one's experience of art, and those reflective, critical movements of the mind that are performed later. A prime duty of the critic is to narrow that gap as much as possible, to remain honest to the experience that he had on the one hand, while raising questions about its value and significance on the other. Clearly there will be occasions on which reflection will lead one to the judgement that one was taken in by the work, unless one is extraordinarily well protected from the lures of pretentiousness and sentimentality; and anyone who is *very* well protected from them may pay the price of being immune to the impact of the genuinely new, the disturbing originality which is manifest in the supreme works of art. But I am not, at the moment, concerned with the value of *Tristan* so much as with the prior question of what it is about— Romantic love as illusion or as sublime possibility.

There are several ways in which the characters in a dramatic work can be 'placed' by the work, or by us in relation to it: thus even when the central figures are as much more the dramatist's concern as they are in *Tristan*, than any of the other characters, they could still be placed within a framework which suggested that they shouldn't be thought of as giving us the 'doctrine' of the work—as Antony and Cleopatra are, for example, in Shakespeare's play. Or, given the opportunities that music affords, the aspirations of the characters might be shown up, one way or another, by the music. Or the work might be one of a series, and should be seen as such, as is the case manifestly with some artists, just as it is equally *not* the case with others. There are further possibilities, but these will do for the time being.

The first alternative clearly doesn't apply in *Tristan*. Indeed, the astonishing construction of the great work, with the wonderfully natural-seeming symmetries between the acts, helps to emphasize that the world we are in as the work ends is the 'Wunderreich der Nacht', in contrast to the savage entry of the world of 'tückischer Tag' at the ends of the first two acts. However illusory Isolde's view of Tristan may be, when she asks the bystanders whether they too can see him smiling, and his eyes open, the effect is not remotely like that of Lear's temporary delusion that Cordelia is still alive, which serves to deepen the already unspeakable pathos of that scene; if anything, we are willing sharers of Isolde's state of exalted delusion, because the music, from the beginning of the *Verklärung* onwards, is wholly Isolde's, or the lovers'. It is the music to which they frenetically strained towards their ultimate climax in the duet in Act II, and for which we have been awaiting the sublime resolution ever since—or, indeed, ever since the opening bars of the whole work. Similarly, Tristan's vision of Isolde in his supreme and calm ecstasy, beginning over that ravishing cushion of horn-tone with 'Wie sie selig', and ending, on great waves of sound from the whole orchestra, 'Ach, Isolde, Isolde, wie schön bist du!', though it is as hallucinated as Isolde's at the end, is supported, and in no way undermined or questioned by, its music. Actually Wagner's music is normally 'loyal' to the character who sings it: though he can use it to undercut, or for purposes of dramatic irony, he generally, like all the greatest dramatists, gives each character the benefit of a proper hearing. So, from the first two points of view, it seems hopelessly implausible to attribute to Wagner a deliberate exposé of the notion of Romantic Love, by taking it to its lunatic extreme, and making clear how lunatic it is. And, however obvious it may be that 'when you are dead you can scarcely enjoy the loss of identity', as Peckham no-nonsensically puts it, Isolde's final words none the less *are* 'unconscious, highest bliss!' Peckham seems to forget that Wagner was writing in a Romantic context where what should be evident nonsense passed for profound sense, as it has done, indeed, throughout the whole recorded history of Western thought and feeling, and especially since the advent of Christianity.

A further, more purely 'aesthetic' point, is that if the impact of the drama was as Peckham and Raphael claim it to be, we would feel, as the curtain came down, with King Marke blessing the corpses (if the producer were freaky enough to notice and obey Wagner's stage directions) something very different from what we do feel. I'm taking it that there is something approaching a standard, normal response, and that it is unclear by what means it could be shown to be mistaken. Peckham and Raphael keep very quiet about how they are affected by Wagner, but I'd be surprised if they weren't 'carried away' by this paradigmatically transporting work. I have found that it is one of the very few music-dramas which doesn't precipitate an immediate burst of applause, and yells of 'Bravo!' as the final chord fades away: the audience remains temporarily silent in the face of the sublime work, the 'miracle' as its creator correctly called it when he looked at the score a few years after its completion, but before its first performances. No other work so instantly effects a suspension of disbelief, and keeps it up without a single false touch. Those people who regard it as dangerous, corrupting and so forth are more honest in their responses to it, I suspect, than anyone who claims that it is a quasi-clinical, diagnostic work.

All this doesn't mean that *Tristan* can't be seen as an exposé of Romantic Love: it *does* mean, though, that in the first place it is a mistake to claim that 'that was what Wagner was doing'—not that we need be too worried about that matter, though equally we shouldn't ignore it; but to the extent that we don't ignore it, the evidence is all on the other

181

side; and it means, too, that to see it as an exposé we have to embark upon some much more complex mental operations than is usually the case with major works of art, where ponderings subsequent to the actual experience of the work are mainly elucidatory of what it was felt at the time to offer, and are attempts to gain a clearer understanding of what, in immediate response, was felt confusedly. Whatever poetry may be, most good criticism is the recollection of emotion in (comparative) tranquillity. But clearly that isn't going to be the case with *Tristan*, if we are intent on an understanding of it along Peckham–Raphael lines.

It is at this point that the notion of critical honesty, which I have characterized as closing, so far as is possible, the gap between experience and reflection, becomes a more intricate matter. There are some works, of which I take *Tristan* to be, probably, the supreme example, though the *St Matthew Passion* runs it a close second, if it doesn't equal it, of which it is a prerequisite that one suspends disbelief, not in this or that aspect of the work, nor in the verisimilitude of events in the work, but in the ethos which the work embodies and promulgates. This means that subsequent reflection, in so far as it involves rejection or critique of the work's ethical and metaphysical dimensions, also involves critique of one's reaction to them; but none the less it is important that one should have had those dubious feelings and near-beliefs. Perhaps it is only when there is a sufficiently rich context of art which can help to fortify us in the true ways of thinking about moral and metaphysical matters that we can allow ourselves the luxury of *Tristan* or the *St Matthew Passion*. It seems to me to imply nothing about the quality of the work concerned, whether it is only 'safe' in a context of other works, or whether it is entirely wholesome by itself.

Put so briefly, this sounds almost like a parody of late Tolstoy, except that it looks as if I'm suggesting that supping with the devil with a long spoon is all right as long as *most* meals are in angelic, or at least non-diabolic, company; a notion Tolstoy would have had no truck with. But it is as always more complicated than it seems at first; for I'm not suggesting a reckless cultivation of wildly disparate *Weltanschauungen*, but rather a preparedness to understand by fully entering into some of the major value-bearing myths of our culture. And there can be no doubt whatever that Romantic Love is a central one of them: 'the most beautiful of all dreams', and one which many people have hoped they might be able to actualize. It may well be true—I think it is—that there is a large element of self-regardingness, even narcissism, in this kind of love. Isolde is entirely concerned with her own feelings in Act I, and

Tristan with his in Act III; and when Isolde arrives and Tristan dies in her arms, her broken-heartedness arises from the fact that he has violated their pact to die together; until she thinks she sees and hears him awakening, she is full of reproaches for him, 'cruel man'. Though Morse Peckham may be overstating the case when he says 'The love-scene in the garden is entirely an analysis of how two lovers exploit one another's emotions', he is more nearly accurate than those who simply talk about 'sublime love-music'; or rather he is more accurate about the text, though not completely so. The trouble with his cursory account is that it suggests, in its use of 'analysis', a detachment that isn't to be found in the lovers, or Wagner, or the audience. Furthermore, 'exploiting one another's emotions' gives a strong impression that Tristan and Isolde are engaged in enjoying themselves by taking advantage of the other, which is grotesque.—I have just listened to the work again, and though it must now be between three and four hundred times, it is still impossible for me to hear it without entering into it with the fervour with which I first heard it—though with a great deal of weather-interference—from Bayreuth in 1952. While one listens, one is oneself a party to this most beautiful of dreams: 'life is poor indeed', says Nietzsche characteristically, 'for anyone who has not been sick enough for this "voluptuousness of hell" '. As so often, one sees what he means. So enormously persuasive is Wagner's eloquence that one forgoes the mean luxury of raising logical or moral objections as much as one does when listening to Bach's *Ich habe genug* or looking at the Isenheim altarpiece. When Tristan embarks on the final, as it were liturgically intoned piece of the love-scene, who wishes to quibble when he sings, 'So let us die together, ever one without end, without awakening, without fearing, nameless in love's embrace, giving ourselves wholly, to live only for love'? By quibbling, at this point, I mean objecting, 'But what kind of living is it that involves never awakening?' The answer is that there *is* no such kind of living that can rationally be valued; but that reason, so used to taking knocks from idealists, is taking another one here. That means that the ideal is incoherent; but one can't say that Wagner *exposes* it as incoherent, if that means anything more than portraying the striving for it and the illusion that it has been attained in supreme art. But that is the sense in which Bunyan 'exposes' the Christian ideal at the end of *The Pilgrim's Progress*, where the sustained exaltation compares in intensity, though not otherwise, to Isolde's. In other words, 'to expound is to expose' must be our aesthetic doctrine about these works, if we wish to make, as we must, a radical critique of the doctrines they embody. And indeed it is a familiar view in twentieth-century literary criticism that the self-sufficiency of a work must be such that it contains, at least implicitly, a judgement on itself, even though it may have taken Thomas Mann to produce, in his novel *Dr Faustus*, a work of which it can be said that it is 'its own critique, and that in the most thorough-going manner imaginable. There is no critical thought which the book does not think *about itself*.'[25] Often put in terms of intimidating jargon, it is expressed with much more persuasive forthrightness by Lawrence in the passages which I quoted at the beginning of this essay. They raise, with wholly typical economy and gusto, so many issues which face us as we deal with the complexities of all 'modern' art: and now that we are so complex, all art has become, in that way, modern. Even so, contrasts can be drawn; and Wagner's art, modern to the point of decadence as it is for his arch-antagonist, Nietzsche, as well as for his passionate admirer, Mann—though one wonders sometimes whether Mann's admiration doesn't spring partly from the torturing agonies of delectable paradox that being Wagnerian involves *him* in—Wagner's art challenges us to deny its supremacy *as art* even while, at least in the case of *Tristan*, we look askance when we recover our balance at its life-in-death metaphysics.

Yet there is a way in which that last formulation must be wrong: for Wagner is, on his own reckoning, the last man to advocate art for art's sake; his art is a series of attempts on the truth—or, not to make him too monolithic, on a series of related truths. One sometimes has the feeling that the people who mind Wagner wouldn't mind him so much if his individual works were less persuasive. As it is, it's rather like finding that the same man wrote the *Mass in B minor* and *A Mass of Life* (but of comparable greatness). Each of Wagner's mature works—counting the *Ring* as a single entity—presents so powerfully imagined a world that anyone who heard just one of them would be bound to feel that the other works, if there were any room left for them in musico-dramatic space, by the same composer, must be the same kind of thing. It's one thing to alternate between ecstasy and depression, or strenuous searchings and comparative relaxations, or even simply tragedy and comedy: but *Tristan* and *Meistersinger*! Surely no one could get into the necessary state to write the first of these masterworks and emerge from the task in excellent shape for proceeding to the second. While they last, they are so compelling: and yet since they both exist, and so do the *Ring* and *Parsifal*, Wagner must have been lacking in artistic integrity. Why? Because he produced such different works. So, but disguised by enor-

184

mous quantities of inaccuracy and moralism, goes the circular anti-Wagnerian argument.

But there wouldn't be so many people travelling round this particular circle unless Wagner's art was especially recalcitrant to comprehension. Clearly from the distinguished number of pathetic botch-shots, it is. But the case, though severe, isn't hopeless. Having aired anti-Wagnerian grievances once more, let me suggest ways in which *Tristan* needn't be seen as a kind of ultimately glamorous cultural catastrophe.

It would be perverse, to say the least, to claim that *Tristan* is not centrally concerned with love; but we should remember that love is always in Wagner an emotional or spiritual synecdoche: when his characters discourse about love, or subject it to trials and proofs, it is always something more that is being tested. Even in *Der fliegende Holländer*, that stupendous first outburst of shattering genius, which none the less is a very raw work compared with everything after *Lohengrin*, we have presented in unambiguous terms the kind of thing that Wagner's characters, like their creator, typically meant by 'love'. As Wagner's first 'Love-duet' gets under way, with its overpowering sense, again so typical, of two separate beings coming together almost somnambulistically—Senta's first line in reply to the Dutchman is 'Versank ich jetzt in wunderbares Träumen?' ('Am I sunk in wonderful dreams?')—what the characters are both concerned with is not fulfilling themselves in any ordinary romantic sense, but in redemption—itself understood in a somewhat personal way by Wagner: hence the irrelevance of Nietzsche's jibes on the subject in *Der Fall Wagner*. In the later dramas, too, the characters will often call their longing for redemption 'love', to our and sometimes even their confusion. But here the Dutchman and his creator are specifically concerned to make the distinction:

> Die düstre Glut, die hier ich fühle brennen,
> sollt' ich Unseliger sie Liebe nennen?
> Ach nein! Die Sehnsucht ist es nach dem Heil:
> würd es durch solchen Engel mir zuteil!

('Should I, the accursed one, call the dull glow that I feel burning here love? Ah no! It is the longing for salvation: would that such an angel should bring it to me!')

It is interesting that Thomas Mann should quote these lines in his great essay, in order to show her how much more complex the feeling behind them is than any that is to be found expressed by earlier operatic figures,

without dwelling at all on what that complex feeling is. For it is, as
much as any one thing is, the key to an understanding of Wagner's
chief preoccupation. Senta shows that she is well aware of what her
mission consists of:

> Wonach mit Sehnsucht es dich
> treibt—das Heil,
> würd es, du Armster, dir durch mich zuteil!

('The salvation that you yearn for—would that it should come to you
through me!')

And as their duet goes on its heady way, punctuated only by a curious
cadential passage which reminds us forcefully how far Wagner has gone
beyond that kind of thing for the rest of the duet, and the Dutchman's
and Senta's *Rausch* continues to grow, we are faced for the first time
with a phenomenon that may well lie near the heart of a great deal of
puzzlement about and hostility to Wagner: the juxtaposition, sometimes even the blending, of the noble and the erotic. We can see how
the Dutchman is concerned, even *in höchste Not*, to be semantically
precise in a way that his successors are not. What he calls the longing for
redemption, and they often call love, is precisely what he does *not* call
love. The aching quality of the Dutchman's monologue, the great
'Die Frist ist um', and of the opening of the duet, is something that
reaches its final fearful expression in Amfortas' agonies in the Hall of
the Grail in Act I of *Parsifal*; no one could claim that *that* was a longing
for love. And if one remembers Wagner's claim, in a letter to Mathilde
Wesendonk, that Amfortas is 'only' the Tristan of Act III taken to his
extreme, one can see that Wagner did have, at least in this case, a very
firm grasp on the meaning of what he was composing.

We are now in a position to get clearer about the controversy between
those who see *Tristan* as the apotheosis of Romantic love and those who
see it as its exposé. It *is* about love, as I am not in the least disposed to
deny. But it is about love as a means to an end, and therefore in a profound way cannot be the ultimate celebration of Romantic love; love is
inextricably, indeed conceptually linked with yearning. And it is precisely the yearnings of the Prelude and much else in the work that
Tristan and Isolde want to transcend by living through their fulfilment
into a state which is 'without fear, without awakening'. Their problem,
which is the problem confronting all Wagner's major characters, is to
find or to create a self. And of course they are not the first people to have
believed that they must lose themselves in order to be redeemed, i.e.

in order to find themselves. Such a doctrine has always proved attractive as well as being paradoxical. It has close connexions with the idea that freedom somehow consists in finding and knowing one's place in a totally determined framework. The version of it that Tristan and Isolde espouse is novel in that each finds him/herself by becoming the other, or at least by feeling as if they have: they actually exchange names at the climax of their love-scene, which they explicitly insist means swapping identities. In one way it is the most intelligible form of the doctrine that one must lose one's life to save it: for in becoming Isolde Tristan finds himself and vice versa. But the intelligibility is only superficial, since to talk of Tristan becoming Isolde is itself nonsense. What is not nonsensical, though, is that each of them should *feel* that he/she has become the other. But even then there are problems. Wagner's characters, sharing their creator's limitless capacity for experience, and being profoundly vital, which is why they are finally attractive, feel imprisoned in their egos. If *Tristan* is Wagner's most Wagnerian work, it is because his *idées fixes* receive their most complete expression in it. There is a desperate feeling of guilt, often supported by or grounded in some outrageous action such as Tannhäuser's sojourn in the Venusberg, which comes from a simultaneous need to expand the boundaries of the ego and an incapacity to do it in a form which does not profoundly disrupt social or moral order. If Wagner's characters have a traditional sin in common, it is clearly that of pride: they pitch their demands on life too high, and commit crimes or sins in order to achieve them.

But pride isn't straightforwardly a vice: and what is heroic about Wagner's characters is precisely their straining for more abundant life, which they feel entitled to, indeed a necessity for their otherwise suffocating existence. This kind of heroism means that Wagner's relations with Christianity are bound to be both intimate and strained. On the one hand there is, as with Christianity, a strongly ambivalent feeling about men: they aren't nearly as grand or fine or pure or good as they should be, and yet they are worth going to enormous lengths to save. On the other hand, Wagner's recommended courses for redemption never involve simply becoming a Christian—not even in *Parsifal*. As for *Tristan*, the question of Christianity doesn't arise, though it nearly did, at the time when Wagner had the bizarre idea of having Parsifal run into Tristan during his (Parsifal's) *Wanderjahre* between Acts II and III of *Parsifal*, and in Act III of *Tristan*. But the bonds between the two great works are too subtle for such a violent incursion of one into the other, as Wagner with his infallible dramatic instinct quickly realized.

So, while not being Christian, *Tristan* is in certain ways decidedly religious: in the need, above all, of its two central characters to transcend themselves. But at this stage they, and Wagner, can only conceive of transcending themselves by becoming someone else under highly privileged conditions. But what they want is not, in any ordinary sense, a completion of love; the eroticism of *Tristan* is in one aspect prior to love: it is vehemently sexual. In another aspect it goes beyond anything that is usually called or thought of as love. So if one demurs at taking it that the climax, or several climaxes, of the duet in Act II are sexual, it isn't because that would demean the feelings of Tristan and Isolde for one another, but because it would make the love which would be finding expression in sexual abandon the kind of love which *can* normally be expressed by love-*making*. One reason why we can't accept Peckham's view of *Tristan* is that it becomes ever less clear that Romantic love is its core: Wagner is dealing with something which we can't but call love, because it involves the innermost feelings of a man and a woman for one another, and their expression. But it would be mistaken, I feel, to regard the nature of their feelings as being either typical or diagnostic of Romantic love; it isn't even an extrapolation to the nth degree of Romantic love, though it's very tempting to take it as that, because it makes *Tristan* more readily comprehensible than it really is. Wagner here, as elsewhere, is working at the outer limits of possible human experience, and at a depth which necessitates the use of the term 'religious'—or, if it should be preferred, 'metaphysical'. But since Wagner is moving so far into unexplored territory, it becomes all the more necessary for him to hold on fast to what we all understand—for he is always desperately concerned to *propagate* the truth. Hence the enormous sensuousness of *Tristan*, the curious tendency it shows to become ever more overwhelmingly sensuous the more it is concerned with transcendence: above all in the 'O sink' hernieder' section of Act II and in Isolde's Transfiguration. The risk that Wagner runs, both here and in his other works, is obvious: as the tension mounts and this supreme master of musical climaxes reveals all his power, his music does become in one sense 'absolute', while in another it is a grievous affront to 'pure' music, as many pure musicians have been quick to point out. But the voice, or voices, become further instruments at many of Wagner's most ecstatic moments, and since voices are the most exciting instruments of all, the fact that they are singing words is not the most important thing, since no listener could discern most of the words in climactic Wagnerian passages. And not only in climaxes: however well one knows Wagner's works, one often doesn't take the precise content of what is being sung into account, for various reasons. For example, in the passage between the end of Brangäne's watch-song and Tristan's 'So starben wir', the lovers are engaged in some remarkable conceptual and verbal niceties, accompanied by the ravishing motif known as 'Love's peace', scored in a variety of ways that seem to define for us, and for Tristan and Isolde, their tenderness for one another in a way that nothing else in the score attempts to do. At this point Wagner the musical dramatist is enchanting us with the beauty of the music, and certainly *not* using the music to highlight the meaning of the words, which have to be worked over purely by themselves if one is to follow the intricate dialectic. I have checked this passage and this point with a considerable number of highly sensitive listeners, none of whom have had more than a vague notion of what is taking place conceptually.

I hardly feel like taking Wagner to task over this: it is true of much of the greatest art that it needs recollection and reflection—as true of Shakespeare as it is of Wagner. The sense of the greatest things often only comes after repeated seeings, readings or hearings: and of course the relationship of experience to reflection varies according to the art form concerned. One can ponder on a picture while gazing at it, or on a poem while reading it to oneself; but a work that is being performed has to be consulted later, or one is left behind. But there is the question of whether Wagner does not defeat his alleged purposes by providing intoxicating music precisely when one needs to be completely sober to grapple with his complex psychological and metaphysical meanings. The answer, with a few possible exceptions, is that he does not. Though the music does not force the text on our attention, it does not go counter to it—except in one entirely satisfying way. It is this: though the central 'doctrine' of *Tristan* is the resolution of love in death, and though (it is often alleged) the general pulse of Wagner's music is slow, or (Thomas Mann's term) sluggish, yet the overwhelming effect is of superabundant vitality. If one is exhausted—and who isn't?—by *Tristan* or indeed by any of Wagner's works, it is because one has witnessed and been compelled to share in such a prodigious expenditure of energy. The sheer ardour of Wagner's characters, whatever their intent, is always in the end energizing, as it is in all great art, even that which is most dynamically negative—Swift, often, or sometimes Lawrence. This is not the

189

morality of life, so much as the morality of liveliness. And of course we cannot accept it straightforwardly, any more than we can accept what I earlier called 'moral vitalism' unreservedly. Vitality, like charm, is a fascinating, alluring and sometimes dangerous gift. Since most people are deficient in it, almost any display of vitality can seem appealing. And Wagner has a kind of primitive vitality, as well as the more sophisticated kind which led Nietzsche to describe him accurately, though with spiteful intent, as a wonderful miniaturist. He *is* that and increasingly so, so that the textures of *Meistersinger* and *Götterdämmerung* are more continuously and richly contrapuntal than any other music since J. S. Bach. But in the case of *Tristan* the vitality, of whichever kind, can seem to be oddly in conflict with the prevailing death-wish ambience of the work. But the death-wish of the lovers and of their creator shows itself clearly in the very intensity, in but not of the moment in which it is expressed, that it is a contrast to 'life' as it is understood by the inhabitants of the 'world of day' who troop on towards the end of each act. The 'most beautiful of dreams', however restfully it tries to express itself, as at the quietly pulsating beginning of the 'O sink' hernieder' section, is always, after a few moments, mounting to a new, even more fervent climax than any that has gone before. And even when, as at the end of that section, the lovers sink exhausted and Brangäne's voice floats on to the scene, there is no loss of intensity: indeed, if anything, the prevailing mood is rendered still more potent as the orchestral web surrounding her vocal line becomes ever more intricate and expressive; this is 'relief' in the same way that the gravediggers' scene in *Hamlet* is 'relief'.

To the extent that the music of *Tristan* is more powerful than the words—a very great extent—it overrules them and carries the day: or rather the night, if we are to keep within the symbolism of the work. It is no paradox to say that *Tristan* is one of art's greatest life-affirmations: it is merely what one has to say if one has listened closely and often, and found oneself recharged, more than ever in love with the deepest forms of beauty in this world. For Wagner's music obstinately refuses to transcend, even when it seems that its creator is most determined that it should. We shall understand more fully why this is so when we come to *Parsifal*. Meanwhile the point about *Tristan* that is most germane to my argument, and which it is most important to bear in mind as we move to consider an aspect of *Meistersinger*, is that in it Wagner exercises his power as supreme rhetorician to the full. It is not a *Gesamtkunstwerk*, thank heavens, but it achieves the effect which Wagner thought could only be achieved by such an aggregative device:

it establishes a total sway over its audience, leaving the receptive listener spellbound, indeed possessed. It is in that sense that it is a total work of art. And among such works which make a bid for a total commitment from their audience it is surely supreme. No wonder it is regarded with suspicious awe—not least by Richard Wagner, whose conscience as an artist, which is not to say his artistic conscience, was sufficiently disturbed by what he had created to make the responsibilities of art the subject of his next work.[26]

5. DIE MEISTERSINGER: THE ARTIST'S CONTROL OVER HIS AUDIENCE

The extent to which people, even music critics, fail to notice Wagner's texts while responding to his music is most forcefully demonstrated by the case of *Meistersinger*. Because of its extreme difference of musical idiom from *Tristan*, especially, but in some respects from all the rest of Wagner's works, *Meistersinger* has been taken to be a 'sport' in the Wagnerian canon; and occasional attempts to fit it in have been at the beckoning of some of the least savoury of the *idées fixes* that Wagner is interpreted by. Once again, the unpretentious and compact pages of Morse Peckham[27] and the expansion of them by Robert Raphael[28] seem to me best in establishing the continuity of this work with the rest of Wagner's *oeuvre*. I shall be concerned with it from strictly limited points of view, simply because I haven't the space here for anything more. So I shall treat *Meistersinger* only as the profoundest study we have of art and illusion. The basic point is very familiar by now: art, especially Wagner's, is extraordinarily powerful but it is also an illusion. How can it defend itself? What has Wagner to offer in reply to his self-arraignment, as we may take Hans Sachs's remarks to the sceptical Walther in Act III to be:

> Eu'r Lied das hat [die Meister] bang' gemacht;
> und das mit Recht: denn wohl bedacht,
> mit solchem Dicht'—und liebesfeuer
> verführt man wohl Töchter zum Abenteuer;
> doch für liebseligen Ehestand
> man andre Wort und Weisen fand.

('Your song made the Masters anxious, and with good reason: for if you think about it, it's with such fire of poetry and love that one seduces daughters to adventure; but for loving and blessed marriage other words and tunes must be found.')

Though such warnings tend to be thought of nowadays as charming period-touches, we must remember, first, that it is the same warning that Plato delivered—and with good reason, miscarriages during performances of Euripides' plays being frequent—and that many other critics and sometimes even artists have offered; and second, that even if as many contemporaries feel our exposure to art is now so incessant that, while much of it hasn't yet become mere wallpaper, none of it is likely to have dangerously strong effects on us, it still remains true that the most serious critics and artists feel the problem of belief to be as worrying as it ever was. That Wagner was of their company seems certain: he is more than half-serious when, writing to Mathilde Wesendonk about Act III of *Tristan*, he says that only bad performances can save him and that he's frightened that his music might drive people mad. And, as convinced as any artist who ever lived that he had found the road to salvation for humanity, and that adequate performances of his work were an indispensable stage on that road, he none the less has to reckon with the fact that salvation takes pretty radically different forms in his works to date; and yet he naturally couldn't bring himself to suppress, say, *Tannhäuser*, when he had moved on to *Tristan*. Indeed, with the skill he had acquired in the intervening years he took the opportunity to expand and intensify the Venusberg music until it becomes a clear depiction of insane sensuality, making the 'pure' elements in the work seem more anaemic than they had before.

It would be as cheap to allege that Wagner's failure to withdraw or suppress his previous works was due to his cravings for fame and wealth as it would be for any other artist ever; he didn't take the works to be exclusive doctrinal tracts. Yet that he did feel the urgency of their message isn't to be doubted either. What can be made of the situation? This is the question that he confronts in *Meistersinger*. Though that work begins with the most radiant generosity of feeling, its heart is to be found nearly three hours later when Sachs sings 'Wahn! Wahn!' ('Illusion! Illusion!'), the great monologue which no one pays sufficient attention to. Its chief point is the absolute pervasiveness of *Wahn*, and its inscrutability. Asking himself the question of how the previous night's madness—in which he himself played a central role—came about, Sachs can only provide a whimsical answer in terms of the magic of *Johannisnacht*, i.e. no answer at all. By this stage, thanks to the Act III Prelude and the *Wahn*-monologue up to this point, we should be feeling sufficiently sombre to agree that the world is hopelessly in thrall to

Wahn, and indeed to agree with Sachs's heartbroken and heart-breaking words:

> Hat keiner Lohn,
> noch Dank davon:
> in Flucht geschlagen
> meint er zu jagen.
> Hört nicht sein eigen
> Schmerz–Gekreisch,
> wenn er sich wühlt ins eig'ne Fleisch
> wähnt Lust sich zu erzeigen!

('He has no reward or thanks for it: driven to flight, he imagines that he is hunting. He does not hear his own cry of pain, when he digs into his own flesh and thinks that he produces pleasure for himself!')

The monologue has become by its end a marvellously condensed feeling-through of the responses that may be made to the recognition of the pervasiveness of *Wahn*. Beginning in tragic accents, Sachs re-enacts, becoming increasingly lively while doing so, the events of *Polterabend*. One of Wagner's great strokes is that of leading Sachs (or because it is so inevitable we feel more as if the composer was faithfully *following* his character's thoughts) to brood on the quiet beauty of Nuremberg for a few moments before emerging from his extremely temporary peacefulness to give a colourful account of the fighting and anger of a few hours earlier: tragic bewilderment is changed to the playful invocation of fairy-magic, again dwelt on briefly but with exquisite effect; and then there is the massive surge into C major at which point no one, even if they have been following Sachs's thoughts up to this point, does so any longer. Wagner the magician in sounds produces his own variety of *Wahn* here, and it is very much of a piece with the spell that Sachs determines to cast; it was preposterous of Wagner to expect anyone in the theatre (and he had no reason to anticipate the advent of the gramophone or radio, which have enabled people to follow librettos and Wagner's meaning *while* listening, which makes a decisive difference from what was previously possible) to do anything except drink in the luxurious warmth of those last lines—certainly not the highly complex set of thoughts they contain. But whether or not he realized it, what Wagner is doing here is a microcosm of what Sachs says *he* is going to do, and what indeed always has to be done:

Jetzt schau'n wir, wie Hans Sachs es macht,
dass er den Wahn fein lenken kann,
ein edler Werk zu tun;
denn lässt er uns nicht ruh'n,
selbst hier in Nürenberg,
so sei's um solche Werk',
die selten vor gemeinen Dingen,
und nie ohn' ein'gen Wahn gelingen.

('Now let us see how Hans Sachs can manage things so that Illusion can be made to do nobler work; for if it will not let us rest even here in Nuremberg, then let it be in the service of such works which seldom arise from ordinary things, and never succeed without a touch of Illusion.')

The movement of feeling from the beginning to the end of the monologue is a whole progress which might well take a man all his mature years to move through, yet which seems quite naturally to take a mere ten minutes: as always concision is one of Wagner's major though least-advertised virtues. *Wahn* can be seen, then, not only as depressingly omnipresent, but what makes the world go round, and as a force which can be channelled and used by someone whose mind is bent on 'nobler works' once he has recognized what the basis of existence is.

Hans Sachs has made a crucial discovery for himself in reflecting on *Wahn*. He begins, like Schopenhauer before him and Nietzsche after him, by seeing all life as reducible, and thus reduced, to a single force. For Schopenhauer the characterization of that force was painfully clear: the Will to Live was manifestly evil, and the only virtues were compassion for everything else that lived, and so far as one's own lot was concerned, resignation. For Nietzsche by contrast the Will to Power had no moral value attaching to it: indeed, it was precisely the realization that the Will to Power was value-free that necessitated the sometimes exhilarating, sometimes appalling task of creating value. Wagner thought of himself as the disciple of Schopenhauer and the mentor of Nietzsche. He was neither, unless we give more weight to his theoretical writings than to his art, which we obviously shouldn't. There is a sense in which he is a pessimist, at least in *Die Meistersinger*, his most desperate work. The high spirits for which it is notable, and which allegedly make it a striking contrast to the inspissated darkness of his other work, are very clearly, once one has understood Sachs's position in the work, the cheerfulness of a man who knows that, terrible as life is, one won't make it any better by crying so one might as well laugh. It is of a piece with this view—which can be shallow or can be profound: it depends *how* it is held, and in *Meistersinger* it is clearly held profoundly—that Sachs tells Walther in the so-called 'composition scene' that it's not difficult to sing beautiful songs in spring, i.e. youth, but that true mastery is shown by someone who can compose beautifully to a background of 'Kindtauf', Geschäfte, Zwist und Streit' ('Baptism, business, discord and strife'). At every point Sachs relates the rules of art to morality and the conduct of life. Thus, when Walther has sung his first stanza, Sachs explains the necessity of a second just like it 'so that people can see you are choosing a wife', and after the second stanza that an 'After-song' is required similar to the first two stanzas, but not identical, so that 'people will find it slender and self-sufficient, such that it makes parents proud of the child'. Clearly these explanations are half-whimsical, but the point is to show that the Masters' rules aren't arbitrary—or need not be.

Walther is not Wagner's ideal artist, nor is Sachs. For several purposes he found it necessary to split the artist into two characters; it is silly, though typical of anti-Wagnerian propaganda, to say that he did it in order to have his cake (i.e. to win Eva) and eat it (i.e. renounce his love for her so that she could marry Walther). He did it because the dramatic structure necessitated it, and to elucidate in a framework of comedy such matters as the relationship between tradition and the individual talent, imagination and form, and above all, the relationship of the artist to his audience.

For Wagner, the superiority of art over philosophy and religion was that no one believed it was 'true', that is, that it could be anything more than a way of organizing experience through the understanding of a drama. Even so, the question with which this section of the discussion began remains: to what extent is the artist committing us to a view of things that excludes other views? For even if we accept Sachs's view that everything is illusion, we have seen that there are discriminations to be made. Morse Peckham again puts the point with perfect precision:

> The power of art is now clear. It introduces value into the world by creating in the hearts of men the experience of order and meaning. To assert the existence of order, meaning, and value, whether natural, divine, or transcendent, is an illusion; to experience them is essential to maintaining life. Art is the source of that experience.[29]

It seems obvious that this was Wagner's view, that in taking it he took an enormous step forward in the understanding of the creativity that inheres in art, and that he set himself at an opposite extreme from aestheticism. For the Nietzsche of *The Birth of Tragedy*, 'the world is only justified as an aesthetic phenomenon'; for Wagner aesthetic phenomena are only justified in so far as they help us to make sense of the world.

But *true* sense of the world? There can't be such a thing, of course, if *all* is illusion. But that is not the kind of approach which it is profitable to make to an artist's work. It remains true, and results in an issue which can't be dodged, that Wagner presents us very forcefully with conflicting views of how to achieve 'redemption'. And if he wants us to take his contribution to the question seriously, as he does, then surely we can't 'take' both *Tristan* and *Meistersinger*, or *Tristan* and *Parsifal*, and so forth?

The first part of an answer which won't involve special pleading is that Wagner is dealing with questions to which it would be (and on the part of many people is) grotesquely simple-minded to think that there is one answer. Wagner's art comes very much into the category of what Leavis calls the 'creative-exploratory'. And by now it is a cliché, though true, that the exploration is a vital part of the participation in grasping the answer. No other artist, not even Beethoven or Lawrence, has made more determined and, in the proper sense, disinterested attempts to find a way to an adequate definition of self-hood. And because we live in a highly pluralistic society, one in which there are serious, intelligent, sensitive people living in pursuit of widely disparate goals, and one cannot be fully alive without knowing that and without being tempted by one of these goals after another, it is as well that they should be presented in as convincing a form as art can manage.

It is at this point that I part company with Peckham and Raphael, to whom I am so heavily indebted for much of what I've written about *Meistersinger*. For they both feel that the status of the artist as portrayed in Hans Sachs is ultimately questionable. But I can't see how, in the society depicted in *Meistersinger*, Sachs at any stage goes beyond the call of duty and intrudes on other personalities in an offensive way. It is *that* charge, however, which is frequently felt and made against Wagner. Indeed *Meistersinger*, which is so heavily concerned with the relation of the artist to his public, is ordinarily thought of as his least assertive work, apart from its concluding few minutes: while in all the other works many people feel, as Nietzsche did, that 'Wagner says something so often until, in despair, one believes it'—a charge dangerously open to a *tu quoque*. Actually Wagner does *not* say things often; what is more alarming is the variety of things he says. But it is also true that he says them with an emphasis, sometimes a stridency, which is characteristic in its positive moods of the convert, and in its negative moods of the apostate. Of course, he can't celebrate or express his convictions with the hugely grand and powerful but calmly believed statements of Bach. Nor, for that matter, could Beethoven: to compare the *Missa Solemnis* with the *B Minor Mass* is to see that Beethoven's Christianity is closer to Wagner's assorted doctrines than to Bach's traditionalism, not to mention Palestrina or Ockeghem. The *Missa Solemnis* presents, in fact, the strange phenomenon of an artist using the most hallowed ritual text of his society in order to try to convince himself that at least the spirit of the thing is true. The comparisons and contrasts that can be drawn between it and *Parsifal* would make an excellent examination topic for relatively advanced Wagnerians. Before going into any kind of detail, though, we may take it as settled that Beethoven is the first *weltanschaulich* musician whose creativity is crucially involved in the very existence of the objects of his belief. Through Bach one might learn, as a Christian, more of the relationship between the oppressiveness of sin and the actuality of redemption: states, attitudes, entities even, might become clearer so that the nature of the objects of belief is helpfully clarified. But in Beethoven, both in the *Missa Solemnis* and in the adagio section of the last movement of the Ninth Symphony ('über'n Sternen *muss* er wohnen'), we have the sense that Beethoven's much-vaunted creativity is coming home to roost. He may be the first man, not only the first musician, who has allotted to art a larger role, or rather a role of a different kind, from any that it can play. It would not be true to say of him, as it is to say of Nietzsche and Rilke, that they do not

> ... praise the praiseworthy. They praise. They do not believe the believable. They believe. And it is their praising and their believing itself that becomes praiseworthy in the act of worship. Theirs is a *religio intransitiva*. Future anthropologists may see in it the distinctive religious achievement of modern Europe, the theological equivalent of *l'art pour l'art*.[30]

That brilliantly perceptive passage of Heller's is true of much more than the works of Nietzsche and Rilke, though it could hardly be more true of anything. But it isn't true of Beethoven, at least not the Beethoven of the Mass in D and the Ninth Symphony; and it isn't true of Wagner. Both are immensely assertive and convinced artists, but their assertions *do* have 'intentional objects', and they are convinced of something—or, to return at last to the case of Wagner, all too many things: so it may seem.

I intend to avoid a general discussion of 'art and belief', not because I would find it tedious or irrelevant, but because there is a more pressing task: to show the contribution of *Die Meistersinger* to this and related debates. One point which, brief though this essay is, I feel needs to be restressed is that there is no warrant for taking Walther or Sachs to be the prototypical artist: I am not sure that, even in this supremely confident-sounding work, any norm of art emerges or is intended to emerge. The Prize-Song itself is one example of art, but hardly something to be imitated—that is part of the point. Its exemplary qualities are, in the drama, independent of what we may happen, outside the drama, to think of it; I regard it as a supreme popular song, but that does not matter. The point is that it has its origins, like all true art, deep in the artist's being; that, having overcome an understandable reluctance to let anyone else hear it, the artist achieves a 'public' expression, makes his art comprehensible by abiding by certain principles of an accommodating kind which make art continuous with, indeed part of the fabric of life; and, supremely, and most contentiously, that the patterning of life which is given by art returning to life in a reshaped form what it took from it as raw material, is necessary as the supreme form of *Wahn*. The Prize-Song embodies all these qualities, as the audience, including the Masters, remark while Walther is singing his partly improvised improvement of it. The symmetry of *Meistersinger*, which is like that of *Tristan* in being clear but unobtrusive, consists partly in each act's ending in a song with crowd reactions. In Act I, Walther perplexes and embarrasses the Masters by failing to distinguish at all between Art and Life, so that 'Fanget an!', the command from without to commence his trial song, is taken over as its impetuous beginning; and though they over-react, the Masters have something to be said for them, as Sachs insists both to Walther alone, and to everyone at the end. Like Henry James in his famous and painful debate with H. G. Wells, Sachs believes that 'Art makes life, makes interest, makes importance', while Walther in his trial song, which is actually less disciplined than his preceding lyrical account of his *Bildung*, is merely adding 'a slice of life' by ignoring rules and being 'spontaneous'. In Act II, by complex contrast, Beckmesser's song is not simply a ridiculous Master-Song with mistakes: it should be sung as beautifully as possible, and by a singer with a fine voice. It is, or is intended to be, a genuine expression of feeling; and the reason why someone as highly trained in the Tabulatur makes so many mistakes is that he is trying to express feelings within a framework which has ossified; Beckmesser's

Act II failure shows what is wrong with the rules, just as Walther's Act I failure shows that they are necessary. Each failure is punished with (at least) due severity. The Prize-Song, both in its 'composition' form and its final flowering, shows how the inspired artist working in a tradition can *achieve* lyrical spontaneity without abandoning 'form', and with sufficiently stunning effect to please the people and the Masters. The fact that Wagner has produced a three-act form which itself is a macrocosm of the Prize-Song has often been remarked; but that by itself is, as it were, a piece of casual and defiant virtuosity. What is more to the point, and I think has not been remarked, is that *Meistersinger*, by being organized roughly as a Master-Song should be, shows that it is to be taken in the way that Sachs sees art in its relationship to life. One emerges glowing from *Die Meistersinger* for very many reasons, and my failure to expatiate on the most obvious and frequently celebrated ones will no doubt earn me censure. But the fundamental reason, though rarely seen in perspective (it is part of the magic spell that it should not be, *at the time*) is that a wise and noble man, by no means a man of mythical-heroic stature, but rather a lovable and vulnerable and sometimes irascible human being, should be able to master his own strong feelings in such a way as to minister to the right working-out of other people's; Sachs is not idealized—at least, not by Wagner—and so we have all the more vivid a sense of that 'everyday reality' which critics exclaim about, in amazement that it should be created by someone who had so bewitchingly captured the 'Wunderreich der Nacht'. But for the artist—and I mean Richard Wagner, not Hans Sachs—who realized that everything was illusion, it was perhaps not so difficult to move from one profoundly expressed state to another. As Wagner matured and his own inner life became ever more rich and varied, so he came to an un-Romantic realization of the nature and stature of the worlds that artists create. It was all of a piece that this deepening, Coleridgean sense of the artistic process as duplicating the original process of Creation should impel Wagner to create not only more beautiful but more spell-binding art-works; for if the artist is like the Creator, it follows— a conclusion that Wagner drew with a rigour denied to Coleridge— that the Creator is like the artist: both are concerned with illusion. If one were God, I have occasionally reflected, it would be extraordinarily difficult, contemplating one's handiwork, to establish satisfactory criteria for what was real and what was deceptive, and the sensible thing to do would be to acknowledge Descartes' alarming insight when he postulated a malicious demon who might deceive a man about everything except his own (the man's) existence, and demur only at the allegation of malice. Such a God, had he existed, might well have claimed to have made artists in his own image, whatever could be said about the rest of illuded mankind. Such an hypothesis would have struck Wagner as lamentably whimsical, granted the seriousness of Art and the miseries of Man: and he would have been right. Yet on his own view of at least one artist, life was a more sombre and indefinitely more prolonged version of this. Other theological parallels, some of them more offensively blasphemous, could be imagined for Wagner's idea of the artist, and his partial embodiment of it in Hans Sachs.

Die Meistersinger is in one way, then, Wagner's most 'private' work, since while beguiling us with the most adorable and gorgeous externalities, he is stealthily developing an allegory of the nature of artistic activity of really alarming boldness; so bold that the pageantry, merrymaking and ceremonial must have been at least as necessary for Wagner not to take fright at what he was doing as it is for us. As it is, it's clear that neither Hans Sachs nor his creator have fully coped with the question: If everything is *Wahn*, and the artist has as his supreme function the manipulation of *Wahn* 'for nobler ends', what check is there that the ends are truly noble, and not only seemingly so? Or if that seems too captious, in talking about a comedy (not that being comic licenses the degree of irresponsibility which it is often taken to do), what is there to check that the artist is not simply a deceiver? We can't reply 'Reality' or 'Life', if both of those are illusions, or contain very large elements of illusion. Of course, Sachs only says that he finds *Wahn* everywhere, he does not say that the world is nothing else. And he does not imply that the artist has a finer apprehension of *Wahn* than anyone else. It seems, to return to Peckham's contention, that it is in imposing form or order on existence that the artist is distinguished from other men. And surely that is right, and the modesty of Wagner's claim for art compounds the boldness of the supreme position he accords it: art is the best we have got, and it is not nearly as good as might have been hoped. Wagner's position, in *Meistersinger*, is thus strikingly like that of the Grand Inquisitor in *The Brothers Karamazov*, with Art substituted for the Church. The artist bears the burden of knowing that life is tragic, and has as his function to persuade people that it's worthwhile going on living, partly by presenting tragedies for them to watch. Indeed it is especially by presenting life in tragic terms that the artist justifies himself: for tragedy gives voice and thus form to the most terrible things that can happen, and is therefore indispensable and not to be transcended. We can never go 'beyond the tragic vision', and it is astonishing that anyone should think we can: at best we can alternate between it and other visions, as we do, thanks to Wagner, in the Prelude to Act III of *Meistersinger*: the motif of Sachs's 'resignation', developed in sombre counterpoint by the strings, gives place to the quiet radiance of what will later be 'Wach' auf!', the heralding of a new dawn; but after the second statement of that chorale on the brass, it is the strings, coming in again with overpowering harmonic-expressive effect with the *Wahn* motive, that bring the Prelude to its close, before David's perky motive wittily takes over and remains to the fore until the beginning of the *Wahn* monologue itself, although we are never allowed to forget that behind and deeper than David's callow joyfulness there lies Sachs's heartbreak.

And yet, though the tragic content of that Prelude and of much else in the opera, and not only in Act III, is evident, it may easily be felt that there is too large a gap between the true *Meistersinger* and the tone of my remarks about it. As I ponder that inevitable complaint, I am torn between agreeing with it and truculently denying it. And it is not self-indulgence to record my self-divided state, since I think it is a more adequate response to the work than either the usual one, couched entirely in terms of warm-heartedness, a sense of the fundamental goodness of ordinary men, and so on, or my account—not by any means unique, but less common than the first. The warmth which *Meistersinger* unquestionably radiates comes not from anything so foolish as an 'apprehension' on Wagner's part of human goodness, but is an accepting geniality: that is its positive side, summed up in such glorious moments as that when Walther asks Sachs, 'Doch, wem der Lenz schon lang entronnen, wie wird er dem im Bild gewonnen?' ('But how can someone from whom spring [youth] has long fled capture it in an [artistic] image?') and gets the reply: 'Er frischt es an, so gut er kann: d'rum möcht ich als bedürft'ger Mann, will ich die Regeln euch lehren, sollt ihr sie mir neu erklären.' ('He refreshes it as well as he can: so, as a man in need myself, I'll teach you the rules, so that you can explain them to me anew.') The casualness with which Sachs refers to his own predicament—that when you are old enough to be wise you are too old to put it to direct use—and moves on to Walther's affairs, shows his benign acceptance at its most generous. By contrast, the outburst which leads to Eva's great 'O Sachs! Mein Freund!' is half mocking, half genuinely bitter about the way in which age is exploited by callous youth.

Actually there is a progression of feeling in the work which hasn't been sufficiently taken account of: it begins as buoyantly as a work can, and the tone of most of Act I is light, and even when grave, as in Pogner's address, only fleetingly so. Anxiety pervades much of the proceedings in all three acts, of course, as it does in many comedies—*Figaro* being an especially conspicuous case: but one of the things that leads us to call them comedies is a sense we get, derived from the general tenor of the works, and usually also from many specific hints, that somehow everything that matters will turn out happily. This is the case in the scene between Eva and her father and Eva and Sachs, in Act II. Oddly, it is only when Sachs's clowning is reaching its height that, besides anxiety, a feeling of sadness begins to colour the great work. As he sings the third, highly 'meaningful' verse of his *Schusterlied*, the motive of resignation makes its first appearance, in counterpoint to the vigorous sung melody, and Eva says to Walther, 'Mich schmerzt das Lied, ich weiss nicht wie!' ('The song pains me, I don't know how!'). And it is pervasive in the whole series of encounters in Sachs's work-room the next morning; the resignation motive punctuates the rehearsal of the Prize-song, tears away into a huge climax as Walther sings the third verse and Eva bursts into tears, and is the orchestra's melancholy reply to the overwhelming grandeur of 'Wach' auf!' And the Sachs who is cheered in the very last moments of the drama is a man who will go back to his loneliness, making do 'as best he can'. Just as one doesn't emerge from *Tristan* feeling tragically oppressed or liberated, so one doesn't emerge from *Meistersinger* feeling comically relieved or equipped to take life lightly. Common to both is the sense of an enormous release of energy, which is imparted to the listener and refreshes and invigorates him—but that is a feature, indeed a criterion, of all the greatest works of art, and is compatible with the temporary sense of exhaustion which arises from the sheer intensity and length of the ordeal to which some of them submit us. What makes *Meistersinger* unusual, at least, is that this refreshing, invigorating force that it very evidently has co-exists with profound and melancholy insights into the absence of value and order in the human world—the only world that exists, or matters, in *Meistersinger*. It is remarkably sparing in consolations, except that, in sum, there are two: first, in view of the grimness with which the human condition is seen, there is the fact that such a work as that which embodies it can exist at all. Some critics go into unnecessary moralistic spasms (as opposed to the absolutely essential moral basis on which all worthwhile criticism rests) about the betrayal of life by form-giving art: and of course form is seductive and in itself consolatory. But I am not praising *Meistersinger* for making life seem finally more patterned than it is, but for rejoicing when it has precious little to construct upon which to rejoice. It is cheering and bracing in the way that all acts of courage in the face of mortality, chaos and the evil in men's hearts are. The second consolation is the Quintet, which is normally accepted as a gorgeous piece of law-breaking by Wagner—a breaking of his own laws, since they forbad ensembles in which it is impossible to tell what sentiments the characters are voicing. It *is* a departure from the rigours of music-drama as it is prescribed in the theoretical works of the early 1850s, but one can see a point in it beyond that—or if one does not, it remains a luscious morsel, or in a vague way the focus of a drama the nature of which is not understood. If my own very selective commentary on *Meistersinger* is so far as it goes correct, then it becomes easier to see why and how the Quintet has the place of honour that it does have in the work. A few minutes before it, emotional chaos has still prevailed: Eva is 'compelled' to marry Walther, not Sachs, she says in her exultant, climatic, but deeply disturbed response to Sachs's grumblings:

> ... hatte ich die Wahl,
> nur dich erwählt ich mir:
> du warest mein Gemahl,
> den Preis reicht' ich nur dir!—
> Doch nun hat's mich gewählt
> zu nie gekannter Qual;
> und werd ich heut' vermählt,
> so war's ohn' alle Wahl!
> Das war ein Müssen, war ein Zwang!

('... If I had the choice, I would choose you alone: you would be my husband, I would give the prize only to you!—But now I am chosen for never-known torment: and if I'm married today, it's without choosing! It's a compulsion, an obligation!')

Making allowances for the fact that she is carried away by Walther's song and the music Wagner provides for her, the Quintet still shows her feelings to be in a state of flux, from which only Sachs, himself deeply upset, can rescue her by defusing the situation in a deprecatory comparison, or rather rejection of a comparison, between himself and King Marke. It is touch and go for both of them; only Walther, a relative innocent and stooge, remains unmoved, because he cannot see what the situation is from any viewpoint other than his own. His Prize-song needs a baptism, just as a child does—'Dass die Weise Kraft behatten zum Leben' ('That the melody may have the strength to live').

It is Sachs's supreme inward moment of organizing and directing *Wahn* 'for nobler ends', balanced by his later intervention after Beckmesser has made nonsense of the Prize-song, and blames Sachs, as its author, for his humiliation. And so in contrast to the rowdy ensembles that have dissonantly concluded the first two acts, before Sachs gained control—or, in the case of Act II, gained and then lost it—we have an ensemble of five harmonious voices, guided but not led by Sachs: indeed, he uses the fact that the other four are going strong to give expression to his true feelings without being noticed—'Vor dem Kinde lieblich hold, möcht' ich gern wohl singen: doch des Herzens süss' Beschwer' galt es zu bezwingen' ('Before the lovely and fair child I would gladly sing out: but the heart's secret burden had to be subdued'). In the glorious harmony of the Quintet the individual words are no more discernible than they were in the chaos of Acts I and II; at their moment of highest consciousness, the characters are simultaneously bound together by sentiments which are too intimate for them to reveal to one another in isolation. So that, far from violating his principles of music-drama, Wagner is fulfilling them *in excelsis*, because public intelligibility of the characters to each other at this stage would be unthinkable; but they are all too emotion-filled to remain silent, so each gives voice to his or her inmost feelings while the other four, both merging and diverging, protect them from exposure. The moment is so true and so beautiful that one knows it must be shorter than one would like it to be, even if Wagner's modification of 'langsam' with 'doch leicht fliessend' is self-indulgently ignored; it is of the Quintet's essence, because of its truthfulness, that it should not requite our longing in the way that the Trio in *Rosenkavalier* does. Hans Sachs can control *Wahn*, but only briefly, being himself a part of it.

There is a sense in which the work ends with the Quintet, and no doubt one of these days an avant-garde producer, abetted by grateful conductor and singers, will actually bring the work to a close there. But needless to say it will be a mistake. Sachs's capacity to control the folk as well as his close circle is crucial; as he insists from the beginning, there is decadence in an art which isn't available for public enjoyment. But he never quite says, though he clearly enunciates all the premises from which we can draw the conclusion—and it is the supremely comic touch of *Meistersinger* that, while Wagner provides all we need to come to a correct understanding, he drags enough red herrings across the path to make it highly unlikely that we shall achieve it—that the art which the folk will appreciate, in being a *Morgentraum* ('Morning-dream') is a species of day-dream.

Die Meistersinger fascinates partly because on so many levels, and in such intricate ways, it enacts its significance; to think about it is a joy continuous with hearing it; to criticize it, in the sense of discursively understanding it, feels gratifyingly like enjoying it: the interpretation of the morning-dream, which, Sachs tells Walther, is the poet's task, is continued by us if we do our best to interpret the fabulous dream that is *Meistersinger*, this most beautiful of all day-dreams, and thus a fitting complement to Wagner's description to Liszt of *Tristan*. One of the privileges that we are granted by Wagner in this divine act of artistic generosity is the invitation to devote ourselves to doing for him what Sachs does for Walther. An extraordinary, awesome privilege and honour, which may well make us react as Sachs does when the crowd greets him with the overwhelming cry 'Awake!'

6. PARSIFAL: THE REFUSAL TO TRANSCEND

So much heavy weather has been made of *Parsifal*, not least by its creator in christening it a 'Stage Consecration Festival', which seems a wantonly bizarre piece of creative taxonomy, and in attempting to confine performances of it to Bayreuth (for which there is a good deal to be said, but not with Wagner's reasons looming largest) that it is hardly surprising that people are even more prejudiced or nervous in approaching it than in tackling the other great dramas. Among common and well-advertised grounds for viewing the work with distaste are that Wagner is exploiting Christianity for 'merely theatrical' ends, that he actually does, or (perhaps worse) merely appears to slump prostrate at the foot of the Cross, as Nietzsche famously phrased it, that it is a morbid and unintelligible *fin de siècle* brew of religion and sex, that it centres round an incoherent concept of redemption, and more straightforwardly that it is a merely slow-moving, anti-dramatic product of senile prolixity. There are more exotic charges, such as that there is a link

> between the monastic homosexuality of *Parsifal*, centred around the leadership of an intuitively inspired youth, and the not dissimilar fellowship of Ernst Röhm's troopers. Not the *Ring* but *Parsifal* was the Wagner work whose mythology was powerful enough to leave an indelible mark on Germany.[31]

There is no point at this stage of cultural development in getting upset about such inanities—or insanities: though it may be worth mentioning that Hitler forbad performances of *Parsifal* at Bayreuth after the outbreak of the Second World War, which suggests a disagreement as to its significance between him and Robert Gutman.

With so large a quantity of nonsense, delectable and otherwise, written about *Parsifal*, it is tempting to produce a new edition of Tappert's *Schimpflexicon*, devoted solely to this work. But so far as possible I shall eschew polemics and instead produce an account of *Parsifal* which shows it at once to be a supreme dramatic masterpiece and the satisfying climax of Wagner's investigations into the central questions that had obsessed him throughout his life. The first thing to get straight and hold to firmly is that *Parsifal* is not a religious work, except in the sense in which all the greatest art is religious, the sense that Lawrence had in mind when he said, 'One has to be so terribly religious to be an artist': a true and helpful remark in many contexts, but not when it is all-important to distinguish firmly between a mass by Palestrina, the *St Matthew Passion* of Bach, or even Beethoven's *Missa Solemnis*, on the one hand—they are religious works in that they set parts of the liturgy or the Bible to convert to or to fortify people in the Christian faith. They are not *about* religion: which, on the other hand, *Parsifal* is. So the fact that in Act I the knights celebrate the Eucharist is not an injunction to us to join in, but rather is there so that we can see what varied effects it has on Amfortas, Gurnemanz, the other knights, and Parsifal himself.

The fact that it is not a religious work should be obvious from the Prelude to Act I: certainly the first few bars, monodic, orchestrated with bewildering subtlety, arhythmic, and with no harmony even implied, suggest a chant; but as soon as the arpeggiated accompaniment begins, and the trumpet takes the theme up to its (the trumpet's) highest range, it is clear that the long, obviously dissectable theme is going to serve psychological purposes before ritualistic ones; and the restatement of the theme in C minor, with the trumpet nearly shrieking at the F G F pinnacle, leaves no doubt that we are in for *individual* anguish. Actually the Prelude, which is extremely easy to follow and *can* be thought of as mere mood setting, is as startlingly original— *elementarisch*, to use Wagner's term—as anything Wagner did, even more than the Preludes to Act I of *Lohengrin* or *Tristan*. For Wagner employs silences in a wholly novel way, and also uses blocks of orchestral sound, dramatically contrasting and imposingly hieratic, in a way that had no precedents, and from which Bruckner clearly learnt a great deal, though nothing in the Prelude reminds us of changes of organ registration in the way that Bruckner so often does. The central section of the Prelude, with its hushed strings and astonishingly bold brass statements, gives us the poles of tenderness and strength which delimit the range of virtues that the work celebrates, and, even more movingly, as the so-called Faith motive undergoes its final transformations for the time being, shows the combination of both which will only re-emerge in Parsifal's great closing benedictions. Then the gruelling last section of the Prelude, with the opening theme trying to rise and receive harmonic resolution, while the violins almost howl at its failure, and at last the resolution which caused Nietzsche to ask (but in a letter, while he retained his public façade of scorn and contempt), 'Has any painter ever depicted so sorrowful a look of love as Wagner has done in the final accents of his Prelude?'

If the Prelude does 'set the scene', it is, in the first part, by taking us into a disturbed and lofty ambience; in the second part, by giving us the sense of value which we shall keep and develop as we go through the work; and in the third, by involving us in untold anguish and getting us prepared for a long wait before the release from it. There is no question of its being concerned with anything other than the 'purely human', which Wagner's ideal of music-drama had always to give pride of place to. And when the curtain rises, it is on a peaceful and simple human scene. While the pace of the music is, of course, mainly very slow, it is as always with Wagner, thanks to the sureness of his harmonic sense, whatever strange regions it may lead us into, clear that things are moving: one never gets, as one does with the much more allegro-minded Berlioz, the sense of a static tableau not contributing to a dramatic process, or the far worse impression of breathlessly running on the spot.

If Wagner's instructions to conductor, singers, producer and scene-designer are followed, our first impression must be of Nature, fresh, benign (Gurnemanz and the Esquires have spent the night out of doors), but vulnerable and deserving and needing reverence. The point is reinforced by the arrival of Amfortas on the scene; though his syncopated, exhausted-sounding motive disturbs us, initially, more than Kundry's dissonant rending cry, because of its suggestion of a chronic state scarcely to be relieved, none the less in the miraculously blooming phrases surrounded by ravishing wind solos and a wonderful stillness, we have a sense of what nature can do, without any aid from 'Supernature':

207

Nach wilder Schmerzensnacht
nun Waldesmorgenpracht!
Im heil'gen See
wohl labt mich auch die Welle:
Es staunt das Weh,
die Schmerzensnacht wird helle—

('After a night of wild pain, now the glorious morning of the wood!
In the holy lake may the waters refresh me: my anguish is eased, and
my night of pain brightened.')

At every stage in Acts I and III one is reminded of Debussy's famous
phrase about *Parsifal*'s music being 'lit from the inside'. Certainly, as
Amfortas speaks of his relief, he is surrounded by a halo of beauty, but
a halo that is entirely *immanent*; and that makes my basic point about
the whole wonderful work. The radiance that streams from it, as well
as the sometimes frightening agonies of spirit, come from within the
characters and their natural settings; only at one or two uncertain
moments does Wagner betray what is unquestionably his central insight
and allow something transcendent to appear, causing momentary
embarrassment—the solo voice at the end of the Act I, as out of place
as the Heavenly Voice promising the heretics salvation at the end of
Act III of *Don Carlos*; and the dove at the end of the whole work,
fluttering above Parsifal's head. But even they don't matter: they only
show what we know from every other supreme artist, that when Wagner
has ventured into alarmingly strange regions of the soul he clutches at a
reassuring banality for a moment.

What relief Amfortas can get, then, at least for the moment, comes
from the waters of the lake and balsam from Arabia—exotic, but by no
means transcendental. Wagner's infallible dramaturgy is displayed
yet again in this first act as, having introduced us to all the characters
except the redeeming and the damned ones, he launches Gurnemanz
on his enthralling and heart-achingly beautiful narration: it is every bit
as dramatic as it would be if the events it retails were being enacted
before us, and makes all the points far more succinctly than if they *were*
presented. Sovereign economy is, as always, a hallmark of Wagner's
greatness. If one tries to summarize baldly what Gurnemanz narrates,
one finds that one is taking longer than he does! And his narration leads
so inevitably to the poised moment of hope that the 'pure fool', sufficiently ill-defined to be unrecognized even by such a professional pure-
fool spotter as Gurnemanz, should come as has been promised; instead
of which we get Debussy's 'perfect idiot', as lost and ignorant as if he

had strayed out of *Pelléas et Mélisande* itself. But unlike the characters in Maeterlinck–Debussy's unhelpful drama, he is eager to get things sorted out: and his pathetic incapacity even to give an answer to Gurnemanz's exasperated last question, 'Your name, then?' is a sure sign that he is in an archetypally Wagnerian identity-crisis, even if he does not yet know it. By the end of the act he does, however, know two things, both extremely painful: that his mother is dead, and that Amfortas's anguish is something that he can share. But he cannot do anything with either of these pieces of knowledge, the first retailed by Kundry and the second experienced at first hand as Amfortas cries for mercy.

The whole act, complex as it is, is set out in such masterly orderliness by Wagner that it should not present interpretive problems; but as soon as we try to see *Parsifal* as a 'religious work', it presents nothing else: for everything seems either irrelevant, blasphemous or banal. But seen as the most penetrating study we have of the psychopathology of religious belief in artistic terms, it is an incomparably involving experience. The peak of involvement comes in the Transformation Music, that incredible piece which needs to be reheard constantly for reminding us that however expressive one had thought art could be, Wagner can go one better. It combines, with the march-like tread and the bell motif on the one hand, the relentless counterpoint in the centre, and the threefold annihilating volleying forth of the syncopated, ultimately jagged and vehement motif of Amfortas's anguish on the other hand, some of the most extreme states of the human soul in a shatteringly brief period. By contrast with these sufferings, given verbal expression in Amfortas's great cries of 'Erbarmen!' ('Have mercy!'), we have the forthright extroversion of the knights, whose music, after their taking the bread and wine, is often felt to be inappropriately cheerful or even jaunty. But so long as it is taken with the requisite deliberation and firmness, it is a perfectly apt expression of their resolve to go out in the world and do good deeds: the Grail Brotherhood is not an enclosed, contemplative order, as their words after taking the wine make clear: 'Take of the wine,/Turn it anew/into life's fiery blood. Rejoicing in the unity/True to the brotherhood/To fight with blessed courage.' But though a chivalric order, and neither other-worldly not comparable to Röhm's homosexual troopers, it is not perfect, and even if Amfortas had not lost the spear to Klingsor all would not have been well. There is an inherent instability in it because it is at a loss as to how to cope with 'the flesh', or with Kundry (not a representation of 'the eternal feminine') or with the sheer ignorance of

Parsifal; complacency, over-confidence and self-righteousness characterize the order, and it is a telling touch when, early in Act I, the Third Esquire asks Kundry hostilely, 'Why do you lie there like a wild beast?' and she replies, 'Aren't the beasts holy here?' Gurnemanz's narration is told from the point of view of one of the order, so that we should recognize that he is not simply a purveyor of objective facts: he has a decided slant on the knights' plight; he calls Amfortas 'all too bold', but Amfortas lost the spear in attempting to vanquish the foe, which it was clearly someone's duty to do. The knights have failed to come to terms with their own latent sexuality, and those who have ventured forth have become Klingsor's knights, whom he loathes; both he and Kundry are pleased, in their different ways, as they see Parsifal wounding them. Wieland Wagner's famous 'Parsifal Cross', with its many misplaced ingenuities and bogus symmetries, is none the less valuable in opposing Klingsor's Flower Maidens, who are naturally unchaste but can be redeemed, and Titurel's knights, who are unnaturally chaste and therefore corruptible.

The first and third acts are of a piece; Act II is quite different in every respect, and plunges us into Klingsor's ambience as decisively as the Preludes to Acts I and III take us into the land of the Grail. The Prelude to Act II is energetic with a vile malevolence providing its dynamism, and in the opening scene we have, in the gruesome dialogue between Klingsor and Kundry, the most powerful expression in art of the hateful bondage in which one person can be to another, and, in its presentation of Klingsor, it shows Wagner once again pregnantly presenting the loathesome complexities of evil: like Hagen, he is intent that all should bend to his will, and, also like Hagen, he sees and recognizes the good. Klingsor becomes temporarily moving as he contemplates Parsifal and says:

> Ha! Wie stolz er nun steht auf der Zinne!
> Wie lachen ihm die Rosen der Wangen,
> da kindisch erstaunt
> in den einsamen Garten er blickt!

('Ha! How proudly he now stands on the rampart! How happily his cheeks are flushed as he gazes, childishly amazed, at the deserted garden!')

Perhaps it is Wagner's most memorable portrayal of the hellishness of being evil, and the futile capacity of the evil for recognizing the good—a cruel futility, but with no suggestion that it does anything to mitigate the evil which endures it.

The long and distinguished tradition of inane commentators, beginning with Nietzsche, who think that Parsifal is pure solely because
he does not lose his virginity to the Flower Maidens or to Kundry, and
therefore take the 'reiner Tor' to be synonymous with a chaste boy,
fail to notice that the only references in the whole of *Parsifal* to chastity
are in connection with Klingsor's self-castration, and that the most
striking is Kundry's cruel question, followed by a derisive laugh:
'Bist du keusch?' ('Are you chaste?') which is the one point she can
yet score at Klingsor's expense; and it is because he is chaste, thanks to
his self-mutilation, that he has power over Kundry, because he is
immune to her charms, though still plagued with longing, the Wagnerian *Furchtbare Not*. That is at least *prima facie* evidence that an identification of 'Reinheit' with 'Keuschheit' is at best an oversimplification,
more likely a fatal misunderstanding.

The scene of the Flower Maidens which follows is, in its languorous
sensuality, with its outrageous key-changes, a portrayal of Nature in
quite a different aspect from that of Act I, where it was restful and
healing; here it (for the Flower Maidens are more properly categorized
as vegetable than animal) is lulling, inducing will-lessness, indolent
sensuality, an attempt to reduce man to his merely animal element—
not vicious, but mindless. The lulling waltz-rhythms of 'Komm, komm,
holder Knabe!' and the maddeningly frivolous chattering of their
rivalry conveys their sub-human nature perfectly, and is vanquished by
that marvellously seductive and imperious 'Parsifal! Weile!' of Kundry.
As they disperse, with their final giggling moment of truthfulness:
'Du—Tor!' ('You—fool!'), Wagner embarks on the most complex,
exhausting and difficult scene in any of his works. Not only are the
processes of thought and feeling as expressed by the words often obscure and mystifying; the music which accompanies much of the scene
makes no pretence, much of the time, to being in any way appealing.
Only if insights of rare depth are being communicated can Wagner's
procedure be justified—the extreme demands he makes on the spec-
tator-listener: and there are moments when he had doubts, which we
may share. And yet it is hardly surprising, since he is operating at a
level so far beyond or beneath that of any previous dramatist, or artist
of any kind, that the odd moment of faltering is reassuring. The one
that I am thinking of in particular, and which I felt to be strange from
my earliest encounters with the work, turned out gratifyingly to be
a place where Wagner, Curt von Westernhagen and Raphael—and
probably others—felt comment called for. It is the moment when

Parsifal is being subjected to the fiercest spiritual blackmail which Kundry can bring to bear—her laughter at Christ, and her consequent desire to be redeemed by one hour in Parsifal's arms. Parsifal, arguing at a remarkably sophisticated level, replies that such an hour would damn them both; what is needed to end her suffering does not come from the source from which it (the suffering) flows—that is, her desire. But this is where the going gets really rough, and Wagner told Cosima that, 'I have never gone so far: this almost goes beyond the bounds of the permissible into the didactic.'[32] For once, that is, Wagner is unable to display, at least at this stage, his meaning; he has temporarily to lapse into telling us what it is, and the give-away is in the music, where a peculiarly banal version of the Faith motive comes in with a very 'willed' effect. For Parsifal has to explain that neither the way of desire nor the way of asceticism will bring salvation; and the complexities are such that, while the first alternative can be rejected by refusing Kundry's advances, the second has to be explained rather than enacted.

By this stage in the proceedings, Wagner has involved his characters and his audience in a web of moral and psychological themes which could only be explored in a very much fuller analysis than I can produce here. Kundry's first attempt on Parsifal, by which she brilliantly forces him to receive from her as 'love's first kiss' the dying kiss of his mother, is simultaneously a moment in which Wagner impresses on us the force of his vision with profoundly disturbing effect, as the strings rise and fall twice over extraordinarily uneasy harmonies, until Parsifal jumps up and shouts, 'Amfortas! The wound!' To suppose, as Nietzsche at least pretended to, that Parsifal is rejecting sexuality as such is grotesque. It is sexuality which, for one thing, is masquerading as something quite other; and for another thing, it is sexuality divorced from any healthy connotations at all—it is, to combine the points, sheer lust pretending to be mother-love; and it is in the doubleness of the falsity that Parsifal is enabled to achieve clarity of vision, and, as von Westernhagen says, to feel with full comprehension of its significance what had been merely gruesome sensation during the Grail scene. Simultaneously, Kundry is becoming more confused: she really believes that, by seducing Parsifal, what will happen will be that, instead of robbing him of his purity, she will regain hers. She will, to put it at its strongest, regain her virginity—an impossible ambition, but one which it makes perfectly good psychological sense to possess or postulate. She, like most of the characters in the drama, is confused about chastity and purity; hence one reason for her desperation, for most of the time she knows that to regain chastity is out of the question. And Parsifal is still a fool in that his only certain knowledge is that he must find the way back to Amfortas; Kundry becomes less and less the seductress in Klingsor's power, and more and more bent on her own salvation; but she has, as one might put it, turned up too late in the Wagnerian canon for Parsifal to save her by anything he does without her active co-operation. Already everything is pointing towards the truth that constitutes the final words of the drama, chanted by the boys, youths and knights—the last words Wagner produced as art:

> Höchsten Heiles Wunder!
> Erlösung dem Erlöser!

('Miracle of highest salvation! Redemption to the Redeemer!').

The point is that Parsifal has found what every other Wagnerian character was looking for: redemption begins at home. He cannot redeem Kundry until she has shown him the way to Amfortas, not because it is a bargain he is making with her: 'You show me the way to Amfortas, and I'll redeem you.' It is only when he has returned to the land of the Grail, and by virtue of recovering the spear has achieved the blessing of the water from the holy spring and the anointing by Gurnemanz, that he can redeem anyone else. It *is* possible to redeem other people, but only on the basis of having redeemed oneself first: redemption being, we must always remember, a metaphor for self-knowledge, self-fulfilment. Raphael, who has once again many illuminating things to say about *Parsifal*, makes a serious mistake when he writes:

> [Parsifal] actually redeems no one: he only *knows*. Others may be redeemed solely by seeing, and then pursuing, the example of Parsifal's perception of the world. [33]

It is perfectly clear that Parsifal *does* redeem Kundry, Amfortas and the fast-disintegrating Grail brotherhood: the final words are 'Redemption to the redeemer', not 'Redemption to the self-redeemer', though he *is* that.

Bewildering and hard-going as Act II is, it remains not only extraordinarily interesting but also moving, for even without grasping the moral-spiritual intricacies of it, Kundry's predicament is plain. She is in the position which for a human being is least appealing, if he has, as Kundry oddly and movingly still does have, self-respect: she cannot initiate *any* course of action wihch will purify or redeem her—she can only count on someone else's grace and mercy. The situation is not all that uncommon—Amfortas is in it too; and if the only redemption were

213

self-redemption, these creatures would be damned, which they are not so long as they desire redemption. Wagner's astonishing maturity as a dramatist enables him to present this desperate specimen, bent on destroying the hero, and playing one card after another, yet still retaining our sympathy for her. Her plight and Amfortas's are, in fact, strikingly similar, though he is a man prone to self-pity. Parsifal, through Kundry's kiss, learns the all-important *Mitleid* ('compassion'); he actually suffers with Amfortas, and thus understands Amfortas in understanding himself. Not surprisingly his understanding of Kundry is less complete, but he knows enough to realize where her salvation lies, and where his damnation would lie. But for complete enough knowledge he has to endure the *Wanderjahre*, or more accurately for him the *Irrejahre* that lie ahead, desolatingly conveyed in the Prelude to Act III, which is still more *elementarisch* than that to Act I. But that incredible piece of music, the most 'progressive' that Wagner wrote, conveys very much more; it may even be said to sum up in a uniquely concise fashion the emotional import of what has led to it: the beginning in resigned, gentle disintegration, the chromatic wanderings, and then the attempt of the Grail motif to assert itself as a pillar-like block of strength against the dissolving forces; but that motive itself, instead of reaching its resounding goal as it has so often in Act I, becomes Kundry's motive—the Grail is powerless against lust, indeed turns hideously into it. A decade after Wagner wrote this Prelude his enemy Nietzsche wrote *The Genealogy of Morals*, with its great long third part, 'What is the Meaning of Ascetic Ideals?'. In the end, he shows himself oddly hesitant: he could have found help to answer this, as so many of his other most searching and urgent questions, if he had been patient enough to attend to *Parsifal* instead of shrieking hoarse derision. However, Wagner has still more to say in the Prelude to Act III; for jerkily but insistently, recognizable through rhythmic distortions, the motive of the Pure Fool emerges and continues, supported by more and more powerful statements of the four consecutive notes which form the end of the first motive of the whole work, and which are especially associated with the Spear. And on that promise the turbulence exhausts itself and we are prepared for the last Act, Wagner's greatest musico-dramatic achievement, as intense as it is profound, and evidently one of the supreme utterances of the human spirit.

Once again, it is Nature that we are brought into contact with almost immediately, recovering from winter, and bringing even the aged and decrepit Gurnemanz fresh vitality, which he vainly tries to impart to

Kundry. But Nature's burgeoning is all the comfort that Gurnemanz has: he, like each of the other characters in the last act, is on the verge of despair when we first encounter him. One of the reasons why the act is so moving is that, seemingly gradually, but in fact at a remarkable pace, one after another of the agonies which it presents is assuaged or turned to triumph. Parsifal's arrival is a moment of extremely low vitality, his motive fragmentarily muttered in minor keys, Gurnemanz watching morosely; it is only when Parsifal has thrust the Spear into the ground and knelt before it, to the great rising and falling of unison strings, which finally move into the Spear motive, that Gurnemanz turns with growing excitement to Kundry and the beginning of the greatest of all recognitions in drama is enacted. We relive the wearisome, terrible years of both Parsifal and the Grail brotherhood before, following an explosion of self-recrimination, all the more moving for its irrationality—Parsifal is no superman—Parsifal is anointed and Gurnemanz sings the great phrase, full of solemn rejoicing and poignancy: 'Gesegnet sei, du Reiner, durch das Reine!' ('Be blessed, you pure one, by this purity!') From then on it is clear that all troubles will be resolved, and it is further proof of the total mastery Wagner had achieved in every dimension and on every level that, with the assurance therefrom comparatively early in the act, we still hang on every moment. The supreme dramatic moment, of course, is Gurnemanz's anointing of Parsifal with ointment, and as King. What follows, the so-called 'Good Friday Music', is not a chance for Wagner to extend himself lusciously over a lovely theme, but is of crucial significance. For it is as soon as Parsifal has been anointed that he notices for the first time the beauty of the meadows and flowers, no longer seductive or even, for the moment, sustaining, but simply existing, at rest and radiant. Wagner is at his most daring here, but with a cunning fully worthy of Sachs he has rendered his message into terms so headily sensuous that attention is diverted from the extraordinary words of Gurnemanz:

> Wie des Erlösten Leiden du gelitten,
> die letzte Last entnimm nun seinem Haupt!

('As you have endured the sufferings of the redeemed one, now lift the last burden from his head!')

I have no doubt that Raphael is right when he says that Parsifal, 'having now redeemed himself by insight and empathy, symbolizes a Christ who *does not have to die*, but lives'.[34] The point about not having to die is that Wagner, like many people, is repelled by the idea of the

215

Second Person of the Holy Trinity dying in order that the First Person should allow man into Heaven. He is impatient, in fact, with the transcendental, though as a late child of the Christian era he found it a handy mythology for expressing his own idiosyncratic, indeed epoch-making, insights. But once having got Christ down from the Cross, or rather stopped him getting on to it, Wagner reinforces his anti-transcendental redemptivist vision by directing our attention to Nature, to what, at the climax of the 'Good Friday Music', Gurnemanz refers to as 'all da blüht und bald erstirbt' ('all that lives and soon must die'). It is in *entsündigte Natur* ('transfigured Nature') that Parsifal will find what he has been looking for *beyond* Nature; for when Gurnemanz tells Parsifal that it is Good Friday, Parsifal breaks out into bitter lament, but is corrected with ineffable gentleness, and Gurnemanz stresses that 'All creatures now rejoice', because—and here the point is made again—

> Ihn selbst am Kreuze kann (Natur) nicht erschauen:
> da blickt sie zum erlösten Menschen auf.

('No more can (Nature) see Him Himself on the Cross: it looks up to redeemed mankind.')

Wagner achieves here the most remarkable balance; while Nature has never been painted in more exquisite colours, it is none the less no longer, in its unconscious loveliness, a temptation: it looks up to man who, in transcending Nature, has no need to transcend himself. And as the beauty of the scene plays itself out, Wagner produces perhaps the most lovely and tender moment of all: as opposed to the kiss of Act II, which precipitated Parsifal's crisis of consciousness, he now gently kisses Kundry's forehead, completing his relationship with her, so that she has only to attend to the return of the Spear to the Grail before she can sleep at last and forever.

The rest of the drama, powerful, tragic and finally calmly ecstatic, is straightforward enough, and there is no need for further commentary, except to say that, with his magnificent 'Nur eine Waffe taugt—' ('Only one weapon serves') Parsifal is singing music which combines an intensity of purity with experience that is elsewhere achieved, I think, only in the slow movement of Beethoven's last quartet, Op. 135, and in the final union of Pamina and Tamino in *Die Zauberflöte*.

I hope that in the light of this brief account of the work, it won't be necessary to argue in detail with starkly opposed views of it, especially ones which see it as a total *bouleversement* on Wagner's part: on the contrary, it was his *summum*, the work in which he came as near as possible to providing answers to those torturing and hydra-headed questions which by their nature can't have answers of a pat, formulable kind. Actually, in his other works he had investigated issues that he doesn't so much as touch on in *Parsifal*; but the great problem of erotic love *versus* asceticism has received here a development both decisive and surprising. So much is surprising about *Parsifal*—it is one of the most original works of art ever created—that it's not altogether surprising that it should have been so thoroughly misunderstood, even if the grossness of the misunderstandings is perplexing. The only one I am at all concerned to combat here is that *Parsifal* is 'decadent' and 'morbid'. The atmosphere of the work is often unhealthy *in the sense that* the atmosphere in a hospital is unhealthy, and in no other way. Thomas Mann, always thrilled by the equivocal, the suspect and so forth, remarks:

> Take the list of characters in *Parsifal*: what a set! One offensive and advanced degenerate after another! A self-castrated magician; a desperate double personality, composed of Circe and a repentant Magdalene, with cataleptic transition stages; a lovesick high-priest, awaiting the redemption that is to come to him in the person of a chaste youth; the youth himself 'pure' fool and redeemer, in his way also an extremely rare specimen.[35]

That is a reasonably accurate account of the leading characters, so far as it goes, but the intention behind it is clear: it is to get us to share Mann's view of the work as 'languorously sclerotic', gorgeously over-ripe, fascinating by virtue of its unhealthiness. He is merely reacting positively to what he sees as the same phenomenon as Nietzsche, where in *Der Fall Wagner* he exclaims: 'Indeed, transposed into hugeness, Wagner does not seem to have been interested in any problems except those which now preoccupy the little decadents of Paris. Always five steps from the hospital.'[36] One resists yet again a *tu quoque*, just as one fleetingly recalls, reading the Mann passage, that he chose as the location for his diagnosis of modern life a sanatorium. Of course, one finds such people in a hospital: and Wagner, Nietzsche and Mann all agreed in thinking the modern world a sick place. The whole question is about the attitude which is taken up towards the sickness, or many sicknesses, that the artist discerns. And there can be no doubt that Wagner's urgent desire in *Parsifal* is to find a treatment of the most efficacious kind; there is even less ground for attributing to him than to Nietzsche a fascination with sickness, decadence or depravity for their own sakes, and very much less than in the case of Mann, who would have suffocated in clear air.

Nietzsche's charge is all the more strange since he spent almost all his adult sane life preoccupied with the 'patient', i.e. modern civilization in its decline. But by the time he wrote *Der Fall Wagner* he was so exhausted with his own non-artistic attempts at diagnosis and prescription that he looked to art as a relaxation, a refreshment—and found *Carmen*. Not that any musical person has anything but admiration for that work, but it's odd that Nietzsche should not have felt that Don José has *his* problems, and so does even Carmen herself. But we don't feel that they matter so much as the problems of Amfortas and Kundry; and that was, for Nietzsche, a relief. Even so the grounds for accusation of Wagner remain strange—at least, *these* grounds. What is true, and may account for Nietzsche's frantic search for plausible criticisms, is that *Parsifal* is an extraordinarily taxing and shattering experience, not to be undertaken lightly. Those who, having heard it or some of it once or twice, withdraw from it on grounds of its 'religiosity' or morbidity, might ask themselves whether what they really object to is not simply the extreme demands it makes on them—demands, they may feel, which are in excess of any that art should ever make. Hence the tendency to recategorize it as 'ritual', and then conclude that it is bogus.

If my quotations from Erich Heller about the *religio intransitiva* of Nietzsche and Rilke are correct, then it is they rather than Wagner who are getting art or pseudo-art (*Zarathustra*) to do the work of religion; on the contrary, *Parsifal* demonstrates how in detranscendalizing Christianity it is possible to find value in a world not created and governed by incomprehensible Goodness and Power.

A last point about *Parsifal*: in the greatest art there has always been transmitted a sense of some fundamental inscrutability, and it has normally been attributed to Fate, or God, or the gods, or to something external to man. And tragedy, where inscrutability tends to be given its head, has often been thought to be the expression of some final element of the ineffable at the heart of things: we are condemned always to remain in darkness about what matters most. But increasingly in the modern age, with the collapse of Christianity and the rise of the novel and of music-drama, inscrutability has been relocated as being in the heart of man. Going with that relocation is the faint hope that we might finally become less opaque to ourselves and to each other. One way in which that could happen would be by understanding better the art of Wagner, and above all of *Parsifal*.

CONCLUSION: EROTICISM AND NOBILITY

'Literary criticism can be no more than a reasoned account of the feeling produced upon the critic by the book he is criticizing,' writes Lawrence, and the same applies to criticism of any of the arts. 'We judge a work of art by its effect on our sincere and vital emotion, and nothing else,' he continues, and one wishes he were speaking for more than the tiny proportion of critics who even try to do that. It is, at least, what I have been attempting; and it therefore leaves the way open— but then it always is—for my readers to simply disagree. In the case of Wagner, that danger is especially likely to be realized. For it does seem that, more than any other artist whom many people regard as being of the highest stature, he just repels many musically and operatically sensitive listeners. The sheer sound of his music is painful to them, in a way that isn't true of Bach, or Mozart, or Schubert, or Beethoven. Nothing I write can do anything to alter that situation. But I feel it incumbent upon me to do my best to explain it. It seems to me that the roots of non-ideological anti-Wagnerism are two. First, there is the sense of a peculiarly insistent voice which is dominating and aggressive to an altogether overpowering extent. And second there is the strange blend of eroticism and nobility to which I have already referred in discussing *Tristan*, and which makes many listeners feel a curious kind of insincerity to be characteristic of Wagner's art.

It is in the very nature of these objections that they resist precise formulation, and *a fortiori* that replying to them is probably out of the question. However . . . I am in the position of seeing what people who raise the first objection mean, but not myself being able to feel it: just the contrary. A few bars of Wagner out of context, and encountered almost anywhere, are liable to have a strong effect on me—an effect unlike that of a few bars of other composers whom I love strongly. There *is* a difference, one which I shall have to move on to the second objection to characterize more adequately; but before doing that I want to scotch the idea that Wagner is especially insistent. Or rather, I want to refine it. He is an enormously eloquent advocate, but for everyone in turn. Just as Mozart can work one up into a passion of jealousy with the Count's aria in Act III of *Figaro*, so Wagner gets one to share the rage and frustration of Alberich at the callous flirtations of the Rhine-maidens. Wagner is dealing very largely with characters who are, and often take themselves to be, built on a grand scale. There is consequently a portentousness about the atmosphere of almost all Wagnerian drama which I would not for a moment deny. The only question is whether it is justified. I have tried in my brief accounts of some of the leading elements in the post-*Lohengrin* dramas to show why I think that it is. What is unfair, and has been and for that matter still is practised at Wagner's expense, is the playing and judging of his work by those 'bleeding chunks' which at one time were excusable, perhaps necessary, but which no longer have a place in the repertoire. I do not wish to be priggish, or only mildly so. Obviously the Overture to *Die Meistersinger* is indispensable for many festive occasions. But the Preludes to *Tristan* or *Parsifal*? Almost never. Since nearly all Wagner's music, including most of his preludes and overtures, is dramatic, to listen to them, or other extracts such as the gruesome 'Forest Murmurs' (Toscanini's favourite Wagner excerpt), is bound to give a gravely misleading impression. It is also the main factor, I suspect, in the formation of the vulgar view that Wagner's music is typically loud. But I hardly need to descend to that level.

Anyone who claims to be unable to bear the typical Wagnerian sound should be carefully interrogated to find out whether he knows what it is. I am perfectly serious about this, since my campaigning efforts on Wagner's behalf have lasted a quarter of a century, and prejudice and ignorance (I refer still to non-ideological objections) are still amazingly prevalent. Once they have been effectively eliminated, it is a matter of getting people to listen intelligently to at least a whole act of one of the works, preferably Act I of *Die Walküre*, which effectively disposes in the course of one hour of many deep-dyed myths of anti-Wagnerism. If that doesn't do the trick, it is most probably because of the Wagnerian fervour or *Rausch*, which may be resisted either because *any* intoxicant is regarded with suspicion, or because this particular one so blatantly has designs on its imbibers. Pressed on this point, people usually become incoherent since it isn't clear how Wagner has designs on his listeners in a way that other composers do not. And at this stage the only way to make progress, if progress is to be made, is to move on to the second type of objection—that the characteristic Wagnerian 'smell' is an undesirable one, rather like a potent perfume being used to disguise either a very raw or a putrescent odour. That is one way of stating the feeling of a distasteful alliance between eroticism and nobility. I use both these terms synecdochically, as gestures in the direction of congeries of at least contrasting states. Many listeners would agree, I take it, that there is a typically noble sound which is instantly recognizable as Wagnerian, and which is to be found in its least adulterated form in the Wanderer's music in Act I of *Siegfried*, and in a great deal of Act III of *Parsifal*. What is disturbing, though, is that it is also pervasive in *Tristan*, even in the love scene and in Isolde's *Verklärung*. That this phenomenon should upset many people, members of the 'permissive society' though they are, is not surprising. For what Wagner does a great deal of the time is what other major artists have only wanted, or been able to do for a comparatively small part of it, and that is to use the resources at his disposal—and in his case they were unusually rich—to reveal different layers of the mind working simultaneously. It can be done, though with difficulty, in poetry, but song or opera is its obvious home. But it would be a mistake to say that the words carry the nobility while the music looks after the eroticism. It is rather that it is in the power of music to a unique degree to express or evoke diverse or even conflicting states simultaneously. The presence of words just makes it quite clear that that is what is happening.

I do not want to expand much on this theme here, because it seems to me to need pretty thorough treatment if it is to be made convincing to anyone not predisposed to conviction. I ask those who have frequented Wagner's music whether something on these lines doesn't tally with their experience. It is easy to feel oneself liberated in the now vulgar sense if one recognizes and welcomes this basic feature of Wagner's art. That would be a pity, because one of the tasks of the greatest art is always to disturb, and it strikes me as a genuinely and properly disturbing feature of Wagner's art that he so often disturbs our complacencies about the relations within the psyche between radically disparate elements. To revert to the Lawrentian terminology of the introduction, Wagner often gives us the 'single undifferentiated element' of carbon, but more often, and more alarmingly, gives us simultaneously the 'diamond' aspect and the 'charcoal', or in approximately equivalent Freudian terms, the ego and the id. But that *is* very approximate, because Wagner, though he is perfectly capable of seeing and depicting the id more or less as Freud saw it, as entirely egotistic, asocial, violent and sexual, is more concerned with that part of the self which, while it is not usually on public display, may have nothing objectionable about it. To put it at its simplest, which is over-simple, his characters are often remarkably uninhibited, and when they are not obviously being so, Wagner often gets the orchestra to give them away, as it were.

Wagner was astonishingly unillusioned about man, without being disillusioned. No doubt his own uniquely protean, passionate and fervently intellectual nature helped him to achieve and maintain his extraordinary degree of insight, and his own fearlessness gave him the courage and love of humanity which enabled him to present it with the limitless audacity and respect which characterizes this unparalleled art, its candour, ardour, lack of all pretence and its underlying, when not overriding grandeur. How can one praise it adequately without lapsing into gushing banalities? (The reader may feel that I have raised that question a bit late.) And yet the terms in which one man expresses his love and admiration may be very close to those in which another man expresses his revulsion. This art which claims to tell us all about ourselves is clearly going to create a sensation not unlike Freud—or, rather, did create such a sensation half a century before the founder of psychoanalysis. I find myself invoking Freud again, and again only partly willingly. But the kind and extent of the hostility which both of them did and still do suffer is so similar that it would be arch to avoid mentioning it. In attempting to rid men of false ideas about their nature and the mixture of wildly divisive forces in it which always make possible the most monstrous vileness, and which under very privileged circumstances make possible astounding heroism, and in their stress on the omnipresence of the erotic in man, above all that last element, they inescapably incurred the wrath of Christians, utopians and egalitarians. And D. H. Lawrence was to suffer still more cruelly, since his art lacked the seductiveness of music, and did not daunt by virtue of being scientific, genuinely or allegedly.

It is characteristic of revolutionaries to be unclear about the nature of the revolution which they want, or are engaged in creating. Wagner's own unclarities on this subject are notorious, and I have dealt with them at sufficient length—i.e. very briefly—in the introduction to this essay. Lawrence was a lot clearer about what he wanted to do, but even he sometimes confused different issues. In his defence of the novel as the supreme art form, he is, as we saw, very insistent on everything in a novel being relative to everything else. But while the fact that nothing is taken as absolute in a novel is extremely important, if it is true, it is independent of that other element which Lawrence stresses, and which is actually a much more personal concern of his: that no one in a novel can get away with being grand but bogus, in the way that blank verse or a surging orchestral accompaniment makes possible. In fact that isn't true, since incantatory and magniloquent prose can help a character in a novel a great deal, and do in fact do so frequently in Lawrence's own works. The point which he really wanted to make was that there should be checks in a work of art against letting a single character, often the artist's mouthpiece, have things all his own way. And since he was for obvious reasons keen to argue for the supremacy of the novel, and the novel had been a more obviously 'realistic' or naturalistic art form than any other, it was an easy slip for Lawrence to make to think that the vulnerability of characters in a novel was related to there being a w.c. on the premises. It might be a help, but it most certainly is not a necessity. And Lawrence is notoriously capable of special pleading on behalf of his most cherished views. In short, there is no special advantage in being a novelist if what you are concerned with is fairness. The checks which can be applied by a novelist to stop anyone, including himself, from getting away with anything, can equally well be applied by a music-dramatist. And we do in fact find Wagner using his rich resources freely in order to question the candour or capacities for self-deception of his characters. The most straightforward example is the entry of the gods into Valhalla at the end of *Rheingold*, where the genuine grandeur unquestionably co-exists with an uneasy grandiosity on Wotan's part, which Loge punctures in his final words.

In dealing with these very deep resistances to Wagner's art in a very sketchy way, I have deliberately reinvoked the name of D. H. Lawrence, and made mention of Freud. For all these three trail-blazers have encountered, and still do, the most colossal amount of hostility, and evidently the grounds for the hostility are to a considerable extent overlapping. For all of them put the erotic element in man into the centre of their picture of him: all of them agree with Nietzsche, to bring in the last crucial name in this list of great geniuses who have determined to an enormous extent how we think and feel about ourselves, that 'the kind and degree of a man's sexuality reach up into the very pinnacle of his spirit'.

It seems to me to be appropriate to end with the invocation of these non-musical names, because it is a commonplace that Wagner has been hugely influential in general cultural fields in a way unique among composers. I wanted to do something a little less trite than merely place him among familiar figures—to suggest that other people besides me might find their understanding, and so their gratitude and love, growing as each of these heroes of the spirit illuminates the others. Love notoriously cannot be commanded; I feel, though, that it is more than simple good fortune that my love for the works of Wagner has grown over the years as I have come to know not only his *oeuvre* better, but also those of Freud, Nietzsche and Lawrence. And so it would have been, to me at least, artificial to make my parting salute to Richard Wagner while refraining from a similar gesture towards those other figures who may even now give us hope, if there is hope to be had.

SEVEN

Wagner's Musical Language

DERYCK COOKE

WHAT REALLY MATTERS to us about Wagner—without which nothing else would have mattered at all—is his great series of music-dramas; and what really matters to us about these music-dramas—without which they would soon have been forgotten—is the magnificent music which is their ultimate means of expression. But understanding and appreciation of Wagner's music have been largely bedevilled and obscured by a misguided obsession with his so-called 'system of leading-motives'.

For example, when Brünnhilde, in Act II of *Die Walküre*, comes to Siegmund to tell him that he is doomed to die in his forthcoming fight with Hunding, her appearance is accompanied by an orchestral passage (Ex. 1). This complex of two thematic ideas, entering here for the first time in the tetralogy, has an overwhelming musico-dramatic impact; and with any composer but Wagner, commentators would surely concentrate on the stuff of the music itself, as a superb piece of musical dramatization, throwing the shadow of death irrevocably across the dramatic action. There is the oppressive solemnity, due to a bold reliance on the sound of brass and timpani alone; the uncanny stillness, achieved by a liberal use of silence, punctuated by hushed drum-beats; and the supremely tragic-heroic character of the music itself, with its sense of posing a dark question—some attempt might even be made to account for the emotional effect of the music by examining the actual notes employed to create it.

With Wagner, however, nothing of this kind is thought necessary, since it has long been understood that idea A is the 'Fate' motive, and idea B (itself ending with a modified double restatement of A) is the 'Annunciation of Death' motive: they enter here simply because

Siegmund's fate is sealed, the Valkyrie having come to announce his death, and nothing more needs to be said.

Ex. 1

But is this in any way a sufficient response to the music? We have to remember that it was not the composer himself who attached these labels to his musical ideas, but the commentators who came after him. Their intentions were entirely laudable, since when *Der Ring des Nibelungen* (and *Tristan* and *Parsifal*) first impinged on the world, the complexity of the music baffled many listeners, and so some kind of 'thematic guide' to it was thought necessary by Wagner's admirers. But unfortunately, the names they attached to his musical ideas were essentially intellectual (and therefore circumscribed), whereas for Wagner these musical ideas—as he said in *Oper und Drama* (*Opera and Drama*), written before the works themselves but with some of the musical ideas for them in mind—were to be 'the carriers of feeling' (and therefore completely uncircumscribed). As a composer he was caught up, during the act of creation, in the *emotions* of his characters— their loves and hates, their hopes and despairs; but the commentators, *thinking* about his scores, and trying to explain the significance of the musical ideas, came up mainly with labels relating them in the most factual way to the characters, objects and events of the outward dramatic action.

And since they very rarely gave any musical reasons for attaching a given label to a given thematic idea, they have left it open to the exponents of 'pure music' to ridicule the whole 'system of leading-motives'. How, it is asked, can music possibly convey conceptual ideas— how can concepts like 'fate' and 'annunciation of death' be expressed by, respectively, a three-note thematic phrase over two chords (*A*), and an eight-note theme over a sequence of seven chords (*B*)? And this argument is absolutely right, of course—they cannot: looked at from this point of view, Wagner's practice can only seem arbitrary, and hence misguided and futile. However, it was not Wagner who was misguided, but the point of view of the commentators. He never intended his music to convey the conceptual ideas of the drama—the drama itself was there for just that purpose; the music was intended to express the profound emotional and psychological realities behind the concepts.

Let us ignore here that group of 'pure-music' theorists who hold the extreme view that music is incapable of conveying not only conceptual ideas, but also aspects of human feeling and psychology: the whole history of opera, and of the reactions of audiences to opera, makes their position *ipso facto* untenable. One recent commentator on Wagner, Robert Donington,[1] is surely right in at last setting aside the conceptual labels so long attached to our two thematic ideas *A* and *B*, and saying that these ideas have to do with 'our awareness of mortality . . . an emotion which goes very deep into our hearts, with a suggestion of finality such as the acceptance of our mortal destiny must necessarily bring'. Even so, his opinion, which we instinctively feel to be justified, is not backed by any musical reasoning. Is it possible to provide any?

Turning to idea *A*, and considering first its three-note melodic phrase on its own, one feels instinctively that its rising inflexion—an overall rise of a tone, achieved through a fall of a semitone and a rise of a minor third—asks a question (Ex. 2a). Instinct is one thing, facts are another: Wagner's melodic phrase follows something like the same pattern as the opening three-note melodic phrase of the finale of Beethoven's last string quartet (Op. 135 in F major). This is a rise of a semitone through a fall of a minor third and a rise of a diminished fourth (Ex. 2b), and underneath it Beethoven himself wrote the question 'Muss es sein?' ('Must it be?').

'Must it be?' is a metaphysical question, involving the whole idea of fate. Whether Beethoven intended the question metaphysically or humorously has long been a subject of argument (and the answer is probably—to use Hans Keller's phrase—'the one does not exclude the

Ex. 2

other'). However, there is a much more simple and exact musical precedent for Wagner's melodic phrase: in its actual form, it was one of the immemorial cadential clichés in German operatic recitative,* when a character asked a question, going back to Mozart, and probably earlier. Wagner's operatic horizon, in the past, was bounded by Mozart, and so here are four examples from Mozart, Spohr, Weber and Marschner (Ex. 3). Ex. 3a is from Mozart's *Idomeneo* (1780): Elektra expresses her consternation at the news that Idomeneo's ship has been sunk, in the words 'Idomeneo is dead?' Ex. 3b, from Spohr's *Faust* (1813), shows Faust asking Mephistopheles whether the paltry sensual pleasures he has brought him were what he was really seeking—'Was that my goal?' In Ex. 3c, from Weber's *Der Freischütz* (1820), Aennchen asks Agathe, 'Can you think that I don't sympathize with you?' And in Ex. 3d, from Marschner's *Hans Heiling* (1832), Anna reproaches Heiling for having wooed her with empty pleasures: 'Why have you tempted my heart with vanities?'†

These examples could be multiplied indefinitely from German operas of the period, and there are examples to be found even in Wagner's own works. Ex. 4a, from *Der fliegende Holländer* (1841), occurs when the Dutchman asks Daland, 'Shall I see your daughter today?' And even as late as *Die Walküre* (1856), there is a subtle, only partly harmonized example (Ex. 4b), when Sieglinde asks herself a question about the unexpected stranger: 'Who has come into the house, and lies there on the hearth?'

So much for the *melodic* aspect of *A*: clearly its mood would seem to be a questioning one, and even—with its solemnity and its resemblance to Beethoven's 'Must it be?'—a profoundly questioning one. But we still have to take the harmony into consideration, and the harmony is something quite revolutionary. The conventional way of harmonizing

---

* In calling it a cliché, one is not making any value-judgement. Cadences, even in the greatest music, are often clichés.

† In the Mozart, of course, according to contemporary notational conventions, the first of the two C sharps would have been sung as a D, making an appoggiatura; but this practice dropped out long before Wagner's time, when Mozart's operas were performed exactly as written.

Ex. 3

Ex. 4

the 'question-cliché' of German recitative was as an imperfect cadence, as Exs. 3 and 4 show, except for Ex. 3d, which is quite exceptional, and Ex. 4b, where an imperfect cadence is implied. And an imperfect cadence, ending on the dominant, is itself a musical 'question' (to which the simplest answer is a tonic chord, though it is hardly ever given, since it would greatly weaken the 'question' effect of the imperfect cadence). It will be noticed that Wagner himself uses this conventional imperfect-cadence harmonization for the melodic phrase of *A* at the point where it rounds off idea *B* (the last two bars of Ex.1); and during the actual dialogue between Brünnhilde and Siegmund, some of Siegmund's questions are set to *B*, so that its concluding melodic phrase of *A*, conventionally harmonized, retains its old function as the 'question-cliché'. But at one point this is followed immediately by the revolutionary harmonization of it (idea *A* itself), with the melodic phrase at the same pitch, as Brünnhilde gives her tragic answer. It happens when Siegmund asks, 'Tell me, who are you, who appear before me, so beautiful and grave?', and Brünnhilde replies, beginning on a deathly monotone against the statement of *A* on the brass, 'I appear only to those who are doomed to die' (see page 231).

With the two harmonizations of *A* set side by side in this way—first the conventional one and then Wagner's revolutionary one—we can hear clearly how he turned the old 'question-cliché' into something rich and strange. Never before, in the history of music, had this well-worn phrase been supported by such an extraordinary harmonic progression. In bars 5–6 of Ex. 5, the first chord is a perfectly simple E minor triad,* using the first melodic note, B, as its dominant; but the second chord, amazingly, is the major chord a *semitone lower*, making, with the final melodic note, C sharp, a dominant seventh on D sharp.†

Strictly speaking, one supposes, this form of *A* can still be analysed as an imperfect cadence in G sharp minor—a minor triad on the flat submediant (E) followed by a dominant seventh on the dominant (D sharp). But since what we *hear* is an E minor triad leading to a dominant

---

* In the full score, Wagner uses the easiest possible notation for the Wagner tubas, which are transposing instruments. In the vocal score, to make the best ocular sense, the chord is notated enharmonically as C flat, G natural and F flat; likewise, in the first bar of Ex. 1, the F natural is notated as E sharp, and in the fifth bar, the G natural as F double-sharp. I have notated what we actually *hear* in each case—triads of E minor, D minor and E minor respectively, to make clear the harmonic sense.

†Again, in the vocal score, to make the best ocular sense, the chord is notated enharmonically as a dominant seventh on E flat, but I prefer to notate it as a dominant seventh on D sharp, as in bar 6 of Ex. 1.

Ex. 5

seventh on D sharp (or, in the first two bars of Ex. 1, a D minor triad leading to a dominant seventh on C sharp), the progression is one of those in which Wagner slips outside normal tonality altogether. This is enhanced by the fact that the dominant sevenths do not resolve at all: the one on C sharp in bars 2–3 of Ex. 1, which implies the tonality of F sharp minor, is followed by a second statement of idea *A* a tone higher —a triad of E minor leading to a dominant seventh on D sharp; and *this* dominant seventh (bars 6–7), which implies the tonality of G sharp minor, is followed by a statement of idea *B*, in purest F sharp minor. The whole passage, of course, is now revealed as having been in F sharp minor; but the tonality of bars 1–8 is uncertain in the extreme, and is only anchored to F sharp minor by the dominant pedal (C sharp) of the timpani.

Wagner's revolutionary harmonization of the old 'question-cliché' modifies its conventional questioning character extremely. The replacement of the normal dominant, expected as second chord, by a remote dominant seventh implying a far-reaching key switch, gives the idea a mysterious, enigmatic character; also the failure of that dominant seventh to resolve leaves it floating on the air, homeless, and this greatly intensifies the slight element of mournfulness inseparable from any quiet, sustained dominant seventh.[2] Moreover, when it follows the conventionally harmonized form of itself, at the same melodic pitch, thereby echoing the simple melodic question in a much darker harmonic context (as in Ex. 5, bars 3–6), it implies that the question is far more serious than is imagined by the questioner—a tragic one in fact. as is conveyed by that lost, homeless, mournful dominant seventh, fading into silence on the sombre but noble voices of the Wagner tubas,

There is another, very long-term way in which Wagner reveals the difference between the conventional harmonization of the old 'question-cliché' and his own revolutionary one. At the very end of *Die Walküre*, when Brünnhilde lies asleep, surrounded by the wall of fire, the melodic phrase of *A* takes on yet another harmonic form—a kind of imperfect-cadence harmonization (a rather different one from that used for its appearance at the end of idea *B*), with the D minor triad followed by a triad of E major (Ex. 6a). This, although very near to the conventional harmonization of the 'question-cliché', is still new and strange by reason of its tonal context: the conventional harmonization would really be the *first inversion* of the D minor triad leading to the triad of E major as the *dominant* of the key of A minor (Ex. 6b), but what we have (Ex. 6a) is the *root position* of the D minor triad (necessary to refer back to idea *A*, as in Ex. 1) leading to the triad of E major as the *tonic* of E major (*Die Walküre* ends in E major ten bars later). This is a *very* strange cadence; the best way to explain it is to say that Wagner brought an imperfect cadence, with its open ending on the dominant, into a closed tonic context; and in this context the cadence no longer asks a question, but has an air of finality. The implication is that the question of fate is to remain peacefully closed until Brünnhilde awakes.

Ex. 6

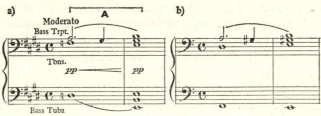

And when she does awake (some twenty years later, in Act III of *Siegfried*), she sings 'Lang war mein Schlaf' ('Long was my sleep') to

Ex. 6a from *Die Walküre*, in the same key of E major, followed immediately by 'Ich bin erwacht' ('I am awake') to idea *A* as in bars 5–7 of
Ex. 1, which now answers Ex. 6a a tone higher as it originally answered
bars 1–3 of Ex. 1 a tone higher. The implication is that, although the

Ex. 7

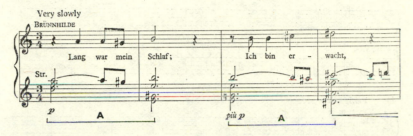

question of fate was closed while Brünnhilde slept, it is immediately
resumed now that she is awake; also that the question is again far more
serious than she or Siegfried for the moment imagine, and that it is
in fact a tragic one, as is confirmed by the events of *Götterdämmerung*.
And this placing of Ex. 6a (so similar to the conventional harmonization
of the 'question-cliché') side by side with idea *A* from Ex. 1 (Wagner's
revolutionary harmonization of it) reveals once more the profoundly
expressive character of the latter.

To return to the Valkyrie's annunciation of death to Siegmund
(Ex. 1). If there could be any doubt concerning the answer to question
A, that answer is provided by idea *B*: its ascending minor melodic line
begins with a slow phrase often used before as a lament for the death of
a hero (which is then put in question again by its concluding double
restatement of *A*). In *The Language of Music*, I attempted to show that
ascending minor music, generally speaking, expresses an outgoing
feeling of unhappiness, or of protest against unhappiness, and that to
move upward firmly and decisively from the lower dominant, through
the tonic, to the minor third, gives a strong infusion of courage or
heroism, in that it boldly acknowledges the existence of tragedy (aiming
at the minor third, which is the essential tragic note of the minor scale),
and moves onward (upward) into the thick of it. Examples—in very
different emotional contexts—are Purcell's 'In the Midst of Life We
Are in Death'; Handel's 'At Persecution I Can Laugh' from *Saul*, and
'Since by Man Came Death' in *Messiah*; the song 'Muth' ('Courage')
from Schubert's *Winterreise*; Otello's suicidal cry 'Ho un arma ancor!'

('I have a weapon yet!') from Verdi's opera; and three examples from
Wagner's *Ring*—idea *B* in Ex. 1 which we are discussing, and (Ex. 8a
and b) the so-called 'Volsung Race' and 'Siegfried' motives.[3]

Ex. 8

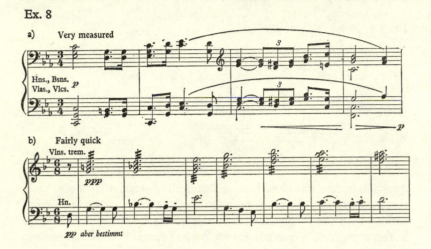

A great deal depends on the speed of the phrase, of course: the
'Siegfried' theme is normally lively and so expresses heroic vitality;
both our idea *B* and the 'Volsung Race' theme are extremely slow, and
so have something like the effect of a funeral march for a hero. Wagner's
half-conscious model here was undoubtedly the Funeral March of
Beethoven's 'Eroica' Symphony. A change of speed necessarily changes
the emotional effect. By greatly slowing down the vital 'Siegfried'
theme, and giving it the greatest possible weight, Wagner was able to
use it with magnificently poignant effect in Siegfried's Funeral March,
together with the 'Volsung Race' theme at less than its original slow
tempo; conversely, the slow 'Volsung Race' theme, greatly speeded
up, is used to express heroic vitality in Act I of *Die Walküre*, when
Siegmund turns to draw the sword from the tree ('Siegmund heiss ich,
und Siegmund bin ich!'/'Siegmund I am called, and Siegmund I am').
Likewise, our idea *B*, greatly speeded up and turned to the *major*,
expresses the change from lamentation to exultation when Brünnhilde
changes her mind and decides to support Siegmund in his forthcoming
fight with Hunding ('und Siegmund lebe mit ihr!').

At the moment of its first appearance, however—the moment of the
Valkyrie's annunciation of death to Siegmund (Ex. 1)—it is extremely

slow, and it sounds like Siegmund's death-knell. The hard tone of the trumpets and trombones, even in pianissimo, and the powerful crescendo leading to the 'question' of the concluding statement of *A* in its conventional harmonization, give the whole theme a protesting character—which is nevertheless rendered rather tentative by the sudden drop to pianissimo on the last chord. And as we have seen (Ex. 5), the tendency is for it to be followed by *A* in Wagner's own mysterious harmonization—also with a crescendo followed by a drop to pianissimo on the mournful dominant seventh—which implies that both questioning and protest are, alas, quite useless.

This fairly detailed examination of ideas *A* and *B* shows why they are so appropriate as an expression of an emotional situation in which a hero comes face to face with his tragic destiny—his imminent death—and as the expression of his question-and-answer dialogue with the arbiter of that destiny, in which his questions receive much more tragic answers than he imagines they will.

And it also serves to show the unique nature of Wagner's music—its phenomenal power of compressing into a few bars the most profound emotional and psychological experience, which makes conceptual thematic labels quite pointless. How are we to account for this phenomenal power of Wagner's? In two ways, I believe, both stemming from the composer he admired above all others, Beethoven. In the first place, he possessed Beethoven's ability to conceive short, basic, concentrated thematic ideas, which go to the roots of musical expression; often, simple ideas which had been used by other composers, in passing, but which were now isolated, transformed in some way or other, and forced to express the powerful emotion which had always lain there latent in them. For example, Beethoven based the first movement of his *Eroica Symphony* (1803) on a simple major triadic theme which must have been a commonplace of earlier music: it had been notably used, as is well known, by Mozart (Ex. 9a), as the main theme of his brief, light-hearted overture to his childish operetta *Bastien and Bastienne* (1768), which he wrote when he was twelve (and which was almost certainly unknown to Beethoven). This cheerful theme had been in the air for a long time, but it took Beethoven to realize what it was capable of expressing. He seized it, and made it the basis of a 'heroic symphony' (Ex. 9b), by bringing out its serious expressive potential in several ways. First he gave it to the cellos in their middle register, where it does not merely sound naïvely cheerful, as on Mozart's violins, but swings forward with committed joyful confidence; and he extended it by two descending semitones, leading from the tonic down to the dark flat seventh (the C sharp is a D flat), which is reluctant to move back up to the normal seventh and tonic, and therefore introduces a feeling of discouragement which conflicts with the original confident momentum.

Ex. 9

Later he developed it in all kinds of different forms and ways through distant keys, major and minor, making it grim, mournful, furious and hopeful by turns, and thereby gave it the central role in a great symphonic conflict. And eventually, in the coda, he brought it out triumphant, at the climax, removing the two discouraging notes and presenting the pure major triadic phrase only, now ending on the upper dominant instead of the tonic, successively on horns, p; on violins, p; on violas, cellos and basses, crescendo; and finally on trumpets, f.

Likewise, Wagner based *Tristan* (1857) on a languishing chromatic sequence which had long been in the air. It had been used, notably, by Mozart in the slow movement of his String Quartet in E flat, K 428 (1783), by Spohr (a great follower of Mozart's chromaticism) in the slow movement of his String Quartet in C, op. 4 no. 1 (1807), and by Spohr again in his opera *Der Alchemist* (1830)—Exs. 10a, b and c.*

* The first two of these three examples have been transposed into the key of the *Tristan* example, for ease of harmonic comparison; the last is actually *in* the key of the *Tristan* example.

Ex. 10

In *Der Alchemist,* Spohr anticipated Wagner's use of it as a love-motive (since it appears there in a ballad representing a Moorish woman's lament for her dead lover); and he also anticipated Wagner's initial development of it—a repetition a minor third higher. But in taking it as the basis of *Tristan* (Ex. 10d), Wagner brought out its deeper potential for expressing the infinite longing of romantic love and the yearning for its appeasement in death.[4]

He did so by simply intensifying the first of the two chords. He brought together simultaneously into a single pungent dissonance—which raised chromaticism to a level of ambiguity heralding the dissolution of tonality—the various harmonic tensions found separately, and partly *un*simultaneously, in all previous examples. Comparing it with

237

the three examples quoted—which Wagner may or may not have known
—it shares its G sharp and E natural with all three, but its D sharp
with the third only, and its B natural with the first two only. (The
form of the second chord is the same as in all three—where the second
Spohr is concerned, the same as in the second statement of the idea.)
Moreover, the significance of Wagner's intensely chromatic idea is
further enhanced by several other things, which are not to be found in
the earlier examples. In the first place, he used it as a main theme, at the
beginning of his work, whereas in the earlier examples it was used as a
passing idea in the middle of a work, where at that time chromaticism
was more easily justified, after a diatonic beginning. Secondly, he
preceded the harmonic sequence with an extra 'yearning' melodic
phrase (A, F, E, D sharp), to go with the old one (G sharp, A, A sharp,
B). And finally, no less than Beethoven, he developed his idea in all
kinds of different forms and ways, through distant keys, giving it the
central role in a great symphonic conflict; and in his coda he let its
passion be exorcised by resolving its unresolvable A minor tensions
into the opera's final cadence in B major (the key of the concluding
Liebestod).

This developmental power was the second of Wagner's two abilities
stemming from Beethoven, closely interwoven with the first: his short,
basic, concentrated thematic ideas were conceived in such a way as to
sustain a large amount of development. In fact, he deliberately modelled
himself on Beethoven's developmental method, particularly in the
matter of rising sequence. For example, in the development section of
the *Eroica Symphony*, we find that its main theme (Ex. 9b) has become
contracted, and is lifted through two ascents of a semitone:

Ex. 11

And in *Tristan*, when the two lovers have drunk the love-potion, and
are in each other's arms, we find the opera's main theme (Ex. 10d) con-

238

tracted, and lifted through three ascents of a tone, and a climactic one of a minor third:

Ex. 12

The musical texture could not be more different, but the technique of musical development is very much the same.

Again, Wagner was able, like Beethoven, to pick up some small fragment of one of his themes, and develop it in rising sequence, to produce a tremendous working-up of excitement. For example, in the first movement of the Seventh Symphony, Beethoven picks up a figure of three notes from his main Allegro theme (marked W in Ex. 13a), and works it up in rising sequence to bring about one of the early climaxes of the movement (Ex. 13b Likewise, Wagner, in the second act of *Tristan*, picks up a three-note fragment of one of his love-themes (marked X in Ex. 14a), and works it up in rising sequence to produce one of the early climaxes of the act (Ex. 14b). The voices of the lovers follow the upper line, taking alternate phrases, as far as bar 5, then broaden out in octaves and arrive on a climactic sustained G in bar 10.

Development certainly plays a most important part in any composer's musical expression; but it would take us too far afield to make a full examination of Wagner's methods of development, which would, as can be seen, require some very large music examples. What we can do here is to consider some more examples of the *vocabulary* of Wagner's musical language—those short, basic, concentrated thematic ideas which are its foundation—and examine its growth and scope. But first a word about Wagner's own conception of music as a language.

Ex. 13

Ex. 14

b) Very animated

The whole idea of music as a language, of there being a 'language of music', has been severely challenged, but Wagner took it for granted. It is, of course, a metaphor, using the word language, not in its strict sense of *verbal* language, but in the broad sense of a means of communication. And what music communicates is emotions, feelings and moods, as Wagner was well aware. In 1851, in his pamphlet *Eine Mitteilung an meine Freunde* (*A Communication to My Friends*),[5] he wrote of the change that had come over him between *Rienzi* and *Der fliegende Holländer*:

241

But now I had completely mastered the language of music [die Sprache der Musik]; I had taken possession of it, as of a true mother tongue. In what I had to communicate, I no longer needed to worry about the technical problems of the expression; it was entirely at my command ... But what can be expressed in the language of music is only *feelings* and *emotions* ... What remains inexpressible in the language of music by itself is an exact definition of the object of the feeling and emotion ... And this it acquires only by being wedded to verbal language.

Or, as he had put it ten years earlier, in one of his Paris articles, 'Ein glücklicher Abend' ('A Happy Evening'):

What music expresses is general, infinite, and ideal: it speaks, not of the passion, love and longing of this or that individual in this or that situation, but of passion, love and longing themselves ...

No true understanding of Wagner's music is possible without the realization that he was not simply a composer but a musical dramatist, for whom music was a language which, in conjunction with the actions of his characters on the stage, could express the inner meaning of life. Despite his worship of Beethoven's symphonic works and string quartets, he had no desire to compose purely instrumental compositions, because he felt that they could only express universal feelings, not individual ones. He thought that Beethoven had achieved miracles in these forms (the second of the two quotations above arose out of a discussion of the *Eroica Symphony*), but that his achievement should now be taken as a basis for further miracles in the *vocal*-instrumental, musico-*dramatic* sphere. And in his short story 'Eine Pilgerfahrt nach Beethoven' ('A Pilgrimage to Beethoven'),[6] written in Paris in 1840, Wagner made Beethoven point the way, by giving him these (rather difficult) words to say:

The instruments represent the primal organs of creation and of nature; what they express can never be clearly established and defined, for they convey the primal feelings, as they arose out of the chaos of the first creation, perhaps when there were not even yet any human beings to take them to their hearts. It is quite otherwise with the genius of the human voice: this represents the human heart, and its specific individual emotion. Its character is therefore restricted, but definite and clear. Let these two elements now be brought together, let them be absorbed into each other! Let the clear, specific emotion of the human heart, represented by the human voice, be set against the wild primal feelings with their reaching out towards infinity, represented by the instruments. The bringing together of these two elements will have a beneficial, calming effect on the warring of the primal feelings, will channel their torrent into a definite, unified flow; the human heart itself, however, in as much as it absorbs these primal feelings, will be infinitely strengthened and expanded, and will become capable of clearly experiencing within itself the transformation of its former vague intimations of the highest into a godlike consciousness.

Wagner was, of course, putting his own ideas into the dead Beethoven's mouth: it was he himself who was eventually to achieve this particular fusion of the human voice and the instruments, the human heart and the primal feelings, in his mature music-dramas. But only because he had completely mastered *the language of music*—which means, not the technique of composition (though he had mastered that too), but the way of making music express 'the primal feelings, as they arose out of the chaos of the first creation, perhaps when there were not even yet any human beings to take them to their hearts'. The phrase may seem strange, but it is surely a way of describing the feelings that the first human beings inherited from nature—those primordial instincts which have been so severely repressed into the unconscious in the interests of civilization: pleasure, sex, aggression, death-wish.

Beethoven first found a way of making music express some of these repressed instincts: orgiastic pleasure reigns supreme in most of the Seventh Symphony, ferocious aggression in the first movement of the Fifth. But he did so mainly in his absolute music: *Fidelio*, whatever its other merits, cannot be compared with these two works from this point of view—the aggression of Pizarro is as nothing compared with that expressed in the first movement of the Fifth Symphony. Now since absolute music has no words to indicate what it is about, people were able to enjoy Beethoven's expression of the repressed instincts without having to acknowledge doing so. But when Wagner gave his expressions of these repressed instincts 'a local habitation and a name', by providing dramas to go with the music, and made his music even more violently expressive of them than Beethoven's, he was execrated (and also worshipped) as no other composer had been. In the *Ring* cycle, pleasure, sex, aggression and death-wish were explicitly let loose in all their primordial power; likewise, sex and death-wish in *Tristan*. The execrators have found this explicit release of the highly-charged contents of the unconscious extremely dangerous; the worshippers have found in the same thing an experience of the 'godlike consciousness' that Wagner was aiming at. The latter are increasing, the former diminishing: the world is gradually learning to live with Wagner.

But how did he manage to do this, musically? What is it about his short, basic, concentrated thematic ideas that makes them so full of unrepressed emotion? In the first place, like Beethoven's, as we have seen, they penetrate to the roots of musical language, singling out its most expressive elements, which were floating about unharnessed in the air in previous music, and crystallizing them in a definitive form (the main themes of the *Eroica Symphony* and of *Tristan*—Exs. 9b and 10d). But Wagner went a stage further than Beethoven—partly because he was a musical dramatist and not merely a composer, but mainly because he was Wagner. He was an extraordinary psychological type, phenomenally uninhibited, always ready to let his emotions come out to the full, good and bad, conscious and unconscious.[7] And so, having brought up an idea from the roots of musical language, he refined it down to its absolute essence, and then gave it the most powerful presentation possible, by means of pitch, harmony, rhythm, tempo, dynamics, texture and tone-colour.

When I assembled the multiple music examples in *The Language of Music*, each illustrating the use of what I called 'a basic term of musical vocabulary', Wagner was nearly always there with the most fundamental example. For instance, when I gathered together examples from the music of many different composers to illustrate the fact that the major third and the major triad, especially in a rising melodic context, normally express pleasure,[8] there was Wagner with the opening of the Prelude to *Das Rheingold* (Ex. 15): a full ascending major triad over more than two octaves, ending with the third on a strong beat, floating up from the depths in a lazy 6/8 rhythm on the voice of a pianissimo horn—pure, unadulterated pleasure.

Ex. 15

What I did not say was that this theme is given out after sixteen bars establishing the tonic and dominant in the bass, and then taken up by seven other horns for the next twenty-eight bars, all eight continually overlapping at closer and closer intervals of time, until the score becomes nothing more than a single oscillating major chord—an appropriate expression of the unending amoral pleasure-principle of nature, represented by the non-human characters who appear when the curtain rises, the Rhinemaidens. In *The Language of Music*, the fifty-three other examples illustrating the major-equals-pleasure equation were drawn almost entirely from great music; but the only rivals in the matter of getting to the absolute roots of musical language were Handel, with the solo trumpet in 'The Trumpet Shall Sound' from *Messiah*, and Bach, with the three trumpets at the beginning of the allegro chorus 'Et expecto resurrectionem mortuorum' from the *Mass in B minor*.

This is not to say that Wagner was a greater composer than any other except Handel and Bach, but simply that his greatness was of a very special kind. He normally drew on the ultimate sources of musical expression, unadulterated and unadorned, and gave them the most powerful presentation—which does not mean the loudest: it is the hushed character of the prelude to *Das Rheingold* which is the most powerful (intense) thing about it. Of course, the romantics, from Beethoven onwards, tended to make their music much more expressive of human feeling than their predecessors, by giving much more intensity to the simple root-phrases of musical language; but no one used this procedure to such consistent effect as Wagner.

Take one of the pairs of twin poles of musical expression: the appoggiaturas from the sixth to the fifth degrees of the major and minor scales, so similar from the point of view of musical structure, and yet so opposite in their emotional effect—the first expressing pleasurable longing, the second pure anguish.[9] Here again, Wagner was to the fore, isolating these poles completely, giving them great emphasis, and placing them in opposition. The major pole became the ecstatic song of the Rhinemaidens, in *Das Rheingold*, drawn to the life-giving gold like moths to a candle-flame (Ex. 16). It is pitched high and given a very diatonic harmonic progression (dominant ninth to tonic); the appoggiatura is drawn out (dotted minim to crotchet in 9/8), the tempo is quick, the dynamic fortissimo, the texture glittering, and the tone-colour brilliant—three high solo female voices (see page 246).

The minor pole became three different thematic ideas (Ex. 17), all closely connected, and set in opposition to the ecstatic song of the Rhinemaidens. When the life-giving gold is stolen by Alberich and turned into the ring—a talisman of ruthless power—the major sixth of the Rhinemaidens' song is changed to the minor sixth for these ideas, which are all associated with the ring. Ex. 17a, the theme connected with the tyrannical use of the ring by Alberich, which causes so much misery, is a very subtle and sinister minor transformation of the Rhine-

Ex. 16

maidens' song: it is pitched low and given harsh chromatic harmony, with the first two phrases lifted a semitone higher; the appoggiatura is still drawn out (minim to crotchet in 3/4), the tempo is slow, the dynamics menacing (forte dying away to piano and then swelling out to fortissimo), the texture is very heavy, and the tone-colour dark (low brass and woodwind, with cymbal, timpani and tam-tam). Ex. 17b, the theme of the misery of the enslaved Nibelungs as they toil without rest for Alberich, is simply the minor 6–5 appoggiatura played over and over: this is again pitched low and has no harmony at all except for the accompaniment of the 'Nibelung' motive which depicts their ceaseless hammering; still the appoggiatura is drawn out, the tempo is fast and restless, the dynamics brutal (fortissimo), the texture naked, and the tone-colour hard and biting (trombones in octaves). Ex. 17c, the theme of the Nibelung Hagen's consuming desire to possess the ring in *Götterdämmerung*, is a much more chromatic and dissonant variant of the first: here the dynamics are soft, the tempo slow, the pitch fairly high, and the texture and tone-colour mysterious, since Hagen's desire is a secret one. But the intensity of that desire is evident from the fact that the appoggiatura is even longer drawn out this time (dotted minim to crotchet in slow 4/4), and is further emphasized by the extremely pungent woodwind dissonance attached to the first note.

And so on. The idea of purity expressed by the major 1–3–5–6–5: a quiet naked unison statement of it, to open *Parsifal*; the idea of intense suffering expressed by the *minor* 1–3–5–6–5: Parsifal's anguished cry

Ex. 17

'Erlöse! Rette mich aus schuldbefleckten Händen!' ('Redeem, rescue me from guilt-stained hands!'). Here we have another pair of twin poles of musical expression, drawn from the roots of musical language, and used with well-nigh incomparable power.

All this will have illustrated the uniquely direct emotional power of Wagner's musical vocabulary. How early did he acquire this gift? The answer is, he had it from the beginning, at the age of eighteen, when he began composing dramatic music in real earnest. A great deal of nonsense has been talked about Wagner's very early works, composed during the ten years before he wrote *Der fliegende Holländer* at the age of twenty-eight. They have been described as laughably amateurish, but in fact, although they reveal very little of his latent genius (except for *Rienzi*), they are the works of one who was already a thoroughly professional composer, and the few moments in them which do reveal his latent genius already show something of his direct emotional power.

Certainly, if he had not been Wagner, they should have been laughably amateurish, since he had no patience with teachers, but picked up the technique of composition in his own way. He was in fact almost entirely self-taught: he had a little piano tuition and studied a treatise on harmony (general bass) at the age of twelve; he had a few harmony lessons when he was sixteen; and finally, at eighteen, he studied composition for six months with Theodor Weinlig, the Cantor of St Thomas's Church in Leipzig. But all this time he had been absorbing himself in great music: at the age of twelve he was already attending performances of theatre works by Beethoven, Weber and Marschner, and was also working his way through the full score of Beethoven's *Egmont* music. At sixteen, he was studying a string quartet by Haydn and the late E flat Quartet of Beethoven, and trying to master orchestration by wrestling with the full score of Mozart's *Don Giovanni*. And at seventeen, unable to afford a copy of the full score of Beethoven's *Choral Symphony* for his own, he borrowed one from a library, and copied it out from beginning to end, at the same time making a piano arrangement of it.

Copying out great music is one of the best ways of teaching oneself the art of composition. In that way, one does not merely look through the scores, noticing the salient features, but one becomes thoroughly familiar with every detail of the music: melody, harmony, rhythm, texture, orchestration—everything. A musical companion of Wagner's at this time, Heinrich Dorn, wrote later:

> I doubt whether there has ever been a young composer more familiar with Beethoven's works than the eighteen-year-old student Wagner. He had copies, made by himself, of the full scores of most of the master's overtures: he went to bed with the sonatas, and rose with the quartets . . .

So when Wagner went to Weinlig, as a 'green' youth of eighteen, he knew a good deal more about a lot of things than his teacher, who was a conservative, out of touch with 'modern music', which at that time meant primarily Beethoven and Weber. How Weinlig taught, according to Wagner, was to take some eighteenth-century piece, usually by Mozart, and draw attention to its construction: the relative length and balance of its sections, the principal modulations, the number and character of the themes, and the general character of the movement. Then he would set his pupil a task, asking him to compose a work of about so many bars, divided into so many sections with modulations to correspond, each having so many themes and of such and such a character. This was probably good for Wagner: from his copying out of great works, he no doubt had an excellent idea of such things, but he needed to buckle down and do them for himself. Certainly, about a year after he had left Weinlig, when he was nineteen, he began to write his first opera, *Die Hochzeit* (*The Wedding*), and the only number he completed*—an opening wedding chorus and septet, interspersed with passages of recitative—is admirably laid out from Weinlig's point of view. The chorus is conventionally festive, and the septet conventionally lyrical (Weinlig admired the piece, no doubt thinking that his 'modernist' pupil was now on the straight and narrow); but the first recitative, a troubled dialogue between a king's son and his friend, with hints of impending tragedy, is more interesting. There are two things about it which can be called embryonically Wagnerian (we are, of course, being wise after the event): the opening of it, which brings a dramatic change of mood by casting a sudden shadow over the festive atmosphere; and the sombre idea in the bass which is introduced almost immediately, to enhance this effect (marked *Y* in Ex. 18).

Idea *Y* is used three separate times during the thirty-five bars of the first recitative, and again to open the second recitative, which is only six bars long; but this is more an example of Wagner imitating the way that Mozart used an idea to bind an orchestral recitative together—for example, the figure that pervades the recitative preceding Donna Anna's aria 'Tu sai che l'onore' in *Don Giovanni*—than an early case of his using a leading-motive. It is, however, an early case of his conceiving one of those short, basic, concentrated thematic ideas which express so powerfully some aspect of human feeling—here, a deep brooding feeling born of bewilderment, sadness and resentment, since the king's son in *Die Hochzeit*, for some reason, feels all these emotions on hearing that the wedding has taken place. But Wagner, having already hit on one of the basic terms of his musical vocabulary (*Y*), simply used it over and over: he was apparently not able to build on it at this early stage (though for all we know he might have done if he had continued the opera). But he did know how to build on it over twenty years later, when he came to compose *Die Walküre*: it first enters in Act III, to

---

* Wagner did not abandon the opera because of any lack of application. His actress sister Rosalie persuaded him that it would not succeed because the libretto (his own) was too gruesome; and within nine months he had completed his first full-length opera, *Die Feen* (*The Fairies*), five months before his twenty-first birthday.

Ex. 18

round off those angry string phrases which punctuate Wotan's furious denunciation of Brünnhilde, in the presence of her sister-Valkyries (Ex. 19).

There is no intention of cheating the reader. Idea *Y*, as it enters here, is admittedly rather different from its appearance in *Die Hochzeit* (Ex. 18); but as we continue to examine *Die Walküre*, it will become very much the same. This is one of those cases where Wagner introduced a thematic idea in a striking embryonic version, before continuing

Ex. 19

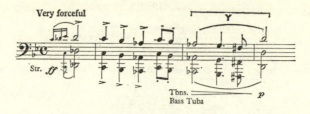

with its even more striking definitive form. Here, the second note and the last note of all are not there (the semiquaver F and the final A in Ex. 18), and the two last notes of what remains are a semitone higher; but the general shape remains much the same—a descent of three notes followed by a leap of a sixth. However, although the omissions are still in operation, the idea becomes much more recognizable when it is used to introduce scene 3 of Act III, in which Wotan and Brünnhilde stand face to face, alone, both brooding on their bewilderment, sadness and resentment caused by the other's attitude (Ex. 20). It is, as in *Die Hochzeit*, a descent of three notes from the minor third of the scale to the tonic, and a leap to the scale's minor sixth:

Ex. 20

Later, when Brünnhilde begins to put forward her self-justification to the angry Wotan, for having disobeyed him, idea *Y* (now only minus its single repeated note, which is merely a case of reducing an idea to its essentials) becomes, in practically its original form, the whole basis of the melody (Ex. 21). The final appoggiatura is now there, though the rising interval varies between a sixth (the second time) and a more elo-quently pleading seventh (the first and third times), before becoming a defiant octave (the last time).

And eventually—another transformation—when Brünnhilde tells Wotan that her disobedience was the outcome of the love that he had

Ex. 21

implanted in her heart, and which, she is sure, is still in his own heart,
idea *Y* turns to the major, the rising interval now becoming first a
yearning seventh, and then a triumphant octave:

Ex. 22

If this still seems bewildering to the reader, he should remember that
musical ideas are not static, but plastic: a large rising interval is a rising
interval, whether an octave, a seventh, a sixth, or even a fifth or a
fourth—probably not less. What matters is the general curve, so long
as it is recognizable as a derivation of the original idea.* So we must now
go back over Exs. 19, 20, 21 and 22. In Ex. 19, the angry phrase is on
fortissimo strings, detached and accented; the brass conclude this with
phrase *Y*, its last two notes a semitone higher, which takes the music
into the key a tone higher, legato and diminuendo: Wotan's rage is
tempered with bewilderment (which Brünnhilde will later dispel).
In Ex. 20, where idea *Y* is half-way back to its normal form, the tone-
colour is quiet strings, and so, despite the heavily brooding atmosphere,
the feeling here is (on Wotan's part) one of 'more in sorrow than in

---

* I am not suggesting that, when Wagner composed Act III of *Die Walküre*,
he was thinking of his youthful idea *Y* of *Die Hochzeit*. It was simply a basic
term of his musical vocabulary—what is often called a 'fingerprint'.

anger'. In Ex. 21, the eloquent rising sevenths and the final defiant octave express Brünnhilde's 'back to the wall' feeling; though since the texture is solo voice only, she seems totally defenceless; and since Ex. 21 is followed by further solo soprano, sadly descending, her sub-servient status as regards Wotan is underlined. However, in Ex. 22, when she feels able to challenge him with the love that is in both their hearts, idea *Y* turns to the major on the woodwind, its pleading minor tensions turning to soaring, yearning major ones—the eventual reconciliation is certain now.

The whole outcome of this confrontation is to be Wotan's acquies-cence in the awakening of Brünnhilde, from the punitive sleep into which he has plunged her, by Siegfried, three acts later; and a glance at the 'Siegfried' motive (Ex. 8b) will show that idea *Y*, in quicker tempo, is a main propellent of its heroic forward momentum (in bars 2–3, and again in bars 4–5).* And since the 'Siegfried' motive is intro-duced into Act III of *Die Walküre* before the altercation between Wotan and Brünnhilde takes place (when Brünnhilde tells Sieglinde that she is to bear a son, who will be the greatest hero the world has ever known, and names him Siegfried), it could be that Exs. 19, 20, 21 and 22 are all derived from the two middle cells of that motive, and are concentrating on the problem behind the altercation, which is ultimately the question whether Siegfried shall be born, and eventually awaken Brünnhilde. (Idea *Y*, in fact, like ideas *A* and *B* in Ex. 1, has a 'questioning' charac-ter, due to its rising inflexion.) But this typical Wagnerian ramification, with all the complexity involved, is too far-reaching to be examined here—though it does give a hint as to the very wide scope of Wagner's musical language.

It may have seemed factitious to have looked at a short idea which the nineteen-year-old Wagner conceived for the recitative of a projected first opera he almost immediately abandoned, and then to have related it to magnificent ideas in one of his great mature works—*Die Walküre*. So I should like to conclude by examining the whole growth and con-sistency of Wagner's musical language, taking a small seed (from a work preceding *Die Hochzeit*), and tracing it through all his music-dramas (with one exception, to be explained later), right down to his last work, *Parsifal*.

Towards the end of Wagner's studies with Weinlig, he wrote his

---

* It should be remembered that the 'Siegfried motive' is a *tragic*-heroic theme.

first musical work for the theatre, a set of incidental music for a play by Raupach—*König Enzio* (*King Enzio*). His sister Rosalie ensured performances of it at productions of the play in the Leipzig Theatre, and it had a certain success. The only part of it which has survived is the overture, which is a perfectly good piece by the eighteen-year-old composer. I do not wish to exaggerate—Mendelssohn wrote his superb Octet at the age of sixteen, and his wonderful overture to *A Midsummer Night's Dream* a year later; but Wagner's *König Enzio* overture is a totally professional piece of work, much better than anything written at the same age by Schumann or Berlioz. And there is one feature of it which is definitely Wagnerian: it looks forward to *Die Hochzeit*, in fact, since it is a moment when the main festive atmosphere is clouded over by a dark bass motive (marked *Z* in Ex. 23).

Ex. 23

Motive *Z*, despite its brevity (or because of it), is essentially Wagnerian —a descent of a diminished seventh through a minor third, with a decidedly oppressive sound about it. Clearly, Wagner must have been pleased with it, since he built on it in later works, introducing an extended version of it into the overtures of his first and third operas, *Die Feen* and *Rienzi*. In the overture to *Die Feen*, written at the age of twenty, it appears slowly, pianissimo, preceded and followed by two ascending steps, and is repeated (Ex. 24). Again, it casts a shadow over the main 'fairy' atmosphere of the music up to this point.

Ex. 24

And in the overture to *Rienzi* (1837–40), completed at the age of twenty-seven, it appears slowly, but fortissimo—this time shorn of its two initial ascending notes, but repeated over and over (Ex. 25). And once more it has the effect of bringing a feeling of trouble into a very confident situation.

Ex. 25

The difficulty is that, in both *Die Feen* and *Rienzi* (and for that matter in the seed-bearer, the overture to *König Enzio*), the idea is not associated with any character, event or emotion in the dramas themselves. It is confined to the overtures (of course we lack the rest of the incidental music for *König Enzio*), and the overtures, being purely instrumental, can only present it as a general expression of the trouble that is to occur in the drama itself. However—looking ahead for a moment, and not forgetting the promise to examine its use in practically all Wagner's works—it occurs, in a most powerful form, in *Die Walküre*, again in a phrase punctuating Wotan's denunciation of Brünnhilde (Ex. 26). The phrase has been transposed into the key of the example from *Die Feen*, to show the close similarity (a repetition of the idea in the dominant of the key of the original statement—though the example from *Die Walküre*, being purely in octaves, rather obscures the tonal context). Again, the plasticity of musical ideas must be remembered, for the idea has lost its intermediate minor third.

Ex. 26

Wotan's attitude to Brünnhilde (at the beginning of this scene) is that of one imposing a terrible prohibition: factually, against her ever more being a Valkyrie, but emotionally, against her feelings of compassion and love for Siegmund, Sieglinde and the as yet unborn Siegfried, which have led her into disobeying him. And the extremely incisive form of idea *Z* in Ex. 26 is an entirely appropriate expression of this state of mind: the descending diminished sevenths (on low woodwind and brass) are emphatically repressive in feeling, and the ascending notes which follow them almost evoke the physical gesture of one sweeping aside all objections or pleadings.

Wotan would seem to be imposing a ban on love, and *Das Liebesverbot* (*The Ban on Love*) was the title of the opera Wagner wrote between *Die Feen* and *Rienzi*—his second, completed when he was twenty-three. In this work, we find him using idea *Z* again, but this time as a leading-motive associated with the idea of the title. The libretto of *Das Liebesverbot* (his own) is based on Shakespeare's *Measure for Measure*, with a difference: the young Wagner viewed the 'ban on love' in Shakespeare's original—a state-governor's prohibition of all extra-marital sexual relations, on pain of death—not as something raising a serious moral problem, but as something to be laughed to scorn and evaded with all the irrepressible sexuality of a pleasure-loving populace. He was passionately, at that time, what we should call anti-establishment, being in sympathy with the group known as 'Young Europe', which hit out right and left at any kind of repression, and especially the moral repression motivated by puritanism.

The 'Ban on Love' motive of Wagner's opera—idea *Z* in a suitably repressive form—makes its first appearance early in the overture, and once more it changes the atmosphere dramatically, bringing to a halt the hectic carnival music (Ex. 27). Again, the idea has undergone a plastic alteration: the descending interval is a minor sixth, not a diminished seventh; the intermediate third of the versions in *Die Feen* and *Rienzi* has vanished, together with the two ascending steps at the beginning; and the two ascending steps at the end are contracted to semitones. The idea has been reduced to its bare essential, as in *Die Walküre* (Ex. 26)—a descent of a large interval, followed by two small ascending steps.

Ex. 27

Those readers who jib at recognizing idea *Z* in its various 'plastic alterations' should realize that they are going against Wagner's own practice. In using his 'Ban on Love' idea as a leading-motive in the opera itself, he changed its descending minor sixth to all kinds of different intervals, if the musical expression demanded it, knowing that the general shape of the idea would still remain recognizable.

Exs. 28 and 29 show this process at work. Ex. 28 is from the duet between Friedrich (the equivalent of Shakespeare's puritanical governor Angelo) and the nun Isabella, whose brother Claudio has been sentenced to death by him for 'living in sin' with his bride-to-be. She pleads with him for her brother's life; and when he finds himself sexually aroused by her beauty, saying to himself, 'How warm her breath! How

I

eloquent her tone! Am I a man?', the music introduces the 'Ban on Love' motive, with a nice touch of dramatic irony.

Ex. 28

Although the two first descending intervals here are a perfect fourth and a perfect fifth, before the third one returns to the original minor sixth, the idea is still recognizable from its general shape. And so it is again, in Ex. 29 (the orchestral opening of the brooding aria sung by Friedrich while waiting for an answer from Isabella to his love-letter), although this time there is no minor sixth, only a major one, a diminished fifth, and a diminished seventh.

Ex. 29

Clearly, Wagner felt idea Z to express the threatening feeling of somebody or something standing between the hero or heroine and their self-fulfilment. The hero of *Das Liebesverbot*, according to the young Wagner's ideas, was the people, with their natural sexual vitality: Friedrich, with his 'ban on love', stood between them and the fulfilment of their desire for free love. In *Die Walküre*, the twin impulses of the heroine Brünnhilde are love and compassion: Wotan temporarily stands between her and the fulfilment of these impulses.

The idea returns in the opera that followed *Rienzi, Der fliegende Holländer*—not as a leading-motive, but fleetingly, in the orchestral recitative given to the Dutchman on his first appearance (Ex. 30). Here it is almost back to its *Die Feen* version (Ex. 24), with its two initial ascending steps, and its intermediary third in the descent of a diminished seventh (though both are chromatically ornamented). It expresses the Dutchman's everlastingly weary and hopeless feeling that the curse upon him stands between him and his redemption:

Ex. 30

It appears in the next opera, *Tannhäuser*, in the vocal line of Venus in Act I, as she vainly tries to stand between Tannhäuser and his desire to return from the Venusberg to the world of humanity and of his true love Elisabeth (Ex. 31). She sings it obsessively to the words 'Nicht wehre stolz deinem Sehnen, wenn zurück zu mir es dich zieht' ('Soon the pride will vanish from your soul; I shall see you humbly come back to me'):

Ex. 31

Here again, Wagner did not use it as a leading-motive, but he did at last hit on the simple, fundamental version of it, reduced it to its absolute bare essentials, which he was to stick to in all his subsequent music-dramas, where he did use it as a leading-motive. This is the version foreshadowed in bars 3–4 of Ex. 28, where the descending interval is a perfect fifth; but he now made these two notes tonic and dominant, and changed the two subsequent ascending steps from chromatic ones to diatonic ones, thereby arriving on the mediant, and thus bringing the idea within the compass of the triad (minor or major).

In the following opera, *Lohengrin*, it became—again in its minor form—the motive of the 'Forbidden Question' (Ex. 32a). Here it is the condition that Elsa shall never ask Lohengrin his name which stands between them and their wedded bliss; and it is seized on by the two villains, Telramund and Ortrud, at the beginning of Act II (Ex. 32b). The fact that this impossible condition is imposed by the hero on the heroine goes far to explain the unsatisfactory nature of the story and symbolism of *Lohengrin*.

Ex. 32

The next time we encounter idea *Z* unequivocally is in the next but one music-drama, *Die Walküre*. It is associated with Fricka in her altercation with Wotan in Act II (Ex. 33), where she firmly stands between Wotan and the fulfilment of his plan, and also between the lovers (Siegmund and Sieglinde) and the fulfilment of their love, since that is part of Wotan's plan. This time, the idea enters as a major triad—but it is harmonized dissonantly in a minor harmonic context, and immediately repeats itself a minor third lower as a minor triad.

Ex. 33

However, this theme is derived from a statement of idea *Z* in scene 4 of the preceding music-drama, *Das Rheingold*, which has been repeated twice in Act I of *Die Walküre*. Fricka's whole argument is that, although Wotan claims that his son Siegmund is a free agent, independent of the gods, he is actually Wotan's pawn, since he is only protected from the punishment of the gods, for his incest and adultery, by the invincible sword that the chief of the gods, Wotan, has provided for him. And so Ex. 33 recalls the statement of *Z* from the theme which Wotan sang when he first conceived the idea of the sword, in scene 4 of *Das Rheingold*, and seizing one, saluted Valhalla with it, to the words 'So grüss' ich die Burg, sicher vor Bang' und Grau'n' ('Thus do I salute the fortress, *free from fear and dread*') (Ex. 34).

Ex. 34

When Siegmund has been left on his own, in Act I of *Die Walküre*, and remembers the sword his father promised him in his hour of need, he sings an almost exact repetition of Ex. 34, at the same pitch, with its statement of idea *Z*:

Ex. 35

And when, later in the act, he turns to grasp the sword and pull it out of the tree, he thinks of his father again, and sings another repetition of Ex. 34 at the same pitch, with idea *Z* repeated:

Ex. 36

Fricka is certainly right. It is not she (Ex. 33) who stands between Wotan and his plans, or between the two lovers and the fulfilment of their love; it is the inherent contradiction of Wotan's plan (idea *Z* in Ex. 34, repeated by Siegmund in Exs. 35 and 36) of supporting his 'independent hero' of a son by providing him with an invincible sword.

In the next music-drama, *Siegfried*, idea *Z* does not appear at all (except in so far as Brünnhilde, in passing, recalls the exact form of Ex. 33 several times, when she begins worrying about the past in her love-scene with Siegfried in Act III); and this is perfectly understandable, since nothing whatever—not even the will of Wotan—can stand between Siegfried and Brünnhilde in this work. In the work that follows, however—*Götterdämmerung*—many things do, especially Gutrune, whom Siegfried is hoodwinked by Hagen into falling in love with, by means of giving him a magic potion which makes him forget Brünnhilde altogether. And so the theme associated with Gutrune is based entirely on idea *Z* (Ex. 37a)—but it takes the major form this time, appropriate to Gutrune's sweetness and seductiveness. And as Siegfried marries Gutrune, the marriage also stands between him and

Brünnhilde, wherefore the 'wedding-call' is a much more powerful statement by the horns of the form of idea *Z* from the beginning of Gutrune's theme (Ex. 37b).

Ex. 37

In fact, almost everything and everybody in *Götterdämmerung* stands between Siegfried and Brünnhilde, and for this reason the oppressive descending interval of idea *Z*, without its continuation, becomes pervasive in various forms, attaching itself to various characters and objects. As a diminished fifth, it portrays the baleful Hagen (Ex. 38a); as a bluff perfect fifth, it portrays the weak strong-man Gunther (Ex. 38b); and as a sharp octave, it portrays Siegfried's misguided sense of honour when, wooing Brünnhilde for Gunther, he places his sword between himself and her in bed, thereby cutting himself off decisively from his true love (Ex. 38c).

One more example from *Götterdämmerung*—the phrase known as the 'Seduction' motive, which is largely attached to Hagen and the potion (Ex. 39). As can be seen, idea *Z* here is almost back to its *Das Liebesverbot* form, with a large descending interval of a minor seventh, followed by two small ascending steps; and so the wheel of plasticity comes full circle (cf. Ex. 27).

Ex. 38

a)

b)

c)

Ex. 39

Tristan and *Die Meistersinger* were, of course, written between Acts II and III of Siegfried, and so have been left to be considered here. In *Tristan*, idea Z makes its appearance as the 'Day' motive (Ex. 40), being associated with (according to Wagner's philosophy) the false values of Tristan's daylight world—honour, chivalry and loyalty—which have stood between him and the night-and-death world of his love for Isolde.

Ex. 40

Ex. 40 is the opening of Act II of *Tristan*, and as the two lovers discuss the day-night antithesis during the act, the idea is (like the 'Ban on Love' motive of *Das Liebesverbot*, written more than twenty years earlier, and with an equal disregard of the actual distance of the descending interval) subjected to intensive development (Ex. 41). The

Ex. 41

descending intervals here all take the form of a perfect fourth, not a perfect fifth as in Ex. 40, and yet the general shape of Ex. 40 is perfectly recognizable.

As with the motive attached to Fricka in Act II of *Die Walküre* (Ex. 33), Ex. 40 is derived from an idea in the foregoing action, the major form of *Z* in the song sung by Kurwenal and the sailors in homage to Tristan—'Heil unser Held Tristan' ('Hail our hero Tristan') (Ex. 42)—which does in fact evoke most forcefully his daylight world of honour, chivalry and loyalty.

Ex. 42

In *Die Meistersinger*, since it is a comedy, we might not expect to find such a serious idea as *Z* at all. However, the comedy has serious undertones, and so *Z* duly appears at the moment when Hans Sachs, the wise old protector of the love between Walther and Eva, prevents them from desperately running away together on that Midsummer Night because he is sure that everything will come out all right in the end, and so this drastic step is unnecessary. It features as the refrain (Ex. 43) of the song he starts bawling out in the middle of the night, so as to ensure a general state of wakefulness in Nürnberg, which will make it impossible for the lovers to slip away. This is the only light-hearted use of *Z* in the whole of Wagner's output, which, for his single comedy, is entirely appropriate.

Ex. 43

Only one work remains—Wagner's last music-drama, *Parsifal*—and here, *Z* enters in the third bar of the Prelude:

Ex. 44

The initial phrase of Ex. 44 is of course the 'pure' and 'holy' ascending 1–3–5–6–5 (deprived of its last note), which stands for the absolute purity of the Holy Grail.[10]

However, this phrase goes over immediately into idea Z, which in the drama is associated with the sacred Spear (the spear which pierced Christ's side on the Cross). The Spear has of course been associated with Christ's passion, and in Wagner's music-drama it retains the idea of suffering: the guardian of the Grail, Amfortas, used it as a weapon to attack the heathen host; but, seduced by the siren Kundry, and laying the Spear aside, he was given an incurable wound with it by the leader of the host, Klingsor, and it was lost to the heathen. Here, *Z* expresses the idea of sin, which stands between the brotherhood of the Grail and ultimate salvation.

However, at the very end of *Parsifal*—the last five bars—when redemption has come through the reclaiming of the Spear by Parsifal, the opening theme of the whole music-drama is brought back for the last time, with its ascending 1–3–5–6–(5); and this time, it does not go over into idea *Z*—the 'Spear' motive, the theme of sin—but resolves on to the upper dominant:

Ex. 45

When Wagner drew the final double barline across *Parsifal*, in 1882, his life's work was finished (he died a year later, in his seventieth year). And so idea *Z*, which he had cultivated for fifty years, and which he had exorcized in the last bars of *Parsifal*, disappeared for ever. Idea *Z* is, of course, only one of the terms of Wagner's musical vocabulary; there are many others.

However, this examination of his use of one idea through all his music-dramas except *Siegfried* will have shown something of the consistency, persistency and scope of his musical language—and also of its absolute precision. One problem remains—was it conscious on his part? But that, of course, is another question.

EIGHT

The Method of Composition

ROBERT BAILEY

MUSICAL CONCEPTIONS can be made intelligible to others only by means of a detailed score, the writing out of which is therefore a composer's ultimate creative task. The more elaborate the medium, the more complex the polyphony—the more difficult is the task of making a score. In creating an opera, there exists first of all the problem of a dramatic conception realized in a poem which can be set to music. The composer then faces several distinct musical problems: setting the poem to music, making an orchestral accompaniment for the voices, and the orchestration of that accompaniment. In his first attempt to produce a full score for a work combining dramatic poetry and orchestral music, Wagner assumed that such a work of art could spring fully formed from the mind of the artist, like Athena from the head of Zeus. He has an amusing account of his procedure in his autobiography:

> At this time [1829], I had already composed a first Sonata in D minor. I had even begun a pastoral play, with whose creation I proceeded in definitely unprecedented fashion. Inspired by Goethe's *Laune der Verliebten* for the form and content of my poem, I barely sketched even a plan of the text and, on the contrary, worked out the poem simultaneously with the music and instrumentation in such a way that while I was writing one page of the score, I had not even given an advance thought to the text for the following page. I recall that in this absolutely fantastic way, without having provided myself the slightest knowledge of writing for instruments, I actually achieved a quite lengthy number which finally turned out as a scene for three female voices which preceded an aria for tenor.[1]

While this naïve attempt is perhaps interesting as an early manifestation of Wagner's later instinct for making the dramatic subject, the poem and the music have something to do with each other, it could not have been anything but a failure, and it is not surprising that Wagner abandoned the project. He soon learned that the final task could be simplified by conceiving and writing down a poem *first*, and by then setting his text to music in some kind of preliminary draft before going ahead with the problems of working out the orchestral accompaniments in full score.

Thus, Wagner began work on each one of his operas by writing out an elaborate prose scenario for it. He was thinking about the music all along, of course, and when he was not able to regard the subject as appropriate to the kind of music he had in mind, he abandoned the project before turning his scenario into a complete poem. The collected edition of his literary writings includes several projects of this sort. *Die Meistersinger* itself was such a project, for after its initial dramatic conception in 1845, Wagner set it aside in favour of *Lohengrin* and did not return to it for sixteen years. Just what music Wagner had in mind before working out a dramatic scenario is largely a matter of speculation. This is undeniably one of the most intriguing aspects of his creative method, but documentary examples relating to this earliest stage are few and far between.

Wagner's very first musical thoughts—his first sketches—seem consistently to have taken the form of melodic fragments—not motifs of the type Beethoven used, which consist of a small number of notes, but instead fully formed melodic units, usually in the form of a closed four-measure phrase. This was natural, since Wagner was essentially a vocal composer. The most curious feature of these four-measure melodies, however, is that Wagner frequently did not use them in their complete form, but rather extracted from them a characteristic motifs element. One is tempted to speculate that Wagner's initial conception corresponded to the motivic idea later used, but that he felt constrained at this early stage to add a cadence for the sake of making the thought 'complete'—four measures long, and with clearly defined tonality.

Wagner never systematically kept sketchbooks, as Beethoven did. He seems instead to have used whatever lay close at hand to write down these ideas: scraps of letter paper; sheets of music paper abandoned from some other project; the small diaries which he carried around with him; and sometimes even manuscripts (or, in the case of the *Ring*, his own printed copy) of the poems. Most of Wagner's earliest musical notations are undatable, a feature unusual in that he was otherwise one of the most methodical of geniuses and nearly always dated his complete musical drafts.

Wagner's prose scenario was designed to fix the dramatic conception, often including the detailed contents of individual speeches, so that he could concentrate on the special problem of versification while writing out the poem. As his career progressed, Wagner gave more and more attention to the problem of constructing versification that would be uniquely appropriate for musical realization. This is the feature of his later dramatic poems so admired and envied by Hugo von Hofmanns-thal, who wrote to Richard Strauss of 'the inimitable excellence with which the way is prepared for the music, that consummate quality through which, as the course of a river determines its landscape, so here the poetical landscape is already figured with streams and brooklets of melodies foreseen by the poet'.[2]

It seems quite unthinkable that a great deal of the musical setting did not suggest itself to Wagner as he was constructing the verse, but once again, there is disappointingly little documentation for the processes of his musical thinking at this particular stage. We have noted that some of the manuscripts of Wagner's poems do contain musical fragments, mostly for the vocal parts. It is impossible, however, to determine when Wagner wrote them down—while he was writing out the poem, or while he had that particular copy in front of him when thinking about setting the text.

In any case, writing the texts himself gave Wagner a distinct advantage over ordinary opera composers. He always felt free to make changes in the text—revisions, additions or deletions—when it did not coincide with his developing musical purpose. He was never quite so bound by a pre-existent text as other opera composers traditionally had been. Small changes might have caused an endless series of delays for a composer who collaborated with a separate and perhaps distant poet, but they posed no problem at all for Wagner.

Once he had a complete poem written down, Wagner could shift the balance of his thinking over to the musical side. Most orchestral composers during the last 150 years have felt the need to make some kind of preliminary draft before writing out a full score. This draft embodies the essence of the musical conception, however abstractly it might be represented, so that a composer can then concentrate on the realization of that conception and on the problem of specific instrumentation. A composer's sketches and even complete drafts are designed simply as aids to his own memory, and are not intended for anyone but himself. As a result, they are always more meaningful, more coherent, to him than they could ever be to anyone else. They convey more of the musical conception to the composer than they ever would to us without our preliminary knowledge of the final result. More of the actual sound of the music may be present in the draft for the composer than for someone else. But realization of that sound in terms of instrumentation is left as a final step.

Mozart's musical conceptions were usually fixed in his mind, rather than on paper. It is no slight to his extraordinary genius to point out that he was nearly always working with a fixed group of instruments—the same basic orchestra. His major orchestrational decisions were which wind instruments from the standard complement to use, and whether to employ trumpets and drums. Once determined by the nature of the musical conception, Mozart's combination ordinarily remains fixed for a movement, or at least for a full structural unit of a movement. Mozart consequently did not need to make a preliminary draft, and he was evidently able to write down a full score almost as if he were copying it.

But Wagner's obstacles were distinctly different. His scores beginning with *Tannhäuser*, are written for quite different orchestras—double wind in *Tannhäuser* and *Die Meistersinger*; triple wind in *Lohengrin* and *Tristan*; quadruple wind in *Parsifal*; and quadruple wind with expanded brass complement in the *Ring*. In addition, these scores served to standardize the modern orchestra by displaying which of all the new instruments of the period were to become permanent additions. Furthermore, within any of his scores, the music turns on a constantly shifting orchestral ensemble. Some kind of preliminary draft, then, was not merely a help, it was an inevitable necessity.

EARLY METHOD

With a complete poem and some preliminary musical sketches before him, Wagner began the musical realization of an opera by making full sketches of individual numbers or whole scenes. The crucial function of these sketches was the setting of the text. The separate pieces could be set to music in any order, not necessarily the order in which they finally appear in the finished opera. In *Der fliegende Holländer*, for example, Wagner began by composing Senta's ballad in the second act. These extended sketches are nearly always on two staves—one for the vocal part, and one for the instrumental bass-line, with perhaps a bit of the harmony indicated abstractly in musical notation. Wagner used figured-bass numerals on only a few exceptional occasions. Throughout his career, this combination of vocal part plus bass-line remained the abstract essence of Wagner's musical conceptions—the fundamental element which generated the remainder of the musical fabric. Wagner made these sketches either in pencil or in ink, and it is likely that he picked up whichever lay closer to hand.

These extended sketches represent an intermediate stage between the finished poem and the complete Composition Draft in ink towards which Wagner was working. In that draft, Wagner elaborated the accompaniment on two staves, and used as many additional staves as he needed for a full representaton of all the vocal and choral parts. The similarity of this draft to a piano-vocal score ends with the mere fact of representation of the orchestral material on two staves in treble and bass clefs. The orchestral material is never written down in an arrangement that would facilitate performance on the piano. Wagner never composed at the piano, but used the instrument only to try out music already conceived at his desk.

While making his Composition Draft in ink, Wagner planned each act as a whole, putting together the separate parts and filling in any portions of text not yet set plus the instrumental interludes or transitions as necessary. This is the stage that Wagner himself regarded as the actual composition. He made the Draft starting at the beginning of an act and working straight through to the end. With such a draft in front of him, he could make a full score whenever the necessary time was available. There are usually only very few changes between the draft and the full score, although the possibility for changes is something that was open to Wagner at any time before the full score was actually written down.

In *Tannhäuser* and *Lohengrin*, Wagner abandoned the convention of numbers and demarcated only scenes in the scores, gradually approaching the ideal realized in his later works of complete structural continuity from beginning to end of an act. For *Tannhäuser*, his extended sketches almost add up to a complete draft by themselves, although Wagner still began each one as a separate entity. The next step was taken for *Lohengrin*, in which Wagner's setting of the text was embodied in a complete draft, although on only two staves. He mentions this draft in *Mein Leben*: 'During this summer holiday [1846] ... I ... succeeded in making a sketch of the music to the whole of the three acts of *Lohengrin*, although this cannot be said to have consisted of anything more than a very hasty outline.'[3]

Wagner made supplementary sketches at all stages of composition. The opening of the first act of *Lohengrin* demonstrates how he gradually worked out a specific passage through several different stages of sketches before arriving at either of his drafts. His first sketch for the orchestral introduction was undoubtedly made very early:

Ex. 1

He made a change in the melody in the fifth and sixth measures, and in this corrected form, he employed the fragment to initiate a more extended sketch in ink:

Ex. 2

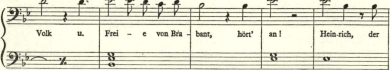

This sketch is dated 1 October [1845]. Wagner evidently thought he would begin his usual complete sketch for the scene, but he broke off and used the remainder of the sheet for fragmentary sketches of various kinds.[4] Wagner did not actually finish the poem of *Lohengrin* until 27 November, so what we have seen so far are sketches made while the poem was being worked out. Wagner later revised the poem of *Lohengrin* more extensively during composition than that of any of his other operas. His original text for the Herald's opening speech runs as follows:

> Ihr Edle, Volk und Freie von Brabant!
> Heinrich des Deutschen Reiches König, kam
> Zu euch, um, so Ihr Klage zu erheben
> Und Streit zu schlichten habt, getreu zu richten
> Und Recht zu sprechen dem, dem Recht gebührt.[5]

Wagner's sketch shown above thus represents an early stage in the revision of the text for this passage. Elaboration of the previous fragment takes the form of indication for the syncopated accompaniment,

275

plus the realization of two parts on the lower staff in the fifth measure. The trumpet fanfare preceding the Herald's speech is substantially different from the one in the opera, and Wagner's next notation on the sheet is the familiar fanfare:

Ex. 3

Wagner's next step was an abstract representation of the harmonic progression of the orchestral introduction on the same sheet, incorporating the new fanfare transposed to C:

Ex. 4

Here he has written in an indication for expansion of the first two measures to four. Having meanwhile revised the text of the Herald's speech, Wagner later used the above sketch for the orchestral introduction to begin his complete Preliminary Draft for the act[6]:

Wagner crossed out the two measures just before the fanfare, which he has added in the Preliminary Draft. All that remains to make the introduction like the final version is to change the initial harmony from B flat to A, making for a smoother transition from the *Vorspiel*. That initial B flat may indicate that Wagner intended to write the *Vorspiel* in that key, or it may simply be an outgrowth of his plan to conclude the first act in B flat without regard to the *Vorspiel*, which he did not compose until the rest of the opera was finished.

The short segment of Wagner's Composition Draft given above shows the typical kinds of elaboration he made at that stage in the orchestral material. At the same time, it illustrates how far from a true representation of the actual orchestral texture this Draft is. One must guard against the temptation to read Wagner's later method into his earlier one. Otto Strobel's term *Orchesterskizze*, rendered into English by Ernest Newman as 'Orchestral Sketch', is not appropriate for Wagner's early operas. Wagner did not define the details of orchestral texture in these drafts, as he did in the final drafts for his works from *Siegfried* on, nor did he work out all the instrumental doublings here. The presence or absence of instrumental abbreviations has, of course, nothing to do with any particular stage of Wagner's method at any time. As the above examples show, he used them at any stage—sketch or draft.

Revision of the poem for the choral finale of Act I (following Lohengrin's speech after the combat) was necessary because Wagner sketched the music *independently*. Afterwards, he wrote a new text to go with that music. He later on worked in the same way for the choral scenes of the second acts of *Die Meistersinger* and *Parsifal*.

The most extensive revision of the poem was made in Act III. It was probably for this reason that Wagner made his final Composition Draft for the third act before that for Acts I and II, a procedure unique in his career. An interesting example is the final scene, beginning at the choral reply to Lohengrin's first speech in that scene and extending through the second quatrain of his narrative, 'In fernem Land'. In the Preliminary Draft for this passage, Wagner set his first version of the poem[7]:

Ex. 6

Maestoso — CHOR — LOHENG

nicht!. Hilf Gott! Welch har – tes Wort er spricht!. Wenn

Al – le ihr zum Ruhm mich wähnt' er – le – sen, wenn Al – le ihr an mei – ne Rei – ne

glaubt, so ist in die – sem Krei – se doch ein We – sen, dem Zwei – fel sei – nes

Glau – ben's Treu' ge – raubt! Das ist ein Weib, wie schmerzt mich, dass ich's

sa – ge!. Ein Weib auf das ich stolz mein Glück ge – baut, das Weib, zu dem ich

rein – ste Lie – be – tra – ge, El – sa, die Gott mir ges – tern. an – ge –

Grave CHOR

– traut. El – sa! Wie moch – te das ge – schehn, wie konn – test so du dich ver –

279

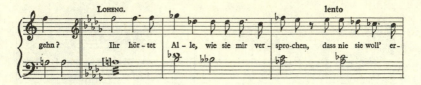

LOHENG.   lento

gehn?   Ihr hör-tet Al-le, wie sie mir ver-spro-chen, dass nie sie woll' er-

[B]
[A]
-fra-gen, wer ich sei-bin?   Nun hat sie ih-ren theu-ren Schwur ge-

-bro-chen, treu-lo-sem Rath gab sie ihr Herz da-hin!   Ihr

keñt das Weib, das ih-ren Zwei-fel rühr-te.   Seht hier den Mann, ver-

-lockt durch Höl-len-trug!   Da

nächtens ich vor sei-ner Wuth mich wehr-te,   Sagt ob ich ihn mit

CHOR Maest
[B]
[A]
Recht er-schlug?   Wie dei-ne Hand ihn schlug auf Er-den, soll

280

dort ihm Got-tes Stra-fe wer-den. O hal-tet: ein, so hart ihn zu ver-

-damen, mocht' er sein' Ehr' u. Tre-ue auch ent-weih'n; liess sich sein

Stolz zu blin-dem Hass ent-flamen, doch schuld' ger nicht mag er als El-sa

sein! O Herr sei gnä-dig, Scho-ne mein!

Sollt' ich der That mit-schul-dig sein? Fern sei es

mir, dich Fre-vels an-zu-kla-gen, vor sol-chem Zwei-fel

ist mein Herz be-wahrt! Doch hör-ten Zeu-gen dein Ver-bot' und Fra-gen.

281

Nun muss ich kün - den wie mein Nam' u. Art!

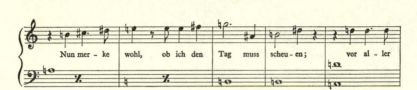

Nun mer - ke wohl, ob ich den Tag muss scheu - en; vor al - ler

Welt vor Kön - ig u. vor Reich ent - hül - le mein Ge - heim - nis!

ich in Treu - en. Nun hört, ob ich an A - del euch nicht

CHOR

gleich! Welch un - er - hör - tes wer - den wir er - fah - ren,

O, könnt' er die er - zwun - g'ne Kun - de sich er - spa - ren!

Largo   Andante

LOHENGR ad. lib.

In fer - nem Land un -

c[olla] p[arte]

282

nah - bar eu - ren Schritten   liegt ei - ne Burg, die Mon-sal-vat ge-nannt

tempo

Ein lich – ter Tem-pel ste – het dort in - mit - ten,   so kost - bar, wie auf

Er - den nichts ge-sehn,   drinn · ein Ge - fäss von   wun-der-thät'gem Se-gen   wird

dort als höch' - stes Hei - lig - thum be - wacht; es ward, dass sein der Men-schen rein - ste

pfle – gen   her - ab von ei - ner En – – – gel-schaar ge - bracht.

FIG. 1

Original Version	Final Version

CHORUS: Hilf Gott! Welch' hartes Wort er spricht!

LOHENGRIN:
Als Streitgenoss bin nicht ich hergekommen;
als Kläger sei ich jetzt von euch vernommen!

LOHENGRIN:
Wenn Alle ihr zum Ruhm mich wähn' erlesen,
wenn Alle ihr an meine Reine glaubt,
so ist in diesem Kreise doch ein Wesen,
dem Zweifel seines Glauben's Treu' geraubt!
Das ist ein Weib, wie schmerzt mich, dass ich's sage!
Ein Weib, auf das ich stolz mein Glück gebaut,
das Weib, zu dem ich reinste Liebe trage,

Elsa, die Gott mir gestern angetraut.

CHORUS:
Elsa! Wie mochte das geschehn,
wie konntest so du dich vergehn?

LOHENGRIN:
Ihr hörtet Alle, wie sie mir versprochen,
dass nie sie woll' erfragen, wer ich bin?
Nun hat sie ihren theuren Schwur gebrochen,
treulosem Rath gab sie ihr Herz dahin!

Ihr kennt das Weib, das ihren Zweifel rührte.
Seht hier den Mann, verlockt durch Höllentrug!

FANFARE: D major . . .

LOHENGRIN:
Zum ersten klage laut ich vor euch Allen,
und frag' um Spruch nach Recht und Fug:
da dieser Mann zur Nacht mich überfallen,

LOHENGRIN:
Da nächtens ich vor seiner Wuth mich wehrte,

284

LOHENGRIN:
O haltet ein, so hart ihn zu verdammen,
mocht' er sein' Ehr' und Treue auch entweih'n;
liess sich sein Stolz zu blinden Hass entflammen,
doch schuld'ger nicht mag er als Elsa sein!

ELSA:
O Herr sei gnädig. Schone mein!
Sollt' ich der Tat mitschuldig sein?

LOHENGRIN:
Fern sei es mir, dich Frevels anzuklagen,
vor solchem Zweifel is mein Herz bewahrt!
Doch hörten Zeugen dein Verbot' und Fragen.

sagt, ob ich ihn mit Recht erschlug?
CHORUS: Wie deine Hand ihn schlug auf Erden,
soll dort ihm Gottes Strafe werden!

LOHENGRIN:
Zum andern aber sollt ihr Klage hören,
denn aller Welt nun klag' ich laut,
dass zum Verrath an mir sich liess bethören

das Weib, das Gott mir angetraut!

CHORUS:
Elsa! Wie mochte das geschehn,
wie konntest so du dich vergehn?

LOHENGRIN:
Ihr höret Alle wie sie mir versprochen,
das nie sie woll' erfragen, wer ich bin?
Nun hat sie ihren theuren Schwur gebrochen,
treulosem Rath gab sie ihr Herz dahin!

Zu lohnen ihres Zweifels wildem Fragen,
sei nun die Antwort länger nicht gespart;
des Feindes Drängen durft' ich sie versagen;

nun muss ich künden, wie mein' Nam' und Art!
Jetzt merket wohl, ob ich den Tag muss scheuen!
Vor aller Welt, vor König und vor Reich
enthülle mein Geheimnis ich in Treuen.
So hört, ob ich an Adel euch nicht gleich!

CHORUS: Welch' Unerhörtes muss ich nun erfahren?
O, könnt' er die erzwung'ne Kunde sich ersparen!

285

Wagner's main concern seems to have been to shorten the passage, and the final version of the text is eight lines shorter than the text shown here. In addition, Lohengrin settles the matter of Telramund with a bit more explanation in the final version, and *before* he accuses Elsa. This represents an improvement in dramatic planning, because it is Elsa who precipitates the revelation Lohengrin will make in his narrative, for which this scene is designed as a preparation. The passage relating to Elsa is shifted intact from the earlier part of the scene to the conclusion, as will be seen in the accompanying diagram (Fig. 1). The only change in the musical setting of this particular passage necessitated by its transfer to a later point occurs in the last line of Lohengrin's quatrain which concludes in B flat in the first version, and in B in the final version.

Aside from the shift of this one crucial passage to strengthen the dramatic structure, it will be seen that the other elements which define the musical structure of this scene—the choral passages and the trumpet fanfare—are left in place, and the musical settings of them were taken over unchanged in the final version. There, Elsa remains silent during this entire scene and does not make her appeal until after Lohengrin's narrative, when it is all the more moving precisely because it is hopeless after he has actually revealed his identity.

The setting of 'In fernem Land' shown above is based on a sketch written on the same sheet as the sketches for the first act discussed above:

Ex. 7

Wagner employed this fragment intact in his Preliminary Draft, changing only the melodic contour in the eighth and ninth measures to resemble that in the fourth and fifth. He transposed it from A flat to

A, and introduced it in the middle of Lohengrin's first quatrain. In the final version, Wagner postponed the entrance of this melody until Lohengrin's second quatrain. By cutting the note-values in half, he was able to fit it exactly to the second quatrain, and it thus serves to delineate the structure of the text.

Wagner's next operatic project was *Siegfrieds Tod*, for which he composed some music in the summer of 1850. His work survives in the form of a sheet of preliminary sketches, plus another sheet on which he began a composition draft in ink on two staves. The first sheet is similar to the sheet discussed above for the opening of *Lohengrin*—it begins with a Preliminary Draft in ink for the opening of the Norns scene, probably based on an earlier sketch of some kind, but is broken off, and Wagner later used the remainder of the paper for other sketches. Most of these are preliminary to his Composition Draft, which extends about a quarter of the way into the duet for Brünnhilde and Siegfried.[8] Wagner was proceeding here with the same method he had used for *Tannhäuser* and *Lohengrin*.

More mysterious, however, are Wagner's attempts to begin the composition of *Der junge Siegfried* the following summer. In a letter of 2 September 1851 to Theodor Uhlig, Wagner claimed that he had 'already the beginning in my head; also some plastic motives, like the Fafner one.'[9] These sketches survive in Bayreuth, but have not been recognized for what they are, since they have been filed with sketches for the later *Siegfried*.

The 'plastic motives' are quite easy to identify. On a blank sheet of paper used for the first draft of a letter to Charles Hanssens of Brussels, with whom Wagner was in correspondence in the earlier part of 1851, Wagner made some sketches in ink and in pencil, drawing the staves free-hand. His first group is in ink. Wagner indicated expansion of his

Ex. 8

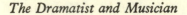

initial eight-measure idea, by stating his bass-line three times and then shifting up a scale-degree to G. The third item, written on one staff rather than two in Wagner's autograph, was evidently designed as a substitute continuation in the dominant, and Wagner has used signs to indicate where it is to appear. The third unit begins with an expansion of the 'Fafner' melody from four measures to twelve, with a change in meter from duple to triple. Having discovered a means for still further expansion, Wagner's next step was to revise his initial bass line and provide a counterpoint against it:

Ex. 9

His Roman numerals indicate two statements: one for the bass alone, the second for the bass plus its counterpoint. Wagner rejected this sketch, and the problem with it is obvious: the counterpoint might well be used to some purpose, but it conditioned modifications in the bass-line which render it altogether less satisfactory than the original one.

On a second piece of blank paper, Wagner made another sketch in ink on free-hand staves based on his variation of 'Fafner':

Ex. 10

He began with a transposition of his melody to F (the pitch-level of the 'Fafner' melody itself) and then continued with the variation in C expanded now from twelve to sixteen measures, supplying a harmonization of the return to F at the end. From there, he reverted directly to his original 'Fafner' melody in duple meter, with which he followed the same plan: a statement of the melody in F in its original four-measure form, followed by a transposition to C with expansion to allow for a return to F at the end. He also included an indication for tremolo strings on C to appear above the original 'Fafner' phrase.

On a piece of music paper, Wagner took his four-measure 'Fafner' phrase and reworked it so that it followed the idea in his second sketch: to present the phrase first as a bass-line alone, then to repeat the bass-line with an added counterpoint (see Ex. 11). To this sketch, Wagner added phrasing and dynamic indications.

In this form, and with this harmonization, the motive plays a crucial role in the later first act of *Siegfried*. It appears in augmentation at the

Ex. 11

end of scene 2 when the Wanderer tells Mime that only someone who has not learned to fear will be able to reforge Nothung. In this passage, Wagner changes the upper-part C and D in the first two bars of his sketch to F and G. The passage reappears twice in scene 3: first, with Mime's initial speech after Siegfried's entrance, where it includes a three-bar interruption for Siegfried; and secondly, when Mime, trying to teach Siegfried to fear, tells him about Fafner. In both the latter passages, Wagner used an initial counterpoint closer to his sketch, beginning on C.

In all three of these passages, the fragment cadences on C, which is Wagner's momentary tonic. On the one hand, this helps to explain the signature of three flats in his third sketch. Wagner was regarding the tonality from the point of view of where the phrase ends, rather than where it begins. When the motive first appears in the first act during Mime's initial monologue, it is transposed down a whole tone: its conclusion here is on B flat, the tonic of that scene. There the conclusion serves to initiate Wagner's triple-meter variation, beginning on B flat, but the change in meter is no longer apparent because of the triple augmentation of the initial phrase.

In Mime's monologue, both forms of the motive thus appear in the context of triple meter. At the end of scene 2 and beginning of scene 3, both forms appear in the context of duple meter: we have noted that the Wanderer has the first phrase at its original pitch-level, and scene 3 begins with the variation at the E-flat pitch-level fitted into the duple-meter context by augmentation.

The last item in this complex is a sketch in ink on still another piece of letter paper:

Ex. 12

Here Wagner took his first bass motive intact, and concentrated on the problem of a new continuation for it, complete with counterpoint. This continuation is employed intact as measures 21–9 of the prelude to Act II of *Siegfried*—not surprisingly, then, Cosima later labelled this slip of paper 'Entwurf zu Fafner's Ruhe' (*Fafners Ruhe* (*Fafner's Repose*) was Wagner's name for this prelude). But the presence of the early rejected phrase as a preface suggests strongly that this sketch, like the others, dates from 1851.

On the same sheet as the first 'Fafner' sketches discussed above are two further sketches in pencil labelled *Waldvogel*:

Ex. 13 & 14

To the right of them, Wagner added in ink the following sketch, transposing his second idea from C to E:

Ex. 15

Rhythm originally different here

This latter sketch probably dates from the later period, when Wagner was actually working on *Siegfried*. In any case, the first of these sketches seems to have prefigured the tonality of E for the *Waldvogel* and the conclusion of Act II.

Finally, upside down on the second sheet discussed above, is the following sketch in pencil:

Ex. 16

Schmieden

LATER METHOD

Sketches such as these were on Wagner's desk when he began work on *Das Rheingold* on 1 November 1853. Aside from his ill-fated attempts to compose music for *Siegfrieds Tod* and *Der junge Siegfried* in 1850 and 1851, *Das Rheingold* represented for Wagner a return to operatic composition after an interval of five and a half years. Wagner used a new method for *Das Rheingold*, which he notes in his autobiography:

> As far as the method was concerned, I soon found myself in difficulty when I started to write down the orchestral prelude, conceived in Spezia in a kind of half-dream, in my usual way of making a draft [in ink] on two staves. I was compelled to resort immediately to a draft of a full score; this tempted me to sketch out in pencil only the very hastiest outlines for immediate elaboration in full score.[10]

The new method, as Wagner suggests, arose from the fact that the prelude to the opera is simply an elaboration of the E flat major triad, and therefore, in principle, an elaborated draft for this passage would come so close to an actual full score that he might as well simply go ahead and make it from the outset.

The first stage in Wagner's new method which was to remain his first stage for the rest of his creative career is a Preliminary Draft in pencil, written on oblong half-sheets rather than the full-sized upright sheets he had used for drafts of his earlier works up through and including *Siegfrieds Tod*. 'Half-sheet' seems the best description as they are approximately half the size of the paper Wagner had used for his earlier drafts. These half-sheets usually have fourteen or fifteen staves, as opposed to the twenty-one or so staves of the paper for his earlier drafts. Wagner's primary concern here is the setting of the text, but the crucial feature is that he worked straight through from the beginning to the end of the opera. He thus planned the work as a whole while first setting the text.

These Preliminary Drafts are always based on earlier sketches, of course, just as the drafts for his earlier works had been. The crucial difference is that, whereas earlier those sketches had largely consisted of settings of sections of text, now they are sketches worked out independently of the text and adapted to text only in the Preliminary Draft itself. The 'cleaner' and freer of corrections per section a Preliminary Draft is, the more certain we may be that earlier sketches were used to make it—before that passage was entered in the Preliminary Draft.

Wagner's decision to use pencil for his Preliminary Draft, rather than the ink he had used for the initial drafts for *Tannhäuser* and *Lohengrin*, is also important. Every composer has felt at some point the frustrating disparity between the speed of the mind in conceiving music and the speed of the human hand in writing it down. Wagner could write more quickly in pencil than in ink. He had in fact two distinct musical handwritings: the extremely hasty one with pencil, and the much neater and more carefully controlled one with ink.

When Wagner was dissatisfied with something he had written, he simply crossed out what he did not like and continued on. If he wished to make changes later on, he either wrote the new version over the earlier one, or employed a separate work-sheet for the purpose. He quite consistently maintained these two distinct levels of revision throughout his compositional practice: (1) changes made while working on a particular passage in a given draft, in which he crossed out the unsatisfactory material and continued with the new version; and (2) changes made at any time afterwards, which are written over the unsatisfactory passage or on separate worksheets.

When proceeding to his next stage, whatever that next stage may have been, Wagner seems to have preferred to work from a draft in ink, perhaps from the habit of his earlier practice. As a result, the Preliminary Drafts for *Das Rheingold, Die Walküre*, the first two acts of *Siegfried*, and most of *Tristan* were carefully traced over in ink by Mathilde Wesendonk. The Preliminary Drafts for the later portions of the *Ring* have also been traced over in similar fashion, but we do not know when or by whom.

Wagner's decision to elaborate directly from his draft in pencil on two staves into full score had its problematic side, however. Wagner complained to Liszt in his letter to the latter of 7 February 1854 that he 'could not find any way of writing down the *Vorspiel* clearly as a sketch'.[11] And indeed his opening in the Preliminary Draft shows the problem clearly enough,[12] for he was able to do little more than indicate the formal outline of it. He had indicated a peroration of the E flat triad for brass in the lowest register, and continued with a hasty indication of string figuration expanding through several registers, but that is all he was really able to do in the way of composition before working the passage out in full score, where he fortunately changed the string figuration. Wagner was in effect 'composing' the passage to a great extent while making the full score, besides working out the instrumentation. Furthermore, Wagner was working with a new orchestra posing new problems of sonority that he could not orchestrate automatically.

The group of eight horns in the *Vorspiel* is just such a case. There are many corrections indicated for these instruments. The *Ring* orchestra itself evolved gradually. One of the discarded sheets from Wagner's full score for the opening scene was later used by Wagner as a trial title-page on the reverse side, complete with a list of instruments:

1 Kl[eine] Fl[öte]	8 Hörner (4 Saxhörner—bass (B),
3 gr[osse] Fl[öten]	baryton (B), tenor (Es), alt (B))
3 Hoboen	3 Tromp.
1 Engl. Horn	1 Saxtromp. (à 4 cyl.) in Es
3 Clarin.	3 Tenor-Bass Pos.
1 Bassclar.	1 Tuba (oder Contrabass-Pos. in B)
3 Fagott.	1 Saxhorn-contrabass.

Pauken (Becken. Triangel. Tamb.) Harfe

Wagner also specified his complete complement of sixty-four strings. The woodwind group is listed as it later appears, but the brass list is certainly curious, as are the indications for tambourine (which Wagner had used in both *Tannhäuser* and *Lohengrin*) and only one harp.

After beginning his full score in the usual way, Wagner decided to switch to pencil somewhere between m. 118 of the *Vorspiel* and Flosshilde's first speech in the opening scene. Just when he switched from ink to pencil cannot be determined exactly, because of a missing portion in the manuscript. The remainder of the document is not really a full score at all, for Wagner also switched to half-sheets like those used for his preliminary draft, beginning at Flosshilde's speech 'Wie thöricht seid ihr, dumme Schwestern, dünkt euch dieser nicht schön [Eul 72/m7]' ('Oh foolish sisters, blind to beauty, can't you see that he is fair?'). When Wagner made the remainder of this document, he first entered the material from his Preliminary Draft, the vocal line on the top staff, the bass line on the bottom one. In between, he added staves for the various instruments as needed: *not* in any fixed order or systematic arrangement on the page. Aside from the opening portion, then, this document is actually an intermediate draft in which Wagner worked out his orchestration, and it seems best to call it an 'Instrumentation Draft'. It is unique to *Das Rheingold*, and Wagner never found it necessary to make such a draft again. Like all the drafts from which Wagner made his full scores, the margin here contains a column of notations in which Wagner determined the layout for a page of full score. He naturally made such notations while working on the full score, and they have nothing to do with the draft in which they are found.

It is scarcely surprising that Wagner felt overwhelmed by the labour that he foresaw the making of a full score was going to pose. For a while, he thought that a copyist might ease the burden by taking his Instrumentation Draft and making a clean full score from it. In his letter to Liszt of the 4 March 1854,[13] Wagner lamented his difficulty and asked whether Liszt could suggest a qualified copyist. Liszt does not seem to have made a suggestion, but Wagner found someone in the Zürich area who started in at the beginning and worked along as far as Flosshilde's first speech, the point where Wagner had switched to pencil for his first draft of full score. Wagner dismissed the copyist and once again made corrections in the horn parts of the *Vorspiel*. After this experience, Wagner never again used a copyist at a preliminary stage of his work. Meanwhile, the gift that spring of an exceptionally fine gold pen-point from the Wesendonks helped to reconcile Wagner to the inevitable task of making his own full scores.

Wagner's Preliminary Draft for *Das Rheingold* is almost entirely on just two staves, and in degree of musical elaboration it resembles the first drafts in ink which he made for *Tannhäuser* and *Lohengrin*. In making his Instrumentation Draft for an orchestral combination with which he was not yet totally familiar, Wagner had to concentrate on orchestration, and with such a meagre 'hasty outline' from which to elaborate, he understandably ignored purely compositional problems to some extent. As a result of his method, then, many vocal portions of the *Rheingold*, particularly in scenes 2 and 4, sound like little more than accompanied recitative. This does not effect the instrumental passages, which Wagner characteristically elaborates on both staves in the Preliminary Draft.

Wagner began *Die Walküre* with a Preliminary Draft in pencil, working as in *Das Rheingold* straight through the entire opera from beginning to end. This time he took pains to see that there would be no 'sketchy' sections, and for a good many vocal sections, he used two instrumental staves rather than just one. These sections are thus as fully worked out as in the final Composition Drafts for *Tannhäuser* and *Lohengrin*. For the passages involving only one instrumental staff, he squeezed in a good bit more of the texture than had been the case for much of *Das Rheingold*.

It is with *Die Walküre* that Wagner's construction of a consistent but constantly shifting texture of orchestral polyphony from the beginning to the end of an act really begins. The prelude to Act I is the first instrumental passage Wagner elaborated on more than three staves. The central section is written on four staves, and at the climax, Wagner included two systems of six staves each.

The thirteen-bar conclusion of scene 2 in Act II provides an excellent illustration of the care with which Wagner put together his Preliminary Draft. He began by writing out a melody in the bass, a variation in triple meter of a theme from Wotan's monologue.

Ex. 17

He decided that this theme would work better in an upper register with a new counterpoint as bass-line, and wrote a new version on top of the preceding (Ex. 18).

He began with the oboe, but changed his mind after he had entered the third note, and shifted the theme down an octave for the English horn. In the ninth bar, Wagner cut the melody off, letting the oboe enter with a direct transition into the material for scene 3. Wagner initiated this transition with the central motive of the opening of scene 3 in augmentation. He crossed the whole passage out and started over again on a fresh system.

Wagner must have noticed that the beginning of his new counter-

Ex. 18

point in the bass had the same outline as bars 4–6 of his original melody. Therefore, he could easily fill out the beginning of the bass-line and make the resemblance exact:

Ex. 19

He could complete the canonic imitation by adding the first three measures of the original melody at the beginning of his new bass-line. The passage would then begin with the melody in the bass after all. Writing on top of the preceding sketch, he produced the sketch shown in Ex. 20, page 298.

Still not satisfied, however, Wagner started over again, entering Brünnhilde's last word and indicating the harmonization (Ex. 21, page 298).

Ex. 20

Ex. 21

After writing the third measure of the bass, Wagner entered the first phrase of the English horn part, beginning the imitation a bar earlier than before, but this would not work out. Returning to the lower staff, he revised the third measure of his bass-line, as shown in the preceding example, and continued on with longer note-values. This time he included the three-note ornament, missing since his first sketch.

Aside from the new rhythm in the fourth bar of the bass, Wagner was back where he had left off in Ex. 20. In order to present his original melody in the bass, the imitation would have to begin after three measures.

From this point on, Wagner corrected and revised on top of the above, and finally continued beyond it. From the confused jungle of what appears at first glance to be an indecipherable maze, made worse by Mathilde Wesendonk's tracing in ink, several stages emerge. Wagner's first step was to apply the idea of longer note values for the bass-line beginning with the English horn entry. To continue the bass part, he added an extra measure before the one with the leap of a sixth. This yielded the following:

Ex. 22

Considering how his original melody would fit against the newly revised bass, Wagner worked out the following:

Ex. 23

This conditioned a small change at the end of the bass part. It also meant that a measure was lacking in the English horn melody, which Wagner duly wrote out in another place on the page, indicating it for insertion at the proper point. He was then able to continue on with little difficulty (see Ex. 24, page 300).

Wagner returned to his original idea of the half-note on F in the fifth measure of the bass part, thus restoring the melodic identity between this line and the English horn part. At the same time, this change serves to strengthen the point of the new A-F leap introduced in the following measure. The passage concludes with the change to oboe two measures before the beginning of scene 3—a change Wagner had had in mind from the time of his second stage. Now, however, the oboe imitates the bass-line of three measures earlier, rather than introducing the musical material of the new scene.

Wagner's work on this passage was now finished as far as the Preliminary Draft was concerned. He had achieved the final form of the passage, except at the beginning. All that remained was to restore the original rhythm of the first two measures of the bass part in the last

Ex. 24

example. In that form, the unit would work perfectly in counterpoint against the second measure of the English horn line. The first measure of the English horn could then be shifted back, reducing the interval of canonic entry from three measures, as originally planned, to one.

Wagner did not need to make an Instrumentation Draft for *Die Walküre*. The experience of scoring *Das Rheingold* left him thoroughly familiar with the *Ring* orchestra. He was now able to make an actual full score in pencil, and later a fair copy of it in ink.

Making the full score caused Wagner considerable difficulties none the less. In connection with *Das Rheingold*, he noted in his autobiography the possible shortcoming in this particular method of composition: 'This process often led to difficulties, as the slightest interruption in my work made me lose the thread of my rough draft, and I had to start from the beginning before I could recall it to my memory.'[14] Wagner had been able to get around this problem in *Das Rheingold* by finishing his Preliminary Draft in a remarkably short time and by proceeding to his Instrumentation Draft almost immediately thereafter, working through to the end with no significant interruption.

Die Walküre, however, is a much longer work than *Das Rheingold*. The Preliminary Draft for the latter opera had taken Wagner less than eleven weeks, while that for *Die Walküre* involved some delays and took a full six months. Wagner experienced further delays while making the full score of *Die Walküre*. All in all, a much longer period of time separated composition of any passage in the Preliminary Draft and the making of full score for it. In *Mein Leben*, Wagner wrote about the difficulties he experienced in England in 1855:

> The instrumentation of the *Walküre*, which I had hoped to finish off here, only advanced a paltry hundred pages. I was hindered in this principally by the circumstance that the sketches from which I had to work on the instrumentation had been written down without considering the extent to which a prolonged interruption of my working humour might affect the coherence of the sketch. How often did I sit before those pencilled pages as if they had been unfamiliar hieroglyphics which I was incapable of deciphering![15]

In other words, Wagner had to concentrate on *compositional* problems while making his full score, even though he had elaborated the Preliminary Draft more than he had for *Das Rheingold*. The orchestra itself was more familiar to Wagner now, but he still could not give his full attention to the problems of instrumentation. It is not surprising that *Die Walküre* represents little if any improvement over *Das Rheingold* in the latter respect. It is not so well scored as the operas from *Siegfried* on.

When Wagner began working on the music of *Siegfried*, he made two significant changes in his method to ensure that he would never again encounter the frustrating problems he had experienced while scoring *Die Walküre*. The first change—and by far the more important one for the problem of scoring—was to make a second complete draft in ink on at least three staves (two instrumental plus one vocal) before proceeding to a full score. In this intermediate draft, Wagner developed the musical conception fully, down to the very details of the orchestral texture, including instrumental doublings. Secondly, he decided to compose one act at a time—i.e. to carry the composition through all stages, from Preliminary Draft to the complete full score, for each act separately— to complete a given act in full score before going on to the next act. In

301

addition, he frequently worked back and forth between the two drafts, so as not to allow too much time to elapse between his setting of text and the final musical elaboration.

The fundamentals of Wagner's method remain constant from now on —two drafts (the first in pencil, the second in ink) plus the full score. At this point in his career, Wagner's preliminary drafts are about as fully elaborated as his second ('Composition Drafts') for *Tannhäuser* and *Lohengrin* had been. About the only perceptible difference is the use of ink for the composition drafts of earlier operas, pencil for these preliminary drafts. His developed drafts, on the other hand, represent a stage of elaboration beyond anything he had worked out in his career before this time. It would therefore be a mistake to think of them as resembling Wagner's second draft for *Lohengrin*.

Wagner began the composition of *Siegfried* in the latter part of September 1856. His Developed Draft is dated 22 September at the beginning, but his Preliminary Draft has no date, an unusual phenomenon for Wagner's drafts. The Preliminary Draft is even more unusual, if not absolutely unique, in the fact that it does not begin at the beginning, but with the setting of Mime's initial monologue. A sketch for the prelude occurs on what is now numbered as the second sheet of the draft—and it is not a complete sketch by any means, but rather a hasty abstraction of the present prelude—in other words, a preliminary sketch. After indicating a short elaboration of the initial F, it begins directly with the characteristic Nibelung rhythm—for practical purposes, at about measure 64 of the final prelude. The familiar opening, with the motif of falling thirds in the bassoons, is not present, nor is that motif used in Mime's monologue as represented on the first sheet of the Draft. Wagner later added a separate sketch for the opening of the prelude below the one just described—it is actually labelled 'Anfang'.

At this point, we return to the remark Wagner made to Uhlig in his letter of 2 September 1851 when he was working on music for *Der junge Siegfried*: 'I already have the beginning in my head.' The conclusion seems inescapable that Wagner's first sketch, now embedded in his Preliminary Draft for Act I of *Siegfried*, was made in 1851 for *Der junge Siegfried*. The main part of this prelude consequently represents the earliest section of music used in the *Ring*. From a stylistic point of view, this particular prelude is less sophisticated than comparable passages from *Die Walküre*, and Wagner could have made the sketch before he composed *Das Rheingold*.

This would also explain the fact that in 1856 Wagner began his

Preliminary Draft with Mime's monologue. He did not start at the beginning, because he already had a sketch for it from five years before. His real task now was to see if he could elaborate that material as a setting of Mime's monologue.

A good example of the kind of sketch Wagner worked from when making his Preliminary Draft is provided by the following:

Exs. 25 & 26

The sketch begins with the modulatory passage leading into Mime's *Starenlied*. Wagner made three different conclusions to the first ten bars. The first conclusion involved only one measure, which would confirm the tonality of C minor. Wagner crossed out that measure, and made the next conclusion of two bars, which would confirm A flat. However, he indicated a change to F in his characteristic manner of simply writing in a letter F for the tonality of the passage to follow. In the third conclusion, he simply reharmonized the uppermost voice from the second, so as to prepare the tonality of F more strongly, and he added the word *nach* to indicate that the tonality of F would follow *after* those two measures.

Then come a group of sketches for the *Starenlied*. Wagner continued in the same meter, working out the melody in triplets. The first two measures present the main motive idea, and Wagner did not ultimately use the first continuation which remains in the tonic. His next alternative continuation represents the final form of the initial phrase. His first idea was the move to D flat in the final measure, which he changed to C. He next tried writing out the phrase in 6/8 meter, with the conclusion on the dominant in the fourth bar, and continuing from there with the final measure as he had conceived it, moving then to D flat.

Wagner used his sketch for the beginning absolutely intact, and he simply added to it a vocal line for Mime, which picks up some elements of the orchestral melody. For the *Starenlied*, Wagner decided to adapt the independently conceived melody itself to the text. He wrote the section in 3/4 meter, but used the indication ♩ - ♪ to preserve the metrical relationship he had planned in his first sketch. The first four bars of his 6/8 sketch worked perfectly for the opening phrase, once he eliminated the change to a C-major chord he had introduced into the third measure of his 6/8 sketch (in short, he reverted to the harmonization of his original sketch for this alternative). He then introduced a balancing phrase for the next group of lines, and continued from there with the last bar of his 6/8 sketch. This procedure is typical of Wagner: he sketched a passage independently of the text, and the Preliminary Draft shows his elaboration of that sketch while setting the text.

Wagner began the full score for Act I on 11 October, but his work was about to undergo a significant interruption of more than six weeks. Liszt arrived for an extended visit on the 13th, remaining until 27 November. A few days before, the two composers collaborated in a concert in which Wagner conducted Beethoven's 'Eroica' Symphony, and Liszt conducted his own symphonic poems *Orpheus* and *Les Préludes*. This marks the beginning of Liszt's influence on Wagner's harmonic language, an influence soon to be manifested in *Siegfried* itself.

Wagner resumed work on *Siegfried* on 1 December, with the setting of Mime's 'Einst lag wimmernd ein Weib' in his preliminary draft. The beginning of scene 2, with the series of chords to be associated through the remainder of the *Ring* with the Wanderer, appears in the preliminary draft in the following form:

Ex. 27

The series of chords is present under the setting of the end of Mime's speech, just as it is in the final version—it appears at the moment the Wanderer comes on stage. Wagner has not yet filled out the full triad on E. Wagner decided to overlap the end of Mime's speech with the beginning of the Wanderer's, but he did not mark the new scene, nor did he change to duple meter until the Wanderer actually begins to sing. The Wanderer's first two words recall the first two chords from the preceding series just as they do in the final version, but instead of continuing with a full second statement of the series a whole tone lower, Wagner makes a cadence in C, the tonality he planned for the Wanderer scene. The rhythmic change at the conclusion of the Wanderer's line is of a type Wagner often made, either in the Preliminary Draft itself or between the Preliminary Draft and the Developed Draft.

Switching to his Developed Draft, Wagner first wrote out the following:

Ex. 28

The indication *Str* and the change from E flat to E natural in the second bar are later additions to this sketch in pencil. He changed the meter at the point where the Wanderer's series of chords begins, and he decided it would be best to change the signature at that same point also. He crossed out his final measure and started again:

Ex. 29

He took Mime's vocal part and adjusted it for duple meter. Wagner forgot to include a staff for the Wanderer's part, and he also had the wrong signature for the orchestral staves, so he crossed out the preceding sketch and began again (see Ex. 30, page 307).

He has now included the full E-major triad as well as the indication for pizzicato strings, which make a complete cadence in A along with Mime. He broke off after the second bar of the Wanderer's speech and returned to his Preliminary Draft to work out the continuation. He

Ex. 30

has already taken away the moving parts in the lower register from the accompaniment of those two bars, and in the Preliminary Draft he took the final step of halving the note-values.

Ex. 31

Here, Wagner stated the series of chords twice, a whole-tone apart just as in the final version. He indicated a contrast in scoring for the two statements, using trombones the first time, the cellos the second.

When he came back to this passage in the Developed Draft, he wrote it out once more, and noted the final form of the scoring (see Ex. 32).

The incipit at the beginning of the orchestral staves is not a sketch, as might be assumed at first glance, but the working out of the spacing of the chords for the so-called Wagner tubas. The uppermost (melodic) element is taken by two horns in unison an octave higher. The second

Ex. 32

statement is given to the trombones, with the melody assigned to a trumpet.

On 19 December thoughts about *Tristan* interrupted Wagner's creative work on *Siegfried*, and he made the earliest dated sketches for material eventually used in *Tristan*. Wagner explained directly in his letter of the same day to the Princess Marie zu Sayn Wittgenstein that he

> ... wanted to work on the composition of *Siegfried* today and unexpectedly fell into *Tristan*. For the time being, music without text. There is a lot for which I would rather write music than poetry, however ...
>
> The Nibelungs are beginning to bore me, though the passage in which Siegfried hears about his mother's death turned out quite well ...
>
> But as I said, today *Tristan* got in my way with a melodic thread that kept springing up whenever I wanted to leave it, so that I could have elaborated it the whole day—which, however, would not be proper at all. Now I am writing to you in order to be rid of it ...[16]

Wagner's work on 19 December survives on a dated half-sheet of sketches labelled 'Liebesscene. Tristan und Isolde' ('Love scene. Tristan und Isolde'). He was elaborating two fragments from a diary.

Ex. 33

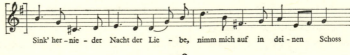

Ex. 34

Hell dann leuch - tet Ster - ne der Won - ne
Glüht im Bu - sen mir die — Son - ne

These fragments first occurred to him in conjunction with poetic
lines. Wagner later used both the texts and the music conceived here in
Act II of *Tristan,* but *separately.* In the sketches of 19 December,
Wagner was not concerned with the texts.

His first step was a four-part harmonization of the first fragment.

Ex. 35

This is not the usual four-part 'harmonization', but rather an abstract
realization. He was evidently not thinking of strings, since his alto
and tenor voices go outside the ranges of the violin and viola. It will be
noticed that in his third measure, Wagner originally placed the two
half-notes, F and E flat, in the alto part, but later lowered those notes
an octave and assigned them to the tenor. His problem was how to
accommodate the transition from the lower register of the first two
measures to the higher register of the third.

He must have seen that the alto voice could make that transition quite
easily in the latter half of the second measure. He needed only to
elaborate that voice by filling out the three notes of the tonic triad. That
in turn suggested the elaboration of the same voice in the first half of
the measure, where Wagner duplicated the melody of the fourth
measure.

Similarly, in the tenor, he could fill in the triadic note as the last
eighth-note of the measure, thus making a transition up to the F natural
at the beginning of the third measure. This in turn made for the revision
of the part-writing in the third measure already described. The alto
could retain the D it had reached in the previous measure, and this made
for better spacing of all four parts.

Wagner then supplied a balancing four-measure phrase, beginning with the same melodic configuration as the first:

Ex. 36

He has marked an increase in tempo and a *crescendo* towards the dominant which is reached in the third measure. With a *diminuendo*, the phrase resolves back to the tonic at the end of the fourth measure.

Wagner provided an alternative modulation for the end of the second phrase in his next sketch:

Ex. 37

He retained the *g* pedal-point, which he had had to change to *d* in the third measure of Ex. 36 in order to accommodate the change to the dominant harmony. In Ex. 37, then, he moved to the sub-dominant.

So far, Wagner's exploration of possible changes of harmony has been timid, to say the least. His main concerns have actually been the making of fluid melodic counterpoints for the two inner voices (as in Ex. 35), and the completion of the melody itself by the addition of a balancing phrase (Ex. 36).

At this point, Wagner reverted to the second fragment from the Diary, which has the same initial measure as the first. In this fragment however, there is a striking change of harmony from G to A flat. Wagner's concern was to realize the harmonic implications of the melody in a simple chordal harmonization.

Ex. 38

He ignored the problem of giving melodic value to the inner voices. The chromatic implications of the modulation yield movements by semitone in each of the three lower voices.

Wagner later appended an indication for the first two measures of this phrase, suggesting the possibility of treating it sequentially one tone higher.

Wagner continued with an elaboration of the latter half of the second measure. From a melodic point of view, this little unit is a linearization of the interval of a third, which has initiated each of the sketches made so far. The dotted rhythm is characteristic of each one, though now in diminution—from the ♩.♪ of the original leap of a third, to the ♫ at the end of the linearization. Wagner expanded this idea so that it culminated in the original melodic configuration, harmonized now without triads.

The next sketch presents what is in reality a continuation for Ex. 38, using the earlier idea in descending sequence.

Ex. 39

Wagner added a new element, however: the last measure of Ex. 38 and the first measure of Ex. 39 have intensified the chromaticism implicit in the presence of the semi-tone at the end of the original melodic unit (first measure of Ex. 33). Originally, that semi-tone had been in the characteristic dotted rhythm; now we have an ascending chromatic line of three notes in the rhythm ♩ ♫.

Wagner made a continuation of Ex. 39.

Ex. 40

The word 'Trist[an]' indicates some form of contrast, either with the orchestra alone up to this point, or else Isolde. Tristan's first phrase is a slightly expanded form of the second measure of Ex. 39, thus continuing the descending sequence one further step. His 'new' continuation, marked piano, is actually an elaboration of the chromatic idea at the end of the original unit, which we have already seen in an intermediate elaboration in Exs. 38 and 39. As it appears here, however, it has the dotted rhythm of the original melody once again, and seems like another foreshadowing of the famous chromatic motive at the beginning of the prelude to Act I. Once again, Wagner placed this new material over a pedal-point on *g*. By now, the progressive elaborations of the chromatic element in Exs. 38, 39 and 40 in the melodic realm have suggested to Wagner the means by which he could provide the inner parts of Ex. 37 with melodic independence:

Ex. 41

This sketch is fundamentally a revision of the harmonization of Ex. 37, with the inner parts more rigorously worked out. Wagner labelled this fragment '*Var*', presumably indicating *Variante*, or an alternative reading to Ex. 37.

The next two sketches are likewise two different variants of the first two measures of Ex. 38, in accordance with the possibility Wagner had noted there:

Ex. 42

Ex. 43

In Ex. 42, Wagner duplicated the original unit of Ex. 38 and then continued by stating it again a semi-tone higher. In Ex. 43, he did the same thing, but a whole tone higher. He evidently preferred the alternative offered by Ex. 43 to that in Ex. 42 because Ex. 43 is the only one of the two for which he bothered to work out the inner voices of the continuation.

The last sketch represents still another possible means of development of Wagner's original unit:

Ex. 44

Beginning with the first measure of Ex. 39, Wagner repeated it once, and from there on reduced the melodic configuration to just the first three notes, thus leaving behind the chromatic ending which he had explored independently in Exs. 38, 39 and 40. In lowering the first tone of the original generating unit by a half-step, he accomplished an easy modulation from the D of the opening to A flat (functioning here as the dominant of D flat). D flat emerges in the fifth measure and changes back to its dominant again in the seventh measure. This sketch is particularly interesting because it is carried over intact into the second act of the opera, with the dotted rhythm removed and one or two other small changes, like the substitution of G natural for A flat in the melody of the fifth measure of the sketch.

What we have seen here is the progressive development of elements implicit in Wagner's original melody, which he had initially conceived as the setting of a poetic idea. He was particularly intrigued with the motif embodied in the first measure of that melody, and the sketches we have just examined represent expansions of one element or another from that generating idea of only four notes.

At some unknown point, Wagner made use of the ideas embodied in sketches 35 to 43, by combining them in such as way as to make a continuous musical complex. He did this one 'sleepless' night in the form of a little musical letter to Mathilde Wesendonk:[17]

Ex. 45

It will be seen that since Wagner had worked out all the essential problems of his material, he had only to combine the smaller sketches to achieve his result. He began with Ex. 35 followed immediately by 36, smoothing out some of the rougher places in the inner parts, particularly the fourth measure of Ex. 35 and the first measure of Ex. 36, where he wished to vary outright repetition. Wagner then proceeded with the first two measures of Ex. 38 and the continuation of those measures in Ex. 43. He followed this with the last two measures of Ex. 38 and the two complete measures of Ex. 39. All that remained was to add a two-measure cadence. Wagner in addition supplied detailed indications of the dynamics and phrase-articulations in order to make his conception clear to Mathilde.

On 22 December, just three days after these sketches for the love-scene in *Tristan*, Wagner wrote to Otto Wesendonk:

> For my part, I am already forsaken enough; I fear I shall soon be forsaken by everything—finally even by my desire to work. I can no longer feel disposed towards *Siegfried*, and my musical sensibility roams far beyond into the realm of melancholy where my mood fits. Truly everything strikes me as downright dull and superficial.[18]

The mood expressed here remained characteristic of Wagner through the major part of 1857, a period of constant shifting between work on *Siegfried* and a growing interest in *Tristan*.

He was distracted on other occasions from work on *Siegfried* to sketch materials later used in *Tristan*. At one point, for example, he entered in his printed copy of the *Ring* poem the following setting of a line from the third act of *Siegfried*.

Ex. 46

This sketch begins with the chromatic motive that opens the *Tristan* prelude, while the termination involves a characteristic figure associated with King Mark. Wagner's ultimate setting of this line is cadential in function, as the sketch had implied, but it runs as follows:

Ex. 47

Another sketch from Wagner's copy of the *Ring* poem has an even more curious history:

Ex. 48

Wagner probably made the change in the inner voice on the upper staff in the penultimate measure in order to avoid duplicating the B flat of the bass-line. He elaborated the main motivic element from this sketch in ink on another sheet, following the sequential idea of the original sketch but now by a whole tone rather than by a minor third.[19]

Ex. 49

IIIʳ Act oder Tristan

His label indicates that he was uncertain for a time whether this material belonged in the third act of *Siegfried* or in *Tristan*. After deciding for the former, Wagner elaborated the first phrase and incorporated at the end a motif familiar from *Die Walküre*:

Ex. 50

These sketches indicate that Wagner had decided at least as early as 1857 that the later portions of the *Ring* would have a more 'chromatic' musical idiom. Thus, one reason why Wagner broke off work on the *Ring* after the second act of *Siegfried* was in order to make a kind of 'trial run' of the new idiom with *Tristan*, a dramatic subject for which he had sensed its appropriateness.

In spite of the insistence of musical ideas for *Tristan*, Wagner finished his first draft of the full score for the first act of *Siegfried* on 31 March. Some time elapsed, however, before he began Act II. On 28 April, he moved into the Asyl, the house which the Wesendonks had prepared for him on their estate. On 22 May, his forty-fourth birthday, Wagner began his Preliminary Draft for the second act. The day before, he had written to Mathilde Wesendonk:

> The Muse is beginning to visit me: does it betoken the certainty of your visit? The first thing I found was a melody which I didn't at all know

what to do with, till of a sudden the words from the last scene of Siegfried came into my head. A good omen. Yesterday I also hit on the commencement of act 2—as Fafner's Repose: which has an element of humour in it.[20]

Wagner's sketch for the melody he did not know what to do with runs as follows:

Ex. 51

Wagner evidently sent this sheet to Mathilde with his letter, for most of it has been traced over in ink—a situation common in Wagner's drafts during this period, but almost unknown in his individual sketches. Wagner has marked a particular measure *good*—the measure which serves as a pivot between several possible modulations. On the same staff, he continued with a modulation to D, while on the one below, he used that same measure to begin a return to the initial B flat. The passage marked for substitution shows an alternate version in which the imitation in the bass-line could be carried through consistently.

When the proper text from the third act of *Siegfried* occurred to him, Wagner entered the passage in his copy of the poem, transposing the beginning to F in order to accommodate the tenor range:

Ex. 52

For the change to A at the end, Wagner used his first alternative in the sketch but expanded it to include an extra measure. This material was ultimately used in *Tristan*, not in *Siegfried*, and Wagner finally set the above text from *Siegfried* with a crucial motive introduced in the opening scene of the third act, about which more will be said later:

Ex 53.

At some point, Wagner returned to his original sheet to deal with this material again, but now in duple meter:

Ex. 54

Wagner began this sketch in E flat and the modulation thus took him to G, but he used the elaborated version of the modulation, from his text-setting version. He got the bass part in the wrong register, beginning at the seventh measure, and made the necessary change before continuing. He then expanded the second phrase to full length but employed his second alternative in the original sketch to return this particular phrase to its tonic, G.

This material plays an important role in the second and third strophes of the passage known as 'Brangäne's Consolation' in the middle of the first act of *Tristan*. Some time after Wagner finished the poem of *Tristan*, but before he reached this passage in his Preliminary Draft, Wagner adapted lines from the third strophe to the very form of the melody he had achieved when adapting text from the third act of *Siegfried* and at the same pitch-level:

Ex. 55

In the copy of the poem made by Mathilde Wesendonk, from which Wagner worked while composing *Tristan,* he made a sketch in which he adapted the *first* lines of the third strophe to the beginning of this melody:

Ex. 56

When he later worked out 'Brangäne's Consolation' in his Preliminary Draft, he introduced the melody in the *second* strophe, in order to prepare its appearance as the musical basis for the third. This section of the Preliminary Draft is shown in Ex. 57 (see page 322).

When Wagner introduced the theme in the second strophe, he used the F-major version, but in duple meter. The instrumental part agrees with the final version through the twenty-third measure shown above. After the opening lines, Wagner evidently first wrote in the transposition of the first thirteen bars of Ex. 54, and adapted his text to the passage in the manner long since a habit of his (and which we saw earlier in the case of the introduction to Mime's *Starenlied*). He then wrote two transitional measures, continued with a literal recall of measures 3–9 of the strophe, using a newly devised vocal part to accommodate the remaining text, and supplied a cadence. Later on, Wagner considerably expanded the transition, as well as the cadence, a process which necessitated a complete reworking of the vocal part, including a new distribution of the text of the whole strophe in relation to the revised accompaniment.

In setting the third strophe, Wagner used the triple-meter version of this material. He began with the second alternative in his first sketch, which he had meanwhile used as the final portion of Ex. 54 above. Following the implication of the return of the tonic in those sketches, Wagner continued with a second statement at the same pitch-level,

L   321

und warb er Mar - ke dir zum Ge - mahl

wie woll-test du die Wahl doch schel - ten muss er nicht werth dir gel - ten von ed-ler

Art u. mild – em Muth wer gli - che dem Mann

an Macht u. Glanz? dem ein hehr – ster Held so

treu – lich dient wer möch – te sein Glück nicht thei – len,.

als Gat — tin [B]bei ihm wei – len

Iso un – – ge – minnt den hehr – – – sten Mann

nah mir stets zu se – hen wie könnt' ich die Qual be – ste – hen

was wähnst du, A-rge Un – – geminnt! Wo

leb – – te der Mann der dich nicht lieb – – te

der I-

-sol- - -den säh' und in I - sol - - den

se - lig nicht ganz _____ ver - ging.

Doch der dir er - ko - ren, wär' er so

([A] wüsst' ich bald)

kalt zög' ihn von bö - sen wüsst' ich

324

but then invoked the third alternative provided by his first sketch. To these two statements, he could fill in the two sections of text he had already adapted to this melody in the earlier sketches. In between there were five extra measures, for which Wagner had also worked out a vocal part. His first idea was probably to write an additional text of nine syllables for these measures. But he later shifted the initial words forward, thus delaying Brangäne's entrance in this strophe.

He composed on beyond what he had worked out in his second sketch with text, providing a new extended cadence. He was able to adapt the remaining text by using fragments of the orchestral melody, which worked for the lines 'Doch der dir erkoren' ('Yet the man chosen for you') and 'wär' er so kalt' ('if he were so cold'). Looking ahead beyond this, Wagner found it necessary to add four extra bars, in which he took his sequential idea one step further and thus effectively delayed his arresting return to E flat at the double bar of the Preliminary Draft.

To return now to the question of *Siegfried*. We saw that Wagner made the sketches for the material just discussed on 16 May. According to his letter to Mathilde Wesendonk cited above (pp. 317–18), he made a preliminary sketch for the prelude to Act II of *Siegfried* on the 20th. With that in hand, he began his Preliminary Draft for the act on the 22nd. This prelude makes use of material Wagner had conceived for *Der junge Siegfried*, specifically, the triple-meter variation of his 'Fafner' motive, shown in Ex. 8. After a five-bar introduction, Wagner states the first eight bars of the motive in C, the two four-bar phrases separated and extended to six bars each. The extensions utilize the tritone idea which Wagner used as an introduction. A three-bar interlude with ascending scale in the bass leads into the eight-bar phrase taken intact from Wagner's Ex. 12 above, the concluding F of which initiates the return of the first eight bars, but now in F, as in Ex. 10. These two four-bar units are now extended to seven-bar phrases by means of new interjections. The continuation comes fairly close to Wagner's idea of continuation in his early sketches (see in particular Exs. 8 and 10).

Thus Wagner based the opening section of the prelude on sketches from 1851, which determined the tonality of F minor for that section. The second section is in B minor, a tritone away, and Wagner undoubtedly would not have composed with this unusual tonal relationship in 1851. That tritone relationship in turn is prepared in the foreground of the opening section as the material of the introduction and the interludes between phrases from the early sketch on their first appearance.

When Wagner began his Developed Draft for this act on 18 June, he headed it with the significant inscription 'Tristan bereits beschlossen' ('Tristan already decided on'). Later that month, Wagner broke off work on *Siegfried* at the point where Siegfried first stretches out under the linden tree, reaching that point in his Preliminary Draft on the 26th, and in his Developed Draft on the 27th. On the 28th, he wrote to Liszt: 'I have led my young Siegfried into the beautiful forest solitude again; there I have left him under a linden tree, and, with tears from the depth of my heart, said farewell to him: he is better there than anywhere else.'[21] But on 13 July, Wagner took up the composition once again and finished the act in his Preliminary Draft on the 30th, and in his Developed Draft on 9 August. Soon afterwards he wrote to Marie zu Sayn Wittgenstein that he had tried to write a scenario for the *Tristan* poem,

> ... when suddenly I was overcome by so pitiful a longing for *Siegfried* that I took it out again and decided to complete at any rate the second act. This has now been done: Fafner is dead, Mime is dead, and Siegfried has followed the flying Forest Bird; and this, my dear child, has turned out very nicely, so that now I know my hero is all right. Yet all this has been a great strain on me, for while I was once more working at *Siegfried* I could get no peace from *Tristan*. I actually worked simultaneously at them both, *Tristan* taking more and more definite shape, and I being so passionately occupied with it that in the end the double labour was a perfect torment to me.[22]

Given the compositional problem as we have examined it, we can now determine one further element in the elaborate complex of reasons why Wagner put aside his composition of the *Ring* to take up *Tristan* in 1857. Composition of the first two acts of *Siegfried* was for Wagner to a large extent elaboration of materials from earlier periods—from 1851, when he had made sketches for *Der junge Siegfried*; and from *Das Rheingold* and *Die Walküre*. As things stood in 1857, most of the new musical ideas that were occurring to him were not appropriate for these two acts, and Wagner may well have wondered if they could be used in the third. They would in fact require another opera altogether for their realization and elaboration. Working with older materials had gone very well during the autumn and winter of 1856-7, and the first act is masterfully made. But as musical ideas for *Tristan* began to assert themselves more and more during the spring and summer of 1857, Wagner began to lose control of the new act. The second act of *Siegfried* contains some magnificent pages as always, but on the whole it is the weakest in the *Ring*.

Tristan brings one further, though incidental, change in Wagner's method. After the Prelude to Act I, Wagner no longer made a first full score in pencil and then a fair copy in ink. Instead, he made the full score directly in ink. This full score, which has been published in facsimile, thus shows the difference: the Prelude to Act I is a fair copy, the remainder a first draft. Wagner never again took the trouble to make two full scores.

Tristan, like *Siegfried*, was composed one act at a time—through all stages up through full score, for a given act, before the Preliminary

327

Draft for the next act was begun. *Tristan* was actually engraved for printing one act at a time, but had Wagner found a publisher for it soon enough, *Siegfried* could have been engraved in similar fashion, as could the first act of *Die Meistersinger*.

Beginning with the second act of *Die Meistersinger*, Wagner changed his procedure in such a way that he completed the entire opera in his Developed Draft before beginning the full score. His method for making a full score thus comes full circle in the latter part of his career.

Beginning with the second act of *Die Meistersinger*, Wagner increased the degree of elaboration embodied in his Developed Drafts, particularly for the instrumental passages. Wagner elaborated them on at least three, but often as many as four or five, staves. Beginning with his Developed Draft for the third act of *Siegfried*, Wagner used the term *Orchesterskizze* for this stage in his work, and Orchestral Draft seems an appropriate translation, though the customary term for it is 'short score' or 'particell'.

Our final examples come from the third act of *Siegfried*. He had made the full score of the second act in Munich from end of 1864 to end of 1865. During the latter part of 1864, Wagner once again experienced a period of indecision involving *Siegfried*. For some time, he was undecided about whether to finish *Siegfried* or to finish *Die Meistersinger*. Making the full score of the second act seemed to resolve the question in favour of *Siegfried*, but after leaving Munich at the end of 1865, Wagner returned to *Die Meistersinger*. The Preliminary Draft for the third act of *Siegfried* was not begun until March 1869.

For the prelude, Wagner elaborated a sketch which he had jotted on a worksheet some time earlier:

Ex. 58

This is another variation of the melody introduced in the bass in Wotan's monologue in the second act of *Die Walküre*, which he worked out as a cadence to the first half of that act as we discussed above. An interesting feature of the present sketch is the third measure, which seems possibly an outgrowth of the third measure of the bass-line of the *Walküre* sketch shown above in Ex. 21. The tonality is G minor, the key of the prelude, and it is curious that when this theme is first introduced into Wotan's monologue (and into the *Ring* as a whole), it appears in G minor before being shifted up to A, the tonic of the monologue.

Unfortunately, we have no direct evidence about the date of the sketch. The last two measures provide a new termination for the melody —a termination which Wagner used in his Preliminary Draft—but otherwise, the melody in the Prelude is an exact duplication of the G minor passage from the second act of *Die Walküre*, which lacks the unusual third measure of the sketch.

Meanwhile, another sketch in a small notebook from the early 1860s was also at Wagner's disposal when he planned the opening of the third act:

Ex. 59

The Preliminary Draft of the Prelude runs as follows:[23]

Ex. 60

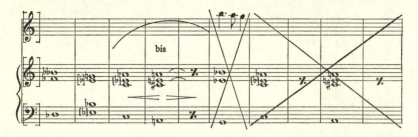

330

[addition in ink]

Version I

[A. = ♩ ♩]
[B]

Version II

Version III
[B]

331

It will be noticed that Wagner uses the termination from his sketch in measures 14/15 of the Draft. Later Wagner added two extra measures between the two measures of the termination, thus carrying the ensuing sequential treatment a step further. A similar situation occurs with the series of chords associated with the Wanderer, which Wagner indicated in the draft to be stated twice as had usually been the case when they appeared earlier in the opera. In each of the two series, Wagner gives the first two of the four chords twice the duration of the remaining two. Later on, but *before* he had finished the prelude in this Draft, as shown by its position on the page, Wagner made an insert at the bottom of the page, which begins the series on D as in the final version. Curt von Westernhagen has perceptively suggested that it was only when he wrote out this insertion that Wagner hit upon the particular means of elaboration of the chordal series.[24] This insertion in turn conditioned Wagner's foreshortening of the third series of chords by removing the extra measures for each of the first two chords, so that the third series in the sequence has the four chords of equal duration.

After juxtaposing the triads of A flat and A the first time, Wagner moved directly to the triad of E flat, but he crossed that out, and made a restatement of the A flat and A juxtaposition, each chord now occupying two measures. This in turn was crossed out, and Wagner indicated the first statement for repetition, so that in each case only the A triad has two measures. He then proceeded with the E flat triad as planned originally. Soon afterwards there follows a juxtaposition of a diminished seventh chord with a G flat triad, similarly marked for a second statement. The elaboration of the G flat triad here was written in later in ink, probably at the time Wagner was working on this passage in his

Developed Draft. The prelude concludes with three different versions of the transition into the opening of the scene, the opening Wagner has had in mind from the sketch given above. Each of the three versions is a little longer than the one before. The second one uses the second sketch and thus anticipates the central motive of the scene to follow; here Wagner concluded his 'Wotan' sketch in the dominant rather than the tonic. The version actually used in the opera represents a still further expansion of the third alternative written in the Preliminary Draft: Wagner removed the eighth measure, and substituted two others, making two balanced phrases, each beginning with the same motivic element.

Wagner began the first scene with two complete statements of the melody of his second sketch, which defines the tonality of the scene at the beginning. The second statement follows the sketch quite literally, but the first statement moves to the dominant, evidently following the suggestion of the second alternative transition given at the end of the prelude. At the same time, the termination for this melody is modified so as to include the termination from Wagner's sketch for the opening melody of the prelude—that very termination which Wagner in effect removed from the prelude by the first insertion he made.

Towards the end of the scene, Wagner introduced a new theme to coincide with the change in the tonic from minor to major. His first sketch for that new theme runs as follows:

Ex. 61

The date of this sketch is uncertain, but Wagner made it before July 1866 when he was at work on his short score for Act II of *Die Meistersinger* and entered a modified form of the theme at the bottom of page 82 of that Draft. This new sketch unfortunately got cut off at the bottom when the short score was bound, but what remains of it reads as in Ex. 62 (see page 334).

In his Preliminary Draft for Act III of *Siegfried*, Wagner preserved this version of the rhythm of his theme, and transposed it to G major (see Ex. 63, page 334). He used the G minor theme as a preface to the new one, which functions as a cadence introducing the change of mode.

333

Ex. 62

Ex. 63

will　　　　was in des Zwie-spalts wil – dem Schmer - ze ver -

- zwei-felnd einst ich be - - schloss　froh　und　freu - dig:

füh - - re ich frei　　es　nun　aus

Wagner immediately reworked this passage into its final form before continuing in the Preliminary Draft. He modified Wotan's last line shown above, making the text less awkward. In the accompaniment, he substituted for the new theme a variation of the G minor theme which now cadences in A flat. The first three bars of the new theme immediately follow this cadence, but in A flat and for the orchestra alone. Wagner thereby reserved the emergence of G major for later in the scene, when he used the rejected passage from the preceding example to accompany Wotan's lines:

> wachend wirkt
> dein wissendes Kind
> erlösende Weltentat.

('Then your wisdom's child will achieve that
deed that will free our world.')

He made one change in the fifth measure of the theme—F natural becomes F sharp, the corresponding harmonization a D major triad. A few measures further on, he recalls the first part of the theme and lets the ascending scale continue up to the high G.

When Wagner began composing *Siegfried* in 1856, his later compositional procedure assumed its final form. From that point on, he worked out each act individually in two successive stages, embodying each stage in a separate draft. He worked back and forth between the two drafts so as not to let too much time elapse between setting the text and elaborating the accompaniment. When he had finished the second draft, he could regard the composition as essentially complete and could then proceed to compose the next act. Making a full score was mere routine mechanical labour to be done whenever time for it was available. For a while, he wrote out the full score of each act as he finished composing it, i.e. before beginning the next act. This is true for the first act of *Siegfried* and the first act of *Tristan*. When he was composing the second and third acts of *Tristan*, he was under such pressure to supply the publisher with full score for engraving that he began the full score before he had finished composing the act. The same is true of the first act of *Die Meistersinger*, but for a different reason: he himself wanted new material for concerts.

Wagner did not begin the full score for the second act of *Siegfried* until the end of 1864, more than seven years after he had composed it.

FIG. 2   STAGES IN THE COMPOSITION OF WAGNER'S OPERAS

	I	II
Early Operas	*Full sketches for individual numbers* 1 inst. staff	*Composition Draft* INK 2 inst. staves
Tannhäuser	*Full sketches for individual sections (approaching character of a complete draft)* mostly INK 1 inst. staff	*Composition Draft* INK 2 inst. staves
Lohengrin	*Preliminary Draft* INK 1 inst. staff	*Composition Draft* INK 2 inst. staves
Das Rheingold	*Preliminary Draft* PENCIL 1 inst. staff	
Die Walküre		*Preliminary Draft* PENCIL 1 or 2 inst. staves
Siegfried (Acts I and II)* **Tristan** (Prelude to Act I)*		*Preliminary Draft* PENCIL 1 or 2 inst. staves
Tristan (Remainder)* **Die Meistersinger** (Act I)*		*Preliminary Draft* PENCIL mostly 2 inst. staves
Later Operas *Die Meistersinger,* Acts II and III *Siegfried,* Act III *Götterdämmerung* *Parsifal*		*Preliminary Draft* PENCIL 2 inst. staves

* Full score made after composition of each act.

		III *Full Score* INK	
		III *Full Score* LITHOGRAPHIC	
		III *Full Score* INK	
	II *Instrumenta-tion Draft* PENCIL	**III** *Fair copy of Full Score* INK	
		II *Full Score* PENCIL	**III** *Fair copy of Full Score* INK
II *Developed Draft* INK 2 inst. staves		**III** *Full Score* PENCIL	**IV** *Fair copy of Full Score* INK
II *Developed Draft* INK 2 or 3 inst. staves		**III** *Full Score* INK	
	II *Orchestral Draft (Short Score)* INK Inst. sections = as many as 4 or 5 staves Vocal sections = 2 or 3 inst. staves	**III** *Full Score* INK	

That long interval of separation may have caused difficulties and may well be partly responsible for the fact that he significantly increased the degree of elaboration in his second draft, beginning with the second act of *Die Meistersinger*. In any case, from that act on, Wagner never again began a full score until the entire opera was finished in second draft.

The development of Wagner's method of composition is summarized in the table (Fig. 2) on the two preceding pages.

III
Prose Writings:
Criticism: Bayreuth

NINE

Wagner as a Writer

CURT VON WESTERNHAGEN

WHEN WAGNER gained his first major success with the première of *Rienzi* at Dresden in 1842, his friend Heinrich Laube asked the composer to supply some details about his life and career as the basis for a short biographical article which he planned to publish in his journal *Zeitung für die Elegante Welt*. In fact Laube published these notes as they stood, remarking in his introductory comments: 'But the pressures of Paris rapidly turned the musician into a writer: I would only ruin this biographical sketch if I tried to change anything in it.' During his years of penury in Paris from 1839 to 1841, Wagner had indeed attempted to earn his living as an author, thereby writing two masterly short stories, 'Eine Pilgerfahrt zu Beethoven' ('A Pilgrimage to Beethoven') and 'Ein Ende in Paris' ('An Ending in Paris'). 'E. T. A. Hoffmann could not have written anything like this,' exclaimed Heinrich Heine in admiration. It is the undercurrent of authentic experience that distinguishes them from mere works of fantasy. Wagner is here already proclaiming his aesthetic ideal—for instance, when he makes Beethoven speak of a marriage of instrumental and vocal music in a 'symphony with choruses', or when his German musician dies in Paris with the words 'I believe in God, Mozart and Beethoven' on his lips. 'All that I wrote was a cry of protest against the state of modern art,' Wagner admitted in 1851 in the autobiographical work *Eine Mitteilung an meine Freunde* (*A Communication to My Friends*).

Nietzsche characterized Wagner the writer in the lines: 'He suffers whenever he writes because he is prevented from stating things in his own fashion, in the form of an inspiring and triumphant example, by a temporarily inexorable necessity.' And when Wagner published the first number of his *Bayreuther Blätter* in 1878 he himself confirmed,

341

'Although the only thing that really mattered to me was concrete, aesthetic achievement, there was a lengthy period when I had to clarify my ideas in theoretical writings.'

This situation of inner and external necessity left its mark on his literary products. 'I have the impression,' Nietzsche continues, 'that Wagner often speaks *as though confronted with his enemies*.' On such occasions he could prove bitter and unjust. When he sent the manuscript of *Oper und Drama* (*Opera and Drama*) to the printer in 1851, he wrote to Theodor Uhlig with regard to the polemic against Meyerbeer which this essay contained: 'I wish I could take back many a point like this: when *I* read it, the mockery never sounds venomous— but when others read it, I must often appear as a passionately embittered man.' And in order to make amends for the criticism voiced here of Rossini, he published in 1868, on receiving word of the death of the Italian composer, *Eine Erinnerung an Rossini* (*A Memory of Rossini*) in which he describes him after a visit in 1860 as 'the first truly great and admirable person' he had met in the world of art.

In addition to the polemics in which Wagner strove to expose 'the idolatry of our age', there were essays, especially from the later years of his life, where he seemed to be conversing with a circle of friends, touching on one idea or another, now and then making a point more sharply, suddenly making a very serious personal declaration, only to round it all off on a note of light-hearted irony: 'But what will the audience have to say to this?—It seems to me that the play is over and we go our separate ways.'

Wagner's writings are extremely diverse both in style and subject-matter, but on the whole they represent a valuable contribution to the history of his intellectual and artistic development. When he wrote the preface to the nine volumes of his *Gesammelte Schriften und Dichtungen* (*Collected Writings and Literary Works*)[1] in 1871, he wrote that the reader would see 'that he is confronted not with the collected works of a man of letters but with the written record of the career of an artist who sought life in his art, beyond all conventional patterns'.

However, despite the personal, confessional character of his writings, we must not overlook the fact that they rested on an extremely wide range of knowledge. Although Ernest Newman feels constrained to criticize Wagner's 'amateurishness in the field of Greek scholarship', a glance at Wagner's Dresden library (1842–9)[2] and the library at Wahnfried would have shown him how many-sided the composer's interests were—not only in Greek scholarship but also in German studies, literary criticism, philosophy, theology and above all the standard works of historiography (including Gibbon in the original and in a German translation, and the main historical works of Carlyle). A visitor relates how Wagner handled the large library that filled the walls of the 'hall' at Wahnfried 'like an instrument', producing with a sure touch from among thousands of volumes printed evidence to support whatever opinion he happened to be championing in conversation.

Wagner's controversial reputation as a writer is associated in the public mind above all with his Zürich manifestos *Die Kunst und die Revolution* (*Art and Revolution*, July 1849), *Das Kunstwerk der Zukunft* (*The Art Form of the Future*, November 1849) and *Oper und Drama* (January 1851).

In *Die Kunst und die Revolution* the results of his studies at Dresden of the ancient Greeks from which he had 'forged' his aesthetic ideal are suffused with a revolutionary *élan* which may be interpreted as a sublimation of his political ideas. Newman expressed regret that we have no information about his political reading in that decisive year—'the mere titles of some of the books might have told us a good deal we should like to know about Wagner's reading and thinking', in particular whether he read the works of 'Marx and his associates'.[3] We now know, however, that no political writings of any kind existed in his library at Dresden. He adopted his revolutionary ideas at second hand, from the Russian anarchist Michael Bakunin (albeit with a strong tendency to contradict him), and above all from the disciple of Proudhon, August Röckel. Wagner himself did not read Proudhon's *De la propriété* until June 1849 in Paris, and so *Die Kunst und die Revolution* originated under the immediate impact of this book.

The inspiration for *Das Kunstwerk der Zukunft* sprang quite spontaneously from a recollection of the watercolour 'Dionysos Educated by the Muses' by Bonaventura Genelli[4] which had first given him an inkling of the 'Greek spirit of Beauty' in his youth and which he now suddenly saw vividly before his mind's eye in Zürich. Twenty years later the picture was a silent witness to the meeting between Wagner and Nietzsche at Triebschen where it inspired the philosopher on his own admission with *Die Geburt der Tragödie aus dem Geiste der Musik* (*The Birth of Tragedy from the Spirit of Music*).

The visionary origins of *Das Kunstwerk der Zukunft*, which are manifest in the ecstatic language, account for the difficulties many readers experience in trying to comprehend it: nor indeed should it be read as a theoretical treatise but as a vision of an aesthetic ideal. In the emphasis on sensual experience in contrast to abstraction, we recognize the influence of the philosopher Ludwig Feuerbach, to whom Wagner dedicated his essay: 'I can dedicate this work . . . to no one but you, for here I have given back to you what is rightfully yours.'

Das Kunstwerk der Zukunft gave rise to two immortal catchwords. Professor Bischoff from Cologne attained a kind of universal renown through his jibe *Zukunftsmusik* ('futuristic music'). And the circle of Wagner's supporters associated with the *Neue Zeitschrift für Musik* seized on the word *Gesamtkunstwerk* with endless discussions about *Sonderkunst* ('particular art') and *Gesamtkunst* ('comprehensive art') which exhausted Wagner's patience. Thus the concept of *Gesamtkunstwerk* eventually gained currency in music criticism as the term for Wagnerian music-drama.

We can accept this usage provided we realize that to Wagner himself the term meant something rather different: it represented for him not only a totality of the *arts* but also—in accordance with the collectivist social principles which he held at that time—a totality of the *artists* involved. Wagner did not therefore apply it to his own works, and when he later discussed the problem of finding the correct terminology for his art in the short but significant essay 'Über die Benennung "Musikdrama"' ('On the Term "Music-drama"') he stated that he would have liked to call his dramas 'deeds of music made visible':

> That would have been a fittingly aesthetico-philosophical title and would have been well suited to the catalogues of a future Polonius[5] . . . And so I had no option . . . but to resolve to deliver up my hapless efforts to the theatres without giving any indication of the genre to which they belonged . . .

When Wagner had finished his *Kunstwerk der Zukunft* and desired in August 1850 to turn his attention to the task of composing the music for his heroic opera *Siegfrieds Tod (The Death of Siegfried)*, he became forcibly aware in this 'crucial moment' of his life of the need to think his ideas out to their ultimate conclusion: 'I had to tidy up a whole life that now lay behind me, to articulate each half-formed intuition on a conscious level, to master through its own devices the urge to reflection that had inevitably arisen within me.' With these words he opened his draft of an article on 'Das Wesen der Oper' ('The Essence of Opera') which expanded during the winter of 1850–51 into his principal theoretical work, *Oper und Drama*.

On 21 November 1928 Richard Strauss wrote to Hugo von Hofmannsthal:

> I happen to be reading Richard Wagner's *Oper und Drama* once again,
> a splendid book as relevant today as it was eighty years ago and still
> every bit as uncomprehended and unknown. But to the likes of us it is
> a comfort and an encouragement, do read it yourself again!

And in a letter to Roland Tenschert on 15 November 1944, he called
it 'the book of books about music'. It was not easy to grasp, he went
on, but one had to remember that it contained ideas which demanded
the compiling of a new dictionary, since they were original creations of
Wagner's own mind. In the struggle for new modes of expression, the
style often grew cumbersome, while the meaning sometimes remained
obscure and had to be guessed at even by musicians.

Wagner was himself aware of this difficulty, and when in 1868—
much to his astonishment—a second edition was required, he admitted
in his preface that his desire to get to the bottom of the matter and not
to leave any stone unturned had led him into an 'obduracy' of style
which inevitably appeared as a confusing prolixity to the reader who
was merely in search of diversion. Yet, in now considering revisions to
the text, he had come to the conclusion that he would not make any
material changes precisely because the widely published difficulty of
his book commended it to the serious scholar. These problems, he
argued, had never been dealt with before by artists, only by theoretical
writers on aesthetics who had applied a dialectical form of presentation to subjects like music which in fact eluded the methods of a
dialectical philosophy.

But despite the 'obduracy' of his style, he can still write whole
sections which set out the problems involved clearly and unambigu-
ously. Among these are:

(1) The problem of reconciling the verse stress with the rhythm of
the melody. It had already caused him to abandon the iambic meter
still predominant in the *Lohengrin* text and to turn instead to free
rhythm with the libretto for *Siegfrieds Tod* (1848). Thus in *Oper
und Drama* he could now base his theory on practical experience.*

(2) The problem of form in music—which should not follow the

* Wagner was of the opinion that this form could best be imitated in English.
'In a speech he made in 1877 . . . in London he praised the English translation
of the *Ring* by Alfred Forman as "sehr korrekt".' (Ernest Newman, *The Life of
Richard Wagner*, Vol. IV, p. 475.)

operatic pattern of joining together autonomous aria forms but should develop according to the organic principle of 'poetic and musical periods' which differed in length and passed through various keys, being finally rounded off by a return to their original key. This notion became the point of departure for Alfred Lorenz's studies of *Das Geheimnis der Form bei Richard Wagner*.

(3) The function of musical motives which not only accompany the immediate events in the plot but at the same time evoke memories of the past and anticipate future developments. Wagner links this with the novel idea that an age-old demand for unity of time and place in drama was thereby being met in a new way, for the musical motives joined together in one present moment things which were temporally and spatially remote. The rather infelicitious term *Leitmotif* ('leading-motive') which was later coined for this did not originate with Wagner himself.

Wagner himself emphasized the overtly personal character of even this theoretical essay. 'It is a very strange work,' he remarked to Cosima in 1879, 'and I was greatly excited when I wrote it, for it is without precedent in the history of art and I was aiming at a goal which nobody else could even see.'[6]

That *Oper und Drama* was not constructed according to an abstract plan but evolved on the basis of his own creative experience is likewise confirmed by the fact that in later years Wagner at times departed from the ideas outlined here. Several things were pertinent only to the conception of the *Nibelungen* on which he was working at the time— e.g. the exclusive stress on *Stabreim* (alliterative verse) which he then abandoned again wholly or in part in *Tristan, Meistersinger* and *Parsifal*. As he once humorously intimated: 'There's no rhyme or reason to my art . . .'

Immediately prior to *Oper und Drama* Wagner had written an article on *Das Judentum in der Musik* (*The Jewish Spirit in Music*) which appeared in two instalments on 3 and 6 September 1850 in Brendel's *Neue Zeitschrift für Musik* under the pseudonym 'K. Freigedank'. 'That everyone will guess I am the author is of no account: I'll still avoid unnecessary scandal by using the fictitious name.' But he was not spared the scandal. Indeed, it proved worse than he had ever dreamed possible. Wagner regarded the essay as one of his occasional pieces stimulated by day-to-day events and having no more than the immediate relevance of journalism.

But what experiences could have provided the sudden impetus for this unusual attack? Shortly before, in *Das Kunstwerk der Zukunft*, he had cited 'the poor Israelites' as a model: 'The people, the chosen people, journeyed safely through the sea to the Promised Land.' Moreover, he had never taken offence at the Jewish origin either of people close to him or of distant acquaintances. On learning of the death of his companion in misfortune in Paris, Samuel Lehrs, he mourned: 'Lamentable, heartbreaking! These are the only words I can think of. This brave, splendid—and so unhappy man will never be forgotten!'[7] We see that this was no empty phrase from a later reference to Lehrs in *Mein Leben* (*My Life*) as one of the few 'friends truly devoted' to him.[8]

The polemic was basically directed at Meyerbeer, as Wagner admitted in a letter to Liszt on 18 April 1851. Though he had once praised the composer of *Les Huguenots* as the culmination of a whole epoch in the history of dramatic music (in an article not published until after his death, but which Richard Sternfeld dates back to 1837 on the basis of internal evidence), his ideas had subsequently undergone a major transformation with the conception of *Der fliegende Holländer*. After seeing *Le Prophète* in Paris in 1850, he regarded Meyerbeer as nothing less than his 'complete opposite'.

The catchphrase which prompted his polemical essay was a devastating review of the opera in the *Neue Zeitschrift für Musik* which alluded to an alleged 'Hebrew taste in aesthetic matters'. Since, moreover, he believed himself to have been deceived by Meyerbeer, whose patronage had availed him nothing—a suspicion which we now know to have been wholly unfounded[9]—he felt absolved from any obligation of gratitude. 'It was time for me to free myself completely from this hypocritical relationship,' we read in the letter to Liszt cited above; 'this was an act necessary for the proper birth of my mature being.'

'And so I let fly . . .' But the public inevitably felt that he was unjust and offensive in insinuating that Meyerbeer's weaknesses as a musician were due to his racial origin, or in transferring his criticism to Jewish artists in general. Only his numerous Jewish friends and colleagues of later years refused to hold this attack against him: they knew that in the heat of the moment he had once again allowed himself to be carried away further than his real opinion warranted. Hermann Levi, who conducted *Parsifal* for Wagner, wrote on 13 April 1882 to his father, the Chief Rabbi of Giessen:

> His fight against what he calls 'Jewishness' in music and in modern literature springs from the noblest of motives, and the fact that he does

not harbour any petty *risches* (antisemitism) . . . is clearly demonstrated by his relationship with me and with Joseph Rubinstein, and by his earlier intimate friendship with Tausig whom he loved dearly.*

While he was engaged upon *Oper und Drama* during the winter of 1850–51, Wagner was at the same time toying with the idea of a comic opera based on the folk-tale '*Von einem, der auszog, das Fürchten zu lernen*' 'The Boy Who Set Out to Learn to Shudder' by the brothers Grimm. 'Imagine my alarm,' he wrote to his friend Uhlig, 'when I suddenly realized that this young lad was none other than young Siegfried!' Within a week he had sketched out the prose draft, and in three more weeks he had completed the verse libretto. But although he had hoped that this artistic effort would free him once and for all from all publicist activity, he was once again to be disappointed. The publication of his *Drei Operndichtungen* (*Holländer*, *Tannhäuser*, *Lohengrin*) (*Three Libretti* . . .) by Breitkopf and Härtel induced him to write the major autobiographical preface *Eine Mitteilung an meine Freunde* (completed in August 1851) in which he tried to elucidate 'the ostensible or real contradiction' between his operas hitherto and the ideas explored in *Oper und Drama*.

Apart from the opening section, where Wagner criticizes the 'monumental' (today we would say 'antiquarian') tendency in art and advocates 'complete modernity', he has the advantage in this piece of not having to present abstract theories but of being able to base himself on concrete examples. In the description of his artistic development we are given instructive insights into individual works. When comparing the two operas of his youth, *Die Feen* (1833–4) and *Das Liebesverbot* (1834–5), he notes that we can see from these the two completely opposite directions in which he might have developed: 'the solemn seriousness of my original sensibility was confronted by . . . a bold tendency to wild sensuous turbulence, a defiant joyfulness'. *Rienzi* (1838–40) is described as dramatic material which set all his nerves tingling with sympathetic desire, but which at that time he could view only as if through the spectacles of grand opera. He vividly depicts how he struck out along a new path in Paris, 'that of revolution against contemporary audiences'; from this painful mood emerged *Der fliegende Holländer* (1841).

---

* Here we should also mention Halévy whose gift 'for writing music which springs forth from the innermost . . . depths of the richest human nature' Wagner praised in 1842 (*Sämtliche Schriften* . . ., Vol. XII, pp. 131ff.) and of whose *La Juive* he was a lifelong admirer.

He thereby makes an illuminating admission about the role his literary work played in his life and creative career. After he had 'deposited and vented' all his irony and sarcasm in his essays, he could then turn his attention to artistic creation proper. Perhaps he too might have followed in the wake of those men of letters whose writings and dramas remain confined to mere didacticism, 'if I had not been endowed with a higher capacity, my absorption in *music* . . . I pay tribute to it here as my guardian angel who preserved me as an artist, in truth first made me into an artist.'

This admission applies particularly to his social essays. When, for example, Bernard Shaw[10] reads these preoccupations into the work at length—and they did, of course, play a part in the conception of the *Ring*—he overlooks the fact that they are 'deposited and vented' in the revolutionary writings and that the remnants were sublimated into pure art in the creative work, especially the music. Those directors who deem themselves progressive when they transform the *Ring* back into a drama with a 'message' have no idea how regressive this approach is in relation to the genesis of the work itself.

In recounting the history of the *Holländer*, Wagner mentions an epoch-making development in his technique of composition as a whole. In Senta's ballad, which he composed in advance, he unconsciously set down the 'thematic kernel' of the whole music, and when in the summer of 1841 he began to jot down the outline of the composition, this existing thematic image spread involuntarily like a complete web over the whole drama—although, it should be added, not nearly as consistently as in the *Ring*, for it is still interrupted by 'operatic' passages.

We learn with regard to the libretto for *Tannhäuser* (1843; the score finished 1845) that Wagner had been familiar with the legend for some time, but that he did not feel impelled to dramatize it until he found it associated with the *Sängerkrieg* (the contest of singers) in a book entitled *Über den Krieg auf Wartburg* by C. T. L. Lucas. Lucas's thesis was in fact untenable, but it fired the composer's imagination. The German philologist who is mentioned in the *Mitteilung an meine Freunde* as having brought the treatise to his attention in Paris was his friend and companion in misfortune, Samuel Lehrs.

When Wagner put aside the draft of *Die Sarazenin* (*The Saracen Girl*, 1843), a tale from the history of the Hohenstaufens, in order to work on *Tannhäuser*, he set the seal on his abandonment of grand historical operas in the manner of *Rienzi* in favour of a recourse to myth and legend. Only in the case of a comic opera like *Die Meister-singer*, which he drafted in 1845 as a satyr play to complement the *Sängerkrieg*, did he subsequently depart from this principle—and then the result was a bourgeois comedy.

It is surprising to learn from the autobiographical *Mitteilung* that *Lohengrin* (1845–8), which is commonly held to be a less impassioned work than *Tannhäuser*, filled him with such pity for the two lovers as he wrote it that he himself sometimes lost sight of the tragic necessity for their separation. Incidentally, he here protests against the wide-spread misapprehension that, by drawing on these medieval legends, he had subscribed to the 'Romantic' school. 'The man who sees in *Lohengrin* no more than the category "Christian-Romantic" has grasped only a superficial and contingent feature, not the substance of the work.' He stresses that this implied no commitment to medieval ideals: 'All our aims and fervent desires which in fact point into the *future*, we try to body forth using images from the past, thus endowing them with a form which the modern age cannot supply.' And Thomas Mann makes a similar point: 'Any philosophy directed to the future can claim [Wagner's] patronage.'[11]

The manuscript of *Eine Mitteilung an meine Freunde* ended with the announcement of the forthcoming publication of *Der junge Siegfried* and *Siegfrieds Tod*; but because Härtel thought he detected here a retrospective declaration of support for the revolution, publication was delayed. They were businessmen, he argued, and did not meddle in politics; and since Wagner resided outside the German Federation, it was they who would be called to account. By the time the offending passages had been altered and preparations for publication resumed, the situation had changed fundamentally.

On 15 September 1851 Wagner had begun a cure in the hydro-pathic clinic at Albisbrunn. Only a fortnight later he was reporting to Uhlig that the miasma of theory which had plagued him at the outset had lifted from his brain. And after another two weeks he announced to him the plan of the tetralogy: 'I've great things in store for *Siegfried*: three dramas with a three-act prelude [later to become four scenes].'

This entailed a change in the concluding passage of the *Mitteilung*. 'I intend to present my myth *in three complete dramas*,' we now read, 'which will be preceded by a great prelude.' And at the same time the idea of the festival was born:

In a festival specially devised for the purpose, I envisage staging these three plays and the prelude *over a period of three days and a preceding*

350

evening ... Very well, I give you time and opportunity to reflect on this: for you shall not see me again except I bear my work completed!

In a dramatic manner we witness here how his literary activity and his art were intertwined.

'Utopias! utopias!' was what Wagner had caused his hypothetical reader to exclaim at the end of his first revolutionary manifesto. And indeed, to the contemporary reader who did not know either the *Ring* or *Tristan*, the author's aesthetic theories must have appeared to be those of an unworldly dreamer. For this reason, when the essays were published as part of his collected writings, Wagner also included the *Entwurf zur Organisation eines deutschen Nationaltheaters für das Königreich Sachsen* (*Plan for the Organization of a German National Theatre for the Kingdom of Saxony*), written in Dresden in 1849:

> In reproducing this almost irritatingly detailed essay I was concerned to refute the common prejudice of unimaginative people who deem the imaginative, productive artist, the man they call a 'genius', to be utterly impractical and incapable of soberly grasping the reality of a situation ... To inform those who are totally unproductive and never have a practical idea themselves how clumsy they are in practice, and to demonstrate to them how they most outrageously waste and squander the very means whereby purposeful and significant achievements might be carried out ... —this temptation was difficult for me to resist at the time.[12]

On the advice of a commission of inquiry, which included his colleague Reissiger, the scheme was turned down. If the exiled Wagner decided in passing to publish the essay, it was merely in order to prove that, as he wrote to Uhlig, the contemptible revolutionary had occupied himself to the end with practical plans for reform (18 September 1850).

This piece was supplemented in 1910 by the publication of a memorandum 'Die Königliche Kapelle betreffend' ('Concerning the Royal Orchestra') dated 1 March 1846.[13] It covers fifty printed pages and represents one of the most revealing documents about Wagner's life. 'I have spent the last three months passing everything that appeared necessary to me under the most thorough and intensive review ...,' he explains in an accompanying letter to Intendant von Lüttichau. 'May Your Excellency accept the result of my labours with your customary graciousness and above all may I who am so indebted to you already continue to find favour in your regard.'

Newman comments that there is not a single sentence in this memorandum which is not fully justified. It is the work of an idealist but not of a dreamer. Above all, he concludes, it is the work of a man who puts art before self-interest. Why should Wagner have troubled himself about the future of the Royal Orchestra? The fact that he sacrificed three months of his by no means ample spare time to this endeavour is, in Newman's view, an example of selflessness unparalleled in the history of musical institutions.[14]

For a whole year Wagner waited for a reply. Finally, early in 1847, he received notification that his scheme had been rejected. This experience was a decisive factor in persuading him to throw in his lot with the opposition and the revolution.

These plans for reform are only two among a whole series of similar memoranda relating to Zürich, Vienna and Munich, the earliest of which only became known with the editing of the documents in the Burrell Collection. It was written when Wagner was a young orchestral organizer at Riga on 11 September 1838 with the intention of urging the members of his theatre orchestra to organize symphony concerts.

> What true musician would not be saddened to see an ensemble of this ability rest content with a mere subsidiary function and never produce anything really gratifying and stimulating of its own? At all events it is largely this consideration alone that has driven me to make this proposal to you. For the rest, I declare in advance that I . . . am prepared to forgo financial reward and to decline any fee.[15]

The *Mitteilung an meine Freunde* brought to a provisional close the period of major aesthetic writings. Wagner now devoted himself to the literary and musical composition of the tetralogy. But alongside this and after it was finished, various occasional essays continued to appear for which he liked to use the more personal form of the 'open letter'.

As early as 1851, when Liszt issued an appeal for the instituting of a 'Goethe Foundation', he replied in an 'Open Letter' of 8 May that Liszt's high-minded suggestion would be taken to apply to the visual arts alone, as the first reactions in the press showed; it would lead to nothing more than the establishment of joint-stock art societies with the usual artistic lotteries. The 'roots of the splendid tree of the future for which we yearn' lay in the theatre: 'You have a clear illustration of this in Weimar; all we need is the necessary determination, and we would soon attain a goal which would in itself be the most appropriate "Goethe Foundation" of all.'

Although it might appear that Wagner is here speaking in the interests of his own work, this suspicion cannot attach to the short pamphlet 'Ein Theater in Zürich' ('A Theatre in Zürich', 1851). The impetus was again an urgent practical issue—the Zürich Theatre's need to build up a new ensemble at the beginning of every season. And Wagner's proposal is again highly original and at the same time realistic: he suggests that they should abandon any attempt to imitate the major theatres and instead establish a Swiss national theatre, using local talent. 'This aim is so novel and important, the potential success so extraordinary and far-reaching that for this reason alone many will doubt whether it can ever be attained, particularly since I have suggested such simple and modest means.'

The open letter 'Über Franz Liszt's Symphonische Dichtungen' ('On Franz Liszt's Symphonic Poems'), addressed to Princess Marie Wittgenstein in 1857, resulted from his desire to lend public support to Liszt who was under heavy attack as a composer. During a lengthy visit to Zürich, Liszt had played his *Faust* and *Dante* symphonies from the orchestral score in such a way that in Wagner's words it was almost miraculous. Particularly illuminating—for his own attitude in such matters as well—is the contrast he draws between Berlioz's programme-music and Liszt's symphonic poems: whereas Berlioz in the love-scene from *Romeo and Juliet* followed the action of Shakespeare's balcony scene and thereby lost the musical thread, Liszt realized that the composer must proceed quite differently from the dramatist. The former 'completely disregards the course of events in ordinary life, does away with its contingencies and details and instead sublimates everything inherent in them according to its concrete emotional content which can only be properly expressed in music'.

This throws light on a whole group of *Programmatische Erläuterungen* (*Programme Notes*) ranging from the programme for Beethoven's Ninth Symphony on the occasion of its epoch-making performance at Dresden in 1846 to the programme for the *Parsifal* prelude which was given a private performance before King Ludwig on 12 November 1880. Not that Wagner believed music needed any 'explanation' in words. He merely thought that allusions to a poetical work could establish the right atmosphere for it in advance. In the case of the *Parsifal* prelude, he was able to refer to his own libretto under the simple heading 'Charity—faith—hope?' In the case of the Ninth Symphony, he had selected quotations from *Faust*. And in Zürich he learned that through such explanations, for instance, of the overture to *Coriolan*, he inspired ordinary dance musicians in his orchestra to heights of achievement which they themselves would previously never thought possible.

There is also a series of more or less significant writings on how to perform his own works and those of other composers, which we can discuss here as a single group. They range from the 'Bericht über die Aufführung der Neunten Symphonie im Jahre 1846' ('An Account of the Performance of the Ninth Symphony in 1846') to the essay 'Zum Vortrag der Neunten Symphonie' ('On Performing the Ninth Symphony'), which is illustrated with passages of musical notation and which Wagner wrote in 1873 after conducting the work to mark the laying of the foundation-stone of the Festival Theatre (22 May 1872). Wilhelm Furtwängler conceded: 'One achievement will always re-sound to Wagner's credit; he was the first to demonstrate in words and even more through actual performances into which he threw his whole passionate personality the true nature of Beethoven.'[16] The practical experiences and insights of Wagner the conductor find their theoretical foundation in the classic essay *Über das Dirigieren* (*On the Art of Conducting*, 1869). He reveals, too, where he derived this in-sight: from the dramatic voice of the great soprano Wilhelmina Schröder-Devrient as Fidelio and from the inspired interpretation of the Ninth Symphony by the Paris Conservatoire Orchestra. Only through song, through the understanding of the *melos*, can the right tempo be found on which everything else depends. Wagner was the first, as Furtwängler confirms, to point to the slight yet constant change of tempo which makes a piece of music played from the printed page into what it really is: a living process of generation and growth.[17] 'Pure gold—wonderful!' exclaimed Hans von Bülow after reading it. And Nietzsche compared the irony with which Wagner treated his fellow conductors to that displayed in Schopenhauer's famous essay about philosophy professors.*

The essays 'Bemerkungen zur Aufführung der Oper *Der fliegende Holländer*' ('Observations on the Production of the Opera *The Flying Dutchman*'), and particularly '*Über die Aufführung des Tannhäuser*' ('On the Production of *Tannhäuser*', 1852) occupy a special position since they deal not only with the musical performance of his works, but also with their theatrical production. Wagner had the second one

---

* 'The only work of his that can be said to be really widely known in England is the treatise on conducting, which has been eagerly studied not only by professional conductors but by thoughtful musicians of all kinds.' (Ernest Newman, *The Life of Richard Wagner*.)

printed and sent as a brochure to the German theatres who were applying in increasing numbers to be allowed to include the opera in their repertoire. Twelve years later, when the last copy had disappeared and he asked the Munich Court Theatre to return one of the six brochures originally sent there, it transpired that all six were lying uncut and well wrapped up in the theatre archive. Wagner adds that many of his essays probably suffered the same fate as that brochure. However, perhaps we do the directors of the time an injustice when we accuse them of having ignored Wagner's instructions for the staging of his works. There are producers today who set their hearts on positively *defying* them—in direct contrast to the attitude of Hans Pfitzner, who held that, although one could perhaps take issue with Wagner as a poet or as a musician, he was infallible as a producer of scenic effect.[18]

An external consideration induced Wagner in 1860 to recapitulate the theories which he had developed nine years earlier in *Oper und Drama*. In order to prepare the Parisians for the production of *Tannhäuser*, he published a prose translation of his *Vier Operndichtungen* (*Holländer, Tannhäuser, Lohengrin, Tristan*) with a preface entitled 'Lettre sur la musique à Frédéric Villot', the curator of the paintings in the Louvre and a sensitive student and admirer of his scores. This treatise, which in the German version bears the provocative title 'Zukunftsmusik' and covers fifty pages of print, expresses his principal ideas with superb conciseness and lucidity, so that it can be recommended to anyone who wishes to get to know them at first hand.

However, the composer of *Tristan* (completed 1859) has now further refined the analysis of his musical style. Here we read for the first time of the phrase 'infinite melody':

> I must once again resort to metaphor in order to characterize for you this great melody that encompasses the whole dramatic composition . . . Initially it should have a similar effect on the mood of the piece as a beautiful forest has on the solitary observer on a summer's evening . . . No matter how many voices or individual tunes he hears, the ringing, swelling sound that overwhelms him seems to be merely the one great melody of the forest . . .

For us who are familiar with the *Ring, Tristan* and *Parsifal*, this is of course immediately comprehensible. But as a preparation for *Tannhäuser*, where the 'infinite melody' is not yet developed, it inevitably caused some confusion among the Parisians. Moreover, the translator Challemel-Lacour had made an unhappy mistake at this very point. Wagner continues: how foolish if the observer tried to capture one of the forest singers and train it at home to chirp a fragment of the great melody of the forest—what would he then hear 'but [the question]—which melody?' But in the translation we read 'si ce n'est ... quelque mélodie à l'italienne?' (the dots do not indicate an omission here). Thereby not only was the meaning altered, but an allusion to Italian operatic melody was included which Wagner had never intended.

It is to Wagner's credit that in the open letter to the *Deutsche Allgemeine Zeitung* entitled 'Bericht über die Aufführung des *Tannhäuser* in Paris' he drew a careful distinction between the clique which had mounted the uproar in the theatre and the Paris audiences in general, who, he testified, demonstrated a 'very animated receptivity and a truly generous sense of justice'.

After the fiasco over *Tannhäuser* in Paris and the non-execution of a world première of *Tristan* in Vienna, Wagner resolved in 1862 to lay the text of *Der Ring des Nibelungen* before the literary public as a mere 'piece of literature'. The book's preface closed with a final desperate appeal to the German people and their princes. It would be an easy matter for a German prince to enable Wagner to stage a performance of his work; the ruler in question would not have to add another item of expenditure to his budget but merely utilize the funds hitherto earmarked for the support of our 'worst cultural institution', the operatic theatre. 'Will this Prince be found?—"In the beginning was the Deed".'[19]

These seven pages were to have the most far-reaching consequences of any of his writings. When the eighteen-year-old Crown Prince Ludwig of Bavaria, who had already been fascinated by *Das Kunstwerk der Zukunft* at the age of twelve, read this introduction to the *Nibelungen* poem, he felt that it was addressed to him personally. He did not realize how soon it would be before his father's death would place him in a position to heed the voice of destiny.

Wagner's summons to Munich led to the writing of the only two essays that carry the words 'state' and 'politics' in their title. In response to a request from King Ludwig to explain in writing whether and in what manner his views on the state and religion had changed since his Zürich essays, Wagner wrote the treatise *Über Staat und Religion* in July 1864. But if anyone had anticipated a political programme, he was disappointed. The very fact that Wagner cites Goethe and Schopenhauer shows that this is anything but a political essay.

It is rather a reflective rumination on the ideal of 'justice' in domestic and foreign politics and on the monarch as the personification of this ideal.

Let us recall at this point that Wagner had championed the same idea as early as 1848 in his very first revolutionary article 'Wie verhalten sich republikanische Bestrebungen dem Königtum gegenüber?'[20] ('What Attitude Do Republican Sympathizers Adopt towards the Monarchy?'): 'At the summit of the free state (the republic) the hereditary king will be precisely what he ought to be in his most noble essence: the *first* man of his *people*, the *freest* of the *free!*' Whether we consider such paradoxical ideas realistic or utopian, at all events they show that Wagner had remained consistent in his almost mystical conception of the monarchy. This is echoed once again in the closing line of his poem 'An das deutsche Heer vor Paris' ('To the German Army at the Gates of Paris', January 1871): 'The Kaiser nears: in peace let right prevail!'[21]

After reading *Staat und Religion*, Nietzsche commented that never had a monarch been addressed in a more dignified or more philosophical fashion: 'I was positively inspired and moved to the quick by this idealism which appeared to have sprung from the very spirit of Schopenhauer.'[22]

The second essay which belongs in this context, *Deutsche Kunst und deutsche Politik* (*German Art and German Politics*), began to appear in the Munich *Süddeutsche Presse* in September 1867. The journal, along with the Festival Theatre planned for Munich and the German Music Academy, was among the most important cultural projects devised by Ludwig and Wagner. As the title of the article suggests, these instalments were primarily concerned with art. But the tense political situation, which was rapidly approaching a climax and which Wagner could not ignore, led him to discuss contemporary political events in a more direct way.

What he did was to base his arguments on the *Untersuchungen über das europäische Gleichgewicht* by the publicist Constantin Frantz. According to Frantz, the influence of French policy on the states of Europe depended on nothing less than the power of French civilization. To escape this influence by developing one's own culture 'would be the right propaganda for Germany and an essential contribution to the re-establishment of the balance of power in Europe'. This notion was for Wagner the motto under which he tried to impress upon politicians the *political* importance of his own cultural and aesthetic endeavours. 'By God,' exclaimed King Ludwig, 'whoever is not entranced by the spell of the words, whoever is not convinced and converted by the profundity of spirit revealed therein, does not deserve to live.' The twelfth instalment moved on from criticism of the world of art to criticism of the school system: 'The school is now a bone of contention, especially in the Catholic areas of Germany, between Church and State . . .' Here Wagner touched on the most sensitive issue of Bavarian politics. When in the thirteenth instalment he then ventured to urge a reform of the nobility on the lines of the French Legion of Honour, the cup overflowed. On the morning of 19 December 1867 a ministerial councillor appeared in the editorial offices: His Majesty deemed the articles suicidal and ordered the suspension of the series forthwith. It was clearly a victory for the court nobility who had long been hostile towards Wagner, for to them the 'Lutheran musician' and 'man of the barricades' had seemed from the outset a dubious confidant for their king. As late as 1900, the ministerial councillor Otto Freiherr von Völderndorff still prided himself on having succeeded on that occasion in 'obtaining an explicit command from the king'.

To anticipate somewhat: even if Wagner wrote no more political essays he could not refrain from touching on political questions of the day in his *Bayreuther Blätter*. It is well known that in 1871 he acclaimed the founding of the German Empire with enthusiasm. What is less familiar is that he later voiced sharp criticisms of the domestic and foreign policy of the new Empire. He thereby concurred with Constantin Frantz's criticism of Bismarck's policies which he expounded in his book *Der Föderalismus* (1879). This work provides the key to our understanding of Wagner's political statements which are otherwise easily misunderstood. By 'Federalism' Frantz means—as a counterpart to Marxism—co-operation between the principle of individuality and the principle of community; and in foreign affairs— as a counterpart to nationalism—the creation of an international organization as the foundation of a federation of European states. In the critical year of 1879, Wagner wrote to King Ludwig: 'A book which I would like to commend to the serious attention of the whole world with a flourish of trumpets; it contains an extremely lucid and thorough exposition of the complete solution to the problems of this world such as I myself consider to be the only correct one' (7 July 1879).

As Frantz influenced Wagner's political thinking, so too did Schopenhauer influence his philosophical ideas. Even the strange fate of his writings aroused Wagner's sympathy: ignored for over a generation by German professors of philosophy, they had been brought to light in 1852 by a brilliant article in the *Westminster and Foreign Quarterly Review*. As far as aesthetics were concerned, he was surprised at the special position which Schopenahuer assigned to music compared with the other arts. But this, in turn, provided Wagner with a basis for his own metaphysics of music. Whereas the philosopher had presented his hypothetical explanation of music as a paradox, Wagner wanted to substantiate and heighten it through the example of Beethoven, 'the very composer . . . whose works first disclosed to men that deepest mystery of music'. This was accomplished in the memorial tribute *Beethoven*, written to commemorate the centenary of the master's birth in 1870. From Schopenhauer's hypothesis and from Beethoven's creative example, he concluded that the other arts, especially the visual arts, produce their effect by arousing pleasure in beautiful forms, whereas music which expresses the essence of all things has to be judged not according to the category of the Beautiful but according to that of the Sublime.

Schopenhauer's doctrine in general caused him to emphasize the ancient dignity of music as 'the womb of drama' in subsequent statements about his own music drama, in contrast to the aesthetic essays of the Zürich period. 'The nature of music can only be perceived intuitively; therefore it manifests itself to your gaze in scenic parables, just as a mother imparts the mysteries of religion to her children by relating legends' ('Über die Benennung "Musikdrama" ', 1872).

In the same year, Wagner completed one of his most original contributions to the aesthetic of his creative work: *Über Schauspieler und Sänger (On Actors and Singers)*. Taking two personal experiences as his point of departure—the singing of Wilhelmina Schröder-Devrient as Leonore and the performance of an anonymous puppeteer in Heidelberg—he expounds the argument that dramatic art consists of a kind of transformation of the self, the merging of the self with the souls and bodies of other characters. 'It is yet another way of getting to grips with the problem,' he notes, 'this time I am tackling it directly through the actors.' Nietzsche replied that he had read the essay like a revelation; there was nothing left here of traditional 'aesthetics'.

Over the next four years Wagner employed his pen only in so far as it was necessary in preparing for the Bayreuth Festival of 1876. Significantly enough, in his disappointment over the way the German

public had greeted the festival, it was to the Parisian historian Gabriel
Monod that in October 1876 he communicated his reactions in an
open letter:

> My dramatic festival at Bayreuth . . . has been evaluated more justly
> and more perceptively by Englishmen and Frenchmen than by the
> majority of the German press. I think I owe this to the fact that edu-
> cated Frenchmen and Englishmen are prompted by their own cultural
> independence to acknowledge the independence and uniqueness of a
> cultural product hitherto alien to them.[23]

During the six-year delay in continuing the festival, necessitated by
the large deficit, Wagner wrote a series of essays for his *Bayreuther
Blätter* in addition to working on *Parsifal*. Of the polemical articles,
the series entitled *Publikum und Popularität* (*Public and Popularity*)
deserves particular mention because it rang down the final curtain on
the friendship between Wagner and Nietzsche. In May 1878, Nietzsche sent a copy of *Menschliches, Allzumenschliches* (*Human, All-Too-
Human*) to Wahnfried; in this book he discredited Wagner not only
as an artist but also as a person (e.g. in Aphorism 164 of the first
volume, 'Gefahr und Gewinn im Kultus des Genius'—'Dangers and
Advantages in the Cult of Genius'), and did not even spare Cosima
(in Aphorism 430, 'Freiwilliges Opfertier'—'A Volunteer Blood
Sacrifice'). Although he mentioned no names, the identity of his
victims was obvious to every reader.

Wagner replied with the third instalment of *Publikum und Popularität* in the August number of the *Bayreuther Blätter*. Philologists
and philosophers, when they met on the field of aesthetics, were
given

> . . . special encouragement, nay placed under an obligation to under-
> take an as yet unbounded advance into the sphere of the criticism of all
> things human and inhuman . . . The more these saturnalia of human
> science are ignored, the more boldly and more unmercifully are the
> most noble victims slain on the altar of scepticism . . .

Wagner returned to his natural element with the 'triad' 'Über das
Dichten und Komponieren' ('On Literary and Musical Creation'),
'Über das Opern-Dichten und -Komponieren im besonderen' ('On
the Writing and Composing of Opera in Particular') and 'Über die
Anwendung der Musik auf das Drama' ('On the Application of Music
to Drama'), all three of which appeared in the *Bayreuther Blätter*
of 1879. They are exemplary in their universal validity, wrote Richard
Strauss in the letter to Tenschert already cited (18 November 1944).

And Newman admits: 'In these admirable works we have the ripest fruits of a lifetime of experience in his own special sphere of art and reflection upon it.'[24] They have the further advantage of being written in such a precise and lucid language that they may easily be read by someone with only a limited command of German.

With the 'Offenes Schreiben an Herrn Ernst von Weber, Verfasser der Schrift: "Die Folterkammern der Wissenschaft" ' ('Open Letter to Ernst von Weber, Esq., Author of the Treatise "The Torture Chambers of Science" '), written in 1879, we appear to enter a very remote field. The fact that people appealed to Wagner over this question of vivisection, Newman writes, shows the respect he commanded in Germany by this time. And in his reply, Newman continues, he proved that his heart was in the right place. Without becoming involved in a discussion of this difficult scientific problem, we must nevertheless concede that a warning was necessary against the dangers of sacrificing morality to scientific progress. Wagner adduced Darwin's *Origin of the Species*, which he had read while composing *Parsifal*: a researcher of integrity and a friend of the animal kingdom had disclosed to us the precepts of a vanished primeval wisdom which taught that animals partook of the same element that gave us life. 'Our conclusion with regard to the dignity of man is as follows: this dignity begins to manifest itself at the very point where man is able to distinguish himself from the animals by feeling pity for them.'

The *Offenes Schreiben*, of which Wagner had 3,000 copies printed at his own expense, paved the way for the following pieces: 'Religion und Kunst' ('Religion and Art', 1880), ' "Was nützt diese Erkenntnis?" —Nachtrag zu "Religion und Kunst" ' ('What's the Use of this Knowledge?—a Postscript to "Religion and Art" ', 1880), 'Erkenne dich selbst' ('Know Thyself', 1881), and 'Heldentum und Christentum' ('Heroism and Christianity', 1881). All appeared in the *Bayreuther Blätter* and were included posthumously in the tenth volume of his writings. What troubled Wagner was his concern for the future of Western culture, which he believed to be threatened by militarism and materialism. He foresaw the approach of an age of social and military cataclysms and contended on the basis of historical analogies that Europe could well lapse into barbarism by about the middle of the next century. He considered it ominous that the art of war should be growing increasingly dependent on mechanical devices. 'Here the brute strength of the nethermost forces of Nature is being harnessed to an artificial game in which despite all mathematics and arithmetic

361

blind willpower could still interfere, erupting in its own fashion with elemental force.'

Though Nietzsche mocked the 'bewildered scribbling of [Wagner's] last years'[25] in his polemic against the creator of *Parsifal*, we may well ask what responsible politician of the time had any cogent answer? It is very easy to criticize the makeshift solutions and expedients which the artist put forward; none the less it is a token of far-sightedness and courage to have recognized and articulated the problem in an age of universal faith in progress.

Because of the conversational tone of these pieces with their many allusions and digressions, it is not possible to give a brief summary of their subject-matter. The basic idea of the main essay 'Religion und Kunst' is, in Wagner's words, 'that where religion becomes artificial, it is the prerogative of art to preserve the core of religion'. 'Was nützt diese Erkenntnis?' is significant in so far as the composer who a generation before had pinned his hopes on the revolution now proclaims his faith in regeneration: 'we believe in the possibility of this regeneration [of man in history] and dedicate ourselves to its fulfilment in every respect'.

On 21 November 1878 Wagner had remarked to Cosima: 'If I were ever to write about the Jews again, I would say that I had nothing against them; the trouble is that they approached us Germans prematurely, when we were not yet sufficiently stable to assimilate this element.'[26] Now, at the beginning of 1881, he found it necessary once more to express his opinion on this subject, and did so in the spirit of this remark. 'I stand completely aloof from the contemporary "antisemitic" movement,' he wrote on 23 February to Angelo Neumann. 'An essay of mine which will appear very shortly in the *Bayreuther Blätter* will make this plain in such a way that it should become impossible for *men of understanding* to associate me with that movement.' This essay was 'Erkenne dich selbst', the purport of which emerges clearly from the mere title.

After this Wagner came across the *Essai sur l'inégalité des races humaines* by Count Arthur Gobineau. But it is wrong to suppose that he was thereby converted to Gobineau's racial theories. The argument that mankind had inexorably degenerated through continual interbreeding between the races provoked Wagner to contradict this fatalism and to oppose the belief in the supremacy of 'blood' with his trust in spiritual and intellectual forces. Uniformity brought about by interbreeding was only conceivable on the basis of a 'general moral consensus such as true Christianity seems called upon to develop'. And there was a symbolic significance in the fact that he read an excerpt from the *Essai* aloud to Gobineau, then played the prelude to *Parsifal* which he had once characterized with the words 'Charity—faith—hope?'

Moreover, as a disciple of Darwin, he had confidence in natural selection through sexual love: no medals, however distinguished, could conceal the wan heart 'whose faint beat laments its origin in a union forged without love, though genealogically impeccable'. This idea preoccupied him so much that two days before his death he made it the subject of an essay 'Über das Weibliche im Menschlichen' ('On the Feminine Principle in Human Affairs'):

> Here [in love and marriage] lies the power of man over nature and we call it divine. It is the shaper of noble races. Only through such a union could the races ennoble themselves even in procreation.

He recalls once more his Buddha legend *Die Sieger* (*The Victors*) which treats of the love of the Chandala girl Sawitri, who belongs to the caste of 'untouchables', for Ananda, a disciple of Buddha: 'Love—tragedy'. These were the last words he wrote on the morning of 13 February 1883. Then the pen dropped from his fingers and slipped diagonally across the page.

By and large, Wagner is an example of a writer who simplifies the problems, dramatizes the conflicts and mobilizes his imagination in seeking a solution to them. All these are characteristics which stood the dramatist in him in good stead but were detrimental to the cultural historian, at least as far as the persuasiveness of his arguments was concerned. He was himself aware that it was an activity forced upon him by external considerations. When writing *Publikum und Popularität*, he remarked to Cosima that he persevered with this sort of thing, yet the only hours that seemed truly hallowed to him were those which he devoted to his real work, even though it might take him a whole day to find one single modulation or one phrase, as in the draft of *Parsifal* (Cosima's diary, 12 April 1878).

The problem of the relationship between artistic creation and didactic or polemical writing has already been discussed in connection with the *Ring*. What it amounted to was that while creating he surrounded himself with an aura of kindred ideas—and no more. No one has ever seriously attempted to identify the idea of the *creative work* with the thoughts informing the *publicist writings*, except with a partisan or polemical intent either to 'prove' or 'refute' the aesthetic creation. But the more intimately one probes the process of artistic creation, the more clearly one realizes that it takes place in a sphere far removed from abstract literary theorizing—in the sphere which Wagner himself called his 'true' element.

Translated by Cedric Williams

TEN

Wagner and His Critics

LUCY BECKETT

IN JANUARY AND FEBRUARY 1860 Wagner gave three concerts of orchestral and choral extracts from his works, up to and including the *Tristan* prelude, in the Théâtre des Italiens in Paris. The published reactions of the greatest French composer and the greatest French writer of the day are instructive. Berlioz, in his capacity as a professional music critic, gave a musically sensible account of the concerts. He preferred the *Lohengrin* prelude to the other pieces and found the *Tristan* prelude incomprehensible, and his general conclusion was that the compelling qualities of Wagner's personality 'would have more brilliant effect if they were joined to more invention, less study and a truer appreciation of certain fundamental elements of the art'.[1] In the second half of the essay, the jealous, frustrated composer of *The Trojans* took over from the critic and, in a journalistic *tour de force*, caricatured the supposed programme of 'the music of the future'—raucous noise, the abolition of melody, arias, duets, simple harmony, singable roles and so forth—in order to dismiss it with contempt. There are here several features that would recur in the response to Wagner of musicians: his earlier works—his operas—are to be rated higher than his music-dramas; he is deficient in musical talent and relies too much on orchestral and harmonic tricks; his theories are and will be responsible for all manner of ills in his own music and that of other composers. This reaction, the musical reaction, is alarmed, defensive, protectionist. There was justification for the criticism; and when it became better informed, it would have real attacking power.

Baudelaire, poet, translator, literary critic and art critic, had never written about music before and confessed that his musical education had been confined to the enjoyment of pieces by Weber and Beethoven.

He was bowled over by the concerts, wrote an enthusiastic letter to Wagner himself, and set himself to find out all he could about the 'something new that I was powerless to define'[2] which had so excited him in the music. The result was the essay *Tannhäuser à Paris*, which raised all the recurring issues of the literary response to Wagner: what were the nature of his artistic language, the relation of poetry to music within it, the relation of this mixed means of expression to poetry without music and to music without poetry, the point of his use of myth, the relation of his works to his theories? Upon these questions Baudelaire shed light and darkness in about equal proportions. He refuted, by showing it to be psychologically inept, the commonly held idea that Wagner's operas were being written to validate his theories, and that these theories had overlaid his creative inspiration. His explanation of the essential force of mythological subjects laid an emphasis, peculiarly relevant to Wagner, on the moral permanencies of human life, on the universality of sin and guilt, redemption and grace, under whatever names and whatever fabulous forms. Here he has never been improved on. But his attempt to account for Wagner's expressive language is much less successful, being seriously confused by an eccentric aesthetic theory. He quotes his own sonnet 'Correspondances', and prose meditations on the *Lohengrin* prelude by himself, Wagner and Liszt, to support his unconvincing assertion that ideas may be translated 'by reciprocal analogy'[3] from one art to another, from sound to colour, from either to words, and vice versa. On this shaky basis he identifies the 'something new' in Wagner's music as the self-explanatory quality that makes it, according to him, perfectly intelligible even to those with no knowledge of the libretto. One must remember that he is speaking only of concert extracts from *Lohengrin* and *Tannhäuser* and had never seen a Wagner work in the theatre. Nevertheless the theory of correspondences, even in this connection, would be weaker still without help from Wagner's programme notes, and oddly enough, Baudelaire quotes a passage by Wagner himself that completely overthrows it:

> I realized . . . that . . . by the intimate union of these two arts [music and poetry] one might express with the most satisfying clarity what neither of them could express by itself; that, on the other hand, all attempts to render by means of one of them what could not be rendered except by both together would be bound to lead to obscurity, first to confusion and then to the deterioration and corruption of each art in particular.

This passage, from Wagner's open letter in reply to Berlioz's article,[4] does not merely contradict Baudelaire's theory of perfect analogy in the arts. It announces that Wagner's own art is a hybrid, a new birth, for which neither poetry nor music can be a substitute. There is here a warning to the musical objectors of the present that ordinary musical considerations do not apply to the new art; there is also, though Wagner could not have foreseen the need for it, a warning to literary enthusiasts of the future that the new art cannot be taken as a model for purely literary productions. Neither warning was heeded. The musical point of view continued to be expressed, not only by composers but also by those critics whose musical priorities led them to see Wagner as a menace to the very existence of the musical tradition. Among these were writers as diverse and as varied in their feelings for Wagner as Hanslick, Nietzsche and Ernest Newman. At the same time, literary enthusiasm continued to grow, particularly in France, for the composer whose music had an extra-musical appeal never known before, and for the man whose creative achievement was seen, however indistinctly, to be of towering proportions.

The element of hero-worship in this literary enthusiasm is not negligible. The scrupulous and tormented Baudelaire, always on the point of finding the willpower to emerge from the toils of debt, emotional entanglement and ambitious projects hardly begun, saw in the ruthless, undeviating Wagner a figure tremendously to be admired. Later and less perceptive writers found in him a colossal, wicked and rather mysterious object of devotion in the cult of the artist as hero. In the 1880s, with garbled ideas about total art and the art-work of the future rife in France but his works virtually unknown, the recently dead Wagner was the source of an aesthetic thrill only comparable to that being generated by the elevating poetic ideals of Symbolism. It was the attempt, encouraged by the example of Baudelaire's yoking of the theory of correspondences to the quite incompatible *Gesamtkunstwerk*, to unite Wagner and Symbolism, to lend the vaguely apprehended prestige of the one to the vaguely formulated precepts of the other, that produced the *Revue wagnérienne*. This extraordinary periodical, which lasted from 1885 to 1888, was written mainly by disciples of Mallarmé who were less interested in Wagner's operas than in his aesthetic theories, and were not well-informed about either. The editor, Édouard Dujardin, an enthusiastic dabbler in several arts, at least admitted that the *Ring* 'was for us an almost unfathomable abyss'.[5] The principal contributor, the very young Téodor de Wyzéwa,

announced at the beginning of four massive articles on *Wagnerian Art*
that 'great works, to transform a race, do not need to be known.'[6]
The articles themselves are an inquiry into 'the progress of the
Wagnerian spirit'[7] in literature, painting and music, an inquiry which
involves Wyzéwa in a bizarre theory, derived from some remarks of
Wagner's, ascribing sensation to painting alone, ideas to literature
alone, and emotion to music alone. This divisive attitude, which can
only have in view Wagner's personal synthesis, the 'total work of art'
that is the music-drama, is then wrenched about to justify the demand
for totality in each of the arts separately. Wyzéwa is here up against the
logical absurdity which beset all the efforts of French literature to
absorb Wagner as an influence.

Between Wagner's supposed creation of total art where only music
had been, and the younger Symbolists' proposed creation of total art
where only poetry had been, lay an unbridgeable gulf of misunderstanding. The fact that Mallarmé, the mentor of the Symbolist movement, had for years been speaking of music in relation to poetry in a
sense altogether divorced from the vulgar realities of voices and instruments, let alone the operatic stage, did not help to clarify matters. At
the persuasion of Wyzéwa and other keen young Wagnerians, Mallarmé in 1885 wrote for the *Revue wagnérienne*, 'Richard Wagner:
Rêverie d'un poète français'. This prose-poem on Wagner, of whose
music Mallarmé had not at that time heard a note, reveals a mixture
of envy, alarm and disdain in the fanatical perfectionist who achieved
only a tiny fraction of what he set out to write, for the creative tyrant
who had mobilized huge resources for the achievement of a noisy
popular success. Wagner's fault of being a musician is compounded by
that of being a German; his mythical subjects—'Here is Legend en-
throned behind footlights'[8]—are regarded as uncivilized and un-
aesthetic because neither abstract nor invented; the mass theatrical
audience produces an artistic response very much inferior to that of
the single reader of the single book; those who find in Wagner's art
'final salvation', 'hospitality from the insufficiency of self and the
mediocrity of their native lands'[9] (ills from which Mallarmé did not
suffer), are mistaking for eternal truth what is no more than a shelter
against the vision of the absolute. The absolute is for nobody to reach,
Mallarmé concludes his address to Wagner. 'Nobody! this word gives
no qualms to the passer-by as he drinks at your convivial spring.'[10]

One suspects that Wagner would have been willing to agree that all
art is a shelter against the vision of the absolute; in any case, Mallarmé's

elegant scorn is directed at least as much at Wagner's admirers as at Wagner himself. Later in his life he came to feel that poetry must respond to Wagner's challenge by itself producing a total work of art that would dispense with the whole musical paraphernalia and make its effect between the book and its reader or possibly in some kind of ceremonial performance. The very un-Wagnerian rationale of this scheme was that poetry properly understood was nothing else but music without musicians. Mallarmé by this time had heard some of Wagner's music at the Concerts Lamoureux in 1893, but though Valéry reported that he left each one inspired with jealousy on poetry's behalf, it is unlikely that they made much real impression on him. 'Use Music in the Greek sense,' he wrote, 'basically meaning idea or rhythm between analogies; more divine there than in public or symphonic expression.'[11] There was little in common between the abstruse, solipsistic world of Symbolist suggestion and Wagner's explicit, extravert, above all dramatic art; and Mallarmé was right to feel that the purity towards which he strove in his poetry could best be described by a musical analogy that bore no relation to Wagner's hybrid language. When Mallarmé said in the 'Rêverie', 'There is no simplicity and no profundity that with an access of rapture Music cannot pour into Wagner's drama—except that the principle of Music itself escapes,'[12] he was drawing attention to the very element in Wagner—and it was the essence of Wagner's work—that so disturbed the musical objectors. And when Valéry wrote about the poetic ambitions excited by music in his Mallarméan youth, it was to Bach that he referred, calling 'an absolutely pure musical work which constructs feeling without a model . . . an immense significance drawn from nowhere'.[13]

The fact is that, among the niceties of late nineteenth century French aesthetics, Wagner was a gigantic red herring dragged across the scene by fashion and personal enthusiasm. As the hero of seekers after the exquisite, who would have been amazed by the full-blooded realism of the *Meistersinger* riot or Wotan's quarrel with Fricka, he was inappropriate to say the least. Baudelaire positively and Mallarmé negatively had exposed some of the central critical issues, but *wagnérisme* on the whole was a literary craze compounded of the sensational and the pseudo-mystical that produced neither good new art nor competent criticism of *Tristan* and *Parsifal*, the works from which it chiefly derived. As a modish literary fad, it had spread to England by the 1890s. George Moore affected Wagner in *Evelyn Innes*, getting

Dujardin to check his musical references, and the inexperienced D. H. Lawrence published a weak and over-excited *Tristan* novel, *The Trespasser*, in 1912. Joyce was influenced by the stream-of-consciousness technique used in Dujardin's *Les Lauriers sont coupés* (1887), but though Dujardin thought he had here invented the literary equivalent of Wagner's endless melody, the real-life randomness simulated in interior monologue had little in common, as an artistic aim, with the patterned integration of Wagner's music. Eliot in *The Waste Land*, on the other hand, not only held the poem together with a version of leading-motive but used direct quotations from Wagner's works, partly, of course, for their resonance, but partly also to evoke that very integration, the complex ordering of artistic structures of the past which in the waste land lie in fragments for lack of the emotional assurance which created them.

Each case of Wagner as a literary influence outside Germany has to be looked at individually and with caution. There were by 1900 many routes, some of them far from direct, by which his works or theories or intimations of either could reach particular writers. Germans, music critics and the writers who congregated as disciples at Bayreuth were, of course, in general much better informed. It is perhaps uniquely true of Wagner as a subject for criticism that it was possible for some of them to be too well informed. It was only natural for critics contemplating the difficult work of a major original artist to assume that they would be helped to understand that work by the artist's own extensive prose writings. In the event, one often feels that the critic of Wagner's works succeeds to the extent to which he has been able to clear his mind of Wagner's theoretical writings. Quite apart from the Master's erratic political passage, and his rapid leaps all his life from fact through prejudice to fantasy in any and every matter of opinion, there is a profound inconsistency in his view of music and of his own expressive language between the writings of his Zürich period and, say, the *Beethoven* essay of 1870. The attempt to weld all this together into a philosophical system, an attempt which some of the Bayreuth devout thought their duty to Wagner's shade, is doomed. But even the application to particular operas of the musical, political or philosophical ideas of contemporary prose pieces has to be undertaken with extreme critical tact. In the first place, when the interval between a work's conception and its completion is thirty years or more, as was the case with all Wagner's mature works except *Tristan*, it is hard to say what piece of dashed-off turgid propaganda is contemporary with what piece of slow cumulative creative thinking. In the second place, the Zürich programme Wagner wrote for the music-drama, the new kind of work he felt he had in him, was out-distanced and out-dated by the works themselves as they were composed. In the third place, and most importantly, the insecurity that made him justify, at length, in public, and with all the devices of laboured historical argument, everything he did and thought, is irrelevant to the finished achievement of the works with their tremendous creative confidence.

The possibilities and the pitfalls hereabouts are well illustrated in the 1968 full-scale biography by Robert Gutman. Here the relationship between Wagner's theoretical writings of the Zürich period and his creative practice is traced with care, and the facts are convincingly disentangled from the fictions of previous critics misled by Wagner himself. To point out that, after *Walküre*, Wagner in practice moved further and further away from the principles of *Oper und Drama*, that he abandoned these principles, if piecemeal and confusingly, in his later prose, and that the Wagnerians failed to notice either of these developments, is to perform a valuable critical service. Gutman can give an amusing account of the conglomeration of fads, fancies and philosophical views that Wagner published in 1880 under the title *Religion und Kunst* (*Religion and Art*), and add: 'The most extraordinary thing about the whole affair was that there were those to take it seriously at the time and later.'[14] But when it comes to *Meistersinger*, and particularly *Parsifal*, Gutman takes leave of his detachment and becomes as gullible as the most blinkered Bayreuth devotee. He argues unsoundly that *Meistersinger* is—in some unspecified sense of the verb—a Nazi work on account of antisemitic remarks about Nuremberg made by Wagner elsewhere. He sees Beckmesser as the outcast Jew, tricked by the preserver of German purity, who returns as Klingsor to menace the racist Grail knights. *Parsifal* is to be interpreted as a theatrical version of *The Heroic and the Christian*, Wagner's 1881 antisemitic tract proving Jesus an Aryan and racial pollution the root of ills curable only by eugenics; and Gutman's chapter on *Parsifal* rises to a hysterical flight of prose about the work's racial and political mania, homosexuality, 'mysticism and demonism . . . the Grail of superblood . . . the hostile Storm Trooper Grail knights . . . the satanic, the occult, and black magic'.[15]

To insist that Gutman's is a grossly inadequate interpretation of *Parsifal* is not at all to deny that Wagner's views in 1881, the year in which the scoring of *Parsifal* was finished, were execrable, nor that the backing of these views by his reputation and the earnest proclamation of them by some of his followers contributed to the formation of Nazi ideology. Nor is it to deny that there were elements in *Parsifal* which could be imitated by *fin de siècle* artists to no other end than the mindlessly sensational. It is only to say that the relevance of an essay expressing in 1881 *Gobiniste* views recently acquired and superficially understood to a highly complex, personal work of art conceived in 1845, sketched in 1857, and worked out in detail in 1865 stands in need of more convincing proof than Gutman can offer. His description of *Parsifal* can only be made to fit if the work's content is not only distorted but thought of as quite separate from the music. If a Wagner critic suggests such a separation, there is something wrong with his description. Finally, the fact that, in Hitler's day, the power of Wagner's prose to confuse appreciation of his operas was used by Nazi critics to dress up Siegfried, Walther and Parsifal as heroes of their ideology, should be seen as a warning and not an example.

Wagner himself began the whole unfortunate process by founding the *Bayreuther Blätter*, edited by the faithful Hans von Wolzogen, as an organ of propaganda more for his views than for his works. To this faulty priority was added, after his death, the difficult duty, undertaken by Glasenapp, of constructing a biography from which all traces of unworthy behaviour had been removed. All these topics are treated together in a book that was a synthesis of the Bayreuth view, Houston Stewart Chamberlain's *Richard Wagner* (1895). Chamberlain was an English Wagnerian (he later married Wagner's daughter Eva) who devoted himself to the Bayreuth cause in all its manifestations. He is remembered today largely and with deserved obloquy as an antisemite. But though the section of his book on Wagner's life is made absurd by bland idolatry, and that on Wagner's 'teaching' is made a mixture of the absurd and obnoxious by his own views and by his attempt to construct a doctrine from Wagner's writings, the quarter of the book that concerns the operas is by no means negligible. He knows the scores thoroughly; he can detach himself from the 'teaching', and, indeed, recommends this as essential, saying correctly that 'the influence of abstract thought upon artistic creation is as a rule enormously exaggerated';[16] and, above all, he has an eye for the central. He observes, for example, that the Zürich years of intense reflection divide the first from the second sketches of both the *Ring* and *Meistersinger* and that, though in both cases the old sketch is retained, the action in the second version 'is laid *within*',[17] so that the heart of

Sachs becomes the arena of *Meistersinger* and the heart of Wotan that of the *Ring*, including *Götterdämmerung*, and all that happens in both works is seen and felt through them. To point this out, and to amplify it with perception as he does, is worth a great deal of philosophical and political interpretation. His pages on the *Ring* and *Meistersinger* are among the best short accounts that can be found anywhere. He is weaker on *Tristan*, but on *Parsifal* he again goes straight for the centre, stressing the importance of the Grail as 'the visible symbol, supplying the connection between the processes in Parsifal's heart and his surroundings',[18] and demonstrating the power of Wagner's use of myth along the excellent lines laid down by Baudelaire.

Biographers of Wagner cannot ignore his prose writings, though if they use them to illuminate his operas they must do so with the utmost circumspection. Critics concerned only with the operas have an easier task, though of course a less interesting one if they leave out of account not only Wagner's but any discussion of the general aesthetic issues raised by his work. Édouard Schuré was one of these. An Alsatian playwright and critic—his principal book on Wagner, *Richard Wagner: son oeuvre et son idée*, is the second volume of the otherwise forgotten *Le Drame musicale*—he avoided the hazards created by being on the one hand personally devoted to Wagner, from the moment when he found himself by chance at the first performance of *Tristan*, and on the other hand a French writer looking for a work of art that might manage to be French, literary and Wagnerian all at the same time. His book, which gives a moderate and sensitive account of all Wagner's operas and deals particularly well with *Lohengrin* and *Tristan*, first appeared in 1875 (he added a *Parsifal* chapter in 1894) and became the textbook upon which Dujardin and many of his contributors depended for their knowledge of Wagner. If they had been more aware of the nature and scale of Wagner's music, they might have taken more notice of Schuré's reluctant conclusion that Wagner could only be succeeded by another writer of Wagnerian music-drama. It is significant that Catulle Mendès, one contributor to the *Revue* who had been to Bayreuth in 1876 and who knew Wagner and his works well, came to the same conclusion in the critical dialogue he wrote for the *Revue*, though naturally he required the new music-dramatist to be French.

Wagner himself and the Bayreuth writers had in view the greater glory of Wagner, his works and, with appalling consequences for which those ideas were in some measure to blame, his ideas. Schuré had nothing in view but increased understanding of masterpieces, though those who read him were deflected by literary preoccupations. Many writers from Baudelaire to the present day have found in Wagner confirmation of theories and ideas already held, and have written about him partly or entirely in the interest of these theories. Shaw in 1898 wrote *The Perfect Wagnerite* to show that Wagner was an altruistic proto-Fabian, and the *Ring* a socialist allegory which goes into creative decline after Brünnhilde's awakening because Wagner, disillusioned with the triumph of capitalism and reaction (Alberich and Wotan) in Europe by 1870, could not carry Siegfried through as the successful revolutionary he had originally conceived. Quite apart from the inappropriateness of Shaw's vision of Wagner as a consistent political philosopher, this argument is disproved by the fact that the whole poem of the *Ring* was finished in 1852 and, apart from haverings over the very end, remained unchanged thereafter. Nevertheless, Shaw's sharp wits and keen, if partial in every sense, enthusiasm for the *Ring* could not help giving out at least flashes of light, and he was certainly right to insist that the *Ring* has to do with power and the immemorial conflict of human motives.

In general, personal axes have been ground on Wagner to much less critical effect. In the case of writers who dislike his operas, this is hardly surprising. In 1895, Max Nordau's vast book *Degeneration*, which analysed the psychopathology of *fin de siècle* decadence with incisive learning and its own passionate lack of balance, gave Wagner pride of place as the most influential of all vicious, neurotic, self-indulgent degenerates. With the help of psychology's recent definition of persecution mania, Nordau wrote well on the dangers of Wagner's antisemitism and the other cant beliefs that made contagious Wagnerism part of German nationalist hysteria, but his attempt to prove the operas themselves pernicious is the usual failure. His musical case against Wagner is, however, being borrowed from Hanslick, soundly based. From a point of view utterly different from that of Shaw or Nordau, Jacques Barzun in *Darwin, Marx, Wagner: Critique of a Heritage* (1942: the date only partly excuses the Wagner third of the book) tried to force Wagner into the materialist-determinist mould formed by his other two subjects. The attempt is based on a highly individual combination of contempt for Wagner's works—Barzun does not so much aim to kill them as assume that they have already decomposed into symphonic fragments—and the belief that these same works can be translated back into 'thought' and Wagner's 'philosophy' or 'system' taken seriously as such. The critical upshot is weak formulas: 'That the world is a meaningless round of lust and death must . . . be the philosophy of the *Ring*';[19] 'The simple meaning and obvious fun . . . the jolly complacency of *Die Meistersinger*';[20] and ultimate inertia: 'What Parsifal himself represents in his author's philosophy is not clear.'[21] If Barzun had found Wagner's operas less boring it might have occurred to him that Wagner was perhaps not after all fighting on the same side as Marx and Darwin, or at least could not be destroyed with the same ammunition.

The translation of the content of Wagner's operas into one or another set of abstractions can be done to praise, as by Shaw, or to blame, as by Nordau and Barzun. It can also be done simply to illuminate. Robert Donington's *Wagner's Ring and its Symbols* is a Jungian translation of the *Ring* which sets forth the whole work in terms of anima and animus, shadow, archetype, libido, ego-consciousness and so on, as elements in a single psyche, the psyches of the characters, Wagner's psyche. This translation is assumed to suffice as both explanation and criticism. There are moments of valuable illumination; but one receives the strong impression that anything that might have happened in the *Ring* but does not, and indeed any other work of art, folk-tale or fairy-story, could be explained with equal conviction in the same way. In other words, the fact that the *Ring* is a great work of art, and the fact that it is a flawed work of art, are equally and for the same reasons lost sight of.

Ernest Newman, by far the most important English writer on Wagner, from the start set firm limits to his relationship with the complex phenomenon Wagner had become by 1914, the date of his first major book, *Wagner as Man and Artist*. Newman was not interested in Wagner as a literary example, nor as a subject for general aesthetic speculation. He was not interested in Wagner's political or philosophical views, nor, as a middle-of-the-road English freethinker, did he have any ideas or theories of his own which he looked to Wagner to confirm or into whose terms he wished to translate Wagner's works. Critically he was interested in Wagner only as a musician, the non-musical content of the operas seeming to him important only as the incidental trigger for the music. His admiration for the music sustained the vast judicial labour of his *Life of Wagner* (1933–47) and the painstaking tracing of prose sources, sketches and amendments in *Wagner Nights* (1949), but neither admiration nor labour resulted in any widening of his critical approach and it is even possible to suspect that the admiration may have produced the labour as a kind of substitute for the adequate critical account that Newman could not give. For in his position as a great admirer of Wagner who thought that, 'It is only as a musician that Wagner will live . . . All that concerns us is the quality of the music,'[22] there is a fundamental paradox. Newman himself met it as a critical impasse in *Wagner as Man and Artist*, and on account of this impasse his later books on Wagner are not critical at all. It arises from the fact that the musical approach to Wagner, unless purely technical, as in the huge works of Alfred Lorenz, are not compatible, in the thought of serious critics, with admiration, but with disapproval and suspicion, condemnation and fear.

Berlioz, with nothing later than the *Tristan* prelude to alarm him, had taken this approach. Even earlier, in 1852, the Belgian critic François-Joseph Fétis had written a series of articles in the *Gazette musicale* which formed the French musical case against Wagner for a whole generation, and in the course of which he had hit upon the central musical point: 'To Wagner's mind music presents itself as only secondary, as no more than an aid to expression. He has no conception of the art in its independent omnipotence and having no subject other than the composer's imagination.'[23] But the most considerable statement of this point of view, gaining strength and narrow intensity as each work from *Lohengrin* on was performed, was made by the Viennese critic, and most formidable writer on music of the nineteenth century, Eduard Hanslick. Having hailed the composer of *Der fliegende Holländer* and *Tannhäuser* as a new German operatic master, Hanslick came to see Wagner's art as a menace to musical tradition and continuity.

> Wagner's most recent reform [he wrote from Bayreuth in 1876] does not represent an enrichment, an extension, a renewal of music in the sense that the art of Mozart, Beethoven, Weber, and Schumann did; it is, on the contrary, a distortion, a perversion . . . One could say of this tone poetry: there is music in it, but it is not music.[24]

According to Hanslick's view, content in music is decisively inseparable from form; in music, that is to say, there can be form without content and form dense with (musical) content, but there cannot be content awaiting form, and in ordinary opera, musical content and verbal content are no more than juxtaposed. Hanslick perceived that Wagner, in whose works non-musical content is present in the music and separable from it, had departed from this definition; had, in fact, invented a new, hybrid means of expression, of which it was possible to say, as it could never be of real music, 'It is simply a matter of comprehension.'[25] This remark summarizes what is perhaps the crucial criticism of Wagner as a composer: that non-musical considerations—the expression of content awaiting form—had led him to reduce music to a translatable language. One may feel that Hanslick blinded himself to the fact that in Wagner's music at its best the translatable vocabulary of leading-motive is extended by properly musical processes far beyond the reach of verbal equivalence, and that his music should therefore be described not as a translatable language but as a medium of expression analogous to verbal language as it is used in poetry. One may feel that the invention of this medium is not Wagner's weakness as a composer, but on the contrary his great strength. Nevertheless, Hanslick was clear as to the true grounds for musical objections to Wagner and his case was infinitely stronger than that of those who regarded the main issue as the relative importance Wagner accorded to words and music. In any case, because his priority was the integrity of the musical tradition as he understood it, and because he feared that the methods dictated to Wagner by his peculiar genius would become a universal musical prescription, Hanslick could not suspend his criteria in order to hear Wagner on Wagner's terms. Being an intelligent critic, he realized that the new art was *sui generis*, but being committed to his definition of music, he judged it by his familiar, inappropriate standards and therefore not only judged it badly but judged it bad: he saw Wagner's 'endless melody' as a contradiction in terms dazzlingly orchestrated to conceal a lack of genuine musical invention, and he could not get past his disgust with it to attend to the substance of the works with any patience or sympathy. With the mature operas he therefore failed fundamentally and disastrously, mistaking Wagner's emphasis on the inner conflicts, victories and defeats of his characters for superstitious determinism of no conceivable modern interest, thinking the *Ring* spoilt by gods and dwarfs blighting the heroics of the *Nibelungenlied* and *Tristan* by the plot hinging on a mere magic potion, and calling the *Wahn* monologue an 'unctuous singsong'.[26] But Hanslick's failures on Wagner in particular should never be allowed to obscure the consistency and accuracy of his case against Wagner in general. In 1861 he wrote that Beethoven's Ninth Symphony and *Missa Solemnis* stood 'like colossal Pillars of Hercules at the gates of modern music, saying "No farther!"'[27] By the time of Hanslick's death in 1904, Wagner had

377

triumphed in most elaborate contravention of this command, and Hanslick's warning that Wagner's perilous path was for him alone was being ignored in its turn.

Behind Newman's *Wagner as Man and Artist*, musical as its approach to Wagner is, there is no clear idea of the nature of music such as that by which Hanslick measured Wagner and found him wanting. Newman, having swallowed whole Wagner's own account of the continuity between himself and Beethoven, has in his mind a picture of musical history in which Beethoven is seen not as a consummation, the creator of the ultimate in form dense with musical content, but as an intermediate figure some way along the road to the expression of non-musical content, the road which Wagner reached the end of. This vision leads Newman to say, for example, not only that the symphony is an illogical and arbitrary form, and that 'even Beethoven, giant as he was, could not quite burst the bonds of custom and prescription',[28] but also to see Wagner's substitution of precise dramatic emotion for the essentially imprecise emotion of Beethoven as a mere 'gradual extension of the borders of the Beethoven territory'[29] rather than as a revolution of both means and ends. So heavily is Newman committed to this picture of musical history, and to the continuity proclaimed in it, that he uses it, together with his scorn for what he calls 'the philosophical or pseudo-philosophical ideas'[30] of Wagner's operas, to support the conclusion that: 'So far from Wagner being first and last a dramatist, the whole significance of his work lay precisely in the fact that he was a great symphonist.'[31] That this should ever have been the opinion of the man who was to become the most balanced of all authorities on the facts of Wagner's life and work is remarkable enough. But later in *Wagner as Man and Artist*, Newman goes further still. He reflects that Wagner might have been without the 'personal bias' that made him 'prefer the seen to the unseen'[32] and compose for the stage, thinks that Wagner's ideal would have been better realized 'in instrumental music pure and simple',[33] and in 'Wagner and Super-Wagner', the essay tacked on to the end of the book, finally announces his wish that Wagner had actually written symphonic poems and not operas. At the same time he maintains the quite inconsistent view that Wagner's exactness of expression is an advance upon Beethoven: 'You can only win the full freedom you need for the expression of definite as distinguished from indefinite emotion by telling the hearer the nature and source of this emotion'[34]—a curious use of the word 'freedom', and one which appears to indicate not the inferiority but the superiority of the music-drama to the symphonic poem, let alone the symphony.

This manifold confusion is created by Newman's conflicting critical needs. On the one hand, Wagner must be absorbed into the musical tradition in order to be rendered harmless for that tradition's future. On the other hand, Wagner must be recognized as a unique genius who had transformed the means of musical expression. Newman's English faith in musical progress, more tenable in 1914 than now, is the optimistic compromise that insecurely conceals the conflict. Hanslick, who thought the symphonic poems and mixed musical forms of Berlioz, Liszt and Strauss only less reprehensible than Wagner's music-dramas, had no such faith. In the generous tribute he wrote at Wagner's death, Hanslick said of his own attitude: 'Wagner has been fought, but he has never been denied.'[35] Through repression and inversion of the same fear for music that Hanslick recognized and expressed, Newman created for himself a critical muddle out of which Wagner was denied but never fought.

Critics primarily concerned with Wagner's place in the musical tradition were and still are bound to find it hard to avoid a basic dilemma. Either they acknowledge Wagner's greatness and blind themselves to his pollution of the musical language—not his pushing of tonality to the limit, but his use of music for the expression of non-musical content—or they condemn his pollution of the musical language and blind themselves to his greatness. Critics of other kinds, from Baudelaire on, have not been forced to such a choice, and indeed, as has often been pointed out, musical people who are not trained musicians often form Wagner's most receptive audience. However, only the critical account that is complex, as the artistic figure of Wagner was complex can be fully adequate, and the Wagner critic whose approach is wider than the musical one of Hanslick or the Newman of *Wagner as Man and Artist* must nevertheless feel the musical issue, to him one issue among several, as keenly as they did. The two writers who have dealt most profoundly and most subtly with the whole Wagner phenomenon have been deeply involved with all the critical problems, with the musical issue as with the more general issue of aesthetic classification, with Wagner the man as with Wagner the creative force, Wagner the German and Wagner the abettor of a pernicious if chaotic school of thought. They were also major and many-sided creative figures in their own right, and therefore able to inform their accounts of Wagner with an imaginative sympathy denied

379

to mere critics. In the case of the first of them, Nietzsche, this sympathy was eventually transmogrified into fierce antipathy, its own negative, by the chemistry of violent personal feeling.

Nietzsche's father was born in the same year as Wagner and died when Nietzsche was four. The lonely, brilliant, puritanical boy, brought up by unintelligent and conventional women, became professor of classical philology at Basel in 1869 before he was twenty-five. He was from then until 1873, when the Wagners moved to Bayreuth, a frequent visitor to Triebschen, and his love for Wagner was the deepest emotion of his whole life. The pressure of Wagner's unquenchable demand for self-abnegation in others, and of Nietzsche's need for sympathy, jealousy of Wagner's success, and hatred of Wagner's antisemitism and nationalism deflected this love into deadly mockery and savage spite but never extinguished it. The mixedness of his feelings can be seen in two sentences from a letter Nietzsche wrote when Wagner died: 'Ultimately it was the ageing Wagner against whom I had to defend myself; as for the real Wagner, I myself will be to a great extent his heir . . . Last summer I realized that he had robbed me of all the people worth working upon in Germany.'[36] Because Nietzsche the man and Nietzsche the thinker and writer were to an exceptional degree all of a piece, these mixed feelings became in what he wrote about Wagner—a third of *The Birth of Tragedy*, one book *pro* Wagner and two *contra*, and numerous passages in his other works —a complicated picture of Wagner as a living contradiction. 'Does it not seem almost like a fairytale, to be able to come face to face with such a personality?'[37] he wrote in *Richard Wagner in Bayreuth*, the book he produced, already with some psychological difficulty, in 1876 to further the Bayreuth cause. By 1885, when Zarathustra meets the Sorcerer, the magic has become both false and pathetic: false because Nietzsche has now seen through the great trick that he claims Wagner's art to have been, pathetic because Nietzsche is vainly asserting his own strength and Wagner's need for him. 'O Zarathustra,' says the Sorcerer in the end, 'I seek one who is genuine, right, simple, unequivocal, a man of all honesty, a vessel of wisdom, a great human being. Do you not know it, Zarathustra? *I seek Zarathustra.*'[38]

A great human being, with all these qualities—for Nietzsche the absolute, the goal and standard of all endeavour—was precisely what he had taken Wagner to be. When he discovered that alongside what he called the will to power, the sublimation through self-discipline of powerful emotion into creative strength, there existed in Wagner the mere worldly will to actual power, his disappointment enraged him. Because of it, in *Ecce Homo*, the autobiographical firework display he wrote shortly before his collapse into the darkness of insanity, he claims for himself all the praise and warmth of perception evoked from him by Wagner in *Richard Wagner in Bayreuth*. 'In all its decisive psychological passages I am the only person concerned—without any hesitation you may read my name or the word "Zarathustra" wherever the text contains the name of Wagner.'[39] His painful ambivalence can be seen in the fact that he appropriates even the moving description in the earlier book of the expression on Wagner's face after the laying of the Bayreuth foundation stone, and yet later in *Ecce Homo* looks back at that very moment with nostalgia. Finally he attempts to resolve his contradictory feelings by blaming the Germans for robbing him of the pioneering exile he still loves and turning him into a *deutsche Meister*. Only two years earlier, in *Beyond Good and Evil*, he had told these same Germans that it was 'precisely the distinction' of Wagner's art 'that it derives from supra-German sources and impulses'.[40]

But in Nietzsche the shifting lights, the varying intentions, the apparent changes of mind revealing always something new, are almost endless. *Beyond Good and Evil* also contains a wonderful impressionistic description of the *Meistersinger* prelude as the very quintessence of Germanness, 'at once young and aged, over-mellow and still too rich in future', embodied in 'a magnificent, overladen, heavy and late art which has the pride to presuppose for its understanding that two centuries of music are still living'.[41] This passage (Aphorism 240) is worth whole libraries of books about Wagner. To it might be added the beautiful account, in *Richard Wagner in Bayreuth*, of Wotan's defeat and withdrawal as the clue to the meaning of the *Ring*, and Nietzsche's prediction arising from it that to the people of an unknown future Wagner will be 'not the prophet of the future, as perhaps he would like to appear to us, but the interpreter and clarifier of the past'.[42] The same might be said of Nietzsche himself. He and Wagner shared a fundamental obsession with the post-Christian problem of morality without God which strengthened both Nietzsche's understanding of Wagner and then his fury with him. *The Case of Wagner*, the book which gave this fury its most organized form, shows that Nietzsche's involvement amounting at times to identification with Wagner made it impossible for him to differentiate between the artist and the philosopher. To Nietzsche, the truth or falsehood of ideas was a matter of life and death, while to Wagner ideas were a matter not of reason but of emotion and intuition. It was natural for Nietzsche to mock the philosophical swerves of the *Ring*, and possible for him to maintain that what in Wagner was the neurosis of decadence was in himself the struggle against decadence; but both charges depended upon the false premise (which in any case Nietzsche only sometimes held) that Wagner's attitude to ideas was or should have been the same as his own. We are back again with Nietzsche's baffled disappointment with his fallen idol: Wagner was not the Goethean figure of control and self-creation, the representative of 'that strength which employs genius *not for works* but *for itself as a work*',[43] that he had thought. He rationalized his disappointment in *The Case of Wagner* and in *Nietzsche Contra Wagner*, his very last work, consisting of passages from his previous books collected, ordered and amended. Here, using terminology developed by him for wider uses, he says that works of art must be judged by the value of the need or motive behind them: 'Is it the *hatred* against life or the *excess* of life which has here become creative?'[44] and that, Wagner having suffered increasingly from hatred against life, his later works are morally disastrous. This reasoning leads to an extreme and partial judgement of *Parsifal*—based on the text only—as a nihilistic 'incitement to anti-nature',[45] the celibate Nietzsche furiously attacking the idealization of chastity and failing to notice that Klingsor's self-castration is contrasted and not identified with Parsifal's sublimation of passion.

The savagery of some of Nietzsche's writing *contra* Wagner has led Newman, for example, to dismiss it as the raving of a lunatic, and Gutman, for another example, to use it as almost factual evidence in the case against, particularly, *Parsifal*. But in Nietzsche the surface is always thin ice. His letters show that when he heard the prelude to *Parsifal*—which he had castigated as a noxious manifestation of slave-morality—he was profoundly impressed not only with its superlative quality as expressive art but also with what was being expressed: 'It was as if someone were speaking to me again, after many years, about the problems that disturb me.'[46] And his passionate though horrified admiration for *Tristan* lasted from his youthful infatuation with Bülow's piano reduction to the remarkable passage in *Ecce Homo* where he finally claims Wagner as 'the greatest benefactor of my life'[47] only by calling him a danger that he, Nietzsche, has been strengthened by overcoming.

Tristan is the example Nietzsche used in his first book, *The Birth of Tragedy*, to demonstrate that Wagner was the ultimate vindication of the Dionysus–Apollo dichotomy that is the book's subject. Dionysian music, the adequate idea of the world, is opposed to Apollonian drama, the veiling illusion of myth, symbol, character and event, which is finally dissolved to leave music, Dionysus, tragedy, supreme.[48] If one discards the historical extravagances of the context and the not very helpful classical terminology, this reveals itself as a piece of Wagner criticism which, though for the moment full of admiration, is substantially in accord with Hanslick. In a fragment 'On Words and Music', written while he was working on *The Birth of Tragedy*, Nietzsche goes still further. He says that definite feelings are no more than 'symbols to music', that 'music's Holy of Holies ... cannot be manifested, but only symbolized, by feeling',[49] that, in other words, there is such a thing as untranslatable musical emotion—a concept, derived from Schopenhauer, which would have considerably clarified Newman's critical case. It should never be forgotten that Nietzsche was an extremely sensitive listener to music and that the very musical responsiveness which inspired his most perceptive appreciations of Wagner also motivated his distrust and later inflamed his bitterness and misery. His very fine descriptions in *Richard Wagner in Bayreuth* of the concreteness of Wagner's imagination and the essential impurity of his musical language gave way, in both *The Case of Wagner* and *Nietzsche contra Wagner*, to the concession that Wagner must be praised as the greatest of musical miniaturists, and ultimately to the exaggeration that is an exaggeration of the central truth about Wagner:

> His place is elsewhere than in the history of music, with the grand true geniuses of which he must not be confounded. Wagner *and* Beethoven —that is a blasphemy—and in the end an injustice even to Wagner ... *He has immeasurably increased the speaking power of music* ... Provided always that one grants that music *may*, under certain conditions, not be music, but speech, tool or *ancilla dramaturgica*.[50]

Nietzsche's approach to Wagner as a subject for criticism was complicated and coloured by his feelings for Wagner the man. Thomas Mann's approach was complicated and coloured by his feelings for Nietzsche's work and ideas. Swept, as a young man, by the emotional power of Wagner's music, which he loved from the beginning of his life to its end, he was nevertheless deeply suspicious of it, having been convinced by Nietzsche's more extreme fulminations that it was not only decadent but actually evil. In an early essay, *Nietzsche and Music*,

383

he saw Wagner as the consummation of Romantic debility and Nietzsche as the prophet of post-Romantic health, and the same view
emerges from his first novel *Buddenbrooks* (1901), in which music,
in strongly Wagnerian form, is associated with inturned sexuality,
inertia, decline and death. In the war between the aesthetic and the
moral, the demonic and the *bürgerlich*, the dualism which obsessed
Mann as the key to himself and to Germany and which appears in all
his work, Wagner began squarely on the side of the demonic. As Mann
grew older, however, becoming always subtler, more ironic, more
equivocal, the intense divided view of Wagner he had inherited from
Nietzsche began to expand and diffuse. In *Tristan*, a story of 1902,
Bürger, artist, and Wagner's music as an emotional force are all
mocked, though the girl caught between them is seen with a sympathy
that perhaps amounts to fellow-feeling. The much more complex
story *The Blood of the Wälsungs* (1906) has *Walküre* inciting a pair of
effete young twins to incest—there is a deeply ambivalent echo of
Wotan's love for the Wälsung race in Mann's portrait of these Jewish
decadents—but is also a defence of Wagner the patient creator, 'the
vision, the intention, the labouring will',[51] and Wagner the evoker of
real vitality and passion, against careless and lazy 'cultured' appreciation.

It was because Mann was himself primarily an artist and not, like
Nietzsche, primarily a thinker that he was able to understand the one
essential fact about Wagner that had eluded Nietzsche. Whereas
Nietzsche was irritated beyond endurance by Wagner's amateurishness as a thinker, Mann seized upon this very amateurishness as an
intrinsic part of his genius. In his long essay, 'Sufferings and Greatness
of Richard Wagner', Mann says that: 'Wagner's triumphant performance does not justify his theory but only itself';[52] that: 'Wagner's
art *is* dilettantism, monumentalized and lifted into the sphere of
genius by his intelligence and his enormous will-power';[53] and that the
critic of Wagner should never forget the element of play, the ultimate
unseriousness of his art as of all art. As a perfect illustration, Mann
uses a letter to Mathilde Wesendonck about *The Victors* in which
Wagner is pleased that the intrinsically non-dramatic Buddhist ideal
has one last story to be turned into drama, and at the same time
dismayed to catch himself 'in the act of preferring the play and not the
spirit'.[54]

Mann sees Wagner's dilettantism as particularly revealed in his
invention of a mixed art, a naïve act which only his 'vast genius for

expression'[55] could have brought to success. This view produces a description of Wagner's means of expression that both explains and excuses the musical opposition to it, while not in the least detracting from Wagner's achievement. Wagner's occasional moments of despair, Mann says,

> ... could only come from the error he made at such moments: of isolating his musicianship and thus bringing it into comparison with the best, whereas it should only be regarded *sub specie* of his whole creative production—and vice versa; to this error is due all the embittered opposition that his music had to overcome ... Wagner's music is not music to the same extent that the dramatic basis is not literature ... Too much to ask that the E flat major triad at the beginning of the *Rheingold* be called music. It was not. It was an acoustic idea: the idea of the beginning of all things.[56]

When to this description are added Mann's subtle and moving accounts of the psychological power of Wagner's characterization and use of myth, symbol, leading-motive; when his drawing attention to the distinctiveness of each opera is given weight with such a generalization as this: 'Each work is stylistically set off against the rest; in a way that makes one see and almost feel the secret of style as the very kernel of art, well-nigh as art itself: the secret of the union of the personal with the objective';[57] when Mann stresses, against Nietzsche, both the emotional consistency of Wagner's whole career and the purity of his artistic motives; when all these things and more are taken together, 'Sufferings and Greatness of Richard Wagner' emerges as the best and fullest piece of appreciative writing in the whole of Wagner criticism.

It was delivered as a lecture in Munich on 10 February 1933. On the following day, Mann left Germany for sixteen years. The essay is naturally marked by historical pressures: the arguments exonerating Wagner's operas from pernicious nationalism are well put, though the very end of the essay, on Wagner as a European and the difference between folk and national art, is vague and unsatisfactory. More surprising is the fact that one strand in the essay is still Mann's identification of Wagner with the demonic, the Romantic, all that is involved in the phrase 'pessimism, the musical bond with night and death',[58] or, in a word, Schopenhauer. Mann is now willing to concede that the *bürgerlich* element in Wagner, the moral preoccupation as well as the painstaking creative care, did exist, but the strength in his mind of his familiar dichotomy will not allow him to relieve Wagner of the Nietzschean charge of demonism, however convincing his political defence. In the later, slighter and more high-flown essay 'Richard Wagner and the Ring' (1937), he reinforces the political defence and in his statement of Wagner's dualistic nature uses the neutral terms 'modern intellectuality' and 'mythic, primitive folkishness';[59] but he nevertheless maintains, against the fact that all Wagner's 'bad' characters, including Klingsor, have a certain human warmth (quite lacking in Mann's own diabolical scenes), that 'the theatre knows nothing nearer to the demonic'[60] than the Hagen scenes in *Götter-dämmerung*.

The truth is that on Wagner, as on other topics, Mann never made up his mind. In 1947, when he was an old man, the anti-Nazi Franz Beidler, Isolde Wagner's son, asked him to be honorary president of a denazified Bayreuth. He refused, but not without hesitation: 'I recalled the enormous influence the equivocal magic of this art had had upon my youth . . . The sinister side of this art had been revealed by the role it had played in the Nazi state. Was it now to be restored to its purity (but had it ever been pure?)?'[61] He could not decide; and his indecision was largely thanks to Nietzsche, the strongest of the four great influences on Mann's life and art, the other three being Goethe, Schopenhauer and Wagner. By the time he wrote *Dr Faustus* (completed 1947) Nietzsche had certainly replaced Wagner in Mann's mind as the arch-demonic figure, and the book's possessed Nietzschean hero Leverkühn, who has left Wagnerian naïvety far behind, can only laugh at the beauty of the prelude to Act III of *Meistersinger*. Indeed, the roles Mann assigned to Wagner and Nietzsche at the beginning of his life are now reversed: the cold intellect has become devilish and emotion is the health that Leverkühn is denied.

Immediately after *Dr Faustus* was finished, Mann wrote an essay on Nietzsche, given as a lecture in both America and Europe, which concludes with what was for him a new kind of hope. After the ruin of both *bürgerlich* morality and the Nietzschean aesthetic revolt against it, 'The main thing is a transformation of the spiritual climate, a new feeling for the difficulty and the nobility of being human.'[62] This dissolution of the old dichotomy would seem to have nothing to do with Wagner were it not prefigured in Mann's 1938 essay on Schopenhauer. Here Mann traces, with the utmost sensitivity and a sympathy born of shared experience, Wagner's appropriation of the vitality and passion, if not the exact philosophical import, of Schopenhauer's thought and in particular his psychology. *Tristan* is, of course, the work Mann has in mind. But at the end of the essay, not referring to

Wagner at all, he speaks of Schopenhauer's pessimistic humanity as contrasted to Nietzsche's 'false idea of healthiness which tramples on the spiritual factor that might today heal Europe',[63] and as 'above dry reason on the one hand and idolatry of instinct on the other',[64] substantiating his case with a long argument of which the high point is his account of Schopenhauer's conception of man:

> To man is vouchsafed the opportunity to right the wrong, to reverse the great error and mistake of being; to get the supreme insight that teaches him to make the suffering of the whole world his own and can lead him to renunciation and the conversion of the will. And so man is the secret hope of the world and of all creatures; towards whom as it were all creation trustfully turns as to its hoped-for redeemer and saviour.[65]

This is an exact description of what *Parsifal* is about, yet neither here nor anywhere else does Mann, being always partly faithful to his own sense of Wagner's sinister decadence, give Wagner credit for having had, and not only in *Parsifal*, 'a new feeling for the difficulty and the nobility of being human'.

In this respect, one may say that Mann's equivocalness towards Wagner did not go far enough. For an elaborate and conscious equivocalness is ultimately the only basis for an adequate critical response to Wagner. Time has shown that the fears of the protectionist musical opposition were justified. Time has shown that Wagner's mature operas are masterpieces of rich power and probably infinite resistance to critical explanation. Yet these two statements are both partial, and they are not contradictory. The musicians who realized that in Wagner's hands music had become a translatable language, and therefore in an important sense not music, heaped upon him also the blame for having shattered diatonic harmony and with it the balance between musical expression and musical form in which the European musical tradition subsisted. But if Wagner had never been born, the human impulse to move always forward, outward, beyond, would without doubt have brought music to the same state of fission, as the work of other nineteenth-century composers shows. It was inevitable that the short tradition of European music, a fragile structure of conventions and precarious rules, should collapse; no one could have predicted that at the last moment a major creative imagination would make this structure one element in a new kind of dramatic art. Grief for the inevitable passing, rejoicing at the unexpected achievement: this mixture of feelings is where the good critic of Wagner starts. As Mann perceived, though he put it only obliquely, it is a mixture that informs the very construction of the *Ring*, not to mention its content:

> Back to the beginning, the beginning of all things, and its music! For the Rhine depths with the glittering hoard, round which the Rhine daughters sported and played—all that was the innocent, primitive state, still untouched by greed and curse; and one with it was the *beginning of music*. He, the poet and composer, would produce the myth of music itself . . . all out of the E flat major triad of the flowing depths of the Rhine.[66]

Georges Servières, a French Wagnerian, wrote in 1886: 'To tell the truth, the definitive book on Richard Wagner is still to be written.'[67] Nearly a century and several thousand books later, the remark still stands. Challenging the future to produce such a book, Joseph Kerman said in 1961: 'I suggest only one preliminary axiom: resist all pressure to regard the *oeuvre* as an inviolable, necessary, superbly constructed whole. There is no such artistic entity as "Wagner"; only four fantastic works of art.'[68] In accordance with his axiom, Kerman himself wrote in *Opera and Drama* (1956) a masterly account of the last act of *Tristan*. But to calm examination of the masterpieces there must be added something of the passion and intricate involvement of Nietzsche and Mann. Of course the *oeuvre* is not inviolable, necessary or (all of it) superbly constructed. But Wagner as an 'artistic entity' does exist, a staggering creative feat produced by intuition and intellect out of and for the critical, moralizing, uncreative, spiritually starved world in which we still live; and those who guess, like Baudelaire, that they have something to learn from it are right.

POSTSCRIPT

Since the above was written, the work of a very distinguished contemporary critic of Wagner, Carl Dahlhaus, has begun to appear in English: *Richard Wagner's Music Dramas* (1979). Professor Dahlhaus's article on Wagner's aesthetics and musical works in the New Grove *Dictionary of Music and Musicians* (1979) is the best short account to be found anywhere.

ELEVEN

The Idea of Bayreuth

GEOFFREY SKELTON

Only through this theatre will the world come to learn what sacredness can be invested in a dramatic performance, presented wholly in *my* way—and then all existing theatres, even the most splendid of them, will be bound to appear ridiculous in the eyes of all sensible people.

THESE WORDS, written by Richard Wagner to King Ludwig II of Bavaria on 13 September 1865, refer to the theatre which King Ludwig intended to build in Munich for the presentation of Wagner's works and not to the Festival Theatre in Bayreuth. But they reflect the thought that inspired the composer throughout his life to pursue the dream of a theatre of his own: his conviction that the function of art is basically religious. The erection of a theatre for his music-dramas was not mere vanity, but an integral part of Wagner's attempt, as significant to him as the dramas themselves, to convince the world that art is one of the profoundest influences in the world and, as such, must be approached both reverently and responsibly.

Wagner considered himself to be first and foremost a dramatist, and thus he was fully aware of the vital importance of the place in which his work was presented. Time and time again he voiced the opinion that a drama could not be said to exist until it was performed, and for him a bad or an inadequate performance was the equivalent of, perhaps even worse than, no performance at all.

If Wagner had been an ordinary dramatist, working only with words, he would certainly have spared himself many frustrations, for the spoken drama, both in Germany and outside, occupied a position of respect. The musical theatre, on the other hand, into which the

389

particular nature of his talent pushed him, was regarded at the time
as a purely superficial form of entertainment, in which the singers'
virtuosity and the ballerinas' charms were more important than
anything the composer or the librettist might have to say.

The musical theatre to which Wagner committed himself in 1833,
when at the age of twenty he accepted a post as chorus-master and
occasional conductor in Würzburg, was one he basically despised.
Beginning (like virtually all great dramatists) at the practical end of
his art, he was initially more concerned to establish himself than to
proselytize, though he had already received a vivid impression of what
the musical theatre could achieve when, four years earlier in Leipzig,
he had seen Wilhelmine Schröder-Devrient playing in *Fidelio*. As he
tells us in his autobiography *Mein Leben*, he immediately wrote the
great singer a letter 'in which I briefly told her that from that moment
my life had acquired its true significance, and that if in days to come
she should ever hear my name praised in the world of art she must
remember that she had that evening made me what I then swore it was
my destiny to become'.

In the pursuit of his destiny it can be doubted whether the six years
of his apprenticesihp in Würzburg, Magdeburg and Riga did much
more than merely confirm his view that the modern operatic stage was
basically frivolous, though they did provide him with an opportunity
of developing his composing craft: *Die Feen* and *Das Liebesverbot*
were completed and *Rienzi* begun in this period. And impressions of
all kinds were being registered along the way, the ultimate significance
of which were perhaps not immediately recognized, but were later to
be remembered and acted on. It was, for instance, in the little theatre
in Riga that Wagner first realized that the shape and atmosphere of an
auditorium can greatly influence the impact of a performance. The
seats in the theatre at Riga were steeply raked, the auditorium was
dark and the orchestra was placed low before the stage, almost out of
sight of the audience. The lessons to be learnt from that were not
forgotten.

Two years later, in Paris, where he next went in his search for fame,
Wagner made another interesting technical discovery. Arriving late
at the Conservatoire to hear Habeneck rehearsing a Beethoven symphony, he was put in a room divided from the main concert hall by a
partition stopping short of the ceiling. As he recalled to his friend
Felix Dräseke twenty years later, the sound of the orchestra reaching
him over the partition amazed him: the music, freed of all mechanical

side-effects, 'came to the ear in a compact and ethereal sort of unity'.

Such reminiscences, written down years later when their relevance to the theatre eventually built in Bayreuth was clearly apparent, must of course be treated with some reserve. Certainly they cannot be taken as evidence that Wagner at this early period of his life was definitely thinking of one day building a theatre of his own. All the same, there can be no reason to doubt that the impressions were registered and went, along with Wilhelmine Schröder-Devrient, into the storeroom of his mind for future if still undefined use.

More reliable evidence of the conscious progress of his thoughts as a young man can be found in the essays, short stories and journalistic reports which the composer, thwarted in his attempts to gain a footing in the operatic world, wrote during his stay of two and a half years in Paris in order to gain a living. These provide a fascinating self-portrait, all the more revealing in that it is not always intended. One of the first pieces he wrote for the *Gazette musicale*, entitled 'Über deutsches Musikwesen' ('On German Music'), shows the depth of his national feeling. His analysis of the German spirit, naïve and over-idealistic as it is, accurately identifies the essential gods: Bach, Mozart, Beethoven, Weber. Their moral earnestness, their basic simplicity—scorning superficial brilliance—were the qualities on which German opera, should it ever flourish in its own right, ought to be based. In Mozart's *Die Zauberflöte* and Weber's *Der Freischütz* he discerned the essential qualities, and they were qualities for which French opera, for all its technical competence (and Wagner was sufficiently a professional to acknowledge that), had little use.

In another literary piece, the short story 'Ein Ende in Paris' ('Death in Paris'), Wagner portrays an idealistic young German composer who, unable to compromise with Parisian musical convention, starves to death. These are among his dying words:

I believe in God, Mozart and Beethoven, likewise in their disciples and apostles; I believe in the Holy Ghost and in the truth of the one and indivisible Art; I believe this Art to be an emanation of God that dwells in the hearts of all enlightened men; I believe that whoever has steeped himself in its holy joy must dedicate himself to it forever and can never deny it; I believe that all men are blessed through Art and that it is therefore permissible to die of hunger for its sake . . . I believe in a Day of Judgment upon which all who dared to exploit this chaste and noble Art for the sake of profit, and all who in the baseness of their hearts dishonoured and disgraced it for the sake of sensual pleasure will be fearfully punished . . .

It is an embryonic, still undirected expression of his own creed, but Wagner, being of stronger stuff than his own hero, knew in his heart that mere intentions are not enough. In another essay, 'Der Künstler und die Öffentlichkeit' ('The Artist and the Public'), he examines, admittedly in a somewhat confused and inconclusive way, the irresistible urge of the artist to communicate, even if in his longing to share his divine discoveries he runs the risk of desecrating them. 'It is then,' he writes, 'that he allows himself to sup with the devil, giving himself the right because he knows, however many lies he may tell, that his truthfulness can never be sullied.' It was in this practical spirit, confident of his ability to withdraw before it was too late, that Wagner wrote songs for reigning Parisian singers (though none of them was performed), and in this spirit too he wrote the libretto for a one-act opera which, since it could be used as a curtain-raiser, might win him a footing in the Paris Opéra. It did not, though the Opéra bought the libretto from him for setting by another composer.

This was the origin of *Der fliegende Holländer*. In spite of having sold his libretto, Wagner set about composing music to it himself, and what had been conceived as a curtain-raiser turned in his hands into a full-length opera. If Wagner, still in the process of making discoveries, could have made one here about his own character, he evidently did not do so, for he was to repeat the same mistake on two more occasions during his life: both with *Tristan und Isolde* and *Die Meistersinger von Nürnberg* he set out to write popular and easily producible works to restore his immediate fortunes. It seems that some force was at work inside him which in the end always held him to his artistic convictions and refused to allow him to carry out his own intended compromises. The devil with whom he sometimes chose to sup could, one is inclined to conclude, only have been his guardian angel in disguise!

Paris may have saved him from his rash willingness to compromise by refusing to have anything to do with him on any terms. Dresden, to which he went in 1842 as conductor, provided a far severer test. Both *Rienzi* and *Der fliegende Holländer* had been accepted for production there. The first was a great success, the second a partial failure. It would have been easy for him, encouraged by his wife Minna and most of his friends, to draw the conclusion that he should stay where he was and establish his position by writing more operas like *Rienzi*. At least he would be assured of comfort and respect, and the Dresden Opera, to which his idol Wilhelmine Schröder-Devrient currently belonged, enjoyed a good reputation. Could not his ambition of raising the standards of German opera be achieved better there than anywhere else?

The factor that spoke most strongly in Wagner's mind against this argument was the lack of recognition for *Der fliegende Holländer*, a work which he knew to contain far more of his ultimate beliefs than the pompous and derivative *Rienzi*. And his feelings of dissatisfaction were only inflamed by the reception of *Tannhäuser*, which he had written in Dresden in a spirit of isolation induced by the conflict inside him between his convictions and the temptations of material success. *Tannhäuser*, though it both expressed his artistic beliefs (to the best of his ability at the time) and pleased the public, was, he felt, appreciated for the wrong reasons—for its superficial beauties rather than for its moral message. The fact that Wagner himself had contributed to the misunderstanding by damaging cuts in his work merely proved the difficulty of his self-imposed task. Opera, in Dresden as in Paris, was at the mercy of people—managers and singers (for whose sake the cuts had been made)—who cared for nothing except their own personal glory. What chance had a dramatist, musical or otherwise, of getting his message through to the audience under those circumstances?

It was the culmination of all these experiences and conclusions that led Wagner in 1849 to define for the first time in writing his ideas for the reform of the operatic stage. His study bore the title 'Entwurf zur Organisation eines deutschen National-Theaters für das Königreich Sachsen' ('A Plan for the Organization of a German National Theatre for the Kingdom of Saxony'), and was addressed, as Wagner tells us, to the members of parliament in Saxony, who were threatening at the time (revolution being in the air) to cut the subsidy of the existing court theatre. Wagner felt rather naïvely that to present a plan for a more democratically organized theatre would avert the threat by showing a way to establish the theatre on a broader social and more genuinely artistic basis.

Reading his study now, one is struck both by its thoroughness and the practicality of its approach. It is obviously the work of a man who had learnt much from experience. In this essay he defines in great detail the terms under which singers and orchestral players should be engaged and what steps should be taken to train them—an interesting foreshadowing of later attempts in Munich and Bayreuth to do exactly that. But its most daring proposal was that the director of the theatre should no longer be appointed by the king, but should be democratically elected by a majority vote of the entire theatre personnel, together with members of a society of German authors and composers.

In this document there is no mention at all of theatre buildings as such. It is perhaps not altogether surprising, since Wagner was here concerned mainly with organizational matters. But one feels that, if he had at the time had any definite ideas on the importance of a theatre's shape, he would have found room in his study to define them— in the same way that he seized the opportunity to define his conception of the theatre's social function. 'In theatrical art,' he writes, 'all forms of art combine to a greater or lesser extent to make an impression on the public such as none of the other arts can make in isolation. Its essential character is socialization, while preserving in full all the rights of the individual.'

There is certainly a liberality about this last sentence more appealing than the dictum of Emperor Joseph II which the composer goes on to quote with open approval: 'The theatre should have no other duty except to contribute to the elevation of taste and morals.' This on the face of it is sheer didacticism, and one feels that, had Wagner adhered to such a dictum in his own works, he would hardly have been the powerful artistic force that he later became. His dramas themselves provide the best evidence that he was alive to the need in the theatre to entertain as well as to instruct. His basic complaint about the opera of his day was that it sought *only* to entertain—in other words, that it was trivial. He was profoundly convinced that the operatic form was capable of expressing eternal truths, and had, indeed, already done so in the operas of Gluck, Mozart, Beethoven and Weber—even to some extent in such lesser works as Auber's *Muette de Portici*, Halévy's *La Juive* and Spontini's *La Vestale*. The 'elevation of taste and morals' which he was seeking to secure applied in his own mind mainly to the managers and singers: only if they could be persuaded to approach their task in the proper exalted spirit would the moral influence on their audience be effected. In the power of music as well as words to influence morals Wagner believed implicitly. 'We can maintain with some confidence,' he states bravely in his 'Entwurf', 'that Beethoven enthusiasts are more active and energetic citizens than those under the spell of Rossini, Bellini and Donizetti: these are mere well-to-do and genteel idlers.'

In his vocabulary Wagner here borrowed something from the revolutionary socialists with whom he was associating at that time (1849), and it is not surprising that his proposals for a national theatre on co-operative lines were emphatically spurned by both court and parliament. He himself, as we know, was found guilty of taking part in the revolution and banished from Germany. This is not the place to examine the justice or otherwise of that decision, but it can surely be claimed, whatever rash statements and acts the composer might have been led into in those excitable days, that his thinking was never political in a strictly sociological sense. Fundamentally, he was not out to sweep aside the King of Saxony, but simply the management of Saxony's main opera house.

The special nature of Wagner's socialism can be clearly seen in the long essay *Die Kunst und die Revolution* (*Art and Revolution*), which he wrote in Zürich in the year of his flight from Germany. Here for the first time he makes use of the word *Gesamtkunstwerk*, though in a different sense from that in which it was later applied to the structure of his music-dramas. He used it in relation to the drama of Ancient Greece, which, he claimed, was an integral part of the social structure and not just a recreational excrescence.

> The theatre [he writes, reechoing the claim expressed in his rejected 'Entwurf'], is the most comprehensive, the most influential of all artistic institutions, and before human beings can freely practise their noblest activity, which is art, how can they hope to be free and independent in other, lower directions? Eternally youthful art, always able to refresh itself from the noblest spirits of its time, is better equipped than a senile religion that has lost its hold on the public, than an incapable government, to steer the turbulent currents of social movements past the wild cliffs and treacherous shallows towards their great and noble goal—the goal of true humanity.

In other words, liberate the theatre and the rest will follow of its own accord.

The revolutions of 1848–9 and his banishment from Germany were responsible for a radical change in Wagner's ideas on how to set about rescuing the human race through the theatre. Up to that point all his efforts had been directed towards reforming the existing operatic theatre from within—not only through his own works and those of his equally high-minded predecessors, but also by placing its management in more dedicated hands. Now he came to the drastic conclusion that the only way was to destroy the existing theatre and start again from the beginning.

Writing in September 1850 from Zürich to his friend and fellow revolutionary Theodor Uhlig, he speculated on how this might be done:

Here on a nice meadow close to the town I would build a crude theatre
of planks and beams according to my own design and furnish it simply
with the machinery and decorations needed for a production of
Siegfried. Then I would select the most suitable singers I could find
and invite them to Zürich for six weeks. I would aim at forming a
chorus mainly from volunteers (there are splendid voices and strong
healthy people to be found here!) and I would get my orchestra
together in the same way. In the New Year, announcements would be
published in all German newspapers inviting all friends of the music
drama to my dramatic music festival. Everyone coming to Zürich for
it would be assured of a seat—free, of course, as all admittance should
be. In addition I would invite the local young people, universities,
choirs, etc., to attend. When everything is ready, I shall give three
performances of *Siegfried* in a week. After the third performance the
theatre will be pulled down and my score burnt! To the people who
enjoyed it I shall then say: 'Now go away and do it yourself!'

Allowing for the pipe-dream quality of this letter, admitted by
Wagner himself, we can nevertheless recognize in it the first particularized vision of what was eventually to become Bayreuth. Above all,
it brings in for the first time the idea of a special building. Obviously
one should not read into the 'crude theatre of planks and beams'
anything more than the thought that this would be the cheapest way
of building it. But in fact, as we find in practically all later references
to a festival theatre, Wagner continually stressed the provisional or
temporary nature of the building he wanted to erect (though there
was no further talk of destroying the score after performance!).

Behind his insistence there certainly lay the hope that a temporary
theatre would relieve him of the attentions of philistine court-theatre
directors, who would scarcely be interested in anything so ephemeral.
But there may, even at this stage, have been artistic considerations
involved as well. Wagner was aware that his projected new work,
Siegfrieds Tod, the text of which had been completed before he left
Dresden, would present problems of staging. Many of his friends had
openly told him so. Only Franz Liszt who, after producing *Tannhäuser*
in Weimar in 1849, went on the following year to give the first performance of *Lohengrin*, had sufficient faith in Wagner's genius to
support him unquestioningly, and it was Liszt to whom Wagner in
gratitude promised *Siegfrieds Tod*. However, in his autobiographical
essay, *Eine Mitteilung an meine Freunde* (*A Communication to My
Friends*), written a few months after his arrival in Switzerland, he
admitted a change of mind: 'If I have since felt compelled to revise
my plans very radically, so that it is no longer possible to carry them

out in the form already notified to the public, the reason for this lies primarily in the nature of the poetic material.'

'Primarily' suggests that Wagner had other reasons beside purely dramatic ones for turning *Siegfrieds Tod* into *Der Ring des Nibelungen*, and it is not too rash to assume that among them might have been the feeling that the best way of ensuring a new start would be to write a work which by its very nature demanded the creation of new conditions to present it. This is in fact clearly enough implied in the 'Communication', in which he does not mention the building of a special theatre, though he does, incidentally—in a footnote—provide another important indication of the radical change that had taken place in his approach to his work. The footnote reads: 'I am no longer writing *operas*; but, since I do not wish to invent some arbitrary name for my works, I call them simply *dramas*: this does at least most clearly describe the standpoint from which what I now have to offer should be regarded.' From all of this it seems a reasonable conclusion that Wagner's dogged insistence on a 'temporary' theatre owed something to his feeling that, until his vast new work was completed, he himself could not really know what the right conditions for its presentation would be.

The 'Communication' was already written and the decision to expand the original Siegfried dramas into a cycle of four works proclaimed when Wagner wrote once more to Uhlig:

> The next revolution must necessarily put an end to our whole theatrical structure as it now exists. The theatres must and will all of them collapse—there is no way round that. From the ruins I shall gather together what I need—and I shall find what I want. I shall then erect a theatre on the banks of the Rhine and issue invitations to a great drama festival. After a year's preparation I shall over four days present my complete work: with it I shall reveal to the people of the revolution the meaning of this revolution in its noblest sense. This public will understand me; the present public cannot. Wild as this plan is, it is the only one on which I can stake my life, my work and my endeavour. If I live to see it, I shall have lived splendidly; if not, then I shall have died in a good cause.

Only a few months later he was writing to another revolutionary friend in Dresden, August Röckel, of the possibility of putting his 'wild' plan into effect in Zürich. The preparation for it would be a series of productions of his earlier works in the existing theatre, and in April 1852 he made a start with *Der fliegende Holländer*. In the same year, Liszt came to visit him in Zürich, and Wagner wrote afterwards to one of his new friends in Switzerland, Otto Wesendonck:

To my gratified surprise Liszt agreed with my plans for a festival, and we have decided that it shall be held in Zürich between the spring and autumn of some particular year. A temporary theatre will be built, and everything I need in the way of singers, etc., will be specially engaged. Liszt will go to all corners of the earth to collect funds, and is confident of raising the necessary money.

It appears from this that what happened eventually in Bayreuth could have happened in Zürich some twenty years earlier. Why did it not come about? The immediate reason was undoubtedly the scepticism of the Swiss who, however honoured they were by Wagner's presence among them, were not prepared to pay out money for so bold and unpredictable a plan. But there was certainly a more personal reason involved: consciously or subconsciously, Wagner did not wish his theatre for the *Ring* to be built outside Germany. His work, still uncomposed, was not only revolutionary, but also demonstratively German. How could he, believing as he did in the moral influence of art, have hoped to further his cherished cause of a united Germany by building his stronghold in neutral Switzerland?

Confidently as he may have talked to Liszt and to his friends in Dresden about plans for producing the *Ring*, Wagner had not yet in fact solved the artistic problems posed by the work itself. That was yet another reason for regarding the building of a theatre for it in Zürich as premature. The first years of his Swiss exile were musically unproductive. Instead of writing operas, he sat down to work out his artistic ideas in words: during this period he wrote his long essay *Das Kunstwerk der Zukunft* (*The Art Work of the Future*) and his full-length book *Oper und Drama* (*Opera and Drama*). The gap between theory and practice, as they affected the work of art itself, remained wide until that afternoon in September 1853 when Wagner, in a semi-conscious state, heard the E flat major chord of the *Rheingold* prelude in his mind's ear and at last unleashed his musical inspiration.

Nevertheless, the dream of an early special production persisted. In February 1854 he wrote to Wilhelm Fischer in Dresden:

> In summer I shall start on *Die Walküre*; in spring 1855 it will be the turn of young Siegfried, and in the winter I hope to get down to Siegfried's death, so that everything will be ready by Easter 1856. Then I will set about the impossible: procuring a theatre of my own, in which I shall produce my work before the whole of Europe as a great musical drama festival.

As usual, Wagner fell behind his programme. In 1855 he was in

London, conducting a series of concerts for a living, *Die Walküre* still uncompleted.

London, however, proved profitable in another way. There he met a former close friend from Dresden, the architect Gottfried Semper who, also exiled for his part in the revolution, had settled in London. Here, clearly, was a useful ally in putting his plans for a festival theatre into effect. On his return to Zürich, Wagner lost no time in persuading the Swiss authorities to offer Semper a post at the newly opened polytechnic there. Semper accepted, and during the next three years Wagner and his architect friend were close neighbours.

Semper was no ordinary architect, but a man passionately devoted to the theatre. The opera house in Dresden in which Wagner brought out *Rienzi, Der fliegende Holländer* and *Tannhäuser* was his creation. It could have been men such as he whom Wagner had in mind when, in a letter to Liszt in 1851 about a projected Goethe Foundation theatre in Weimar, he described the architect as 'the poet of the plastic arts, with whom sculptors and painters should stand in the same relationship as musicians and actors with the genuine poet'.

Whatever discussions Wagner and Semper may have had during those three years in Zürich concerning an actual theatre building, they could have been no more than theoretical. Wagner's growing feeling that his preoccupation with the *Ring* cycle was causing him to lose touch with the world about him (some eight years had passed since a new work of his had appeared on the stage) persuaded him to abandon it in the middle of *Siegfried* and to embark on a new work which would be less problematical and therefore simpler to stage. This was *Tristan und Isolde*.

The next few years can be seen as a renewed effort, born of frustration and despair, to come to some sort of terms with the existing theatre—still very much alive in spite of all the revolutions. But *Tristan und Isolde*, the revised *Tannhäuser* in Paris and finally *Die Meistersinger*, which refused in composition to conform to the modest proportions he had designed for it, must eventually have convinced Wagner that he had now finally passed the stage where compromise, even when he was resigned to it, was practically possible.

The two completed parts of the *Ring* cycle—*Das Rheingold* and *Die Walküre*—were also works with which Wagner could have attempted, even before *Tristan und Isolde*, to prove to his contemporaries that he was still an opera composer to be reckoned with. In 1861 an invitation did in fact come to him from Prague to produce and conduct

Das Rheingold there. He turned it down. With the *Ring* there were to be no compromises: it was to be all or nothing. And in 1862 he decided to make an attempt to win support for a special production by publishing the text of the *Ring* cycle in full. There were two possibilities, he wrote in the foreword, to secure its production in the way he wanted: either with the help of 'a group of well-to-do, art-loving men and women', or under the patronage of a German prince. He had little hopes of the first, but could the prince be found?

As history knows, he was found. Wagner's book came into the hands of the young crown prince of Bavaria, whose first act, when he became King Ludwig II two years later, was to summon Wagner and offer him unlimited freedom to put his ideas into practice. Their partnership started out auspiciously enough. Within a few months of their first meeting Ludwig wrote to the composer: 'I have decided to have a large stone theatre built, so that the production of *Der Ring des Nibelungen* can be a complete one; this immortal work must be given a framework worthy of its presentation.'

Wagner at once sent for Semper, who came to Munich to show the king the plans which Wagner and he had already worked out. The projected theatre's main features—the amphitheatrical auditorium and the concealed orchestra—were already familiar to Ludwig from Wagner's foreword to the *Ring* poem. 'If one has ever listened,' Wagner had written there, 'to the pure, ethereal tone of an orchestra heard through an acoustical sound barrier, freed of all the unavoidable non-musical sounds an instrumentalist makes in producing his notes, and if one imagines how advantageously the singer must appear to the onlooker when the space between them is uninterrupted, then one has only to add the ease with which the words can be understood, to be persuaded of the success of my proposed arrangement.' Here one is forcibly reminded of that early acoustical experience in Paris of which Wagner had once told his friend Dräseke.

The decision to build an interior on these lines as a temporary structure inside an existing exhibition building in Munich—and later to transfer it *en bloc* to a grandiose permanent outer shell on the banks of the river Isar—was one with which Wagner was for the moment content. It would give him a chance to try out his ideas in practice before committing himself to them finally, and it would enable him to present his *Ring* cycle to his eager patron without delay. (In the timetable he drew up for the king in those early intoxicating Munich days, the first performance was scheduled for 1867-8.)

There were certainly also other, unspoken reasons why Wagner preferred a temporary to a permanent theatre in Munich. The first lay in the nature of his dream—that romantic dream, nursed for so many years, of some hastily erected wooden structure which would be pulled down as soon as the performance was over. There was still in Wagner's mind, when he wrote his foreword to the *Ring* in 1862, the idea of its production as a grand solitary gesture: subconsciously perhaps he wanted Brünnhilde's liberating act at the end of *Götterdämmerung* to wipe out the old order entirely—including the very place at which it was performed. However, if this idea is too fanciful, one can certainly assume that Wagner had not entirely forgotten one of the basic conditions for his theatre—that it should be erected in one of 'the less large towns in Germany' so that visitors could approach the performance in a proper receptive spirit, unburdened by daily cares and undistracted by rival entertainments. Munich by its very size could not fulfil this condition, and the grudging spirit of its inhabitants, which rose to a positive fury when the news got about that Ludwig was proposing to build not only a festival theatre but a wide road and bridge leading to it as well, could not have failed to remind Wagner that this was not the theatre of which he had dreamed.

He continued, however, to support Ludwig's plans, even after his own indiscretions and the jealousies of the Munich court circles had forced him once again to take refuge in Switzerland. In order to give the king an impression of the proposed theatre, he asked Semper to make a model of it, and after viewing this in Zürich he wrote to Ludwig on 2 January 1867: 'It is a miracle: my idea, my suggestions and stipulations have been completely grasped by Semper's genius and carried out in so novel and practical a way that the noble simplicity of this conception must meet with the admiration of every connoisseur.'

A letter from Semper to Wagner, dated 26 November 1865, shows the nature of their collaboration:

> In the next few days you will receive a set of sketches from me on which I particularly want your opinion. I need to know whether its specifications match your intentions and ideas entirely . . . I should add that the present plan for the temporary festival theatre differs from the previous plan mainly in the fact that the central point of the concentric seating has been shifted in order to avoid from all angles a view into the orchestra. Then, in line with our discussion, I have put in two prosceniums, one behind the other, divided by the sunken orchestra. The narrower second proscenium is a smaller replica of the large one in front. This

produces a change of scale and in consequence an apparent enlargement of everything on the stage, as well as the desired separation of the imaginary stage world from the real world on the other side of the intervening orchestra . . . This last is completely invisible, though the pit is not sunk all that low . . . I have not made the stage deep, as you can see, though with no intention of tying you and the stage mechanic (and/or scene designer) down in advance. On the contrary, I consider it most important to have your and the mechanic's view on this very point—whether the proposed depth is sufficient . . .

This letter leaves no doubt at all that in the design of the festival theatre Semper saw his role as that of simply turning Wagner's ideas into practical architectural terms.

Only a few weeks after his letter to Ludwig in January 1867 praising the model of his theatre, Wagner wrote rather petulantly to Semper: 'If I were to think only of my own peace and security, I should feel bound to advise the king against building the theatre now, for everything to do with it that can be presented in an odious light will—as I do not need to tell you—be placed entirely to my account, while the whole credit will go to you.' However, he consented to continue supporting the plan, 'although my personal interest would not now urge me in that direction: in order to do justice to my artistic intentions I must concern myself with my creative preparations, which for the moment are still far removed from monumental buildings'.

In this letter one can see the resistance which was beginning to build up in Wagner's mind against the whole Munich project. Semper himself recognized it, as his reply (4 February 1867) shows:

For me creation is a joy in itself, the aim of my life, which can in any case last only a few more years. The putting off of this project to a later date would therefore mean my withdrawal from it—though incidentally I may say that I have always regarded my part as a secondary one, leaving you all credit for the ideas and inventions . . . If, as usual, it does not get beyond the planning stage, I shall have to comfort myself with . . . the thought that these preparatory sketches may prove useful to others when the work is taken up again—at least to provide a standard of comparison for even better things.

Semper's forecast proved correct. Ludwig told Wagner in October 1867 of his decision to put off construction of the Munich theatre on financial grounds, and Wagner received the news without protest. Semper himself, denied by ministerial prevarication the promised consolation of a professorship at the Munich polytechnic, made himself unpopular both with the king and Wagner by insisting on full payment for the work he had put in on the sketches and models. He received his fee in the end—but at the cost of Wagner's friendship.

The idea of a festival theatre in Munich was now effectively dead, and perhaps for that very reason one can detect an improvement in the relations between Wagner and the king, rising to its climax at the first performance of *Die Meistersinger* in Munich the following year. What followed shortly after was, however, to flaw their friendship for ever: the king insisted on an immediate production of *Das Rheingold* and *Die Walküre* in the court opera-house.

Wagner's first reaction to the proposal was surprisingly mild: he merely told Ludwig that he himself could not undertake the production of *Das Rheingold*, but would from his Swiss home supervise its staging by persons of his own choosing. In a later letter (22 March 1869) he pointed out to the king: 'This production will certainly differ in many ways from what you have so long intended: all the same, it should be possible in important points to demonstrate and justify its exceptional character.' Above all, it should not be more than a special private occasion, with guests admitted free on the king's direct invitation.

When it became clear that the king had no such intentions, and when Wagner heard of the difficulties his chosen henchmen were experiencing at the hands of the court theatre staff, his tone became more peremptory, and he attempted finally to stop or at least postpone the performance. This in turn roused Ludwig's fury—to an extent that would have shocked even Wagner if he had seen some of the private memoranda which the king was addressing to his secretary Düfflipp.

> The behaviour of Wagner and the theatre rabble can only be described as criminal and brazen. If Wagner's disgusting intrigues are allowed to succeed, the whole pack will become more and more impudent and shameless and will in the end be impossible to control . . . I have never heard of such insolence [and so on].

Though not directly addressed in such terms, Wagner could read between the lines and recognize that in the final analysis Ludwig was no different from all the other princes with whom he had had to do during his life: the royal whim was paramount. That calamitous production of *Das Rheingold*, followed in the ensuing year by a no more satisfactory one (from Wagner's point of view) of *Die Walküre*, convinced the composer that he had been right all along: the *Ring* did by its very nature demand the special production he had always dreamed of. The prince had failed him: he must now place his hopes in the other category of sponsors mentioned in his foreword to the *Ring*—the 'group of well-to-do, art-loving men and women'.

It is possible that Wagner would not have explored this possibility, which he himself had dismissed in his foreword as hopeless, if it had not been for another person whose importance to him waxed as Ludwig's waned. Indeed, there was some connection between the two events, for Ludwig's disillusionment with Wagner began when he realized how deliberately he had been deceived concerning the intimate relationship that had developed under his very nose between Wagner and Cosima, the wife of his conductor Hans von Bülow.

Without Cosima, said Nietzsche—who was a close friend of the Wagner household in Lucerne—Bayreuth would not have been possible. It is a judgement one can accept, and not only because Cosima had more resilience and courage than Ludwig: her idealism and her belief in Wagner and his work were also far more practical. In addition to all that, she had supplied a new incentive by presenting him with children of his own. Fatherhood, coming to Wagner late in life, was an event of profound significance to him. A family man by nature, devoted to his mother, and to all of his sisters, he had alleviated the frustrations of his childless marriage to Minna, his first wife, by taking a whole series of young musicians (as well as a young king) under his wing. Now these surrogate children had been replaced by real ones of his own. When, after two daughters, Cosima in 1869 bore him a son, his pride and joy assumed almost absurd proportions. He informed his friend Pusinelli in Dresden: 'A fine strong son with high forehead and clear eyes, Siegfried Richard, will inherit his father's name and keep his works alive.' Without the rejuvenating effect of this primary fulfilment, and without the driving force of his young second wife, who can say for certain whether Wagner would have found the strength and will to pursue his dream to the end?

When he first thought of Bayreuth as the place to launch his *Ring* cycle, Wagner did not in fact contemplate building a special theatre for it, but envisaged making use of the existing theatre there, the Markgräfliches Opernhaus, which possessed the largest stage in Germany. Certainly on paper Bayreuth fulfilled the conditions he had himself laid down for the site of his festival theatre: a small town, centrally situated in Germany and offering no rival distractions. It was also in the realms of his royal patron—an important consideration since, however much their friendship might have cooled, their mutual indebtedness remained. Besides, Ludwig was the legal owner of all rights in the *Ring* and he could, if he had a mind to, prevent a production of it even by the composer himself.

A single glance at the Markgräfliches Opernhaus, when he at last inspected it in April 1871, was enough to convince Wagner that this elaborate rococo building, erected a century earlier by Frederick the Great's sister, the Margravine of Bayreuth, could never provide a setting for the *Ring*. 'So we must build—and all the better,' wrote Cosima in her diary. Within a fortnight of his visit, Wagner was writing to Ludwig's secretary, asking him to send on Semper's plans for the Munich theatre. He would, he assured Düfflipp, use in Bayreuth only such parts of it as were based on his own ideas.

The decision to build in Bayreuth was made before it was known where the money was to come from, though the proposed method of raising funds had been defined by Wagner in a 'Mitteilung und Aufforderung an die Freunde meiner Kunst' ('Communication and Appeal to the Friends of My Art'), written even before his visit to the town. It was a straightforward invitation to supporters to band together to provide funds. The details were worked out in more practical form in Berlin, the whole operation being placed in the hands of Countess Marie von Schleinitz, one of Wagner's powerful admirers, and the pianist Karl Tausig. Certificates of patronage (*Patronatscheine*) would be offered for sale to well-to-do persons, entitling their holders to seats at each performance. This would constitute the only means of admittance.

Here we see Wagner still sticking adamantly to his conviction, expressed as early as 1849 (in *Kunst und Revolution*), that, the theatre being in the nature of a social necessity, entry to it must be free. Making admittance dependent on the advance purchase of an expensive certificate has, however, little to do with socialistic principles, particularly since this system would confine participation to a moneyed minority and such of their friends with whom they were willing to share their tickets. It was an essentially paternalistic system, and the credit for bringing Wagner back more into line with his early socialism must be given to Emil Heckel, a Mannheim bookseller who suggested the foundation of so-called Wagner societies (*Wagnervereine*) throughout Germany, which could buy certificates for sharing between their members drawn from less opulent circles.

On 22 May 1872, his fifty-ninth birthday, Wagner laid the foundation stone of his festival theatre in Bayreuth and made a long speech to his assembled supporters. When they next met, he told them, they

would find on this spot a building in which they would be able to read
the history of the thought that lay behind it.

> You will find, constructed with the cheapest of materials, an outer shell
> which will at best remind you of those sketchily built festival halls
> erected on odd occasions in German towns for singing and similar
> social occasions, to be immediately dismantled when the festival was
> over. On the other hand, you will on entering the building soon begin
> to see which of its aspects have been designed for permanence. Here
> too you will find very cheap materials, a complete lack of decoration;
> you will perhaps be surprised by the lack of ornament with which those
> traditional festival halls were pleasingly hung. But in the proportions
> of the interior and in its seating arrangements you will find the expres-
> sion of an idea which, once grasped, will transform your expectations
> into something quite different from what you have ever before ex-
> perienced in visiting a theatre. If this effect is fully achieved, the mys-
> terious entry of the music will now begin to prepare you for the unveil-
> ing and display of scenic pictures which, by appearing to emanate from
> an idealistic dream world, should demonstrate to you the complete
> reality of the simulating powers of a noble art. Here nothing must be
> permitted to speak in mere provisional, sketchy forms; in scenery and
> in acting you will be offered the best that the artistic skill of our times
> can achieve.

The things in which he placed his trust, Wagner went on, were the
German national spirit, the spirit of German music, which awaited
only the master's touch to rouse it, and the talent of the actors and
singers who, as he knew from experience, could in the right hands be
brought to an eager acceptance of the seriousness of their calling.
Perhaps in times to come others would begin to believe in the things
he believed in, and a splendid national theatre would be built somewhere in Germany. In the meantime, all he could do was to set the
example with his own work.

One may doubt whether Wagner's reference to a national theatre,
with its implications that this would provide a home for works other
than his own, was in fact more than a piece of tactical window-
dressing. In any case, as he tacitly admitted in his speech, what had
started out in the youthful composer's mind as an attempt to reform
the German theatre generally had been channelled by events into a
desire to provide an ideal setting for the production of one single work,
the *Ring* cycle. Can one believe, for example, that, when Wagner
referred in his speech to 'the mysterious entry of the music', he was
thinking of anything except the low E flat of *Das Rheingold*? And how
unerringly he gauged in advance the effect of that is evident to any-

one who has ever heard it in his Festival Theatre at Bayreuth. The story of the erection of the theatre, with all its attendant difficulties, is told in the next chapter of this book and need not be anticipated here. We can move straight on to the summer of 1876, when three complete performances of the *Ring*, produced by the composer himself, were given in the presence of a distinguished gathering of supporters and even crowned heads, including the Emperor Wilhelm I of Germany. From the material point of view Wagner had indisputably triumphed. But how had he succeeded artistically?

It was inevitable that he should have been disappointed with his production: the gap between the imagined and the actual performance is bound to be wide, if only because it is dependent on the combined efforts of so many people. Though Wagner had expressed in his speech at the stone-laying ceremony his confidence in actors and singers, this was little more than the expression of a pious hope. Throughout his long life Wagner found only two singers for whom his admiration was unbounded: Wilhelmine Schröder-Devrient (his first Adriano, Senta and Venus) and Ludwig Schnorr von Carolsfeld (the first Tristan). And though, after lengthy searchings and negotiations, he managed to assemble a suitable cast for his *Ring* production, some of the singers proved disappointing and some of them difficult to work with. The scenery, the costumes, the movements—all these, so vivid in the imagination, fell for one reason or another far short in the execution. 'Fantasy in chains' was Nietzsche's description for them, and after the last performance Cosima noted in her diary: 'R. is very sad, says he wishes he could die!'

This need have been no more than normal post-production depression. But Wagner's later remark to one of his assistants, Richard Fricke, reveals a persisting disillusionment, though expressed with more resilience: 'Next year we shall do it all differently.' It is not clear whether he meant to suggest by this that his whole production might have been wrong in conception, and that he had doubts about the basically realistic style, with its elaborate machine for the Rhinemaidens, its rickety wooden rainbow bridge, its Valkyries mounted on model horses and its dragon from the pantomine workshops of London. Both in writing his *Ring* drama and in building his theatre for it, Wagner had deliberately aimed to achieve a synthesis between the ancient and the modern worlds. His production, on the other hand, however much it improved on existing methods in respect of the care lavished on its preparation, does not appear—visually at any rate—

to have attempted anything so definite. Unfortunately there was no opportunity in the following year or after to present the *Ring* again, owing to the huge financial deficit with which the festival ended, and we are therefore denied the knowledge of Wagner's second thoughts— except in so far as they may be reflected in the work to which he now turned his attention: *Parsifal.*

The essential technical difference between the two works is that the *Ring* was written for an imaginary theatre, whereas *Parsifal* was written for that same theatre after it was actually built. The difference is audibly reflected in the orchestration, which in *Parsifal* is of a clearer, more translucent quality. But there are differences in other aspects too, leaving aside those which arise inevitably from the difference in subject. *Parsifal* is a far more static and less visual work, and the dramatic impact is less direct. Its confrontations are mainly retro- spective, more spiritual than physical, and its episodes are few. The synthesis of ancient and modern, which in the *Ring* is buried in the story, is in *Parsifal* embodied in the presentation. One can easily in the *Ring* become so gripped by the story as to forget its moral implica- tions; the same temptation can scarcely arise in *Parsifal.*

Parsifal was conceived long before the Festival Theatre was built, though both poem and music were not written down until after the *Ring* had been launched. There was no suggestion, in all previous references to it, that it had been designed from the beginning to occupy a special position in Wagner's theatrical plans. His subsequent de- cision, not only to write it for his Festival Theatre, but to confine its presentation strictly to that theatre, consequently raises certain questions regarding his attitude towards the festival he had brought into being.

Considering how closely it had been bound up with the *Ring*, it seems surprising, whatever the circumstances, that during the re- maining seven years of his life he made no attempt to restage this work. More than that, he handed over all production rights in it to an outsider, Angelo Neumann, who not only in Wagner's lifetime pre- sented it in several German opera houses, but also took it on tour abroad. Wagner excused this decision by claiming that, having shown at Bayreuth how the *Ring* should be done, he could now afford to release it to other theatres. But this argument is as inconsistent with his own view of his single production of 1876 as it is with the protec- tive attitude he adopted all his life towards all his works. Even allowing for the very genuine financial difficulties which stood in the way of staging repeat performances of the *Ring* at Bayreuth, one cannot avoid the conclusion—one subsequently borne out by Cosima's diaries—that disillusionment played a significant part in Wagner's decision virtually (according to his own concepts) to abandon the *Ring* and concentrate on the creation of a work whose overtly religious character would unmistakably reflect his conception of the theatre as a place of divine revelation. And by confining *Parsifal* to Bayreuth, he would additionally ensure that the physical nature of the place of offering would be given a chance to demonstrate its vital function in his scheme of things.

The production of *Parsifal* in 1882, the last summer of his life, can be regarded sentimentally as a happy ending to a life of superhuman endeavour and achievement. Even if the strain of rehearsals at one time wrung from the composer the confession to King Ludwig that, having invented the invisible orchestra, he now wished he could invent the invisible stage, the production, performed sixteen times, was by all accounts (including his own) a very successful one. But in one particular at least it fell short of the original dream: admittance to the theatre was not free. Even the fiction of certificates of patronage was abandoned. Tickets were offered to individual members of the public through the box office in the usual way.

This, though it might seem to us a small point, was certainly not so to Wagner. The principle of free admission was an integral part of his vision of post-revolutionary theatre. Its abandonment, forced on him by the realization that he could not rely on his professed supporters in his effort to keep the single outcome of his vision alive, was a recognition that his bid to revolutionize the theatre as a social institution had failed. His sense both of isolation and of time running out emerges clearly in the letter he wrote to King Ludwig on 18 November 1882:

> I wish to stage all my works one after another in our Festival Theatre in such a way that these productions will at least serve as models of correctness for those who follow immediately after me. For this I am relying on some ten years of robust health, during which my son will reach full maturity: to him alone can I entrust the spiritual and ethical preservation of my work, knowing no other to whom I could hand over my office.

Those ten years were denied him. Three months after writing that letter, he died, and it fell to his widow Cosima (of whom, strangely, he never appears to have thought in all his references to the future) to carry out the limited tasks—far short of the original ambitions—defined in it. Her achievement was certainly a very great one. Not only did she present in the space of fifteen years every one of his works from *Der fliegende Holländer* onwards (including a new production of the *Ring*), she also founded in Bayreuth a school for music and acting which, though it has received little attention in this essay for reasons of space, had always been an important part of the composer's dream.

But the value of her work was inevitably limited. Her productions were memories of the composer's own, and they made no allowances for any second thoughts he himself might have had. How indeed could they? Any successor, whether in the family or not, would have been in the same position. The difference between Wagner's successors and those of any other composer was that he left behind him, in addition to his written works, a theatre—and not just any theatre, but one that had been built as a pointer to the future in all its artistic and social aspects. The world, willing enough to accept Wagner's works, showed no inclination to follow his theatrical aspirations—except in Munich, where a theatre on the lines of the Bayreuth Festival Theatre was built at the turn of the century, though more in a spirit of rivalry than emulation.

So that finally the theatre itself, rejected as a model, even if recognized as an asset (but not necessarily an essential one) in the performance of Wagner's own works, became—ironically—a limiting and not a liberating factor. Cosima's successors—her son Siegfried and then Heinz Tietjen working with Siegfried's widow Winifred—certainly strove to move with the times in their production styles and to incorporate technical improvements, but basically they conformed to the realistic approach which Wagner initiated and Cosima converted into doctrine. Radically new approaches were tried outside Bayreuth, but it was not until 1951 that a member of Wagner's own family, his grandson Wieland, showed the courage and spirit of independence to put into practice in the Festival Theatre itself those words his grandfather spoke to his assistant Fricke after the first festival of 1876: 'Next year we shall do it all differently.'

Wieland Wagner's style of production, much closer in spirit to the mythological and classical origins of the works than Wagner's own, was born of a study of the works themselves rather than of previous attempts to stage them. Its significance can be measured by the impact it immediately made on Wagnerian production throughout the world. But it is not the last word on the subject: that can clearly never be spoken as long as the works continue to live.

And it is to them, of course, and not just to the theatre in Bayreuth, that one must look in judging the success of Wagner's intended revolution. He may not have achieved his goal of revolutionizing the theatre or even decisively altering the course of operatic development. His influence on composers after him, apart from a few lesser spirits whose work is now forgotten, has been only partial. But the works themselves, which were the result of his dream, remain to illuminate the idea that originally inspired it—the idea of art not as mere entertainment, but as a fundamental need of the human spirit.

TWELVE

Wahnfried and the Festival Theatre

ZDENKO VON KRAFT

RICHARD WAGNER saw two of his most fervent wishes fulfilled in Bayreuth, though only towards the close of his troubled and strife-ridden life: the acquisition of his own home and the building of his own theatre. From his early manhood these two things had represented the ultimate goal of his career. Many references in his correspondence over the years bear this out. One such passage, in a letter to Mathilde Wesendonk on 6 July 1858, reads: 'There is a voice within me which yearns for peace, for the peace which my flying Dutchman longed for many years ago. It was a yearning for "home".' Admittedly here this 'home' denotes a spiritual dwelling-place, refuge and solace at the side of a kindred soul. But a purely material 'residence', a secure place where he could be on his own, was also dear to Wagner's heart. Such a place he hoped he had found in the 'refuge on the Green Hill' near Zürich: but he lost it through the tragic confusions of an unfulfillable passion. But his longing for it remained with him for the rest of his life. Several years earlier he had written to his Dresden friend Theodor Uhlig: 'The desire to have a cottage with a garden in the country, here in the distance on the hillside overlooking the lake, to tend my small estate, to surround myself with flowers and animals . . . has now grown so strong within me that I am determined to satisfy it at all costs.' Similar passages can be found in numerous letters from the following period: from Paris, from Biebrich, from Penzing near Vienna, from Munich and finally from Triebschen where he came closest to realizing this aim during six happy years. But not until Wahnfried could he say of a house—as he wrote joyfully to Ludwig II: 'My' garden, 'my' house . . . my 'own'. Here the fulfilment was complete right to the end.

And his own theatre? It is not as if an inherent conceitedness impelled him to nurse high-flying ambitions from the outset. Up to the end of his career as an orchestral organizer in Dresden, he accepted the prevailing theatrical conditions and entrusted his operas to them without demur. The conflict did not arise until the emergence of his most characteristic and important work, *Der Ring des Nibelungen*. Developing compulsorily but organically out of its kernel *Siegfrieds Tod*, it acquired a greatness (in terms of its practical demands as well) which outstripped the capacity of routine theatrical productions. How soon Wagner realized this can be seen from a letter of 1850 to the same Theodor Uhlig, where he voiced the thought 'of constructing a crude theatre of planks and beams according to my own design, on a lovely meadow near the town'. He elaborated this notion to Franz Müller in Weimar five years later to the effect that he would like to mount his 'stage festival' in some place 'which by virtue of having been completely neutral hitherto would remove me from all contact with our conventional theatrical world'.

This initially utopian plan crystallized into more and more compulsive images in his mind as the composition proceeded and the completion of the work drew nearer. For a brief time it even appeared to be on the brink of fulfilment: at the end of 1864, King Ludwig II, suffused with Wagner's ideals, commissioned Gottfried Semper, the most important architect of the age, to build a festival theatre in Munich in complete accord with Wagner's desires. The model exhibited in the royal palace at Munich in January 1867 won the enthusiastic acclaim of the king. Yet his insight was greater than his patience. Avid to see the completed parts of the *Ring*—*Das Rheingold* and *Die Walküre*—as quickly as possible, he prematurely ordered that they should be produced in his court theatre—against the express wish of the composer. Thereby he broke the pact of friendship between them and prevented Wagner from carrying out his basic intention of waiting until the work as a whole could have its first performance at one and the same time in its proper sequence. Wagner reacted with unconcealed sorrow and displeasure, his friendship for the king cooled and he retreated to Triebschen. He became more and more firmly convinced of the need to make himself completely independent even of the king's favour; he could only find true fulfilment on his own. Munich was lost to him as fertile ground for his artistic goals; and his beloved Triebschen refuge too was not his own (it stood on somebody else's land). In the end a small miracle occurred: the opportunity to combine his creative activity and a home of his own in one place, Bayreuth.

Why did he select this particular 'quiet little town on the Red Main' to fulfil his lifelong ambitions? As a twenty-two-year-old orchestral organizer in Magdeburg, he had visited it briefly on the journey from Karlsbad to Nuremberg. It was the middle of March 1866 when he reached this point in the course of dictating his autobiography *Mein Leben*, and he recalled it in these words: 'The journey through Eger, over the Fichtel mountains and to Bayreuth, basking charmingly in the evening sunshine, made a pleasing impression upon my memory which has lasted to the present time.' A few years later a musician told him of the unusually large stage in the old opera house there, originally built for the local margrave. And now on 5 March 1870 he remembered this: he looked up the article 'Bayreuth' in Brockhaus's encyclopedia and discovered that this opera house was described as one of the largest in Germany. It was like a sign. On the second day of his first 'journey into the Empire', on 16 April 1871, Wagner arrived in Bayreuth in order to see the stately edifice for himself. But without success: for his personal artistic needs, the splendid baroque theatre was unsuitable. But the peaceful charm of the old town itself proved all the more attractive to him. By the following morning Wagner had made up his mind to settle nowhere else. The next day he was taken through the castle gardens by the castellan and shown the meadow-land which at that time had not yet been built upon. Making a quick decision, he opted for a plot of land between the Rennweg and the royal gardens, a piece whose area corresponded to what would later become the garden of Wahnfried. (He became the legal owner on 1 February 1872 after paying a price of 12,000 guilders.) The initial scheme for acquiring the much larger piece of land at the rear for the building of the Festival Theatre had to be dropped. No matter, the town and the site for his own house had now been decided upon: Bayreuth and the plot on the Rennweg.

By 1 May 1871 Wagner was writing a courteous letter to the Royal Secretary, Hofrat von Düfflipp:

> I am sticking to my choice of lovely, peaceful Bayreuth as a home for the rest of my days because it is a Bavarian town . . . Just on the outskirts I have already discovered a satisfactory plot of land for sale on a meadow site, the rear of which adjoins the far end of the castle park . . . So I beg you, dear friend, earnestly and urgently to obtain permission from His Majesty to meet me in Bayreuth as soon as possible, in order to arrange with me the relevant details with regard to this building plot and the home that is to be erected on it for myself and my family.

Wagner's easily ignited optimism produced rapid results. Even before the desired meeting with Düfflipp could be arranged, the confidence which had suddenly blossomed in his heart impelled him to make a premature decision: on 12 May he announced from his home town of Leipzig that the first Bayreuth Festival, with a performance of the *Ring* in its entirety, would take place in the summer of 1873—even though he had not yet found a site for the Festival Theatre. For, after a quick inspection, the prospective meadow site at the end of the castle garden had to be abandoned on purely technical grounds: the land had inadequate drainage. Negotiations on the part of the town council over a piece of land on the Stuckberg near St Georgen fell through because of the injured pride of one of the owners. Indeed, for a moment it looked as if the whole enterprise would collapse. Not until January 1872 was a solution acceptable to all parties found: the town council managed to acquire an extensive site on the 'lovely hill under the Bürgerreuth' for a price of 14,000 guilders and presented it to Wagner *gratis*, while for the building of the private residence the king himself had advanced a subsidy of 25,000 thalers. Now work could begin.

Rival offers prompted by envy or by a nose for business had sprouted overnight in response to Wagner's Leipzig manifesto. All wanted to usurp the position of the small and insignificant town of Bayreuth. They included Baden-Baden, Bad Reichenhall, even Darmstadt, which, having recently lost its theatre in a fire, hoped for rich rewards in future from an association with the Festival Theatre. But all were turned down flat. As quickly as Wagner had opted for the quiet town on the Red Main, so, too, he now remained stubbornly loyal to it. Admittedly he was not a patient master. House and theatre had to be built simultaneously and it was not easy to do justice to both demands.

Before Richard Wagner's old dream of having his own theatre could be turned into bricks and mortar, two essential preconditions had to be met: the necessary finance had to be found and the right architect chosen. Gottfried Semper, estranged from Wagner since the collapse of his Munich project (see p. 413), was out of the running. However, the plans which he had drawn up for Ludwig II became the basis for discussions with the Berlin architect Wilhelm Neumann, upon whom Wagner's choice had fallen, and the Darmstadt stage-machinist Karl Brandt, one of the most brilliant theatre directors of his day. Wagner's joy at being able to employ him was expressed in a letter to Brandt on 20 August 1871:

The success of a large part of my enterprise is now assured by your agreeing to join us. It has truly strengthened me to find you so intimately familiar with my intentions . . . Certain decisions which you imparted to the architect were a positive surprise to me: to bring the proscenium forward still further was an inspiration on your part which set the seal on the whole vision of the interior of the theatre.

Karl Brandt completely justified the trust placed in him: when Neumann was guilty of an intolerable delay in submitting the plans, he suggested that he should be replaced by Otto Brückwald, an architect from Leipzig 'with whom he reached such a clear and successful understanding about the special features of the Festival Theatre that this building . . . arouses admiration in every expert [familiar with it]'. Thus Brückwald was promoted to the status of chief architect. It is to him, his younger colleague Carl Runkwitz from Altenburg who took over supervision of the day-to-day work, the master-mason Karl Wölfel and the two master-carpenters Hans Weiss and Christian Vogel from Bayreuth that credit is due for having, through their collective labours, given tangible shape and substance to the theatre on the hill.

As far as money was concerned, the estimated cost of the building and its furnishings was reckoned at 300,000 thalers. According to a plan worked out by Karl Tausig, this sum was to be raised by issuing 1,000 patronage-certificates at 300 thalers apiece. But by the end of 1873, only 300,000 marks, in other words, a third of the total cost, had been forthcoming. The sum outstanding was made up early in 1874 by royal credits and various private donations, including money which Wagner himself raised by giving concerts.

And the house on the Rennweg? Although Wagner already had the 'very fine' drawings and plans of the Berlin architect Neumann to hand by the end of March 1872, the contract with the builder Karl Wölfel was not signed until 15 July 1872. The ceremony of laying the foundation stone of the Festival Theatre had long since passed when work started on digging the foundations at the far end of the castle gardens. To keep an eye on both sites, and to speed up construction wherever possible, it was essential for Wagner to be there in person. So he and his family left their beloved Triebschen towards the end of April 1872. To begin with, they took an apartment in the Hotel Fantaisie in Donndorf, near the castle of the same name and its beautiful park. Here Wagner completed the orchestral sketch of *Götterdämmerung* and wrote his essay *Über Schauspieler und Sänger*. From here he set out on his portentous journey into the future—when he went to lay the foundation stone of the Festival Theatre. Unfortunately, the weather was by no means attuned to the solemn mood of the moment when Wagner raised his hammer to deliver the three symbolic blows before committing the foundation stone to the earth. On it was carved the well-known dedication:

> A secret I enclose within,
> Here many aeons may it rest,
> As long as it survives in stone,
> Its power to all make manifest.

Profoundly moved, he thereby pronounced the words: 'Blessed be thou, my stone, stand long and hold firm!' His face was grey, his eyes full of tears. Friedrich Nietzsche, who was one of the witnesses of this event, recalled it in a particularly impressive fashion:

> On that day in May in the year 1872 when the foundation stone was laid on the hilltop at Bayreuth, in pouring rain and under a black sky, Wagner travelled back with some of us to the town; he was silent and engrossed in his own thoughts, his eyes expressing something impossible to describe in words. His sixtieth year had commenced that day; everything that had gone before was as but a preparation for this moment. It is well known that in a moment of extreme peril or some other crucial decision in life, men see all the experiences of their past life flit with infinite rapidity across the mind's eye and recognize the most recent and most distant events equally with extraordinary clarity. What Wagner saw within himself that day—how he had become what he was, what he would be—we, his intimates, could share to a certain extent: and only in the light of what his gaze there beheld can we comprehend his great deed properly—that, armed with this understanding, we may guarantee its fruitfulness.

Wagner's basic mood remained buoyant and full of confident anticipation. 'What would I know of Bayreuth at this moment,' he wrote to King Ludwig before the end of the month, 'if I had not found you, if you had not summoned me. Here then I will abide and in supreme happiness close my weary eyes in the warmth of your gracious favour.' And five months later, on 7 October, he wrote:

> I have come across the greatest modesty and the most unqualified devotion, along with the most skilful expertise and most energetic industriousness. The whole friendly town does all it can for me . . . Oh, my King! This miracle coincides with the magic of your summons . . . In my sixtieth year I can thus build a secure home, look to my domestic affairs in the most felicitous company, and discharge a creative task which is reserved for the man who is well and truly prepared!

o

Whereas the earliest tours of inspection from the Hotel Fantaisie to the building site of the Rennweg had been protracted and time-consuming, they were reduced from the end of September 1872 onwards to a mere fifteen-minute stroll. Wölfel's new building in the Dammallee, which had been envisaged from the start as a provisional residence, was finally ready, and the move into the town could be made. In this comfortable house opposite a copse known as the Dammwäldchen, Richard Wagner and his family spent an enclosed and eventful period in which the future was already foreshadowed. By October, Franz Liszt had become their first visitor, spending a happy week with them. The year 1873 brought with it the celebration of Wagner's sixtieth birthday; Anton Bruckner submitted the scores of his Second and Third Symphonies for appraisal, so that he might dedicate one of them to the 'unsurpassed genius'; at the end of October, members of the Bayreuth patronage committee and delegates of the Wagner societies met for a conference, and finally Professor Josef Hoffmann arrived from Vienna to present his designs for the *Ring* in the presence of Karl Brandt. Only one thing was denied Wagner in 1873: he was unable to move into his own house next to the castle gardens, despite the fact that, according to the contract, the keys should have been handed over on 15 July. Small wonder that, in the light of this slow progress, there were disputes with the craftsmen, and that the prospective occupant christened the house unofficially 'my house of chagrin'. The Dresden sculptor, Gustav Adolf Kietz, who was one of the first to be allowed to look over the half-finished building (in which he would one day execute the busts of Wagner and Cosima and undergo a comic adventure in the company of Anton Bruckner), noted on 18 July:

> There was still a lot to do but the impression of the whole was very distinguished. I admired the harmonious layout of the large hall with the gallery up above and the beautiful room adjacent to it with the rotunda facing the castle park, a room designed for Wagner's own use. He told me that the room above, the finest in the whole house, with an uninterrupted vista out over the garden and the park, had been set aside for his daughters. He also said that he had drawn up the ground plan of the house himself.

Strange to relate, almost dearer to his heart than the completion of the house itself seemed to be that of another structure: the last resting-place for himself and his wife at the southern end of the garden. It is this tomb which is referred to in a letter to his royal friend dated 2 June 1873 and expressing gratitude for a particular favour:

My kind and generous King! You have granted me in these last few days the fulfilment of a heartfelt desire; henceforth I am to have direct access to your gardens at Bayreuth from my own garden. The unobtrusive door . . . leads, as you enter from the royal gardens, first to a small newly planted coppice, in the middle of which . . . I am now having a simple grave prepared for me and my dear wife: a modest vault which shall one day enclose us both. It is an inexpressible solace to us to be familiar with the spot that will receive us unto eternal rest and to be able to tend it daily on land which we owe to your generous affection and which will one day be handed down to my son as his inalienable home.

Midsummer brought with it a special event: while Karl Wölfel's workmen slowly continued work on the villa on the Rennweg at barely half their normal pace, its 'big brother' up on the hill, the future Festival Theatre, towered to its full height. Overshadowed by four corner-towers, the enormous cube of the theatre had risen from below. The walls had already risen above second-floor level, the scaffolding in the stage area had reached a height of 100 feet. Now the moment had come to erect the mighty roof—and then the long-awaited day of the topping-out ceremony arrived.

It was 2 August 1873. In contrast to the rainy conditions that prevailed when the foundation stone was laid, it was a wonderful summer's day. Wagner's daughter Isolde, who was not quite nine years old, captured in an amusingly naïve drawing the main participants sitting next to each other in the topmost rafters: Wagner himself, her mother Cosima, the five 'organ pipes' of the children and Grandfather Liszt. The man responsible for the whole venture crossed out the verse referring to himself in the celebratory poem that was to be recited by the foreman carpenter Hoffmann and substituted the following one:

> Now set we on this house a roof;
> May God protect it from collapse!
> To toast the one who had it built,
> What name should I bestow on him?
> Should it be Wagner's or his patrons'?
> Or his whose sceptre rules us all?
> The one who gives the best commissions—
> Long live the spirit of German song!

It was a moving ceremony for all concerned. With the chorale 'Now Thank We All Our God' the official proceedings came to an end; but only after a long and merry gathering of all those present,

419

lasting far into the night, did the splendid day draw to a close with a magnificent firework display.

The building was 'topped-out' but nowhere near completed. With the erecting of the framework of the roof the financial reserves were as good as exhausted. A grave crisis loomed, threatening a lengthy interruption or even complete suspension of the work. There seemed no hope of assistance from private means; the only recourse was to the king. Help came after an anxious period of waiting and misleading hesitation in the form of a letter bearing the date 25 January 1874:

> My dearest, most precious friend! From the bottom of my heart I beg you to forgive me for not writing to you sooner . . . I console myself with the thought that you know me and must realize that . . . it would be madness to believe in any abating of my fervent feelings for you and your great endeavour.—No, no and thrice *no*! it shall not end thus! Help must be found. Our plan must not be allowed to fail. Parsifal knows his mission and will expend his entire resources . . . Do not despair and make me happy again soon with another letter!

On 20 February, the administrative board of the Richard Wagner Theatre was accorded a credit of 300,000 marks by the Royal Secretariat. The project thereby became solvent again, work proceeded at an accelerated pace and completion was only a matter of time.

The 28 April 1874 was a red-letter day in Wagner's life: he and his family finally moved into their home, a home they would never again have to abandon. Wahnfried—in fact, the villa did not bear this name yet—welcomed him, the heartfelt longing endured throughout decades of restless wandering was finally stilled in the heart of the sixty-year-old composer. Now, in his own words, he could wrest 'from the demon of all earthly existence as much peace and serenity as possible', in order to 'meet to the full the demands made [upon me] in the service of genius . . .'.

The house that now received its builder and master was redolent of dignity and repose. Although it was not yet completely finished or furnished, it perhaps revealed its designated purpose most clearly in its newness. A short flight of steps led up to the heavy, beautifully carved front door. On the outside its two panels bore the ingeniously intertwined double 'W', based on Dürer's motif for the prayer book of the Emperor Maximilian; above the door was a panel of stained glass showing two coats of arms through which light entered the vestibule—

the 'cooking-spoon arms' from the old refuge in Triebschen and the family arms designed by Wagner himself. These showed a hawk (in German *Geier*, in memory of his stepfather, Ludwig Geyer) bearing the 'Plough', a cluster of seven stars, on its breast. The constellation was symbolic of the orphaned family of seven which Geyer had once selflessly adopted.

A door opposite led directly into the interior of the house. It consisted mainly of two spacious rooms taking up the greater part of the ground floor. One was meant as the music room proper, and stretched up through two floors with a graceful gallery running round it half-way up the walls; it was illuminated by an enormous double-glazed skylight in the roof. A gleaming frieze with a gold ground and a Scandinavian serpent motive which encompassed copies of Echter's paintings inspired by the *Ring* (another gift from the king) ran round the walls below the gallery. The centre of the room was occupied by the black grand piano that stood on a flagstone floor. The Pompeiian red of the walls showed off most effectively six marble sculptures which represented the major characters of his work and which the king had presented to Wagner when he was still living at Triebschen: the Dutchman, Tannhäuser, Lohengrin, Tristan, Stolzing and Siegfried. Two doors to right and left led to the simple dining room and the 'lilac sitting room' of the mistress of the house. A middle door, flanked by the marble busts of Wagner and Cosima, sculpted by their old friend Gustav Kietz, opened into the main room of the house, the *Saal*.

This 'hall', a combination of drawing room and library, was the focal point around which the other rooms were arranged. It was forty-two feet long and twenty-eight feet wide and, together with the semi-circular bay window, it covered almost half the floor area of the whole house. Wagner himself said that it 'contained all his possessions'. And with good reason. All that it contained in the way of books, scores, paintings and manuscripts combined to form a rich unity. The famous library, including almost all the standard works of European literature, filled twelve plain book-cases along the walls—although it was far from complete at the time when the family moved in. Christian Senfft, the bookbinder who had already bound hundreds of volumes for the house in the Dammallee according to Wagner's precise directions, would need years yet to complete the work awaiting him at Wahnfried. Pictures from various phases in Wagner's career decorated the walls. Next to the portrait of King Ludwig II by Dürck, of Wagner's mother Johanna and his stepfather Ludwig Geyer (copies of the originals painted by

Geyer himself), hung pictures of Schiller, Goethe, Beethoven, Liszt, Marie d'Agoult and his uncle Adolf Wagner. Franz Lenbach's master-piece, the head of Schopenhauer, was not yet included—and, in fact, other works were to be added all the time: the portraits of Wagner and Cosima by Lenbach and Herkomer, the portrait of Cosima again by Paul von Joukovsky. The latter's canvas of the 'Holy Family' repre-sented a charming portrait of the five Wagner children with the painter himself as Joseph. (It disappeared after the Second World War.)

The spacious room was furnished informally with Wagner's large desk and the Bechstein grand piano, various armchairs, ordinary chairs and stools, while on small tables lay folios of select prints and beauti-fully bound scores. In a word, this was the throne room of Wagner's self-communing and his social life, the scene of special celebrations, but also the place where he and Cosima retired each evening after dinner to read together or to spend the last hour or two in the company of the young musicians of the 'Nibelungen chancellery' and other guests. By comparison with this room, all the other private rooms were rela-tively small and of overt simplicity; the spiral staircases between the floors were narrow (in fact, a reasonably impressive main staircase for visitors was completely lacking). The real Wahnfried was represented exclusively in the two main rooms on the ground floor, and the two guest rooms alongside the larger 'hall'.

'Wahnfried'? No, not yet. The house had not yet been christened. Now and then Wagner called it affectionately 'The Inn of Ultimate Happiness' or 'My adopted home'. Not until three weeks after he finally moved in did the 'safely fenced-in' owner think of the name which was to become part of our cultural vocabulary. On 25 May 1874 he reported to his royal patron:

> My house is now completed: thanks be to God! I had to find a name
> for it and thought about this for a long time: but in the end it came to
> me and I am having it inscribed in the following verse:
> Here where my troubled mind found peace—
> Wahnfried
> So let this house by me be named!

On three tablets of pink marble to the right and to the left under the windows of the upper floor and above the main entrance the words were carved and inscribed in letters of soft gold. But in the autumn of the same year, a further embellishment was added to the façade which had hitherto remained curiously plain. The bare, uninteresting section of wall between the two pairs of windows on either side had been a thorn in Wagner's flesh from the outset. As the sketches in the plans show, a rather ugly and oversized clock was originally envisaged as occupying this space. However, as Wagner informed the king in October, a far better, indeed 'excellent', solution was found by Cosima. It consisted of a large graffito covering the whole wall—a kind of colourless fresco on which the picture is scratched with a pointed iron tool uncovering the black undersurface of chalk, sand and coaldust, so that when finished it looks like an engraving. The work was commissioned from their friend Robert Krausse, a historical painter from Weimar. The details of the picture, an allegorical representation of the 'Art Form of the Future', were minutely described by Wagner in the letter to the king:

> The centre is occupied by Germanic Myth; since we wanted to have characteristic physiognomies, we resolved to use the features of the late Ludwig Schnorr; from either side Wotan's ravens fly towards it and it proclaims the legend imparted to it to two female figures, one of which represents Ancient Tragedy and whose features resemble those of [Wilhelmine] Schröder-Devrient, while the other represents Music, with the head and figure of Cosima; a small boy, clad as Siegfried and with my son's head, holds her hand, gazing up at his mother Music with an expression of mettlesome joy. I think the whole thing will be a splendid success.

Wagner's confidence was justified: the graffito unveiled in the late autumn made a powerful impact and the façade of Wahnfried was now harmoniously rounded off. Yet it was not until the following summer that the noble building presented the image which was to become familiar to posterity: the final touch was added by the circular bed of rose bushes with the bronze bust of Ludwig II which was situated in front of the entrance steps. Even when the small lawn was being laid out, the master of the house had a pedestal erected for an already existing life-size bust (later to adorn the staircase in the 'Royal Wing' of the Festival Theatre); however, against the background of the expansive façade, it appeared so insignificant and paltry that it could not possibly remain where it was. But a cautious hint that Wagner dropped in the letter of 1 October produced the desired effect: the king presented his petitioner with the twice life-size bust of himself by Zumbusch. Wagner duly had it installed upon the pedestal on 22 July 1875 as the crowning glory. In a telegram to Hohenschwangau, he thanked his ever-generous royal patron: 'In wonderful beauty, gently inspiring and augustly awesome, radiant and grave like the slayer of the Python, the bust is now on show, suffusing each visitor with thrilling reverence and the occupants of the house with sublime solace.' The exterior of Wahnfried was complete.

The interior continued to be enriched year by year. The bookcases were filled with new acquisitions; the splendid portrait of Schopenhauer by Lenbach was accorded its place directly above Wagner's desk, so that he could commune with him eye to eye at any time. Over the door that led to the music room, a cloth of golden damask which Cosima had given to Wagner in Naples as a birthday present was spread out like an awning (he used to call it the 'love banner' or 'Isolde's sail'). The thirty hollowed-out sections in the coffered ceiling of the *Saal* were painted with the colourful arms of all the towns that up to then had formed a Wagner society—this too was Cosima's idea. 'In this manner,' Wagner wrote in delight, 'I have acquired an ancestral gallery whose colourful decoration animates the whole most gaily.'

This was the last substantial adornment of the interior of Wahnfried which Wagner was to witness in his lifetime. The summit of his domestic ambition had been achieved. He testified to this more than once. In February 1878 he wrote to the king: 'We are filled with horror at the thought of any potential interruption of our so hallowed retreat at Wahnfried; on the other hand our sense of well-being here is unparalleled . . . I am now experiencing the happiest years of my life.' And just before the end of 1878: 'Everything else I learn from the outside world compresses my whole being almost convulsively into an ever narrowing space, into these narrow confines which can only be expanded into a friendly spaciousness through my boundless domestic happiness, the peace of mind I bring to my work, in short, through what I understand by the term "Wahnfried".'

There is no doubt that, with Wahnfried, Richard Wagner attained the goal towards which he had striven so painfully and for so long. Only one drop of wormwood falls into the overflowing cup of happiness: the physical ailments occasioned by the raw, sunless, all-too-bracing climate of Upper Franconia. Wagner's sensitivity to weather, which had always been pronounced, increased with age. Even in the prime of life he had looked on bad weather as a feared adversary. What a tragedy that to preserve his well-being, or rather to regain his seriously impaired health, he had to leave his 'own' home which he had desired for so long! As though anticipating a premature but inexorable leave-taking, he wrote on 19 September 1881, immediately before his departure for a stay of several months in Sicily: 'How it fills my heart with heaviness to know that this dear, fine house which I owe to your generosity stands in a spot where it can only so very rarely be warmed by a ray of the sun!—This is what grieves me at the present time!'

From 28 April, the day on which Wagner and his family moved into Wahnfried, it took more than two years for the Festival Theatre to reach completion; only then was it possible to realize the monumental work for which the master had built it—*Der Ring des Nibelungen*. It was a day of unique triumph that had sometimes seemed as if it would never come. Nevertheless this triumph was fraught with personal hardship, like most things which grow from the seed of an initial vision to tangible maturity. It endured its share of doubt, toil, trouble and mockery. Even Wagner himself called it a 'peculiar building' in a remark to the king, while contemporaries gave it many a disparaging nickname. They scarcely ever reflected that its builder had thought of it from the start as something provisional, a kind of expedient which he hoped would be fittingly completed by posterity. His own share in it was his constant self-sacrifice. 'This building is tinted with our blood', he once said to Cosima, and to the king he described it frankly as a 'fight for the impossible'. That it nevertheless did prove possible constitutes one of the great achievements of human tenacity.

As late as the summer of 1875, the auditorium was still scarcely more than a huge hall full of scaffolding and wooden props, in which there were about eighty shabby seats for the benefit of the intimates who were admitted to the early rehearsals. Other onlookers had to be content with boxes and joists. The work neared completion the following spring with ever more urgent speed, until finally the day dawned which had been dreamed of for decades. The stately but unpretentious edifice opened its doors to visitors from all over the world. For the first time, thousands could see for themselves the architectural vision which had preoccupied Richard Wagner with increasing clarity for half his life.

It was no ordinary theatre. Even the vast undivided sweep of the stalls, whose furthest rows contained up to sixty seats, was reminiscent more of a theatre of antiquity than of conventional designs. One looked in vain for an orchestra: it was situated in a deep pit and therefore invisible. A grey sound-board hung over that much discussed and admired 'mystical chasm' whose acoustical beauty was unique, unsurpassed even to this day. There were no boxes along the side-walls to distract attention from the stage. In their place, massive pillars, tapering towards the rear, stretched on either side as far as the edge of the stage and did away with the otherwise inevitable 'blind spots'. Since their upper sections were of wood, these acted as acoustical reflectors just like the wooden ceiling. The latter was decorated symbolically by the brothers Max and Gotthold Brückner, to give the effect of a huge awning, such as used to cover the tribune of the Roman Emperors, in pale yellow over a pale blue sky. All in all, it was a fundamental departure from existing European opera houses, a renunciation of the ornate splendour of the old court theatres in favour of practicality, the effective presentation of the creative work. Even the curtain was allotted an essential function. Instead of being gathered upwards from under the very feet of the performers, it divided to either side so as to reveal the whole set almost simultaneously. And at the end it did not fall, but 'closed' like the dramatic action itself. What we nowadays take for granted was still a novelty in 1876.

The first illustrious 'guest' to enter the finished building as a spectator and there to witness the final rehearsals for the *Ring* was King Ludwig II. He dedicated it, so to speak, as Wagner's co-builder in the spirit and his ever-faithful patron. This occurred on 6 August 1876. Immediately after hearing *Rheingold*, he wrote to Wagner from Schloss Eremitage at about two o'clock in the morning: 'My great, splendid, loyally and dearly beloved friend!—I cannot possibly bring this day to a close without joyfully proclaiming to you how truly happy this evening has made me. Those impressions will remain with me for ever more.' And upon his return to Hohenschwangau at midnight, after seeing *Götterdämmerung*, he wrote:

> With what impressions I returned from my visit to the rapturous Festival at Bayreuth and my happy meeting with you once again, my revered friend, I cannot describe. I went there with great anticipation, and even though I had such high hopes, they were all surpassed *by far* ... Happy the age that saw such a genius rise from its midst! How future generations will envy all those who had the inestimable good fortune to be your contemporaries!

King Ludwig saw the *Ring* cycle for a second time on the occasion of the third performance between 27 and 30 August. He was as deeply moved as he was enthusiastic, and his mode of expression, for all its hyperbole, came from the heart. But he dashed, almost cruelly, Wagner's subsequent hopes—indeed his justifiable expectation—six years later when, after the first performance of *Parsifal* on 26 July 1882, he abstained from delivering a similarly favourable verdict, being by now morbidly shy of social contact and increasingly turning his back upon the world. And this after Wagner had gone to the trouble of ensuring that the comfort of his royal friend would be especially enhanced on this visit by having the hitherto undecorated semi-circle of the brick façade of the Festival Theatre extended to form the so-called 'Royal Wing'. This was a decorative projection constructed of expensive materials by the architect Brückwald at a cost of some 27,000 marks. Its sole purpose was to provide the king with a worthy appartment in which he could spend the intervals—he already had his own entrance and his own separate box—so that he might at all times be kept completely apart from the rest of the audience. But the effort was all in vain: King Ludwig never used the extension. It was the most bitter disappointment he caused Wagner throughout their years of friendship. The composer never completely got over it. It is referred to in the lines which he addressed to his 'faithless' friend on 25 August, the king's birthday:

> Though spurn thou didst the Grail's cool draught,
> It was my All thee to endow.
> Let not the impoverished soul be scorned
> Who cannot give thee, only wish thee more.

With the building of the 'Royal Wing' the Festival Theatre was finished. The façade has remained in this form down to the present day. Of course, it is clear that other changes have become necessary in the course of the last hundred years. Renovations, extensions, modernizations proved unavoidable with the passage of time. The first alterations occurred as early as 1888 when the gas lighting, which had been the only illumination available at the time of construction, was replaced by electricity. 'To the astonishment of the town', Cosima Wagner wrote to a friend, 'the frightful machine for electric light . . . was yesterday transported up the hill with tremendous effort; it took eight hours and sixteen horses . . . We have also built a structure to house this monster.' Having regard to the increasingly substantial scenery, Siegfried Wagner was compelled after the 1924 festival to extend the backstage area by building on a large annexe. Five years later, his widow Winifred built the so-called 'administrative wing' on the north-west corner to house all the various offices previously scattered about the town, including the box-office. At the same time the 'press boxes' were inserted between the Royal Box and the circle. Now known as the 'balcony boxes', they are today in great demand.

The increase in motor traffic produced new problems: parking space for hundreds of cars had to be found. International audiences made costly demands. With the outbreak of the Second World War, of course, circumstances changed once more; and on 9 August 1944 everything was suddenly brought to an end and the Festival Theatre closed its gates.

It is a small miracle that the struggle between warring nations, which destroyed an immeasurable wealth of the cultural heritage throughout Europe, did not leave these two buildings in charred ruins. It passed the Festival Theatre by without leaving any visible traces. But it dealt grave blows to Wahnfried: the *Saal*, the very soul of the house, together with the rooms next to it and above it, was hit by a bomb on 5 April 1945. Many valuable items were destroyed or disappeared without trace. On entering the garden from the avenue in front, one would have found the façade unblemished, as in the early days—and yet this was a deceptive illusion concealing the ruin behind. During the emergency restoration of the parts that had survived, the music room was also split up and thereby destroyed. Whether this grave, even decisive wound can ever be healed by national sacrifice, only the future can tell. Posterity will, one hopes, be mindful of its duty!

The idea of the Bayreuth Festival itself remained unaffected, as was seen after five years of uncertainty. When performances began again in the summer of 1951, the vicissitudes of time had left their mark only in the new modes of production which broke with tradition. Not until the end of the 1950s was a thorough renovation of the fabric of the building added to the spiritual renewal within. The rotten beams of the largest half-timbered building ever erected had to be replaced by steel and concrete without the surgery becoming visible from the exterior. The walls of the auditorium also had to be rebuilt, but the historic design as such was preserved. On the other hand, its almost pastoral setting underwent a major transformation through many additional buildings and extensions: a multi-purpose building to the north of the theatre, wings for dressing rooms and new rehearsal rooms and stages, enlarged refreshment areas for the audience, and a canteen for the staff which can only be reached from within the theatre. The most recent change was in the Grand Restaurant; it was rebuilt completely in a contemporary style. The adjoining gardens also underwent some changes. With this the final adaptation to the demands of the modern age seems to have been accomplished.

These necessary changes, though judicious, do not wholly reflect the modest but solemn and dignified spirit of the festival hill as it used to be years ago. Admittedly the foreign visitor walking up the Siegfried-Allee for the first time and seeing in front of him the almost unchanged main body of the theatre may still be able to conjure up an illusion of the past—of the days when the massive building stood in dominating simplicity in the almost empty square. It still has an air of the 'Great Barn' about it, the mocking nickname which it once earned for itself from ignorant critics who insisted on measuring it by the standards of conventional opera houses. The hope of its creator, that posterity would one day honour it with a more magnificent structure, has not been fulfilled.

APPENDIX
THE WAHNFRIED ARCHIVE

The real founder of the Wahnfried Archive was the composer's son, Siegfried. Without him the documentary wealth of manuscripts, letters and papers would never have been preserved in their present form. This is clearly attested in two of Wagner's letters to King Ludwig II—the emotional passage of 1 October 1874 when the happy father announced with regard to this male heir: 'Now, of course, my life has gained a completely different meaning . . . it has a purpose which it never had for me before.' And the extension of this feeling articulated in the letter of 9 February 1879:

> In days gone by I would simply discard anything which might have served as a memento of me . . . Then one morning I called out all over the house, 'I have a son!' All of a sudden the whole world looked different! The happy mother realized immediately that my whole past and future had acquired a completely new meaning . . . From then on every relic was preserved: letters, manuscripts, books which I had once used, every line I had ever written, were tracked down and collected; my life was recorded in ever greater detail, pictures of all the places and houses I had lived in were accumulated. My son, for all his tender years, shall on reaching maturity, know exactly *who* his father was.

It is to Cosima Wagner's great credit that, with the help of friends, she brought this scheme to fruition and realized her husband's wishes as completely as possible. Throughout years of toil she sought to collect everything that was still accessible, in particular the letters written by Wagner in the course of half a century. Of the period after Wagner's death, her biographer Du Moulin writes: 'The papers written by Wagner's own hand were now unearthed on all sides and Frau Cosima came to the painful realization that her husband's literary legacy was scattered far and wide. But the legal and especially financial means to recover it all were lacking. For everyone tried to profit from his valuable possession and few complied with the request to deposit at least a copy in the Wahnfried archive.' Nevertheless, its riches have increased from year to year, its contents have been steadily enlarged by donations down to the present day, and the total material is now of an overwhelming abundance.

The contents can be divided into four categories, although there is a degree of overlap between them:

(1) The literary and musical drafts, sketches and completed versions of the music dramas, together with other compositions and literary drafts.
(2) The critical and analytical prose writings of the artist and philosopher.
(3) The letters which Wagner wrote and received, together with letters from Franz Liszt's literary remains.
(4) Pictures, documents and mementos from the seventy years of Wagner's life.

What follows is a necessarily brief outline of the material stored under the various headings.

1a. *Die Feen*: libretto and orchestral sketch.
Das Liebesverbot: libretto and orchestral sketch.
Rienzi: various composition and orchestral sketches.
Tannhäuser: prose draft, libretto and (hand-written) score; score of the Paris version.
Lohengrin: prose draft, sketch of composition and orchestration, score.
Das Rheingold: libretto, sketch of composition, fragment of first completed version of the score.
Die Walküre: libretto, first version of the score, sketch of composition.
Siegfried: libretto, sketch of composition, orchestral sketch, first version of score and final draft of score (Acts I and II).
Götterdämmerung: libretto, sketch of composition and orchestration, score.

Tristan und Isolde: libretto, sketch of composition and orchestration, score.

Die Meistersinger von Nürnberg: prose drafts, libretto, sketch of composition and orchestration.

Parsifal: libretto, sketch of composition and orchestration, score.

1*b*. Copy of Beethoven's Ninth Symphony (1830) and piano arrangement of this work (1830); scores of two concert overtures and the overture to *König Enzio* and *Polonia*; scores of the *Huldigungsmarsch, Kaisermarsch* and *Amerikanischen Festmarsch*; *Eine Faust-Ouvertüre*, scores of 1840 and 1855; 2 *Sonatas* and the *Fantasia* for piano; *Siegfried-idyll*; *Albumblätter*; *Lieder* from the Parisian period and the five *Wesendonk-Lieder*, etc.

1*c*. Drafts, literary works and poems such as: *Friederich I, Jesus von Nazareth, Wieland der Schmied, Antikes Lustspiel* (*The Capitulation*) along with fifty-four poems, poetic dedications, etc.

2. *Die Kunst und die Revolution, Das Kunstwerk der Zukunft, Das Judentum in der Musik, Oper und Drama, Über Staat und Religion, Deutsche Kunst und deutsche Politik, Über das Dirigieren, Beethoven, Religion und Kunst, Heldentum und Christentum*, together with all the appeals, addresses and instructions concerning the founding of the Bayreuth Festival and the performances of 1876 and 1882.

3. 750 original letters from Wagner to Franz Liszt, Hans von Bülow, Eduard Devrient, Theodor Uhlig, Wilhelm Fischer, Otto Wesendonk, Graf and Gräfin Schleinitz, Josef Standhartner, Ludwig and Malvina Schnorr, Vreneli Stocker.
265 original letters to Minna Wagner.
350 original letters to various recipients during the years 1830–83.
292 telegrams.
258 letters and 70 telegrams to King Ludwig II, and 183 replies from the king (copies).
2,815 letters to other correspondents in the form of copies or photocopies.
353 original letters from Franz Liszt and his family.
912 original letters, 142 photocopies and 304 other copies of letters from Cosima Wagner to various correspondents.
6,392 original letters and 882 telegrams from friends, contemporaries and participants in the Bayreuth Festival.

4. The original MS. of *Mein Leben* in Cosima Wagner's hand. Pictures of the places and houses in which Richard Wagner lived, together with pictures of places he visited in Germany, Switzer-

land, Austria, Italy, Russia, etc. Rare portraits of Wagner and his friends. The 'Brown Book' (copy). 156 certificates concerning Wagner's genealogical tree. Files, tributes, etc. 17 small *Festspiele* for family occasions. Cartoons by E. B. Kietz from the Parisian period. 65 water-colours by Isolde Wagner to commemorate 22 May 1880. Anton Bruckner's Third Symphony (copy) with the dedication to Wagner. Folio with plans for the Munich Theatre, the Bayreuth Festival Theatre, Wahnfried, etc.

These are the essential contents of the Wahnfried Archive, which since 1973 has been incorporated into the Richard-Wagner-Stiftung in Bayreuth. In October 1978 it was enriched by acquisition of the chief items from the great Burrell Collection, formerly in the possession of the Curtis Institute of Music at Philadelphia. Although the Wahnfried Archive cannot claim to be complete—there are other important manuscripts and documents in such collections as those of the Wagner museums in Triebschen-Lucerne and Eisenach—it is *the* source of documentary evidence about Wagner, the man and the artist, and has thus become the focal point of historical and musicological research.

Translated by Cedric Williams

Notes

CHAPTER 2

1 W. D. Robson-Scott, *The Literary Background of the Gothic Revival in Germany*, Oxford, 1965, p. 293.
2 Ibid., p. 296.
3 Ernest Newman, *The Life of Richard Wagner*, New York and London, 1933, Vol. II, p. 431.
4 Ernest Newman, *Wagner as Man and Artist*, London, 2nd edn., 1924, p. 151.
5 Schopenhauer's marginalia are given by W. Ashton Ellis in his *Life of Richard Wagner*, 6 vols., London, 1900–8, Vol. IV, pp. 440–6.
6 Present author's translation.
7 Act I (present author's translation).
8 *The World as Will and Idea*, para. 54.
9 loc. cit.
10 Ibid., para. 71.
11 *Götterdämmerung*, early draft of final scene (present author's translation).
12 Goethe's *Faust*, transl. Bayard Taylor, Part II, Act V, sc. vii.
13 *The World as Will and Idea*, para. 35.
14 Act III, sc. ii (present author's translation).
15 See, however, F. R. Love, *Young Nietzsche and the Wagnerian Experience*, Chapel Hill, 1963.
16 See the index of the edition and translation by Walter Kaufmann and R. J. Hollingdale, London, 1968.
17 Nietzsche, *The Case of Wagner*, final paragraph of the Epilogue (present author's translation).
18 Nietzsche, *Nietzsche contra Wagner*, section 'How I escaped from Wagner', end of first paragraph (present author's translation).
19 Nietzsche, *The Case of Wagner*, para. 9 (present author's translation).
20 Thomas Mann, 'Leiden und Grösse Richard Wagners' in *Adel des Geistes*, Stockholm, 1945, p. 467.

CHAPTER 3

1 The leading ideas in this essay have been expanded in Michael Black, *Poetic Drama as Mirror of the Will*, London, 1977.
2 G. E. Lessing, *Hamburg Dramaturgy*, New York, 1962, pp. 198–9.
3 Ibid., pp. 41–2.

P

Notes

4 G. E. Lessing, *Hamburgische Dramaturgie*, Nr. 34, in *Werke*, Vol. 4, p. 150 (cited in R. Wellek, *A History of Modern Criticism 1750–1950*, Vol. I, London, 1955, p. 173).

5 A. W. Schlegel, *Über dramatische Kunst und Literatur*, Heidelberg, 1817, Vol. 3, p. 8. (Translated as *A Course of Lectures on Dramatic Art and Literature* by John Black, rev. A. J. W. Morrison, London, 1846.)

6 F. Schlegel, ed. J. Körner, *Neue philosophische Schriften*, Frankfurt, 1955, p. 103 (cited in R. Wellek, *A History of Modern Criticism 1750–1950*, Vol. II, London, 1955, p. 33).

7 'Lettre à Richard Wagner' and 'Richard Wagner et *Tannhäuser* à Paris' in C. Baudelaire, *Oeuvres complètes*, ed. Y.-G. le Dantec and Claude Pichois (Pléiade edition), Paris, 1968, pp. 1205–44.

CHAPTER 4

1 *My Life*, pp. 34–5 (English transl., 1911, of *Mein Leben*).

2 Ibid., p. 44.

3 Letter to Hans von Wolzogen, 12 January 1879, in Wolzogen, *Erinnerungen an Richard Wagner*, 1883, pp. 26–7.

4 *Der Zuschauer*, 7 (OS)/19 (NS) December 1837.

5 Details of Wagner's Magdeburg period are in Wilhelm Hasse, *Richard Wagner in Magdeburg* (*Magdeburger Zeitung*, Nos. 251–3, 19–21 May 1898); summary in Carl Glasenapp, *Das Leben Richard Wagners*, Vol. I, p. 222 et seq. (1905 edn.).

6 Details of Wagner's Königsberg period are in A. Woltersdorf, *Geschichte des Königsberger Theaters von 1744–1855*, Berlin, 1856, p. 83; summarized in Glasenapp, op. cit., Vol. I, p. 276.

7 Details of Wagner's Riga repertory are summarized in Glasenapp, op. cit., Vol. I, pp. 308–9.

8 *Briefe an Hans von Bülow*, 1916, pp. 125–6.

9 'Halévy et *La Reine de Chypre*' in *Revue et Gazette Musicale*, 27 February 1842.

10 'Erinnerungen an Auber' in *Musikalisches Wochenblatt*, November 1871.

11 H. F. Redlich, 'Wagnerian Elements in Pre-Wagnerian Opera' in J. A. Westrup (ed.), *Essays Presented to Egon Wellesz*, Oxford, 1966.

12 *My Life*, p. 184.

13 *Journal des Débats*, 9 February 1860.

14 *Revue et Gazette Musicale*, 27 February, 13 March, 24 April and 1 May 1842. He had previously published in the *Dresden Abendzeitung*, dating it 'Paris, 31 December 1841', a 'Bericht über eine neue Pariser Oper' (26, 27, 28 and 29 January 1842).

15 *Oper und Drama* (1851), in *Gesammelte Schriften und Dichtungen*, Vols. 3 and 4 (1872).

16 *My Life*, pp. 153–4.

17 Robert Gutman, *Richard Wagner: the Man, his Mind, and his Music*, London, 1968, pp. 78–9.

18 See Harold Truscott, 'Wagner: the Growth of an Art' in *Listener*, LXIX, 16 May 1963, p. 849.

19 'Über das Opern-Dichten und Komponieren im Besonderen' in *Bayreuther Blätter* (September 1879). For Wagner's further views on *Jessonda*, see 'Über eine Opernaufführung in Leipzig' in *Musikalisches Wochenblatt*, January 1875.

20 See Alan Walker, *Franz Liszt*, London, 1970, p. 72.

21 Humphrey Searle, *The Music of Liszt*, London, 1954, p. 52.

CHAPTER 5

1 e.g. *Oper und Drama* in *Gesammelte Schriften und Dichtungen, von Richard Wagner,* Vol. III, Leipzig, 1871, p. 82.
2 *Richard Wagners Briefe an Theodor Uhlig, Wilhelm Fischer, Ferdinand Heine,* Leipzig, 1888 (present author's translation).
3 *Gesammelte Schriften,* Vol. II, p. 115.
4 e.g. *Zukunftsmusik* (1861) and *Über die Bestimmung der Oper* (1871).
5 Ernest Newman, *Wagner Nights,* London, 1949, p. 636.
6 See *Oper und Drama,* III, in *Gesammelte Schriften,* Vol. IV, pp. 218ff.
7 See p. 227 below.
8 *Gesammelte Schriften,* Vol. IV, p. 191.
9 Jack M. Stein, *Richard Wagner and the Synthesis of the Arts,* Detroit, 1960, pp. 51–2, 84–5, 102–4.
10 Robert Gutman, *Richard Wagner: the Man, his Mind and his Music,* London, 1968, p. 94 (in paperback edn., p. 54).

11 *Eine Mitteilung an meine Freunde* (1851) in *Gesammelte Schriften,* Vol. IV, p. 320.
12 C. Dahlhaus, *Richard Wagners Musikdramen,* Velber, 1971.
13 Shakespeare, *Macbeth,* III.iv.22.
14 e.g. by Francis Fergusson, *The Idea of a Theater,* Princeton, 1949.
15 Joseph Kerman, *Opera as Drama,* New York, 1956; London, 1957.
16 *Das Kunstwerk der Zukunft* in *Gesammelte Schriften,* Vol. III, pp. 180–3; *Oper und Drama,* II, in *Gesammelte Schriften,* Vol. IV, pp. 16–17; and see Gutman, op. cit., p. 488 (in paperback edn., p. 346).
17 *Meine Erinnerungen an Ludwig Schnorr von Carolsfeld* (1868) in *Gesammelte Schriften,* Vol. VIII, pp. 223ff.
18 Shakespeare, *Richard III,* III.v. (stage direction in First Folio).
19 *Gesammelte Schriften,* Vol. III, p. 282.
20 Ibid., Vol. IV, p. 302.
21 See p. 225 below.
22 Quoted on pp. 116–17 above.

CHAPTER 6

1 W. Furtwängler, *Ton und Wort,* Wiesbaden, 1956, p. 21.
2 T. S. Eliot, 'The Function of Criticism', in *Selected Essays,* London, 1934, p. 25.
3 Erich Heller, *The Ironic German: A Study of Thomas Mann,* London, 1959, p. 135.
4 See Francis Fergusson, *The Idea of a Theater,* Princeton, 1949, Chapter 3.
5 On this subject and related ones, see Jack M. Stein, *Richard Wagner and the Synthesis of the Arts,* Detroit, 1960.
6 D. H. Lawrence, *Phoenix,* Vol. II, London, 1968, p. 416.
7 Ibid., pp. 417–18.

8 D. H. Lawrence, *Phoenix,* Vol. I, London, 1936, p. 535.
9 *The Collected Letters of D. H. Lawrence,* ed. Harry T. Moore, Vol. I, London, 1962, p. 282.
10 D. H. Lawrence, *Phoenix,* Vol. I, p. 539.
11 Aldous Huxley, 'Tragedy and the Whole Truth' in *Music at Night,* London, 1931.
12 F. Nietzsche, *Der Fall Wagner,* section I.
13 Ibid.
14 They are considered, together with some other issues related to the concerns of this essay, in my book, *Wagner, Nietzsche and Tragedy,* Cambridge, forthcoming.

15 *New York Review of Books*, 31
October 1975. In reprinting this
article in his book *Current
Convictions*, he rewrites this as
'one of the most rabidly
misogynistic of all great works of
art', op. cit., p. 90.
16 Dorothea Krook, *Elements of
Tragedy*, London and Yale, 1970,
pp. 66–7.
17 Robert Gutman, *Richard Wagner:
the Man, his Mind, and his Music*,
London, 1968, p. 91.
18 Robert Craft, *Prejudices in
Disguise*, New York, 1975, p. 161.
19 An interesting discussion of the
Act II difficulties can be found in
the Bayreuth *Festspielführer* for
1937 (if *that* can be found!) in an
article by Walter Engelsmann,
entitled 'Von keinen Weib kam
mir das Reif'.
20 Ernest Newman, *Wagner Nights*,
London, 1949, p. 666.
21 R. Raphael, *Richard Wagner*, New
York, 1969, p. 61.
22 One mistake is so rife that it is
worth putting it right firmly: at
the beginning of *Götterdämmerung*
the First Norn tells us that when
Wotan came to drink at the
spring 'seiner Augen eines zahlt'
er als ewigen Zoll' ('he paid as
forfeit for ever one of his eyes');
and it is common to allege that
this is inconsistent with what
Wotan says to Fricka in
Rheingold: 'Um dich zum Weib
zu gewinnen, mein eines Auge
setzt' ich werbend daran.' ('To
win you for my wife, I pledged
my single eye as forfeit'), i.e. he
did not sacrifice it, though he
might have ended up blind if he
had lost his 'eines Auge'. Yet one
translation after another gets it
wrong—the one accompanying
Karajan's recording, for example
has 'I sacrificed *one of my eyes* to
woo you'; William Mann has 'I
gave up one of my eyes to court

you'; and after mistranslating the
passage in *Rheingold*, Ernest
Newman, when he gets to
Götterdämmerung in *The Wagner
Operas*, has a footnote that runs
as follows: 'It has often been
pointed out that in the second
scene of the *Rheingold* Wotan had
told Fricka that when wooing
her he had forfeited one eye as
pledge of his love. Wagner is
following different legends in the
two instances' (*The Wagner
Operas*, London, 1961, p. 625).
Perhaps he is: but they are
perfectly consistent, and it is
important to get the passage
right, because Wotan was taking
a bigger and more dangerous risk
in gambling his remaining eye for
Fricka than in losing one and
keeping one.
23 Raphael, *Richard Wagner*,
p. 61.
24 Morse Peckham, *Beyond the
Tragic Vision*, New York, 1962,
pp. 256–7.
25 Erich Heller, *The Ironic German:
A Study of Thomas Mann*,
London, 1958, p. 277.
26 See Peckham, *Beyond the Tragic
Vision*, pp. 210–11.
27 See Peckham, op. cit.
28 See Raphael, *Richard Wagner*,
Chapter 5.
29 Peckham, op. cit., p. 260.
30 Erich Heller, *The Disinherited
Mind*, New York, 3rd edn.,
p. 171.
31 R. Gutman, *Richard Wagner: the
Man, his Mind, and his Music*,
p. 300.
32 Curt von Westernhagen, *Richard
Wagner. Sein Werk, sein Wesen,
seine Welt*, Zürich, 1956, p. 365.
33 Raphael, *Richard Wagner*, p. 110.
34 Ibid., p. 121 (Raphael's italics).
35 Thomas Mann, *Essays of Three
Decades*, trans. H. Lowe-Porter,
London, 1947, pp. 336–7.
36 Nietzsche, *Der Fall Wagner*.

Notes

CHAPTER 7

1 *Wagner's 'Ring' and its Symbols,* London, 1963, 1969 and 1974.
2 See Deryck Cooke, *The Language of Music,* London, 1959, Ex. 32c, h and j.
3 Ibid., Exs. 56a, b, c, d and f.
4 See *The Language of Music,* pp. 190–3, for an analysis of the expressive functioning of the *Tristan* idea.
5 *Eine Mitteilung an meine Freunde,* 1851, in *Gesammelte Schriften,* Leipzig, 1871–83, Vol. IV, Eng. transl. as *A Communication to My Friends* by W. Ashton Ellis, Coll. Ed., London, 1892–9, Vol. I, pp. 267ff.
6 'Eine Pilgerfahrt zu Beethoven',

No. 1 of *Ein deutscher Musiker in Paris,* in *Gesammelte Schriften,* Leipzig, 1871–83, Vol. I, Eng. transl. as 'A Pilgrimage to Beethoven' by W. Ashton Ellis, Coll. Ed., London, 1892–9, Vol. VII, Ia.
7 See Bryan Magee, *Aspects of Wagner,* London, 1968, pp. 63–4, for three contemporary descriptions of Wagner's almost unbelievable everyday behaviour.
8 *The Language of Music,* Exs. 25, 53 and 54.
9 Ibid., Exs. 29 and 61, Exs. 30 and 62, and Ex. 31.
10 See *The Language of Music,* Ex. 64.

CHAPTER 8

1 *My Life* (London, 1911; reissued 1963) pp. 39–40. This is the 'Authorized Translation' of *Mein Leben,* and page refs are to the 1963 reissue. I have modified the translation. (= *Mein Leben,* 'Erste authentische Veröffentlichung' (Munich, 1963), pp. 44–5.)
2 Hanns Hammelmann and Ewald Osers (trans.), *The Correspondence between Richard Strauss and Hugo von Hofmannsthal* (London, 1961), p. 174.
3 *My Life,* p. 408 (= *Mein Leben,* p. 396).
4 This sheet is published in facsimile in the *Neue Musikzeitung,* xiv/7 (1893), pp. 82–3. Except where specified otherwise, all transcriptions presented here are from autographs in the Richard-Wagner-Archiv, Bayreuth, which now incorporates the holdings of the former Richard-Wagner-Gedenkstätte.
5 For a study of the unpublished original version of the poem, with some citations from

Wagner's autograph, see Julius Kapp, 'Die Urschrift von Richard Wagners "Lohengrin"-Dichtung', in *Die Musik,* xi/14 (April 1912), pp. 88ff.
6 Facsimiles of the initial pages of the Preliminary Draft, Composition Draft and autograph Full Score are given in Herbert Barth, Dietrich Mack and Egon Voss (eds.), *Wagner: A Documentary Study* (London, 1975), plates 69–71.
7 This particular sheet from the Preliminary Draft, numbered 18 by Wagner, is in The Pierpont Morgan Library, Mary Flagler Cary Music Collection.
8 For a detailed discussion of this problem, see Robert Bailey, 'Wagner's Musical Sketches for *Siegfrieds Tod*', in Harold Powers (ed.), *Studies in Music History: Essays for Oliver Strunk* (Princeton, 1968), pp. 459ff.
9 *Richard Wagner's Letters to his Dresden Friends, Theodor Uhlig, Wilhelm Fischer, and Ferdinand Heine,* trans. J. S. Shedlock,

(London, 1890), Letter no. 30, p. 115. The date for this letter is supplied in John N. Burk (ed.), *Letters of Richard Wagner: The Burrell Collection* (London, 1951), p. 620.

10 *My Life*, pp. 610–11 (= *Mein Leben*, p. 587). I have modified the translation.

11 Erich Kloss (ed.), *Briefwechsel zwischen Wagner und Liszt*, 3rd edn (Leipzig, 1910), Vol. 2, p. 11. (The translation is my own).

12 A photographic reproduction of the first page of the Preliminary Draft will be found in Curt von Westernhagen, *Die Entstehung des 'Ring', Dargestellt an den Kompositionsskizzen Richard Wagners* (Zürich, 1973), pp. 32–3. (Published in English as *The Forging of the 'Ring'*, Cambridge, 1976.) A transcription of the Preliminary Draft for the *Vorspiel* is given in Bailey, 'Wagner's Musical Sketches for *Siegfrieds Tod'*, op. cit., pp. 473–4.

13 Kloss (ed.), *Briefwechsel zwischen Wagner und Liszt*, Vol. 2, pp. 15–16.

14 *My Life*, p. 611 (= *Mein Leben*, pp. 587–8).

15 *My Life*, p. 635 (= *Mein Leben*, p. 611).

16 Richard Sternfeld, 'Richard Wagner in seinen Briefen an "das Kind" ', in *Die Musik*, xix/1 (1926/7), p. 4. Unfortunately, Sternfeld published only excerpts from the letters.

17 A facsimile of this musical letter will be found in Otto Strobel,

' "Geschenke des Himmels": Über die ältesten überlieferten "Tristan"-Themen und eine andere—unbekannte—Melodie Wagners', in *Bayreuther Festspielführer* (1938), opp. p. 160.

18 Wolfgang Golther (ed.), *Briefe Richard Wagners an Otto Wesendonk, 1852–1870*, 5th edn. (Leipzig, 1911), Letter no. 19. p. 44.

19 A facsimile of this sketch and the following one will be found in Otto Strobel and Ludwig Deubner (eds.), *Bayreuth, Die Stadt Richard Wagners*, 2nd edn (Munich, 1943), p. 44, and also in *Das Bayreuther Festspielbuch 1951*, p. 90.

20 William Ashton Ellis (trans.), *Richard Wagner to Mathilde Wesendonk*, 3rd edn. (London, 1911), Letter no. 28, p. 13.

21 Kloss (ed.), *Briefwechsel zwischen Wagner und Liszt*, Vol. 2, p. 171. Translated in Ernest Newman, *Wagner Nights* (London, 1949), p. 192.

22 Sternfeld, op. cit., p. 5. Translation, slightly changed here, in Newman, *Wagner Nights* p. 194.

23 For a photographic reproduction of the Preliminary Draft for this passage, see Westernhagen, *Die Entstehung des 'Ring' . . .*, pp. 196–7. The beginning of Wagner's short score is reproduced in Barth, Mack and Voss (eds.), *Wagner: A Documentary Study*, plate 167.

24 Westernhagen, *Die Entstehung des 'Ring' . . .*, p. 195.

CHAPTER 9

1 vols. I–IX: 1871–80; vol. X: 1883; vols. XI–XVI (*Sämtliche Schriften und Dichtungen*): 1911.

2 Thanks to the co-operation of the publishing house of F. A. Brockhaus (Wiesbaden), the present author was able in 1966 to publish a catalogue of and commentary on the *Dresden Library of Richard Wagner*; the library is now in the possession of the Richard-Wagner-Stiftung, Bayreuth.

3 Ernest Newman, *The Life of Richard Wagner*, 4 vols., London and New York, 1933–46, Vol. II (2nd print), p. 51.
4 Now in the Wagner Archive in Bayreuth.
5 Shakespeare, *Hamlet*, II, 2.
6 *Bayreuther Blätter* (1937), p. 106.
7 *Sämtliche Briefe*, II, p. 319.
8 *Mein Leben* (authent. edn.), p. 571.
9 Heinz Becker (ed.), *Giacomo Meyerbeer, Briefe und Tagebücher*, Berlin, vol. I, 1960; vol. II, 1970.
10 'The Perfect Wagnerite' in *Major Critical Essays*, London, reprinted 1955.
11 Thomas Mann, *Wagner und unsere Zeit* (Sammelband) Frankfurt a.M., 1963, pp. 120f.
12 *Sämtliche Schriften . . .*, vol. II, pp. 1f.
13 Ibid., vol. XII, pp. 151–204.
14 Newman, *The Life of Richard Wagner*, New York, 5th print 1949, Vol. I, pp. 464ff.
15 John N. Burk (ed.), *Letters of Richard Wagner/The Burrell Collection*, London, 1951, pp. 341ff.: 'Wagner as Orchestral Organizer in Riga and Zurich'.

16 *Ton und Wort*, Wiesbaden, 1954, p. 11.
17 Ibid., p. 12.
18 *Werk und Wiedergabe*, in *Gesammelte Schriften*, vol. III (Augsburg, 1929).
19 Goethe, *Faust*, Part I.
20 Found among his papers after his death and published in *Sämtliche Schriften . . .*, vol. XII, pp. 220ff.
21 Ibid., vol. IX, pp. 1f.
22 To Gersdorff (4 August 1869).
23 The letter was published by Monod on 17 February 1883 in the *Revue politique et littéraire*. The German text can be found in volume XVI of *Sämtliche Schriften . . .* pp. 120ff.; the French version is in Julien Tiersot, *Lettres françaises de R. Wagner* (Paris, 1935), pp. 381ff.
24 Ibid., vol. IV, pp. 615f. The writings are included in vol. X of *Sämtliche Schriften . . . .*
25 *Zur Genealogie der Moral: Was bedeuten asketische Ideale?* Abschnitt 3.
26 'Aus Cosimas Tagebuch' ('From Cosima's Diary'), *Bayreuther Blätter* (1937), p. 59.

CHAPTER 10

1 Hector Berlioz, *A Travers Chants* Paris, 3rd edn 1880, p. 311.
2 Charles Baudelaire, *Oeuvres complètes*, ed. F.F. Gautier, Vol. IV, Paris, p. 278.
3 Ibid., p. 276.
4 For the full text of the letter, see G. Servières, *Richard Wagner jugé en France*, Paris, 1887, pp. 309–13.
5 Quoted in A. G. Lehmann, *The Symbolist Aesthetic in France*, London, 1950, p. 196.
6 T. de Wyzéwa, *Nos Maîtres*, Paris 1895, p. 4.
7 Ibid., p. 11.
8 Stéphane Mallarmé, *Oeuvres*

complètes, Paris (Pléiade), 1951, p. 544.
9 Ibid., p. 546.
10 Ibid., p. 546.
11 Letter to Gosse, quoted in S. Bernard, *Mallarmé et la musique*, Paris, 1959, p. 75.
12 Mallarmé, *Oeuvres complètes*, p. 543.
13 Paul Valéry, *Écrits divers sur Stéphane Mallarmé*, Paris, 1950, p. 95.
14 R. Gutman, *Richard Wagner: the Man, his Mind and his Music*, London, 1968, p. 404.
15 Ibid., p. 438.
16 Houston Stewart Chamberlain,

Richard Wagner, London, 1895, p. 297.

17 Ibid., p. 298.

18 Ibid., p. 328.

19 Jacques Barzun, *Darwin, Marx, Wagner*, p. 291.

20 Ibid., pp. 306 and 312.

21 Ibid., p. 309.

22 Ernest Newman, *Wagner as Man and Artist* (2nd edn., 1924), pp. 320 and 324.

23 Quoted in G. Servières, *Richard Wagner jugé en France*, p. 27.

24 Eduard Hanslick, *Music Criticisms 1846–99*, trans. H. Pleasants, London, 1963, p. 139.

25 Ibid., p. 142.

26 Ibid., p. 115.

27 Ibid., p. 73.

28 Newman, *Wagner as Man and Artist*, p. 267.

29 Ibid., p. 266.

30 Ibid., p. 320.

31 Ibid., p. 265.

32 Ibid., p. 275.

33 Ibid., p. 349.

34 Ibid., p. 278.

35 Hanslick, *Music Criticisms*, p. 208.

36 F. Nietzsche, *Gesammelte Briefe*, Berlin and Leipzig, 1900–09, pp. 135–6.

37 F. Nietzsche, *Richard Wagner in Bayreuth* in *Complete Works*, Vol. I (1909, trans. A. M. Ludovici), p. 126.

38 F. Nietzsche, *Thus Spoke Zarathustra*, trans. W. Kaufmann, *The Portable Nietzsche*, London and New York, 1971, p. 369.

39 Nietzsche, *Ecce Homo* in *Complete Works*, Vol. 17 (1911, trans. A. M. Ludovici), p. 74.

40 Nietzsche, *Beyond Good and Evil*, trans. R. J. Hollingdale, London, 1973, p. 171.

41 Ibid., pp. 151–2.

40 Nietzsche, *Richard Wagner in Bayreuth*, p. 204.

43 Nietzsche, From 'Dawn' (Aphorism 548), quoted in R. J. Hollingdale, *Nietzsche*, London, 1965, p. 166.

44 *The Portable Nietzsche*, p. 671.

45 Ibid., p. 675.

46 Nietzsche, *Gesammelte Briefe*, Vol. V, 1909, p. 710.

47 Nietzsche, *Ecce Homo*, p. 44.

48 Nietzsche, *The Birth of Tragedy*, section 21.

49 Quoted in 'Nietzsche's Attitude to Wagner' in Gerald Abraham, *Slavonic and Romantic Music*, London, 1968, p. 315.

50 From Nietzsche, *The Case of Wagner*, section 8, quoted in and trans. by Abraham in *Slavonic and Romantic Music*, p. 320.

51 Thomas Mann, *Little Herr Friedemann and other stories*, Harmondsworth, 1972, p. 165.

52 Thomas Mann, *Essays of Three Decades*, trans. H. Lowe-Porter, London, 1947, p. 315.

53 Ibid., p. 316.

54 Ibid., p. 328.

55 Ibid., p. 316.

56 Ibid., pp. 319–20.

57 Ibid., p. 322.

58 Ibid., p. 307.

59 Ibid., p. 365.

60 Ibid., p. 369.

61 Thomas Mann, *The Genesis of a Novel*, trans. R. and C. Winston, London, 1961, pp. 180–1.

62 Thomas Mann, *Last Essays*, trans. R. and C. Winston, London, 1959, p. 177.

63 Mann, *Essays of Three Decades*, p. 407.

64 Ibid., p. 410.

65 Ibid., p. 403.

66 Ibid., pp. 367–8.

67 Servières, *Richard Wagner jugé en France*, p. 303.

68 Joseph Kerman, 'Wagner: Thoughts in Season', *The Score* January 1961, pp. 23–4.

Bibliography

Compiled by RICHARD SUTTON

SECTION I: WAGNER'S OWN WORKS

Collected Works

COMPLETE WORKS
Richard Wagners Werke: Musikdramen-Jugendopern-Musikalische Werke
(ed. Michael Balling):
Vol.   III *Tannhäuser und der Sängerkrieg auf Wartburg*
      IV *Lohengrin*
      V *Tristan und Isolde*
    XII *Die Hochzeit*
   XIII *Die Feen*
   XIV *Das Liebesverbot*
    XV *Lieder und Gesänge*
   XVI *Chorgesänge*
 XVIII *Orchesternwerke, Part 1*
   XX *Orchesternwerke, Part 3*
Leipzig, 1912–23 (no more published).

VOCAL SELECTIONS AND ARRANGEMENTS
Lieder: Schlaf ein holdes Kind. Die Rose (Ronsard). *Die Erwartung* (V.
Hugo). *Der Tannenbaum* (Scheuerlin) (with German, English,
French and Italian texts), Berlin and Dresden, 1875.
Richard Wagner-Album für Gesang mit Pianofortebegleitung (with German,
English and Italian texts, ed. Otto Lessmann), Berlin and Dresden,
1877.
Songs and Arias for a Female (Male) Voice with Pianoforte accompaniment
(with English and German words): 1: Soprano, 2: Mezzo-soprano,
3: Tenor, 4: Baritone, 4 vols., London, 1901.
Zehn Lieder aus den Jahren 1838–1858 (ed. and introduced by Professor
Dr Wolfgang Golther. With a portrait), (one of the Musikalische
Stundenbücher), Munich, 1921.

Operas and Music-Dramas

Die Feen, Romantische Oper in drei Akten (founded on Gozzi's *La*

441

Bibliography

Donna Serpente), Vollständiger Klavierauszug. Mannheim, 1888.
Das Liebesverbot: The Ban on Love: La Defense d'aimer, Oper, Vollständiger Klavierauszug mit Text von Otto Singer (English translation by Edward Dent, French by Amédée and Frieda Bautarel), Leipzig and Berlin, 1922.
Rienzi der Letzte der Tribunen: Rienzi L'ultimo dei tribuni, Grosse tragische Oper in 5 Akten, Vollständige Partitur, Berlin, 1899.
Der fliegende Holländer, Romantische Oper in 3 Aufzügen, Partitur, etc., Berlin and Dresden, 1877.
Der fliegende Holländer, Romantische Oper in 3 Aufzügen, Vollständiger Klavierauszug (vocal score), Dresden, 1861.
Tannhäuser und der Sängerkrieg auf Wartburg. Grosse romantische Oper in 3 Akten. Partitur (reproduced from a stone engraving taken from the autographed manuscript of the composer), Dresden, 1845.
Tannhäuser und der Sängerkrieg auf Wartburg, Vollständige Partitur, etc., Berlin and Dresden, 1880.
Tannhäuser und der Sängerkrieg auf Wartburg, Partitur, Alte und neue Fassung (Anhang: Pariser Bearbeitung) (ed. Felix Mottl), 2 vols. 'Edition Peters 3810', Leipzig, 1925.
Tannhäuser und der Sängerkrieg auf Wartburg, Romantische Oper in drei Akten, Vollständiger Klavierauszug, Dresden, 1855.
Lohengrin, Romantische Oper in drei Akten, Partitur, etc., Leipzig, 1852.
Lohengrin, Romantische Oper in drei Akten, Vollständiger Klavierauszug von Theodor Uhlig (with libretto inserted), Leipzig, 1870.
Der Ring des Nibelungen, Ein Bühnenfestspiel für drei Tage und einen Vorabend, Partitur.
Vorabend: *Das Rheingold*, 1873.
Erster Tag: *Die Walküre*, 1874.
Zweiter Tag: *Siegfried*, 1876.
Dritter Tag: *Götterdämmerung*, 1876.
Mainz, 1873–6.
Tristan und Isolde, Handlung in drei Aufzügen, Vollständige Partitur, Leipzig, 1861.
Tristan und Isolde, Vollständiger Klavierauszug von Hans von Bülow, Leipzig, 1859.
Tristan und Isolde (facsimile of the autograph score), Munich, 1923.
Die Meistersinger von Nürnberg, Opera, Vollständige Partitur, Mainz, 1868.
Die Meistersinger von Nürnberg (facsimile of the autograph score), Munich, 1922.
Die Meistersinger von Nürnberg, Vollständiger Klavierauszug von Karl Tausig, Mainz, 1867.
Parsifal, Ein Bühnenfestspiel, Orchester-Partitur, Mainz, 1883 (No. 4 of an edition of five copies printed on Japanese paper).
Parsifal, Das Autograph der vollständigen Partitur von Richard Wagners 'Parsifal' (Facsimile Ausgabe), Munich, 1925.
Parsifal, Ein Bühnenweihfestspiel ... für das Klavier übertragen von Joseph Rubinstein, Mainz, 1882.

Bibliography

Songs

5 Gedichte für eine Frauenstimme mit Pianoforte, Begleitung in Musik gesetzt von Richard Wagner . . ., Mainz, 1863.
Les Deux Grenadiers (traduit de l'Allemand de M. Henri Heine. Mélodie de Richard Wagner), Paris, 1840.

Orchestral Music

Grosser Festmarsch der hundertjährigen Gedenkfeier der Unabhängigkeits-Erklärung der vereinigten Staaten von Nordamerika, Partitur, Mainz, 1876.
Seiner Majestät Ludwig II König von Bayern. Huldigungs-Marsch für grosses Orchester, Partitur, Mainz, 1871.
Fanfaren für 3 Signal-Trompeten (dedicated to the Königl. Bayr. 6.Chevaulegers-Regiment), Munich, 1933.
Siegfried-Idyll, Partitur, Mainz, 1878.

Instrumental Music

Ein Albumblatt für das Klavier, Leipzig, 1871.

Choral Works

Gruss seiner Treuen an Friedrich August . . ., bei seiner Zurückkunft aus England den 9ten August 1844, Dresden, 1844.

Posthumously Published Works

Fantasia Fis-Moll für Pianoforte, Nachgelassenes Werk, Leizpig. 1905.

Wagner's Poetry and Prose Works

COLLECTIONS
Gesammelte Schriften und Dichtungen, 12 vols., Leipzig, 1871–1911.
Richard Wagners gesammelte Schriften (ed. Julius Kapp), 14 vols., Leipzig. 1914 (part of the Deutscher Klassiker Bibliothek).

SMALLER COLLECTIONS: GERMAN AND ENGLISH
Nachgelassene Schriften und Dichtungen von Richard Wagner, Leipzig, 1895.
Gedichte von Richard Wagner (ed. C. F. Glasenapp), Berlin, 1905.
Der junge Wagner: Dichtungen, Aufsätze, Entwürfe, 1832–1849 (ed. Julius Kapp), Berlin and Leipzig, 1910.
Skizzen und Entwürfe zur Ring-Dichtung: Mit der Dichtung 'Der junge Siegfried' (ed. Otto Strobel), with many facsimile enclosures, Munich, 1930.

443

Bibliography

Richard Wagner's Prose Works (translated for the Wagner Society by W. A. Ellis), London, 1892.

Stories and Essays (selected and ed. by Charles Osborne), London, 1973.

Wagner writes from Paris, Stories, essays and articles by the young composer (edited and translated by Robert L. Jacobs and Geoffrey Skelton), London, 1973.

BOOKS

Das Liebesverbot: Zur Erstaufführung an der Berliner Staatsoper (Wagner's account of the conception and production of the opera, with an introduction to the opera by J. Kapp), Berlin, 1933.

Beethoven, E. W. Fritzsch, Leipzig, 1870.

Bericht an Seine Majestät den König Ludwig II von Bayern über eine in München zu errichtende deutsche Musikschule, Munich, 1865.

Das Bühnenfestspielhaus zu Bayreuth: Nebst einem Berichte über die Grundsteinlegung desselben . . . Mit sechs architektonischen Plänen, Leipzig, 1873.

Deutsche Kunst und deutsche Politik, Leipzig, 1868.

Ein Einblick in das heutige deutsche Opernwesen (Nos. 1–3 of the Musikalisches Wochenblatt of 1873), Leipzig, 1873.

Das Judenthum in der Musik, Leipzig, 1869.

Judaism in Music, being the original essay together with the later supplement . . . (translated from the German and furnished with explanatory notes and introduction by Edwin Evans), London, 1910.

Die Kunst und die Revolution, Leipzig, 1849.

Das Kunstwerk der Zukunft, Leipzig, 1850.

Mein Leben, 2 vols., Munich, 1911.

Mein Leben: Kritisch durchgesehen, eingeleitet und erläutert von Wilhelm Altmann (with portraits and facsimiles), Leipzig, 1933.

My Life (authorized translation from the German), London, 1911.

Oper und Drama, 3 Parts, Leipzig, 1852.

Opera and Drama (translated by Edwin Evans), 2 vols., London, 1913.

Eine Pilgerfahrt zu Beethoven, Munich, 1920.

A Pilgrimage to Beethoven (A novel . . . translated by Otto W. Weyer, with a preface by Paul Carus, and a portrait of Beethoven), Chicago, 1897.

Rede bei der Grundsteinlegung des provisorischen Festtheaters in Bayreuth, Bayreuth, 1872.

Richard Wagner's Lehr und Wanderjahre (autobiographical), Leipzig, 1871.

Über das Dirigieren, Leipzig, 1870.

On Conducting: A treatise on style in the execution of classical music (translated by E. Dannreuther), London, 1887.

Über die Aufführung des Bühnenfestspieles. Der Ring des Nibelungen: Eine Mittheilung und Aufforderung an die Freunde seiner Kunst von Richard Wagner, Leipzig, 1871.

Über die Aufführung des Tannhäuser: Eine Mittheilung an die Dirigenten und Darsteller dieser Oper vom Dichter und Tonsetzer derselben, Zürich, 1852.

444

Bibliography

Über die Bestimmung der Oper: Ein akademischer Vortrag, Leipzig, 1871.
Über die Vivisection (Offener Brief an Ernst von Weber . . .), Berlin and Leipzig, 1880.
Über Schauspieler und Sänger, Leipzig, 1872.
Die Wibelungen: Weltgeschichte aus der Sage (Insel Bücherei Nr. 104), Leipzig, 1914.

Letters

Briefwechsel zwischen Wagner und Liszt, 2 vols., Leipzig, 1887.
Echte Briefe an Ferdinand Praeger: Kritik der Praeger'schen Veröffentlichungen von H. S. Chamberlain (Foreword by H. von Wolzogen), Bayreuth, 1894.
Richard Wagners Gesammelte Briefe. 1830–1850, 2 vols., (ed. Julius Kapp and Emerich Kastner) Leipzig, 1914.
Bayreuther Briefe von Richard Wagner: 1871–1883 (ed. C. F. Glasenapp), Berlin and Leipzig, 1907.
Familienbriefe von Richard Wagner: 1832–1874, Nos. 1 to 5000 (ed. C. F. Glasenapp—with portraits), Berlin, 1907.
Richard Wagner an Theodor Apel (ed. Theodor Apel the younger), (one of Breitkopf und Härtel's Musikbücher). Leipzig, 1910.
Briefe an Hans von Bülow (with an editorial introduction), Jena, 1916.
Die Briefe Richard Wagners an Judith Gautier (und Catulle Mendès) (with an introduction 'Die Freundschaft Richard Wagners mit Judith Gautier', ed. Willi Schuh, etc., with portraits and facsimiles), Leipzig, 1936.
Richard Wagners Briefe an Theodor Uhlig, Wilhelm Fischer, Ferdinand Heine, Leipzig, 1894.
Richard Wagner an Mathilde Wesendonk: Tagebuchblätter und Briefe 1853–1871 (edited, introduced and expanded by Wolfgang Golther . . . appendix Mathilde Wesendonk to Richard Wagner; 14 letters, 24 June 1861 to 13 January 1865; with the words and music of *Fünf Gedichte für eine Frauenstimme* and with a portrait of M. Wesendonk), Leipzig, 1915.
Briefe Richard Wagners an Otto Wesendonk, 1852–1870 (new complete edition—edited with an introductory sketch of Otto F. L. Wesendonk by Wolfgang Golther, with portraits), Berlin, 1905.
Briefe Richard Wagners an Emil Heckel: Zur Entstehungsgeschichte der Bühnenfestspiele in Bayreuth (ed. K. Heckel), Berlin, 1899.
Briefe Richard Wagners an eine Putzmacherin (unabridged edition issued by D. Spitzer), Vienna, 1906.
Richard Wagner an Minna Wagner, Berlin and Leipzig, 1908.
Zwei unveröffentlichte Briefe Richard Wagners an Robert von Hornstein (in explanation of Wagner's references to Robert von Hornstein in *Mein Leben*. Edited by Dr Ferdinand Frh. von Hornstein), Munich, 1911.
König Ludwig II und Richard Wagner: Briefwechsel, 5 vols., (with portraits), Karlsruhe, 1936.

445

Bibliography

The Nietzsche-Wagner Correspondence (edited by E. Förster Nietzsche and translated by C. V. Kerr), London, 1922.

Richard Wagner's Letters to his Dresden friends, Theodor Uhlig, Wilhelm Fischer, and Ferdinand Heine (translated with a preface by J. S. Shedlock), London, 1890.

Richard to Minna Wagner: Letters to his first wife (translated and prefaced, etc., by William Ashton Ellis), 2 vols., London, 1909.

Family Letters of Richard Wagner (translated by W. A. Ellis). London, 1911.

Richard Wagners Briefe an Frau Julie Ritter, Munich, 1920.

Richard Wagners Briefe nach Zeitfolge und Inhalt (ed. Wilhelm Altmann), Niederwalluf bei Wiesbaden, 1971.

SECTION II: WORKS RELATING TO WAGNER STUDIES

Books

Barth, Herbert, Dietrich, Mack, and Egon, Voss, *Wagner: sein Leben, sein Werk in zeitgenössischen Bildern, und Texten*, Vorwort von Pierre Boulez, Vienna, 1975.

—— Mack, Dietrich, and Egon, Voss, *Wagner: A Documentary Study*, Preface by Pierre Boulez, translated by P. R. J. Ford and Mary Whittall, London, 1975.

Barzun, J. M., *Darwin, Marx, Wagner: Critique of a Heritage*, London, 1942.

Bélart, H., *Friedrich Nietzsche und Richard Wagner: Ihre persönlichen Beziehungen, Kunst und Weltanschauungen*, Berlin, 1907.

Bergfeld, Joachim, *Von Tribschen nach Bayreuth: Richard Wagners Weg zur Verwirklichung seiner Festspielidee*, Zürich, 1957.

Bohe, W., *Richard Wagner im Spiegel der Wiener Presse*, Würzburg, 1933.

Bournot, Otto, *Ludwig Heinrich Christoph Geyer, der Stiefvater R. Wagners*, Leipzig, 1913.

Buesst, Aylmer, *The Nibelung's Ring*, London, 1952.

Chamberlain, H. S., *The Wagnerian Drama*, London, 1923.

—— *Richard Wagner*, London, 1900.

Coeuroy, André, *Wagner et l'esprit romantique*, Paris, 1965.

Cooke, Deryck, *The Language of Music*, London, 1959.

Dahlhaus, Carl, *Das Drama Richard Wagners als musikalisches Kunstwerk*. 'Studien zur Musikgeschichte des 19. Jahrhunderts', vol. 23, Regensburg, 1970.

—— *Die Bedeutung des Geistischen in Wagners Musikdramen*, Munich, 1970.

—— *Richard Wagner: Werk und Wirkung* (Studien zur Musikgeschichte des 19. Jahrhunderts, vol. 26), Regensburg, 1970.

—— *Wagners Konzeption des musikalischen Dramas*, Regensburg, 1971.

—— *Richard Wagners Musikdramen*, Velber, 1971.

Dannreuther, Edward G., *Wagner and the Reform of Opera*, London, 1904.

—— *Richard Wagner: his tendencies and theories*, London, 1873.

Bibliography

Dippel, P. G., *Nietzsche und Wagner: Eine Untersuchung über die Grundlagen und Motive ihrer Trennung*, Bern, 1934.

Donington, Robert, *Wagner's 'Ring' and Its Symbols: The Music and the Myth*, London, 1963; second edition 1974.

Dubitzky, F., *Von der Herkunft Wagnerschen Themen*, with musical examples, Musikalisches Magazin No. 50, Langensalza, 1912.

Einbeck, W., *Der religiös-philosophische Gehalt in Richard Wagners Musikdramen*, Buenos Aires, 1956.

Einstein, Alfred, *Music in the Romantic Era*, London, 1947.

Ellis, W. A., *Richard Wagner, as Poet Musician and Mystic*, a paper for the Society for the Encouragement of the Arts, London, 1887.

—— *Wagner Sketches: 1849. A vindication*, London, 1892.

Foerster-Nietzsche, Elisabeth, *Wagner und Nietzsche zur Zeit ihrer Freundschaft*, Munich, 1915.

Fromme, R., *Richard Wagner; Betrachtungen über sein Drama und über das Mythische in seinem Schauen und Schaffen*, Leipzig, 1912.

Furtwängler, Wilhelm, *Ton und Wort*, Wiesbaden, 1956.

Gal, Hans, *Richard Wagner* (translated by Hans Hubert Schänzeler), London, 1976.

Gautier (afterwards Mendès, Judith), *Le Collier des jours: le troisième rang du collier* (recollections of Wagner), Paris, 1909.

—— *Richard Wagner et son oeuvre poétique depuis Rienzi jusqu'à Parsifal*, Paris, 1882.

—— *Wagner at Home* (translated by E. D. Massie), London, 1910.

Geck, Martin, *Die Bildnisse Richard Wagners*, Studien zur Kunst des 19. Jahrhunderts, vol. 9, Munich, 1970.

Glasenapp, C, F., *Das Leben Richard Wagners*, 6 vols., Leipzig, 1894.

—— *Richard Wagner als Mensch*, Riga, 1890.

Gollancz, Victor, *The Ring at Bayreuth: and some Thoughts on Operatic Production with an afterword by Wieland Wagner*, London, 1966.

Golther, W., *Richard Wagner als Dichter* (ed. G. M. C. Brandes) (Die Literatur vol. 14), Berlin, 1904.

—— *Richard Wagner as Poet*, Illustrated Cameos of Literature, London, 1905.

Graves, Marie H., *Schiller and Wagner: A Study of their Dramatic Theory and Technique* (A Dissertation . . .), Ann Arbor, 1938.

Gregor, M., *Wagner und kein Ende: Richard Wagner im Spiegel von Thomas Manns Prosawerk*, Bayreuth, 1958.

Gregor-Dellin, Martin, *Wagner Chronik: Daten zu Leben und Werk*, Munich, 1972.

Griesser, L., *Nietzsche und Wagner*, Leipzig, 1923.

Hanslick, E., *Music Criticism 1846–99* (translated by H. Pleasants), London, 1963.

Hausegger, F. von, *Richard Wagner und Schopenhauer*, Leipzig, 1878.

Heckel, C., *Hugo Wolf in seinem Verhältnis zu Richard Wagner*, Munich and Leipzig, 1905.

Herzfeld, F., *Minna Planer und ihre Ehe mit Richard Wagner*, Leipzig, 1938.

Hight, G. A., *Richard Wagner: a critical biography*, 2 vols., London, 1925.

Hohenlohe-Schillingsfuerst, M. P. A. von, Princess, *Erinnerungen an Richard Wagner*, Weimar, 1938.

Imbert, H., *Rembrandt et Richard Wagner: Le clair—obscur dans l'art*, Paris, 1897.

Indy, P. M. T. V. d', *Richard Wagner et son influence sur l'art musical français*, Paris, 1930.

Irvine, David, *The Badness of Wagner's Bad Luck: A first exposure of anti-Wagnerian journalism*, London, 1912.

Jachmann, H. (Johanna Jachmann-Wagner), *Wagner and His First Elizabeth* (with a portrait), London, 1944.

Jacobs, Robert L., *Wagner*, London, 1974.

Jacobson, Anna, *Nachklänge Richard Wagners im Roman*, Heidelberg, 1932.

Jung, Ute, *Die Rezeption der Kunst Richard Wagners in Italien* (Studien zur Musikgeschichte des 19. Jahrhunderts, vol. 35), Regensburg, 1974.

Kaiser, Hermann, *Der Bühnenmeister Carl Brandt und Richard Wagner: Kunst der Szene in Darmstadt und Bayreuth*, Darmstadt, 1968.

Kapp, J., *Der Junge Wagner*, Berlin, 1910.

—— *Richard Wagner: Eine Biographie*, Berlin, 1910.

—— *Richard Wagner und die Frauen. Eine erotische Biographie*, Berlin, 1912.

—— *The Loves of Richard Wagner* (with plates, including portraits), London, 1951.

—— *Richard Wagner und seine erste 'Elizabeth', Johanna Jachmann-Wagner ... mit unveröffentlichten Briefen von R. Wagner*, Berlin, 1927.

Kastner, E., *Chronologisches Verzeichnis der ersten Aufführungen von Richard Wagners dramatischen Werken*, Leipzig, 1897.

—— *Wagner Catalog: Chronologisches Verzeichnis der von und über Richard Wagner erschienenen Schriften, Musikwerke ...* (a chronological index of and about Richard Wagner's published writings, musical works, etc.), Offenbach-am-Main, 1878.

Kerman, Joseph, *Opera as Drama*, London, 1957.

Kietz, G. A., *Richard Wagner in den Jahren 1842–9 und 1873–5: Erinnerungen*, Dresden, 1905.

Kirchmeyer, Helmut, *Situationsgeschichte der Musikkritik und des musikalischen Pressewesens in Deutschland: Das zeitgenössische Wagner Bild*.

Vol. I: *Wagner in Dresden*, 1972.

Vol. II: *Dokumente 1842–1845*, 1967.

Vol. III: *Dokumente 1846–1850*, 1968.

(Studien zur Musikgeschichte des 19. Jahrhunderts, vol. 7), Regensburg.

Kobbé, G., *Wagner's Music Dramas Analysed: Niebelung, Tristan, Mastersingers, Parsifal*, London, 1927.

Kolb, A., *König Ludwig II von Bayern und Richard Wagner*, Amsterdam, 1947.

Kraft, Zdenko von, *Tel fut Wagner* (translated from the German by J. Boital), Paris, 1964.

—— *Wagner*, Bayreuth, 1956.

Krehbiel, M. E., *Studies in Wagnerian Drama*, London, 1891.

Kronberg, M., *Frauen um Richard Wagner*, Berlin, 1939.

Kummer, F., *Dresdner Wagner-Annalen 1814 bis 1914*, Dresden, 1914.

Lange, Walter, *Richard Wagners universale Bedeutung* (with a portrait), Leipzig, 1920.

—— *Weib und Welt: Ein Wagnerbuch* (with facsimiles), Leipzig, 1931.

Lavignac, A., *The Music Dramas of Richard Wagner* (translated by E. Singleton), London, 1898.

Lessing, T., *Schopenhauer, Wagner, Nietzsche: Einführung in moderne deutsche Philosophie*, Munich, 1906.

Lichtenberger, H., *Richard Wagner, poète et penseur*, Paris, 1898.

Lippert, W., *Richard Wagners Verbannung und Rückkehr, 1849–1862*, (with portraits), Dresden, 1927.

——*Wagner in Exile 1849–1862* (with plates, including portraits) London, 1930.

Liszt, Ferencz, *Gesammelte Schriften*, vol. 3, section 2, *Richard Wagner*, Leipzig, 1880, etc.

Lorenz, A. O., *Das Geheimnis der Form bei Richard Wagner*, 4 vols., Berlin, 1924.

Lübke, W., *Wilhelm Lübke und Eduard Hanslick über Richard Wagner*, Berlin, 1869.

Lüning, Otto, *R. Wagner als Dichter und Denker* (with a portrait) (Neujahrblatt der Allgemeinen Musik-Gesellschaft in Zürich, No. 8), Zürich, 1900.

Magee, Bryan E., *Aspects of Wagner*, London, 1968.

Mann, Thomas, *Schriften und Reden zur Literatur, Kunst und Philosophie*, 3 vols.:

Vol. I: *Ibsen und Wagner*.

Vol. II: *Leiden und Grösse Richard Wagners*.

Richard Wagner und der Ring des Nibelungen.

Vol. III: *Briefe Richard Wagners*.

The Burrell Collection.

(part of *Das Essayistische Werk*, pocketbook edition in 8 vols.), Frankfurt and Hamburg, 1968.

—— *Leiden und Grösse der Meister*, Berlin, 1935.

—— *Freud, Goethe, Wagner* (contains translation of 'Leiden und Grösse Richard Wagners') New York, 1937.

Matter, Jean, *Wagner l'enchanteur*, Paris, 1968.

Mayer, Hans, *Anmerkungen zu Richard Wagner*, Frankfurt-am-Main, 1966.

Meinertz, Josef, *Richard Wagner und Bayreuth: Zur Psychologie des Schaffens und des Erlebens von Wagners Werken*, Berlin, 1961.

Mensch, E., *Richard Wagners Frauengestalten*, Darmstadt, 1885.

Meyer, F., *Richard Wagner und seine Stellung zur Vergangenheit und 'Zukunft'*, Thorn, 1859.

Michotte, Edmond, *Richard Wagner's Visit to Rossini (Paris 1860) and An Evening at Rossini's in Beau-Sejour (Passy 1858)* (Translated from the French and annotated, with an introduction and appendix, by Herbert Weinstock), 1968.

Millenkovich-Morold, M. von, *Richard Wagner in Wien*, Leipzig, 1938.

Moos, P., *Richard Wagner als Ästhetiker: Versuch einer kritischen Darstellung*, Berlin, 1906.

Moser, Max, *Richard Wagner in der englischen Literatur des XIX Jahrhunderts*, Bern, 1938.

Müller, G. H., *Richard Wagner in der Mai-Revolution 1849*, Dresden, 1919.

—— *Staat, Volk und Recht bei Richard Wagner*, Berlin, 1934.

Muncker, F., *Richard Wagner, eine Skizze seines Lebens und Wirkens*, (Bayerische Bibliothek, vol. 26), Bamberg, 1891.

—— *Richard Wagner: a sketch of his life and works*, London, 1891.

Neumann, Angelo, *Erinnerungen an Richard Wagner*, Leipzig, 1907.

—— *Personal Recollections of Wagner* (translated by E. Livermore), London, 1909.

Newman, Ernest, *Fact and Fiction about Wagner* (with a portrait), London, 1931.

—— *The Life of Richard Wagner* (with portraits), 4 vols., London, 1947. Paperback edition (without portraits), Cambridge, 1976.

—— *A Study of Wagner*, London, 1899.

—— *Wagner* (Music of the Masters series), London, 1906.

—— *Wagner as Man and Artist*, London, 1925.

—— *Wagner Nights* (with plates), London, 1949.

Nietzsche, F. W., *Der Fall Wagner*, Leipzig, 1888.

—— *Thoughts Out of Season*, Part I (translated by Anthony Ludovici. Contains 'Richard Wagner in Bayreuth'), New York, 1964.

—— *Die Geburt der Tragödie aus dem Geiste der Musik*, Leipzig, 1872.

—— *The Complete Works of Friedrich Nietzsche*, vol. 8. I. *The Case of Wagner*, II. *Nietzsche Contra Wagner ...*, translated by A. M. Ludovici, Edinburgh and London, 1911.

—— *Unzeitgemässe Betrachtungen*, Part 4: *Richard Wagner in Bayreuth*, Schloss-Chemnitz, 1876.

Nohl, L., *Gluck und Wagner: Über die Entwicklung des Musikdramas*, Munich, 1870.

Nolte, E. H. L., *Studien zu Richard Wagners dramatischen Fragmenten im Zusammenhang seiner Entwicklung von 1841–56*, Inaugural Dissertation, Berlin, 1917.

Norlenghi, G., *Wagner a Venezia*, Venice, 1884.

Österlein, N., *Katalog einer Richard Wagner-Bibliothek*, 4 vols., Leipzig, 1882.

Overhoff, K., *Der germanisch-christliche Mythos Richard Wagners*, Dinkelsbuhl, 1955; transl. by Rosamond Chapin as *The Germanic-Christian Myth of Richard Wagner: Introduction into 'Nibelung-Tetralogy' and 'Parsival'*.

—— *Die Musikdramen Richard Wagners*, Salzburg, 1967.

Bibliography

—— Wagners Nibelungen-Tetralogie: Eine zeitgemässe Betrachtung, Salzburg and Munich, 1971.

Padmore, Elaine, Wagner, London, 1971.

Panizzardi, Mario, Wagner in Italia, vol. I, Genova, 1914; vol. II, Genova, 1923.

Panofsky, Walter, Wagner: A Pictorial Biography (with portraits and facsimiles), London, 1964.

Parkinson, F., Bibliography of Wagner's Leitmotive and Preludes, London, 1893.

Peckham, Morse, Beyond the Tragic Vision, New York, 1962.

Petzet, Detta und Michael, Die Richard Wagner-Bühne König Ludwigs II. München, Bayreuth: Mit Beiträgen von Martin Geck und Heinrich Habel, (Studien zur Kunst des 19. Jahrhunderts, vol. 8). Munich, 1970.

Pfohl, F., Bayreuther Fanfahren (a criticism of the performance of Wagner's operas at Bayreuth), Leipzig, 1901.

Pfordten, Hermann Ludwig von der, Baron, Handlung und Dichtung der Bühnenwerke Richard Wagners nach ihren Grundlagen in Sage und Geschichte, Berlin, 1911.

Pinkus, H., Friedrich Hebbels und Richard Wagners Theorien vom dramatischen Kunstwerk im Zusammenhange mit ihren Weltanschauungen, Würzburg, 1935.

Praeger, F., Wagner as I Knew Him, London, 1892.

Pringsheim, A., Richard Wagner und sein neuester Freund: Eine Erwiderung auf G. Häblers 'Freundesworte', Leipzig, 1873.

Rabich, F., Richard Wagner und die Zeit, Langensalza, 1925.

Raphael, Robert, Richard Wagner, New York, 1969.

Reichelt, C., Richard Wagner und die englische Literatur, Leipzig, 1912.

Röckl, S., Ludwig II. und Richard Wagner: 1864, 1865 (1866 bis 1883), Munich, 1903.

Romain, L. de, Count, Médecin-philosophe et musicien poète: Étude sur Richard Wagner et Max Nordau, Paris, 1895.

Rosenband, Doris, Das Liebesmotiv in Gottfrieds 'Tristan' und Wagners 'Tristan und Isolde', Cöppingen, 1973.

Ruprecht, E., Der Mythos bei Wagner und Nietzsche (Neue Deutsche Forschungen, Abteilung Philosophie) Berlin, 1938.

Sans, Édouard, Richard Wagner et la pensée Schopenhauerienne, Paris, 1969. Zürich, 1959.

Scharschuch, Horst, Gesamtanalyse der Harmonik von Richard Wagners Musikdrama 'Tristan und Isolde': Unter spezieller Berücksichtigung der Sequenztechnik des Tristanstiles, Forschungsbeiträge zur Musikwissenschaft, vol. 12 with supplement, Regensburg, 1963.

Schmid, Theodor, Das Kunstwerk der Zukunft und sein Meister Richard Wagner, Freiburg-im-Breisgau, 1885.

Schmiedel-Eisenach, Otto, Richard Wagners religiöse Weltanschauung, Tübingen, 1907.

Schrenck, E. von, Richard Wagner als Dichter, Munich, 1913.

Schuh, W., Renoir und Wagner, Erlenbach and Zürich, 1959.

Bibliography

Schultz, Günther, *Das Recht in den Bühnendichtungen Richard Wagners*, Cologne, 1962.

Schultze, Fritz, *Das neue Deutschland, seine Heldensagen und Richard Wagner: Eine elementare Einführung in das Verständnis der Werke und der Bedeutung Richard Wagners*, Leipzig, 1888.

Schuré, E., *Richard Wagner und das musikalische Drama*, Hamburg, 1873.

—— *Richard Wagner: son oeuvre et son idée*, Paris, 1875, vol. 2 of *Le Drame musical*.

Schwerin, Baron C. von, *Richard Wagners Frauengestalten, Brünnhilde, Kundry*, Leipzig, 1902.

Seidl, A., *Hat Richard Wagner eine Schule hinterlassen?*, Kiel-Leipzig, 1892 (*Deutsche Schriften für Literatur und Kunst*, 2nd Series, Part 3).

Semper, M., *Das Münchener Festspielhaus: Gottfried Semper und Richard Wagner*, Hamburg, 1906.

Shaw, G. B., *The Perfect Wagnerite*, London, 1913.

Skelton, Geoffrey, *Wagner at Bayreuth*, London, 1976.

—— *Wieland Wagner: The Positive Sceptic*, London, 1971.

Sommer, Antonius, *Die Komplikationen des musikalischen Rhythmus in den Bühnenwerken Richard Wagners*, Giebing über Prien am Chiemsee, 1971 (*Schriften zur Musik*, vol. 10).

Soubies, A., and C. Malherbe, *Wagner et Meyerbeer: documents inédits*, Paris, 1891.

Stefan, P., *Die Feindschaft gegen Wagner*, Regensburg, 1919.

Stein, Jack M., *Richard Wagner and the Synthesis of the Arts*, Detroit, 1960.

Sternfeld, R., *Beethoven und Wagner*, Berlin, 1886.

Tappert, W., *Richard Wagner im Spiegel der Kritik*, Leipzig, 1903.

Ühli, E., *Die Geburt der Individualität aus dem Mythos als künstlerisches Erlebnis R. Wagners*, Munich, 1916.

Verweyen, Johannes M., *Wagner und Nietzsche*, Stuttgart, 1926.

Voss, E., *Studien zur Instrumentation Richard Wagners* (Studien zur Musikgeschichte des 19. Jahrhunderts vol. 24), Regensburg, 1970.

Wagner, Cosima, *Die Tagebücher, 1869–77* (edited and with a commentary by Martin Gregor-Dellin and Dietrich Mack), Munich, 1976.

Wagner, Wieland (ed.), *Hundert Jahre Tristan: Neunzehn Essays*, Emsdetten, 1965.

—— *Richard Wagner und das neue Bayreuth*, Munich, 1962.

Wagner, Wolf Siegfried, *The Family Albums* (translated by Susan Flatauer), London, 1976.

Waldstein, W., *Richard Wagner: Eine kulturhistorische Studie über die Entwicklung . . . zwischen 'Lohengrin' und der 'Ring'-Dichtung* (Germanische Studien Part 17), Berlin, 1922.

Weil, F., *Victor Hugo et Richard Wagner: leurs conceptions dramatiques*, Zofingue, 1926.

Weingartner, Felix, *Bayreuth: 1876–1896*, Berlin, 1897.

—— *Bayreuth* (translated by L. Antrobus), London, 1904.

Weller, Elizabeth, *Richard Wagner und der völkische Gedanke*, Tübingen, 1927.

Westernhagen, Curt von, *Richard Wagner: Sein Werk, sein Wesen, seine Welt*, Zürich, 1956.
—— *Gespräch um Wagner*, Bayreuth, 1961.
—— *Discussion on Wagner* (translated by Desmond Clayton), Bayreuth, 1961.
—— *Forging the Ring* (translated by Arnold and Mary Whittall), Cambridge, 1976.
—— *Vom Holländer zum Parsifal: Neue Wagner-Studien*, Zürich and Freiburg-im-Breisgau, 1962.
—— *Richard Wagners Dresdener Bibliothek. 1842–1849*, Wiesbaden, 1966.
—— *Wagner*, Zürich. English trans. Cambridge, 1978.
Weston, Jessie, *Legends of the Wagner Drama*, London, 1896.
White, Chappell, *An Introduction to the Life and Works of Richard Wagner*, New Jersey, 1967.
Wiesengrund-Adorno, Theodor, *Versuch über Wagner*, Munich and Zürich, 1964.
Wieszner, Georg Gustav, *Richard Wagner der Theater-Reformer: Vom Werden des deutschen Nationaltheaters im Geiste des Jahres 1848*, Emsdetten, 1951.
Williamson, Audrey, *Wagner Opera*, London, 1962.
Witkowski, Georg, *Richard Wagner in Paris: Novellen, Skizzen und Aufsätze*, Leipzig, 1929.
Wolzogen, Baron H. P. von, *Die Tragödie in Bayreuth und ihr Satyrspiel* (on Wagner's *Ring des Nibelungen*), Leipzig, 1877.
—— *Die Sprache in Richard Wagners Dichtungen*, Leipzig, 1878.
—— *Was ist Styl? Was will Wagner? Was soll Bayreuth?*, Leipzig, 1881.
—— *Erinnerungen an Richard Wagner*, Vienna, 1883.
—— *Richard Wagner und die deutsche Kultur* (Sammlung kunstgewerblicher und kunsthistorischer Vorträge, No. 7), Leipzig, 1883.
Wrassiwanopulos-Braschowanoff, G., *Richard Wagner und die Antike: Ein Beitrag zur kunst-philosophischen Weltanschauung Richard Wagners*, Leipzig, 1910.
Zeh, Gisela, *Das Bayreuther Bühnenkostüm*, Munich, 1973.
Zuckermann, Elliot, *The First Hundred Years of Tristan*, New York, 1964.

Periodical Publications

Wagner-Kalender auf das Jahr 1908 (issued by *Musik*) Leipzig, 1909.
Bayreuther Blätter (ed. H. von Wolzogen), January 1878 to Autumn 1938, Chemnitz, 1878–1938.
Richard Wagner-Jahrbuch (ed. L. Frankenstein):
  Vol. I, Leipzig, 1906.
  Vols. II and III, Berlin, 1907, 1908.
  Vol. IV, 1912.
Revue wagnérienne, 1re–3e année (ed. Édouard Dujardin), Paris, 1885–7.
Parsifal: Halbmonatschrift zum Zwecke der Erreichung der Richard Wagner'schen Kunstideale (ed. Alexander Ortony), 1st and 2nd year, Vienna, 1885.

Index

GENERAL INDEX

Index

INDEX OF WAGNER'S WORKS

1. Music

Index

2. Writings

461